INSIDERS' GUIDE® TO

HOUSTON

HELP US KEEP THIS GUIDE UP-TO-DATE

We would love to hear from you concerning your experiences with this guide and how you feel it could be improved and kept up-to-date. Please send your comments and suggestions to:

editorial@GlobePequot.com

Thanks for your input, and happy travels!

INSIDERS' GUIDE® SERIES

INSIDERS' GUIDE® TO

HOUSTON

LAURA NATHAN

INSIDERS' GUIDE

GUILFORD, CONNECTICUT
AN IMPRINT OF GLOBE PEQUOT PRESS

All the information in this guidebook is subject to change. We recommend that you call ahead to obtain current information before traveling.

To buy books in quantity for corporate use or incentives, call **(800) 962–0973** or e-mail **premiums@GlobePequot.com.**

INSIDERS' GUIDE®

Project editor: Ellen Urban
Layout artist: Maggie Peterson
Text design by Sheryl Kober
Maps by XNR Productions, Inc. © Morris Book Publishing, LLC

ISBN 978-0-7627-5314-7

Printed in the United States of America
10 9 8 7 6 5 4 3 2 1

CONTENTS

Directory of Maps

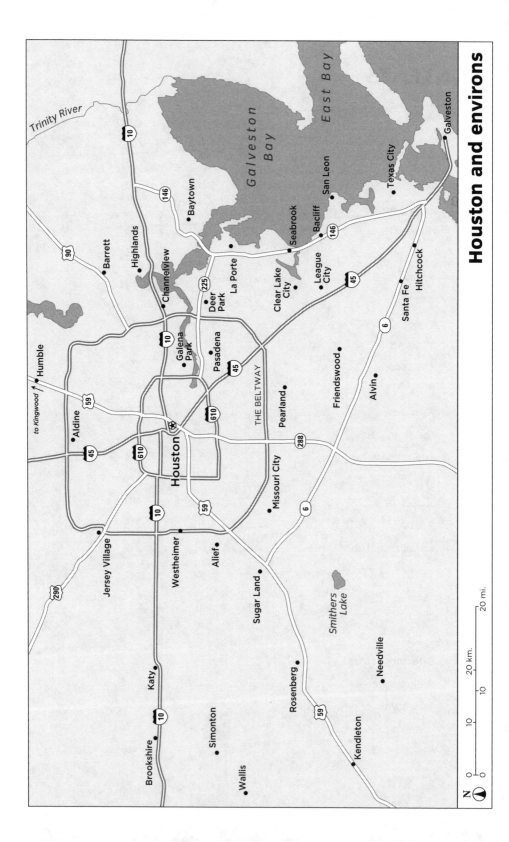

Houston and environs

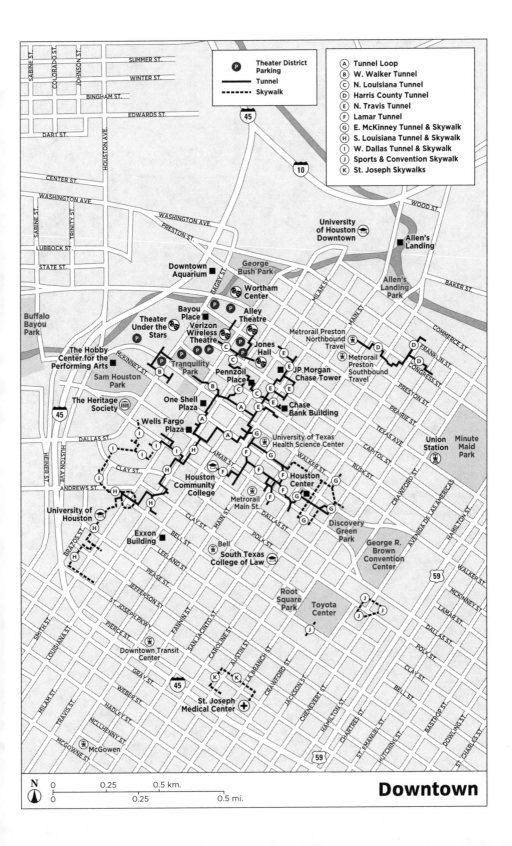

Downtown

Theater District Parking

Tunnel

Skywalk

(A) Tunnel Loop
(B) W. Walker Tunnel
(C) N. Louisiana Tunnel
(D) Harris County Tunnel
(E) N. Travis Tunnel
(F) Lamar Tunnel
(G) E. McKinney Tunnel & Skywalk
(H) S. Louisiana Tunnel & Skywalk
(I) W. Dallas Tunnel & Skywalk
(J) Sports & Convention Skywalk
(K) St. Joseph Skywalks

N

0   0.25   0.5 km.

0   0.25   0.5 mi.

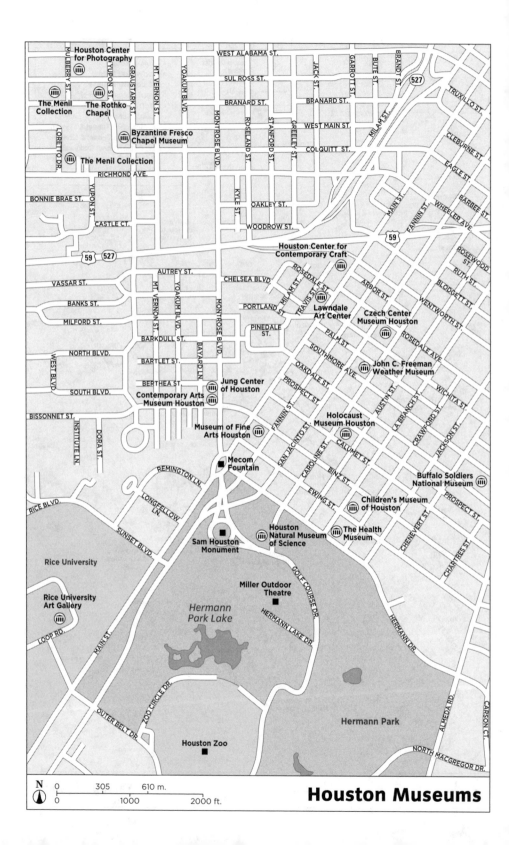

Houston Museums

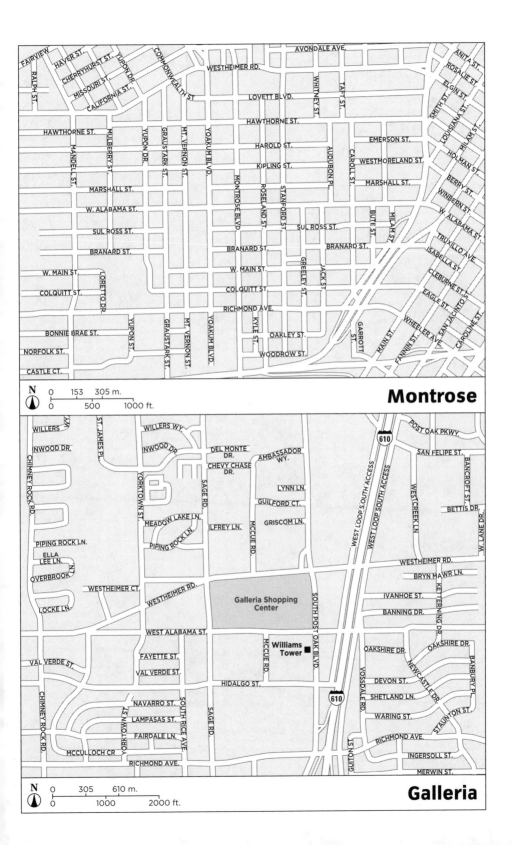

FAIRVIEW
RALPH ST.
HAVER ST.
CHERRYHURST ST.
MISSOURI ST.
CALIFORNIA ST.
YUPON DR.
COMMONWEALTH ST.
AVONDALE AVE.
WESTHEIMER RD.
LOVETT BLVD.
WHITNEY ST.
TAFT ST.
ANITA ST.
ROSALIE ST.
ELGIN ST.
SMITH ST.
LOUISIANA ST.
1ST ST.
HAWTHORNE ST.
HAWTHORNE ST.
MANDELL ST.
MULBERRY ST.
YUPON DR.
GRAUSTARK ST.
MT. VERNON ST.
YOAKUM BLVD.
HAROLD ST.
KIPLING ST.
AUDUBON PL.
EMERSON ST.
WESTMORELAND ST.
CAROLL ST.
MARSHALL ST.
HOLMAN ST.
BERRY ST.
WINBERN ST.
MARSHALL ST.
MONTROSE BLVD.
ROSELAND ST.
STANFORD ST.
W. ALABAMA ST.
SUL ROSS ST.
BRANARD ST.
SUL ROSS ST.
BRANARD ST.
BRANARD ST.
BUTE ST.
MILAM ST.
W. ALABAMA ST.
TRUXILLO AVE.
ISABELLA ST.
CLEBURNE ST.
W. MAIN ST.
LORETTO DR.
COLQUITT ST.
W. MAIN ST.
COLQUITT ST.
RICHMOND AVE.
GREELEY ST.
JACK ST.
EAGLE ST.
SAN JACINTO ST.
CAROLINE ST.
BONNIE BRAE ST.
NORFOLK ST.
CASTLE CT.
YUPON ST.
GRAUSTARK ST.
MT. VERNON ST.
YOAKUM BLVD.
KYLE ST.
OAKLEY ST.
WOODROW ST.
GARROTT ST.
MAIN ST.
WHEELER AVE.
FANNIN ST.

N
0   153   305 m.
0   500   1000 ft.

Montrose

WILLERS
INWOOD DR.
CHIMNEY ROCK RD.
ST. JAMES PL.
YUXM
WILLERS WY.
INWOOD DR.
YORKTOWN ST.
SAGE RD.
DEL MONTE DR.
CHEVY CHASE DR.
AMBASSADOR WY.
LYNN LN.
GUILFORD CT.
610
POST OAK PKWY.
SAN FELIPE ST.
BANCROFT ST.
PIPING ROCK LN.
ELLA LEE LN.
OVERBROOK
LOCKE LN.
MEADOW LAKE LN.
PIPING ROCK LN.
ILFREY LN.
MCCUE RD.
GRISCOM LN.
WEST LOOP SOUTH ACCESS
WEST LOOP SOUTH ACCESS
WESTCREEK LN.
WESTHEIMER RD.
BRYN MAWR LN.
IVANHOE ST.
BETTIS DR.
W. LANE DR.
WESTHEIMER CT.
WESTHEIMER RD.
Galleria Shopping Center
SOUTH POST OAK BLVD.
BANNING DR.
KETTERING DR.
VAL VERDE ST.
WEST ALABAMA ST.
FAYETTE ST.
VAL VERDE ST.
MCCUE RD.
■ Williams Tower
OAKSHIRE DR.
OAKSHIRE DR.
NEWCASTLE DR.
BANBURY PL.
CHIMNEY ROCK RD.
NAVARRO ST.
LAMPASAS ST.
FAIRDALE LN.
MCCULLOCH CR
RICHMOND AVE.
YORKTOWN ST.
SOUTH RICE AVE.
SAGE RD.
HIDALGO ST.
610
DEVON ST.
SHETLAND LN.
WARING ST.
VOSSDALE RD.
RICHMOND AVE.
STAUNTON ST.
UNION ST.
INGERSOLL ST.
MERWIN ST.

N
0   305   610 m.
0   1000   2000 ft.

Galleria

PREFACE

During a recent flight, the man sitting next to me asked where I was from. "But you don't sound like you're from Houston," he said when I told him. I laughed a little—one of those genuine, but somewhat forced laughs of someone who has gotten this reaction many times before—and told him that Houston's a big city and that people here don't have the thick, drawn-out accents that you might find in smaller towns around Texas. "Well, everyone I know from Houston has an accent," he said. I wondered how many people from Houston my companion in row 12 had actually met.

Looking back, there is a little truth to what each of us said. Houston is a big cosmopolitan city filled with people who buck every stereotype that outsiders might have about Texans and Houstonians. Thanks to the city's Gulf Coast location, as well as its role in international trade, oil, aerospace, and education, Houston lures residents from around the world. For someone visiting from a more homogenous area, Houstonians might bear a slight resemblance to a United Nations assembly with their many different accents, beliefs, rituals, and skin tones. Included within this population are people like those my companion in row 12 met—people with deep Southern accents, as well as ranchers who ride horses and breed livestock. (In fact, you'll find thousands of ranchers—as well as hipsters, socialites, and everyone in between—in Houston for the world's largest livestock show and rodeo each March.)

The many interests, beliefs, and backgrounds of people who call Houston home make for a city rich with culture. You'll see this at annual events like the International Festival, the Art Car Parade, and the Shakespeare Festival, as well as at our first-class museums and in our performing arts' companies' unparalleled performances. You'll taste this cultural diversity in our cuisine, which spans from the requisite barbecue and Tex-Mex to vegetarian restaurants and fine dining options that consistently win praise from top foodie magazines like *Gourmet, Bon Appetit,* and *Wine Spectator.* You'll see it at our pro football, basketball, and baseball games, where fans paint their faces and wear their pride on their chests and heads. You'll see it at our parks that fill up on sunny days. And if you're a shopper, prepare yourself: You'll see it in our stores that sell everything from Prada and Tiffany to rare antiques and vinyl records to one-of-a-kind handbags and works from some of today's leading artists. You'll even see it in our hospitality, which many discovered when the city opened its doors to thousands of people displaced by Hurricane Katrina in 2005. These are just a few of the thousands of reasons so many of us call Houston home, even when our current addresses lie elsewhere.

Having been born and raised in Houston, I thought I knew most of what there is to know about this city. But in the course of writing this book and speaking to other Houstonians, I discovered there is so much more to love: A bat colony. A funeral museum. A velodrome. A house made of beer cans. A hole-in-the-wall taco joint that stays open into the wee hours of the morning. A wine bar known for its greasy comfort food. A bookstore that only sells magazines.

I am not surprised to have learned of so many new places to go and things to do in Houston while writing this book. Between the strip malls, skyscrapers, and the routine of everyday life, it can be easy to forget about or never notice some true gems. The big city I have always called home is filled with treasures and quirks just waiting to be discovered. So whether you are a longtime Houstonian, a new resident, or just passing through, cast aside what you think you know about Houston and prepare to be pleasantly surprised.

ACKNOWLEDGMENTS

In the course of writing this book, I asked many friends, friends and family of friends, and family members to tell me about their favorite places and events in Houston. Their recommendations pointed me in new directions and made this book more well-rounded and representative of this dynamic city. While it is impossible to thank each and every one of these people here, I hope all of them know how much I appreciate their contributions to this book, whether they suggested one must-visit spot or 30. Special thanks go to the staff at Globe Pequot Press, especially my editor Amy Lyons, who helped see this book through from start to finish and offered up large doses of insight and guidance along the way. As always, I am grateful to my supportive parents and to Ricky, whose judicious advice and patience helped make this book become a reality.

HOW TO USE THIS BOOK

You've heard the saying: "Everything is bigger in Texas." Houston itself is no exception. With the city itself spanning more than 600 square miles and the surrounding suburbs and exurbs adding another 9,000-plus square miles, there's a lot of ground to cover here. All of the possibilities—where to eat, which theater company to watch, where to shop, where to stay, which festivals to attend—can seem overwhelming, even for those who have lived here for years.

That's where this book comes in. Whether you are in town for a weekend, a week, a month, or a lifetime, consider this your personal tour guide for Houston. In the self-contained chapters that follow, you'll find information on almost everything you might want to know about Houston—where to stay or live, where to eat and go out at night, and where to see a great theater performance. How you read these chapters is up to you: Every trip—or decision to live in a new city—is a little different, so this book is designed to allow you to easily jump around and use the chapters that are most useful for your purposes. Within each chapter, you will find options for every taste and budget, making this something of a *Choose Your Own Adventure* guide. Of course, if you find it helpful, feel free to read this book from cover to cover.

The book begins with a look at Houston's history. Even if you already know a thing or two about the city, you're likely to find a few things you don't know. Perhaps you know Augustus Allen and his brother John founded the city, but do you know how they lured prospective residents to live there? Or did you know that Houston was once the railroad capital of Texas? Check out the "Houston History" chapter to find out even more about the city's intriguing past and present.

After you have gotten a feel for Houston's history, you might want to figure out how you're going to get to and around the city by reading the "Getting Here, Getting Around" chapter. If you need a place to stay, be sure to check out the "Accommodations" chapter as well.

Afterward, follow your stomach to the "Restaurants" chapter, where you will find a sampling of some of Houston's best culinary offerings. Included in the chapter are bakeries and coffee shops, a few of which are great places to hang out in the evening. The restaurants, coffee shops, and bakeries listed are all local or regional, so you can really get a taste of Houston's great dining options. Restaurants are organized by cuisine, then by neighborhood. This way, you can find a place to eat the kind of food you crave—without having to drive 20 miles. Many local restaurants have multiple locations; in many cases, each location is listed. For restaurants that have an abundance of locations, only the most central locations are included in this book.

If you are looking for someplace to go after dinner, check out the "Nightlife" chapter, which includes a little of everything—pubs, bars, wine bars, live music venues, dance clubs, country-and-western dance clubs, gay bars, movie theaters, and readings. The "Nightlife" chapter is organized just like the "Restaurants" chapter.

Houston's cultural scene is part of the city's allure. The "Performing Arts" chapter highlights some of the best theater, ballet, opera, and music offerings, many of which can be found downtown in Houston's Theater District. In the "Museums" chapter, you will discover museums ranging from the requisite (but outstanding) fine arts and natural history museums to the one-of-a-kind Rothko Chapel, a funeral museum, the Holocaust Museum, Houston, and a weather museum.

Flip to the "Attractions" chapter to find out what you must see during your stay in Houston; it will point you to some of Houston's most unique offerings, including NASA's Space Center Houston, the San Jacinto Battleground State Historic Site, and the downtown tunnel system. Also check out the "Annual Events" chapter, which highlights some of the city's best annual festivals, parades, and events ranging from the Houston Livestock Show and Rodeo to the International Festival to the Park to Park Run. Annual events are organized by month so you can flip to the month you're in town and see what is happening during your stay. If you have kids, be sure to check out the "Kidstuff" chapter, which will point you toward Houston's many kid-friendly attractions, theaters, events, and activities like ice-skating and bowling.

Check out the "Parks" chapter if you're looking for a good place to run or to bask in the Texas sun. Here you will learn about some of the city's best parks, which are about as diverse in their offerings and locations as the city itself. Within this chapter, you will also find several off-leash parks where you can take your favorite dog. If you're fond of a particular recreational activity—or just leisure in general—flip to the "Recreation" chapter, which highlights some of the best places to partake in everything from skateboarding to camping. You'll also find a list of gyms and yoga studios that are open to the public in the "Recreation" chapter. If sitting and watching other people play sports is your preferred form of recreation, take a look at the "Spectator Sports" chapter. It includes information about seeing Houston's many professional sports teams in action, as well as a marathon, an annual bowl game, and greyhound and car racing venues.

Whether there's something you need to buy while you are in town or you just like to shop, check out the "Shopping" chapter. Like the "Restaurants" chapter, it highlights only local shops since you can pick up the yellow pages to find a mall. The "Shopping" chapter is organized by store type—antiques, thrift shops, women's clothing, Western wear, kids' clothing, shoes, music, books, and art galleries, just to name a few—and then by neighborhood. If you're using a GPS to navigate your way around town, keep in mind that you should enter the appropriate suburb name rather than "Houston" for destinations located outside of Houston city limits. If necessary, cross-reference with the "Area Overview" chapter to see if a neighborhood is located outside of the city.

Moving to Houston? Be sure to check out the back of the book, where you will find chapters on relocation (including real estate companies, neighborhoods, and what to do when you move to town), primary and secondary school education and child care, higher education, and health care.

In each chapter, you'll find Insiders' Tips, which offer up useful information and tips you might not find elsewhere. Sprinkled throughout the book are Close-ups, which offer detailed looks at some intriguing aspects of Houston.

As you consult these pages, keep in mind that this book should merely be used as a starting point. Houston is a huge city and no chapter is exhaustive in recommendations or information. Often, favorite spots are those discovered by accident, so don't be afraid to stray from this book when deciding what to do here. There are so many great restaurants, shops, clubs, bars, and attractions in this city that you just might stumble upon something fantastic. Also bear in mind that some recommendations and information may be out-of-date by the time you read this book. New businesses are constantly cropping up and older ones are often moving or closing their doors. Even long-standing shops, restaurants, clubs, theaters, and attractions often change their hours or days of operation, so it is always a good idea to call ahead before heading out and seeing the city.

With that in mind, go ahead and start getting to know Houston—whether in your chair (or airplane seat) as you read this book or as you try to navigate your way around the city. If you catch an error or think a particular restaurant, bar, store, or other spot should have been included in this book, please let us know. The *Insiders' Guide to Houston* will be updated periodically, and your feedback would benefit the next edition. Please write to us at *Insiders' Guide to Houston*, GPP, PO Box 480, Guilford, CT 06437-0480 or at editorial@globepequot.com.

AREA OVERVIEW

Houston, the county seat of Harris County, gives a whole new meaning to "the big city." Located just 50 miles from the Gulf of Mexico, this low-lying city covers some 634 square miles—enough space to hold New York, Boston, Seattle, San Francisco, Seattle, Miami, and Washington, D.C. And that's just what lies *inside* Houston's city limits. Add in contiguous cities such as Baytown and Sugar Land and nine additional counties, and the Greater Houston area spans more than 10,000 square miles. Most of this land is—or was—forests, swamps, prairies, or marshes. Buffalo Bayou, the birthplace of Houston, passes through the city, running from the western suburb of Katy into downtown before making its way farther east into the Houston Ship Channel, which produces a sizeable amount of smog. Three Buffalo Bayou tributaries can be found around Houston: Braes Bayou runs along the Texas Medical Center; Sims Bayou runs through downtown, as well as south of Houston; and White Oak Bayou flows through the Heights neighborhood. The combination of these bayous, the city's flat land, and frequent rain makes flooding a common occurrence.

This isn't keeping many people away, though. Houston's population has swelled over the last couple of decades, with a growing number of people coming here in search of mild winters, a relatively low cost of living, and unrivaled opportunities in the aerospace, medicine, and energy sectors. In fact, Houston is one of the fastest-growing metropolitan areas in the United States. Between 2000 and 2007, the population grew 11 percent to 2,208,180 people. Add in the cities and nine counties neighboring Houston, and the population is closer to 5.7 million.

Houston's population defies many of the stereotypes that you might have heard about Texas. Nearly 70 percent of Houston's population represents at least one racial or ethnic minority group, and many residents were born abroad. All told, Houston is home to a substantially larger percentage of blacks, Hispanics, Latinos, and foreign-born residents than the rest of Texas. Thanks in part to the large number of colleges and universities here, Houston's population is also fairly young: The median age is just under 31 years old.

OVERVIEW

The vast majority of this book focuses on activities and spots inside the City of Houston since these tend to be more centrally located and attract more people. The majority of destinations in the city limits can be found inside Loop 610, a major local freeway that circles around the heart of the city, including downtown. Houstonians often refer to locations in terms of whether they are inside or outside the Loop. For this reason, the neighborhoods in this chapter are categorized as either "Inside the Loop" or "Outside the Loop."

This categorization isn't quite sufficient to talk about the Greater Houston area, though. Houston has dozens of neighborhoods, and the Greater Houston area is filled with dozens of suburbs and exurbs. While it is impossible to discuss every Houston neighborhood and suburb in the space of a chapter, it is equally impossible to talk about Houston without talking about some destinations outside the city limits. This chapter highlights a few of the larger suburbs and neighborhoods, particularly those that are home to attractions listed elsewhere in this book. In this chapter, more distant suburbs and neighborhoods are classified under overarching ordinal categories, such as "Northwest" or "East." Because Houston is so large and is home to so many neighborhoods and suburbs, these ordinal directions serve to keep you from becoming overwhelmed: You can look at a map and find a location relative to you. These overarching, ordinal categories include both neighborhoods in Houston (but outside the Loop) and suburbs located outside the city limits. Don't worry, though: Suburbs here have been identified as such; this chapter also includes the distance from downtown to these suburbs, so you have a better sense of how far you'll be traveling if you are visiting the more distant reaches of the Houston area.

CLIMATE

Thanks to its Gulf Coast location and the forests, swamps, and prairies in the area, Houston's climate qualifies as humid subtropical. The city gets roughly 48 inches of rain a year, which makes for more than a few bad hair days.

Winters are mild in Houston, so you don't typically need more than a light jacket. If you're just visiting, you're unlikely to see snow, and on the off chance that you do, it probably won't stick. January temperatures reach a high of about 62°F on average; lows average about 41°F.

If you visit Houston during the summer, be sure to pack sandals, shorts, and sleeveless or short-sleeved shirts. Highs in July average a sweltering 94°F. The relative humidity on summer mornings is about 90 percent, with the humidity falling to about 60 percent in the afternoons. Now for the good news: You'll be hard-pressed to find a place in Houston that isn't air-conditioned—rental cars included.

i Find out the day's weather forecast by calling the local weather line at (713) 630-0222.

INSIDE THE LOOP

Bellaire/Meyerland/ Braeswood/Southside Place

Bellaire, Meyerland, Braeswood, and Southside Place are a collection of neighborhoods that sit in the southwestern part of the Loop and spill over west of Loop 610. These neighborhoods are predominately residential and are filled with large trees and a mix of older homes and newer mansions. There are also some retail developments and restaurants in the area. If you are looking for the city's Jewish community, this is where you'll find it. The Bellaire/Meyerland/Braeswood/Southside Place area is home to two major synagogues, the Jewish Community Center, and some good kosher bakeries.

Downtown

Houston's bustling downtown district is located in the center of the Loop. It is bounded by I-10 on the north, Bagby Street on the West, Chartres Street on the east, and US 59 on the south. Since Houston's founding in 1836, downtown has been the city's primary area for commerce and municipal activities. Downtown is the location of City Hall and Allen's Landing, the spot where the Allen brothers arrived in and first settled Houston; the skyscrapers here are the headquarters of some of the world's largest corporations, including Continental Airlines, El Paso Corporation, Shell Oil Company, and Halliburton. Downtown is also home to the **George R. Brown Convention Center,** which hosts dozens of conventions each year in its 1.2 million square feet of exhibit and meeting space.

For many years the only real entertainment found downtown were the world-class ballet, opera, and theater performances in the **Theater District.** There were some nice restaurants in **Market Square,** an area dating back to the 1800s, but these weren't great evening destinations unless you were attending the theater afterward. So people typically left downtown—and stayed away on the weekends—after work. Over the last decade, though, the city has revitalized downtown to make it a more inviting area to play and even live. Many new restaurants and clubs, an aquarium, a movie theater, and a number of residential lofts and luxury apartments have opened in the area.

In 2004 the city introduced a new light-rail system that runs through downtown along Main Street. More lines are planned for the coming years, which will make it even easier to get around downtown. Dubbed METRORail, the light rail makes it particularly easy to get to Houston's two new sports stadiums—**Minute Maid Park** (baseball) and the **Toyota Center** (basketball and hockey)—as well as to the many festivals that are held downtown each year. Most of these are to be found at one of the parks downtown and a growing number of festivals and other events are held at **Discovery Green,** a Central Park–like green space that opened in 2008 and has quickly become the hub of downtown recreation. All of these attractions are discussed elsewhere in this book. Information about the **Downtown Aquarium** can be found in the "Attractions" chapter; the parks, including Discovery Green, are listed in the "Parks" chapter. The stadiums are discussed in the "Spectator Sports" chapter, the Theater District is discussed in the "Performing Arts" chapter, and the METRORail is discussed in the "Getting Here, Getting Around" chapter.

The Heights

Located northwest of downtown, the Heights is bounded by Loop 610 on the north, I-10 on the south, Yale and Oxford Streets on the east, and Blair and Dian Streets on the west. Whether you're looking for charm, community, or independent spirit, you'll find it in the Heights. This relatively small neighborhood dates back to 1896, when it was established outside what were then the city limits. Built above White Oaks Bayou, the neighborhood is named for the fact that, with an elevation 23 feet higher than that of downtown, it was the highest point in the city.

Today this spirited community is home to a number of thrift shops, artist galleries, plant nurseries, and special events throughout the year.

i On the first Saturday of the month, head to the First Saturday Arts Market in the Heights to check out the work of local artists, listen to music, eat street food, and bond with area residents. The free-to-attend market is held at 548 W. 19th St. from 11 a.m. to 6 p.m., rain or shine. Learn more at www.yalestreetmarket.com.

Midtown

Bounded by I-45 on the north, US 59 on the south, SH 288 on the east, and Bagby Street on the west, Midtown sits on the southwest edge of downtown. After being run-down for many years, this neighborhood has received a big makeover and become one of the hippest areas in town. A younger crowd flocks to Midtown partly for the prime location, but largely to be near some of the best bars, lounges, and restaurants in the city. Midtown is also home to a large Vietnamese population. This community's presence is evident in the numerous Vietnamese restaurants and businesses in the area, as well as the street names written in Vietnamese.

Montrose

Montrose is bounded by Allen Parkway on the north, US 59 on the south, Bagby Street on the east, and Shepherd on the west. It is Houston's most eclectic neighborhood, thanks in part to the neighborhood's proximity to the artsy Museum District and hip Midtown, as well as the youthful Rice and St. Thomas Universities. Montrose is perhaps best known for its large gay and lesbian population, but the area is also home to and frequented by plenty of students, artsy types, families, and a growing number of young professionals. The dozens of independent shops and thrift stores and trendy restaurants and bars lining the streets of Montrose make this a popular place to shop and socialize, day or night. Montrose is also one of the city's most pedestrian-friendly areas. The neighborhood is the site of two of the city's biggest parades—the Art Car Parade in May and the Gay Pride Festival and Parade in June. More information about both of these parades can be found in the "Annual Events" chapter.

Museum District

Nestled between West University and Montrose, the Museum District is home to 18 of Houston's best museums. The district covers a 1.5-mile radius from the Mecom Fountain, a three-pool-high fountain that stands in the traffic circle at the entrance to Houston's prized Hermann Park. Inside the park, you'll find the **Houston Zoo**, a beautiful Japanese garden, the Houston Museum of Natural Science, and more. **Rice University** is located right across the street from the park.

The Museum District has a sophisticated feel, with trees and well-manicured landscaping lining many of the streets. This makes for enjoyable scenery if you opt to go museum hopping, which is readily possible with several museums here. The **Contemporary Arts Museum, Museum of Fine Arts, Museum of Natural Science, Health Museum, Children's Museum,** and **Holocaust Museum** are within a few blocks of one another. Ten of the museums in the district are free, and all but one offer free admission days or hours. More than 6.6 million people visited at least one of the Museum District campuses from 2007 to 2008. Each year—usually in the fall—the Museum District hosts Museum District Day, when the museums offer free admission and shuttle service to get more people to visit the already popular museums. Activities in the Museum District are handled by the Museum District Association (www.houstonmuseumdistrict.org), which was founded in 1997. The Museum District is easily accessible on the METRORail, which makes stops in the district. US 59, TX 288, Main Street, and Fannin also offer easy access. Learn more about the Museum District in the "Museums" chapter.

River Oaks

River Oaks is one of Houston's ritziest neighborhoods, centrally located just east of the Galleria and west of Shepherd between US 59 on the south and Buffalo Bayou on the north. The area was developed by Michael and William Hogg, the sons of former Texas governor Jim Hogg. With their sister Ima, the Hoggs oversaw the building of Bayou Bend, a beautiful manse and gardens on the Buffalo Bayou. Today the Hoggs' River Oaks home and gardens are owned by the Museum of Fine Arts Houston. At this second museum campus, the Museum of Fine Arts showcases the old architecture as well as centuries' worth of American furniture, ceramics, silver, and decor. The **Museum of Fine Arts–Bayou Bend** isn't the only magnificent home in the area. During the spring, River Oaks homes are surrounded by azaleas, which people from across the city pay to see as part of the **River Oaks Garden Club Azalea Trail.** This affluent area is also home to a number of independent restaurants, bakeries, and boutiques. Many of these can be found in the River Oaks Shopping Center, as well as in Highland Village, an upscale shopping area located along Westheimer.

Texas Medical Center

Sitting adjacent to Hermann Park and across the street from Rice University, the Texas Medical Center—aka the Medical Center or TMC—is the world's largest medical center with 47 medicine-related institutions. Although there are some restaurants and housing around the Medical Center, this area revolves around the hospitals, which are discussed in more detail in the "Health Care" chapter. Most of the hospitals here are located off of Fannin Street (which runs parallel to Main Street) or Holcombe Boulevard and are accessible on the METRORail.

Upper Kirby and Greenway Plaza

Just north of West University and south of River Oaks lies the area known as Upper Kirby. It is

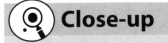

Close-up

The Wards

In and around downtown and east Houston are six former political subdivisions known as wards. Each is named for its ward number (First Ward, Second Ward, and so on). In the late 1830s, shortly after the city's founding, the Allen brothers and other civic leaders divided the city into four geographic political districts known as wards. In the next four decades, two additional wards were added. Rather than defining the wards based on population, each of these six areas was demarcated based on natural and major thoroughfares—Buffalo Bayou, Congress Street, and Main Street.

Today, the wards have lost their political significance, but the neighborhoods continue to be known by their ward numbers. Because most of the wards' residents are minorities, some of these areas have a reputation for being poor and crime ridden. Many of the wards have been undergoing a revitalization, though, allowing some of the old homes in the area to be restored. Unfortunately, Hurricane Ike wreaked significant damage on some of the wards. Below is an overview of the six wards:

Located northwest of downtown just north of Congress Avenue and west of Main Street, the **First Ward** is situated alongside the **Theater District.** Historically a working-class neighborhood, the First Ward is now home to a mix of Latino, black, and white residents. The Old Jeff Davis Hospital, Houston's first hospital, is located in the First Ward. No longer a hospital, this neoclassical-style building has been turned into artists' lofts.

The **Second Ward** lies between Buffalo Bayou on the north and railroad tracks on the south and between Lockwood Avenue on the east and Congress Street on the west. Once an upper-class, white area, the Second Ward lost many of its residents to other suburbs after World War II. Today it is home to a large Latino population, as well as industrial buildings and some lofts.

Settled by freed slaves following the Civil War, the **Third Ward** is a historically black neighborhood that is home to both **Texas Southern University** and the **University of Houston.** The Third Ward was run-down for many years; however, **Project Row Houses**—an innovative community art program—has given the area a significant physical and emotional makeover. Find out more about Project Row Houses on page 105 of the "Museums" chapter.

Nicknamed Freedman's Town, the **Fourth Ward** was founded by freed slaves. Located along the edge of downtown in what is now Midtown, this ward was the hub of black culture in the city but it became run-down over the years. Today, the shotgun-style houses and housing projects are beginning to be replaced by the lofts, apartments, restaurants, and bars that are popping up around Midtown.

Freed slaves created the **Fifth Ward** out of parts of the First and Second Wards. Located just northeast of downtown, the Fifth Ward sits north of Buffalo Bayou and east of its Little Oak Bayou Tributary. It is the city's oldest black neighborhood, but over the years it has attracted large Latino, Asian, and immigrant populations. Today about a third of Fifth Ward residents are of Latino origin. Although the Fifth Ward has one of the city's highest populations of ex-felons, it also has areas filled with organic gardens and blooming flowers.

Created out of the northern portion of the Fourth Ward, the **Sixth Ward** sits along downtown's western edge. It is home to the area's largest concentration of Victorian-era homes, making the neighborhood Houston's first to be added to the National Register of Historic Places in 1978. Many run-down homes here have been restored, but some are at risk of being bulldozed.

bounded by Westheimer on the north, Westpark on the south, Shepherd on the east, and Buffalo Speedway on the west. Much like the neighborhoods that surround it, Upper Kirby is fairly trendy and upscale, with a mix of commercial developments, private homes, and apartments. Even if you don't have a map, you are likely to know when you're in Upper Kirby: Throughout the area stand many red British-style telephone booths, as well as red (as opposed to green) street signs. The bars, pubs, and restaurants in the area make Upper Kirby a popular spot to hang out or meet up with friends. This makes parking spaces tough to come by here, especially on evenings and weekends.

The part of Upper Kirby located along US 59/Southwest Freeway is known as Greenway Plaza. The area is named after a series of office buildings just off the freeway. Today these buildings are joined by a number of luxury apartments, condos, and townhomes, as well as a strip center with a growing number of restaurants and shops.

West University

Technically, West University—also known as West U and West University Place—spans from Bissonnet Street to Bellaire Boulevard/Holcombe Boulevard between Community Drive on the west and Kirby Drive on the east, but "West U" is often used to describe the area as far east as Main Street, where Rice University lies. The neighborhood is home to some beautiful, pricey homes, as well as countless restaurants and shops. Many of these are located in Rice Village, a retail area located just a few blocks west of Rice University. For many years, Rice Village—aka the Village— was comprised almost entirely of independently owned businesses located along just a couple of blocks between Kirby and Greenbriar Streets. In recent years, the Village has expanded to about four main blocks between Rice and University Boulevards on the north and south and Kirby and Greenbriar on the east and west. Many chain stores like Ann Taylor and Banana Republic have moved in. Still, a number of local restaurants, bars, pubs, and stores—particularly women's boutiques—can be found around the Village.

> **i** Parking spaces are tough to come by in Rice Village. Visit during off-peak weekday hours to save yourself the hassle of driving around in search of an elusive spot.

OUTSIDE THE LOOP

West

Galleria/Uptown

Located right on the border of West Loop 610 South, the Galleria area is anchored by the Galleria, Houston's most distinguished mall, which sits at the intersection of Westheimer Road and Post Oak Boulevard. Just a couple of blocks away stands the third-tallest building in the city— Williams Tower—and a unique water wall, which is listed in the "Attractions" chapter.

The Galleria mall is home to an ice-skating rink, restaurants, and elite stores such as Louis Vuitton, Tiffany, Nordstrom, Neiman Marcus, and Dylan's Candy Bar, as well as more mainstream mall fare such as Banana Republic, Gap, Abercrombie & Fitch, and Macy's. More great shopping can be found across the street and in the blocks surrounding the Galleria, particularly on Westheimer on either side of Loop 610 and on Post Oak Boulevard. A few blocks north of the Galleria at Post Oak Boulevard and Loop 610, you'll find the still-new **Uptown Park** development, which is home to several higher-end boutiques and restaurants, including several listed in the "Shopping" and "Restaurants" chapters of this book. There are also several hotels and a growing number of residential developments in the area. Because the Galleria area offers easy access to US 59, Loop 610, and I-10, as well as to River Oaks and other neighborhoods inside the Loop, many out-of-town visitors choose to stay in the area, which is lined with lit trees each December. Depending on the route you take, the Galleria is about 8 miles west of downtown.

Memorial

Located south of the Katy Freeway between West Loop 610 North and West Beltway 8, Memorial is one of Houston's wealthiest and most beautiful neighborhoods. Large homes and tall pine trees line the residential portions of Memorial. There are also many great restaurants and shops in the area, as well as some low-rise business offices. Popular shopping areas here include the recently renovated Memorial City Mall, which has a skating rink and a giant carousel, and Town & Country Village, a well-manicured open-air shopping area. Don't be surprised if you see a familiar looking face when you're out and about in the Memorial area: Among the area's residents are Roger Clemens, former president George H. W. Bush, and former First Lady Barbara Bush. Memorial is about 12 miles from downtown.

Westchase

Located along Westheimer Road near Beltway 8, Westchase is home to many office buildings and strip malls, as well as some good restaurants and apartments. While the stretch of Westchase along Westheimer is too covered in concrete to be attractive, you will find a number of pretty homes if you turn onto some of the side streets in the area. Westchase is about 15 miles from downtown; the area's location near Beltway 8 makes it easily accessible from I-10 and US 59.

Dairy Ashford

Located around Dairy Ashford Road between I-10 and Westheimer Road, Dairy Ashford is largely a residential area, comprised largely of attractive older homes. There are also many retail establishments and restaurants in the area, as well as the popular **Dairy Ashford Roller Rink,** which is listed in the "Kidstuff" chapter of this book. The neighborhood is about 15 miles from downtown.

Katy

One of Houston's most popular suburbs, Katy has a long history as an agricultural town and continues to produce rice today. Katy is comprised of several master-planned communities and golf courses. More restaurants and retail developments have been cropping up here in recent years—most notably, Katy Mills Mall, a mixed retail and outlet mall that is home to a Bass Pro Shop. Located off of the Katy Freeway, Katy is about 25 miles from downtown.

East
Houston Ship Channel

Located east of Beltway 8, the Houston Ship Channel is the hub of the city's industrial and shipping activity. It comprises a large part of the Port of Houston and feeds into the Gulf of Mexico. As one of the country's busiest ports, the ship channel is used to transport general cargo, petrochemical, grain, and other products to destinations around the country and the world. Many oil refineries are located along the channel, which has been widened several times to accommodate larger ships. The sheer amount of industrial activity and ships passing through here makes for some unpleasant scents and high ozone levels. Located along the length of the ship channel are the USS *Texas,* which was used during both World Wars, and the San Jacinto Monument, the site where Texas revolutionaries defeated Mexican troops to secure Texas' independence in 1836. Both the USS *Texas* and the San Jacinto Monument are located in the **San Jacinto Battleground State Historic Site** in the town of La Porte; see the "Attractions" chapter to learn more about these sites. The ship channel is about 25 miles east of downtown.

Baytown

Baytown lies on the east side of the ship channel, about 27 miles from downtown. While there are plenty of homes in this independent city, the area is perhaps best known for its many oil refineries and rubber and chemical plants. Baytown is also home to the **Houston Raceway Park,** a motor-racing complex that you can learn more about in the "Spectator Sports" chapter. Baytown residents and visitors—as well as their cars and bicycles—can travel across the Houston Ship Channel on the **Lynchburg Ferry,** which once transported Texas revolutionaries to the Battle of San Jacinto in 1836.

North

The north side of Houston is home to **George Bush Intercontinental Airport,** the city's largest airport, which sits just north of Beltway 8. Much of this area is devoted to airport operations, as well as to hotels and rental car companies that cater to travelers. There are also several neighborhoods and suburbs north of Houston.

Greenspoint

Just southwest of the airport, right along Beltway 8 at I-45, is Greater Greenspoint. Anchored by Greenspoint Mall, the area has a number of retail establishments and tall office buildings. Companies with offices in the area include Continental Airlines and ExpressJet Airlines. A number of shootings and other crimes took place in the area during the 1980s and 1990s, earning Greenspoint the nickname "Gunspoint." However, crime in the area has decreased in recent years and the number of people moving into apartments and homes has increased dramatically. Greenspoint is about 12 miles from downtown.

Spring

Spring lies about 22 miles north of downtown on I-45 and falls into Houston's extraterritorial jurisdiction. Once home to the Orcoquiza Native Americans, Spring is a predominately residential area whose population has grown significantly in the last few decades, with new residential developments popping up all the time. There are many retail developments in the area, but perhaps the most notable is Old Town Spring, which houses shops in Spring's oldest buildings. Spring is also home to the popular water park **SplashTown,** which you can learn more about in the "Kidstuff" chapter.

Conroe

Located about 40 miles north of downtown on I-45, Conroe is the county seat of Montgomery County. It is also home to **Lake Conroe,** one of the most popular places in the area to go boating, fishing, and waterskiing. While many people come here only on weekends and during vacations, the permanent population has grown dramatically in recent years as the Greater Houston area has expanded outward.

The Woodlands

Located about 30 miles north of downtown off of I-45, the Woodlands offers a serene reprieve from city life. The master-planned community is heavily wooded and elegantly landscaped, making it a popular place for the fairly well-off to call home. In recent years the Woodlands has become home to a growing number of restaurants and retail establishments, including the Woodlands Mall. **Cynthia Woods Mitchell Pavilion,** an outdoor amphitheater that hosts some of the city's biggest concerts, is located in the Woodlands; find out more about it in the "Nightlife" chapter.

Northeast

Kingwood

Located off of US 59, Kingwood is a master-planned community that has been around since the 1970s and was annexed by Houston in 1996. Primarily a residential area, Kingwood is heavily wooded with pine trees and oaks. There are also many retail developments and restaurants here, including a growing number along US 59. While Kingwood is a master-planned community, the villages within it boast a variety of architectural styles. Kingwood is about 23 miles from downtown.

South

Pearland

Located about 20 miles south of downtown on TX 288, Pearland is one of the country's fastest-growing suburbs. The population is more than 80 percent white and predominately white-collar, with many Medical Center employees and downtown workers living here. Pronounced "pear-land," the city occupies three different counties—Harris, Fort Bend, and Brazoria. This master-planned community is primarily residential, with no major industries of its own. There are several retail developments, restaurants, and parks in the area.

Southeast

Head southeast of downtown along I-45, and you'll find **William P. Hobby Airport.** Drive a little farther, and you'll find some of the area's most popular recreational areas, as well as some industrial areas.

Pasadena

Pasadena is located east of the Houston Ship Channel, about 20 miles southeast of downtown, and is filled with odor-emitting refineries and shipping-related businesses. Although there are some million-dollar homes in the area, most Pasadena residents are blue-collar workers who play a central role in Houston's industries. About half of the city's residents are Hispanic or Latino. While the city is largely shaped by its industries, it is also home to an annual strawberry festival and to **Armand Bayou Nature Center,** a beautiful nature reserve listed in the "Parks" chapter of this book on page 129.

Bay Area

Situated between Houston and Galveston, the Bay Area is the name for a collection of communities that sits along Galveston Bay. The crown jewel of these communities is **Clear Lake,** a wealthy master-planned community that is home to a large population of engineers, thanks to its proximity to Houston's petrochemical plants and to Lockheed-Martin, Boeing, and NASA's **Johnson Space Center** and its visitors center, **Space Center Houston.** Clear Lake, as its name suggests, is also home to a lake of the same name, which empties into Galveston Bay. The area is one of the best and most popular places in the Houston region to go boating, sailing, fishing, and water-skiing. Most of Clear Lake is located in Houston, but a small part lies in Pasadena's jurisdiction.

Just a few minutes south of Clear Lake is **Kemah,** a small fishing town that has recently become a popular destination among Houstonians. Spanning less than 2 square miles, Kemah is home to some colorful little cottages and shops—and the **Kemah Boardwalk** Entertainment District, which is home to many restaurants, carnival rides, boardwalk games, shops, an aquarium, and other family-friendly entertainment. The boardwalk, which you can learn more about in the "Attractions" chapter, is a popular place for Houstonians to escape to for a day or a weekend. Like other parts of the Bay Area, Kemah endured significant damage from Hurricane Ike, but most of the boardwalk attractions have been repaired and reopened. Clear Lake is located about 20 miles from downtown; Kemah is about 30 miles from downtown.

Galveston

Galveston sits on the Gulf of Mexico, making it a popular place to go to the beach, surf, sail, water-ski, fish, and partake in other water-based activities. Many of the residences here are beach houses, inhabited only on the weekends and during the summer. The island is home to many hotels, seafood restaurants, and touristy shops, making this a popular spot for Houstonians and other tourists to head for a week or a weekend. Once Texas's most bustling port, much of Galveston was destroyed by the Hurricane of 1900. While the city rebuilt after that storm, it is still struggling to rebuild from Hurricane Ike, which destroyed hundreds of homes and businesses and killed many who didn't heed evacuation orders. Galveston is about 45 miles from downtown.

Southwest

Alief

Located west of West Beltway 8, Alief is one of Houston's most diverse areas, with a large population of Latin American and Asian immigrants, blacks, and people of Caribbean, African, and Middle Eastern origins. Many Louisiana residents who fled Hurricane Katrina moved to this area. There are some good hole-in-the-wall restaurants and ethnic shops in Alief, which is home to part of the city's Chinatown, as well as Little Saigon. There's been quite a bit of crime and gang violence in Alief in recent years, which has a murder rate that is 480 percent above the national average. Alief is about 15 miles from downtown.

Houston Vital Statistics

Founded: 1836 (incorporated in 1837)

Area codes: 713, 281, 832

Population (in 2007): 2.2 million inside the city limits; 5.7 million in the Houston Metropolitan Statistical Area, which includes the suburbs and exurbs

County: Harris

Counties in the Houston Metropolitan Statistical Area: Harris, Fort Bend, Montgomery, Brazoria, Galveston, Liberty, Waller, Chambers, Austin, San Jacinto

Nicknames: Space City, Bayou City, Clutch City

Average temperatures:

> **January:** 62°F (high), 41°F (low)

> **July:** 93.6°F (high)

Average annual rainfall: 48 inches

Major commercial airports: George Bush Intercontinental Airport, William P. Hobby Airport

Major colleges and universities: Rice University, University of Houston, Texas Southern University, University of St. Thomas, Baylor College of Medicine, South Texas College of Law, University of Texas Health Science Center at Houston, Houston Baptist University, Prairie View A&M College of Nursing

Major area businesses: NASA, Continental Airlines, Texas Medical Center, El Paso Corporation, Shell Oil U.S. Division, Landry's Restaurants, Halliburton, Marathon Oil, Pennzoil, ExpressJet Airlines, Sysco, Gulf South Pipelines, Schlumberger Americas Division, Shipley's Donuts, BP America headquarters, ConocoPhillips, Citgo, CenterPoint Energy, Luby's, Al's Formal Wear, Apache Corporation

Daily newspaper: *Houston Chronicle*

Alternative newsweekly: *Houston Press*

Sales tax: 8.25 percent

Hotel tax: 17 percent

Famous sons and daughters: Musician Lyle Lovett; Dell Computer founder Michael Dell; journalists Dan Rather and Walter Cronkite; Broadway star Tommy Tune; actors Dennis and Randy Quaid, Patrick Swayze, Isaiah Washington, Hilary and Haylie Duff, Renee Zellweger, Salma Hayek, Chandra Wilson, Jennifer Garner, and Alexis Bledel; basketball star Clyde Drexler; singers Beyoncé and Solange Knowles; filmmaker Wes Anderson

Famous residents: Former U.S. president George H. W. Bush and former First Lady Barbara Bush; filmmaker, aviator, and billionaire Howard Hughes; baseball stars Roger Clemens and Andy Pettitte; gymnast Mary Lou Retton; NBA basketball coaches Avery Johnson and Jeff Van Gundy

Sharpstown

Located between Beltway 8 and Loop 610, Sharpstown was considered a trailblazer among master-planned communities when it was founded in the 1950s. Today, though, many of the buildings— including apartments, homes, retail stores, and restaurants—look pretty outdated compared to much of the city. Much like Alief, Sharpstown is home to large Asian and Latin American immigrant populations and part of Houston's China-

Visitor Information

Greater Houston Convention and Visitors Bureau
City Hall
901 Bagby, Ste. 100
(713) 437-5200
www.visithoustontexas.com

The Greater Houston Convention and Visitors Bureau is responsible for attracting conventions and tourists to the Houston area. Call or visit the Web site for more advice on where to go, what to do, where to stay, and even what to eat in Houston. The visitors bureau is located downtown in City Hall.

Explore Houston! Visitors Center
George R. Brown Convention Center, Level 2
(713) 853-8258
www.houstonconventionctr.com

If you're attending a convention at the George R. Brown Convention Center, stop in at the Explore Houston! Visitors Center there. In addition to selling Houston souvenirs, Explore Houston! can help you with dinner reservations, touristy questions, and airline, concert, and theater tickets.

Many of the Houston suburbs also have their own visitors bureaus or chambers of commerce that assist newcomers. The contact information for the largest suburbs' visitors bureaus are:

Bay Area Houston Convention and Visitors Bureau
913 N. Meyer Rd., Seabrook
(281) 338-0333
www.visitbayareahouston.com

Galveston Island Convention and Visitors Bureau
2328 Broadway, Galveston
(888) 425-4753
www.galveston.com/cvb

Katy Visitor and Tourism Bureau
23501 Cinco Ranch Blvd., Ste. B206, Katy
(281) 391-5289
www.katychamber.com

Lake Conroe Area Convention and Visitors Bureau
505 W. Davis St., Conroe
(936) 538-7112
www.lakeconroecvb.org

Spring Visitors Bureau
606 Spring Cypress, Spring
(281) 288-2355
www.shopspringtexas.com

Sugar Land Chamber of Commerce/Fort Bend County Chamber of Commerce
445 Commerce Green Blvd., Sugar Land
(281) 491-0800
www.fortbendchamber.org

The Woodlands Convention and Visitors Bureau
10001 Woodloch Forest Dr., Ste. 600, The Woodlands
(281) 363-2447
www.thewoodlandscvb.com

town. You'll find a number of ethnic restaurants and grocery stores in the area, as well as many apartments, residential developments, and some single-family homes.

Fondren Southwest

Located just northeast of Beltway 8 West and south of US 59, Fondren Southwest is primarily a residential and retail area. Up until recently, the neighborhood was home to many deteriorating apartment complexes. In the last few years, though, the most dilapidated of these apartment complexes have been torn down and many orthodox Jewish congregations have cropped up in their place. Fondren Southwest is about 13 miles from downtown.

Stafford

Located predominately in Fort Bend Country, Stafford has a reputation for being a business-friendly community. This has led companies such as Tyco, UPS, and Texas Instruments to set up offices in the city. There are also many retail businesses, hotels, and restaurants in Stafford, where the sales tax is 0.5 percent lower than that of surrounding cities. While there are many single-family homes in the area, the number of people who work in Stafford is believed to be larger than the number of people who actually live in the city.

ℹ️ Although regulations have significantly curtailed pollution in the last few years, ozone levels can be dangerously high in Houston, thanks to industrial activity in the Houston Ship Channel. On days when atmospheric conditions make high ozone levels particularly likely, the Texas Commission on Environmental Quality issues ozone watches, advising children, the elderly, and adults with breathing problems or lung disease to stay indoors. Watch or listen to the local weather to find out about upcoming ozone watch days.

Sugar Land

Once a sugar plantation and the home of Imperial Sugar's headquarters, Sugar Land is now one of Houston's most highly regarded suburbs. An independent municipality, Sugar Land is a master-planned community filled with larger homes, golf courses, and country clubs. Close to 60 percent of residents are white, about a quarter are of Asian descent, and more than a couple are famous athletes. Like other master-planned communities in the area, businesses in Sugar Land are predominately retail and restaurants. Sugar Land is about 20 miles from downtown, just off of US 59.

GETTING HERE, GETTING AROUND

Between the hundreds of domestic and international flights departing from and arriving at Houston's two airports each day and the many interstate and state highways that run through the city, this Texas metropolis is accessible from just about anywhere. Once you get to Houston, you'll need a car—that is, unless you're staying (and don't plan to leave) downtown, where you can walk, take cabs, and ride METRORail. Downtown options aside, Houston is a sprawling metropolis without a sprawling public transportation system. Sure, the city has a bus system, but the frequent stops and traffic mean you could spend an hour or more traveling from point A to point B, even if points A and B are just a few miles apart. The city has a new light-rail system, too, but it doesn't venture into the suburbs, much less to areas like the Galleria, River Oaks, the Heights, or Montrose. As for taking cabs around the city, well, you could. But the cost will add up quickly, and you'll have to call in advance to schedule a pickup.

When trying to get your bearings in Houston, keep in mind that downtown is at the center of the city and that the city's major freeways—I-10, US 59, and I-45—intersect there. Heading south of downtown will take you to Freeport on the Gulf of Mexico; heading southeast will take you to William P. Hobby Airport and to Galveston, which is about a 45-minute drive from Houston. Heading north of downtown will take you to Dallas, which is about a five-hour drive from Houston. Go east of downtown and you'll wind up in the Houston Ship Channel. If you head west from downtown, you will be on your way toward Memorial Park, Memorial, Katy, and eventually San Antonio, which is about a three-hour drive.

i It's okay to turn right on red at stoplights in Houston, unless the signage says otherwise.

BY CAR

When you're driving around Houston during rush hour, expect traffic on major freeways. During weekday mornings and in the early evening, it can take twice—or sometimes even three times—as long as usual to reach your destination. To minimize traffic and encourage carpooling, the city has several so-called HOV lanes and HOT Lanes, located along most major freeways and highways. To drive in an HOV lane, you must have at least two people riding in the car, including the driver. Watch for the HOV signs before entering the HOV lane: Many HOV lanes accommodate inbound traffic during the morning rush hour from 5 to 11 a.m., then switch to accommodate outbound traffic from 2 to 8 p.m. In most cases these special lanes are demarcated with their own concrete separators; along US 59 South, HOV lanes are distinguished only by painted diamonds in the lane. A map of HOV lanes and schedules can be downloaded from www.ridemetro.org/schedulesmaps/hov.aspx.

i You must have three passengers to drive in the HOV lane on US 290 during rush hour or on the Northwest Freeway between 6:45 and 8 a.m. Cars with just two occupants can still drive in these lanes during rush hour by paying $2 each way, however. If you want to pay the $2, you must register to use the lanes by calling (713) 224-7433.

Driving around Houston, it is almost impossible to avoid the freeways, which—along with toll roads—are abundant here. Instead of overwhelming you with highways you'll probably never use if you spend your time in the more central areas of the city, the next few paragraphs offer an overview of Houston's major highways—a crash course, if you will. With that in mind, spend some time looking at a map to acquaint yourself with the general layout of the city before driving around.

> ℹ️ **Tune in to AM 740 or AM 1610 on your radio to get the latest traffic and weather updates.**

As you'll discover, there are quite a few toll roads in Houston. While you can certainly get around without ever driving on a toll road here, the toll roads tend to make it quicker to get where you are going. Beware, though: Houston has tollbooths at the toll-road entrances as well as pass-through tollbooths, which require you to pay a toll even after you've paid the initial entry toll. This means you may have to stop and pay tolls two or three times in the course of a drive. Tolls vary, but they typically run somewhere between 30 cents to $2 for cars; vehicles with three axles or more pay higher tolls. You can avoid the hassle of rummaging through your wallet for money at tollbooths by purchasing an EZ Tag. Just stick it on your window and drive through the EZ Tag lane. A camera will scan your EZ Tag and deduct the toll from your account automatically. An EZ Tag costs a one-time activation fee of $15, plus a minimum deposit of $40, from which your toll charges will be deducted. Purchase an EZ Tag online or by visiting one of the four EZ Tag stores. Call (281) 875-3279 to find these locations, or visit the EZ Tag registration Web site (www.hctra.org). The Web site also includes a downloadable map with the toll roads' entry and exit points and toll plazas.

Now that that's out of the way, here is the lowdown on the freeway and toll-road landscape you have been anxiously awaiting: **Loop 610**—aka the Loop—runs around central Houston, which includes downtown, the Medical Center, Montrose, the Museum District, Midtown, West University, Braeswood, the wards, and the Heights, among other areas. The top part of the Loop is known as the North Loop, the bottom part is called the South Loop, the eastern side is known as the East Loop, and the western side—which runs along the Galleria and Bellaire—is known as the West Loop.

US 59, which cuts through the Loop, runs from northeast to southwest Houston and along the eastern side of downtown. The section in the northeastern part of the city is called the **Eastex Freeway;** the section running from downtown to the southwestern suburbs is called the **Southwest Freeway.**

I-45 cuts through the northern part of the city before running along the western side of downtown and then veering southeast. I-45 North will take you to the northern suburb of the Woodlands and eventually to Dallas, about five hours north of Houston. I-45 South will take you to William P. Hobby Airport, the Bay Area, Space Center Houston, and ultimately, Galveston.

> ℹ️ **Use your EZ Tag to park in the on-site garages at George Bush Intercontinental and William P. Hobby Airports. This will save you the hassle of waiting in line and paying the cashier.**

I-10, which runs from California to Florida, cuts east-west through the upper half of the Loop and intersects with both I-45 and US 59 downtown. The section of I-10 running east from downtown to the ship channel is called the **East Freeway,** or the **Baytown East Freeway.** The recently widened stretch of I-10 that runs west from downtown to Katy is called the **Katy Freeway.** The Harris County Toll Road Authority recently added managed lanes to the Katy Freeway between 610 West and **TX 6,** a state highway that runs from the Texas-Oklahoma border to just northwest of Galveston and intersects with I-10, Westheimer Road, FM 1960 (an old farm-to-market road), and US 290.

Houston Roadways

Here's the CliffsNotes breakdown of some other Houston roadways worth knowing:

The east-west highway **US 290** runs northwest, intersecting with both Loop 610 and the Sam Houston Tollway. You can take US 290 straight to the Texas capital of Austin, which is about two-and-a-half hours northwest of Houston by car.

FM 1960 is an old farm-to-market road that intersects with US 290 and TX 6 in northern Harris County. It travels east for the most part.

Westheimer Road, sometimes referred to as **FM 1093** on signs, is a major road that runs east-west from the Westpark Tollway on the far west side of the city to downtown, where it turns into Bagby Street. Westheimer runs parallel to I-10, which lies to its north. The Galleria mall sits on Westheimer, which goes under West Loop 610 South and through River Oaks' Highland Village shopping area, Montrose, and Midtown.

The **Westpark Tollway** is relatively parallel with Westheimer Road, which lies to the tollway's north. The Westpark Tollway runs from Westpark Drive on the west to **TX 99**, which will eventually make a third loop around the Houston metropolitan area. Tolls here range from 35 cents to $1.25, but there are no tollbooths. You must have an EZ Tag to drive on the Westpark Tollway. If you don't, you can expect to receive a ticket in the mail.

The **Hardy Toll Road** runs from I-45, just north of the city, to Loop 610, near central Houston. For the most part, the 22-mile Hardy Toll Road runs parallel to I-45. Toll charges range from 75 cents to $1.50 for cars; EZ Tag users get a 25-cent discount on each Hardy Toll Road toll.

TX 288 runs south from downtown to Freeport, Texas, along the Gulf of Mexico. 288, as it's known, will also take you to the southern Houston suburb of Pearland.

The Katy Freeway managed lanes run both eastbound and westbound from 5 to 11 a.m. and 2 to 8 p.m., Monday through Friday. The managed lanes are essentially part HOV lane, part toll road. That is to say, vehicles with two or more people can drive in the managed lanes for free; if you don't have passengers to keep you company can drive in the managed lanes by paying a toll. There aren't any tollbooths for these lanes, though. You must have a toll tag—either an EZ Tag (local) or a TxTag (statewide), and the cost of the toll will be deducted each time you drive in a managed lane. Tolls range from 30 cents to $1.60, depending on the time and direction you're driving in. Visit www.hctra.org to download a map of the managed lanes' entry and exit points.

i Drive in the left managed lane of the Katy Managed Lanes if you have two or more people in your car; drive in the right managed lane if you're flying solo with your EZ Tag or TxTag.

Houston has a second loop comprised of the **Sam Houston Tollway,** the **Sam Houston Parkway,** and **Beltway 8.** This intermediate loop circles the more distant reaches of the city, including the area near George Bush Intercontinental Airport on the north, the Houston Ship Channel on the east, and southern exurbs like Sugar Land on the south. It also intersects with I-10 just west of Memorial and east of Katy, ℹ TxTag and EZ Tag are interchange-able in Houston. EZ Tag drivers can drive in TxTag lanes and vice versa, and the toll will be deducted accordingly. TxTag stickers are primarily purchased for use on tollroads in Austin and Tyler, Texas, and are typically used only by those who travel around the state quite a bit. Rates are the same as those for the EZ Tag. If you wish to purchase a prepaid TxTag sticker, you can do so online at www.txtag.org or by calling (888) 468-9824.

making this a popular place to get on the toll road and head to Intercontinental Airport from the west side of town. Each side of the Beltway, as this Texas state highway is often called, is referred to by its compass direction (East Belt, for example). The northern, southern, western, and southeastern sides of the loop are called the Sam Houston Tollway or Beltway 8; the northeastern side is referred to as Sam Houston Parkway. The beltway runs primarily on frontage roads; the toll-way section requires—as the name suggests—a toll. Tolls along the Sam Houston Tollway range from 75 cents to $2, though they're typically 75 cents or $1.

ℹ Find a carpool buddy by contacting METRO at http://ridepro.ridemetro .org/ridepro/service.asp. It maintains a database of local commuters who want to carpool.

Parking

Most Houston businesses and attractions have their own parking lot or parking garage. In some areas, you'll even see plenty of free street parking. The biggest exception to this rule is downtown, where free public parking doesn't really exist on weekdays. Unless the downtown business you're visiting or working for provides a parking permit, you'll either need to pay to park in a garage or

find a metered spot on the street. Bring lots of quarters if you plan to park on the street Monday through Saturday before 6 p.m. Metered parking costs a quarter for every 15 minutes from 7 a.m. to 6 p.m. from Monday through Saturday. The meters (and cops) let you have a free ride—or rather, free park—all day on Sunday.

BY PLANE

Houston is home to two commercial airports—George Bush Intercontinental Airport and William P. Hobby Airport. Together they served more than 50 million passengers in 2008. Between the two airports, you can find service to nearly 200 international and domestic destinations on just about every national and international air-line. Both airports have been renovated recently, which means they're clean, easy to get around, and filled with new restaurants and shops.

The larger of the two airports, George Bush Intercontinental, is located in north Houston, about 22 miles north of downtown and 27 miles northeast of the Galleria. Hobby Airport is located in the southeast part of the city, about 8 miles from downtown and 16 miles from the Galleria. When calculating how long it will take you to get to or from either of the airports, don't assume 60 mph translates to 1 mile a minute. Houston freeways have been known to get congested, particularly during rush hour, so if you're staying 30 miles from the airport, give yourself an hour to get there. Also be sure to account for the extra time you will need to park and return your rental car (if you're driving), check your luggage, go through security, and get to your gate in advance of boarding time. Typically airlines recommend arriving an hour and a half before takeoff, but it never hurts to call your airline to see what it rec-ommends. If you're traveling during the winter

ℹ Need to page a family member or friend at Intercontinental? Pick up one of the white phones located in each terminal and you'll be connected with the airport paging service.

Airlines Serving Intercontinental Airport

Airline	Phone Number	Web Site	Terminal(s)
AeroMexico	(800) 237-6639	www.aeromexico.com	D
Air Canada	(888) 422-7533	www.aircanada.com	A
Air France	(800) 237-2747	www.airfrance.com	D
American Airlines	(800) 433-7300	www.aa.com	A
British Airways	(800) 247-9297	www.britishairways.com	D
Continental Airlines	(800) 523-3273	www.continental.com	A, B, C, E
Delta Air Lines	(800) 221-1212	www.delta.com	A
Emirates	(800) 777-3999	www.emirates.com	D
Frontier Airlines	(800) 432-1359	www.frontierairlines.com	A
KLM Royal Dutch Airlines	(800) 447-4747	www.klm.com	D
Lufthansa	(800) 399-5838	www.lufthansa.com	D
Northwest Airlines	(800) 225-2525	www.nwa.com	A
Qatar Airways	(877) 777-2827	www.qatarairways.com	D
Singapore Airlines	(800) 742-3333	www.singaporeair.com	D
TACA	(800) 400-8222	www.taca.com	D
United Airlines	(800) 864-8331	www.united.com	A
US Airways	(800) 428-4322	www.usairways.com	A

holiday season or other big travel holidays, it's a good idea to arrive at least two hours early. Even though both Houston airports have plenty of security lines and ticket counters, there is always a line during peak travel times.

Both airports have plenty of on-site and off-site parking lots for long-term and short-term parking. At $2 for up to 3 hours and $6 for 3 to 24 hours, each airport's city-owned Parking Cents lot is one of the cheapest places to park. Intercontinental's Parking Cents lot is located at JFK Boulevard and Greens Road as you approach the terminals. Hobby's Parking Cents lot is on-site and within walking distance of the terminals. Look for the signs with a pink piggy bank.

George Bush Intercontinental Airport

Previously called Intercontinental Airport, Houston's largest and busiest airport was renamed to honor the 41st U.S. president and Houston resident George H. W. Bush in 1997. Houstonians tend to refer to the airport—abbreviated

i Get around downtown more quickly— and avoid the heat and rain—by walking through the underground tunnels. See the downtown map on page vii or read about the tunnels on page 115 of the "Attractions" chapter to learn more.

as IAH—as "Intercontinental" or "Bush Intercontinental." Currently, Intercontinental, which is located off the Hardy Toll Road, is served by 17 commercial airlines, as well as some passenger charter airlines. Because this bustling airport is Continental Airlines' biggest hub and Houston is the largest major city near Mexico and Latin America, more than 700 flights depart from Intercontinental each day. These flights give residents and visitors access to more than 185 domestic and international destinations.

To accommodate its many airlines and passengers, Intercontinental has five terminals, lettered A through E. Passengers departing

Houston on international airlines leave out of Terminal D. International inbound flights provided by Continental Airlines arrive in Terminal E. The Inter-Terminal Train provides a quick connection between terminals B, C, and E. Follow the signs for the train, which are located in the ticketing areas and terminals. The airport's sheer size means passengers typically have a long way to walk from the gate to baggage claim. Look for the men and women driving carts around the airport to get a ride if the long distance is a problem.

Intercontinental's many amenities make the airport seem like a city unto itself. There are more than 50 restaurants and bars here, including fast-food chains like McDonald's, Chili's, and—in Terminal E—popular local restaurants like Pappas BBQ, Pappadeaux Seafood Kitchen, and Pappasito's Cantina. You'll also find plenty of Houston and Texas paraphernalia in the airport gift shops, as well as some higher-end shops. Other highlights include an interfaith chapel, a currency exchange booth, and multilingual service representatives.

i **Arriving on an international flight? Grab a free-to-use luggage cart in the customs area.**

William P. Hobby Airport

After stints as Houston Municipal Airport and Howard R. Hughes Airport—yes, *that* Howard Hughes—Houston's oldest commercial airport was renamed in 1967 to honor former Texas governor William P. Hobby. Abbreviated as HOU, Hobby's location, just 7 miles south of downtown Houston off I-45/Gulf Freeway, makes this a more convenient airport to fly in and out for many visitors and Houstonians. With just five airlines and no international flights currently serving Hobby, it is not nearly as crowded as Intercontinental. All five airlines—Southwest, AirTran, JetBlue, Delta, and American—fly out of the Central Concourse. Combined, they provide nonstop or direct service to more than 32 destinations around the United States.

Airport Web Site

George Bush Intercontinental Airport and William P. Hobby Airport share a Web site. Visit www.fly2houston.com for useful information about both airports, including travel alerts and arrival and departure information.

---

i **Baggage carts aren't allowed on the Bush Intercontinental Inter-Terminal Train.**

Hobby Airport has more than a dozen dining and drinking establishments, most of them located in the food court. Food options range from good local restaurants like Barry's Pizza, Pappasito's Cantina, and Pappas Burgers to national chains like Wendy's and Subway. The airport also has newsstands, gift shops, an interfaith chapel, a currency exchange booth, and multilingual special service representatives. Hobby is home to the 1940s Air Terminal Museum, which commemorates the old terminal's classic art-deco architecture as well as its role in early aviation.

From the Airports to the City

The baggage claim level is the place to find transportation options from both of Houston's airports. Head out the door and a ground transportation agent can help you find taxis and limos, hotel and rental car shuttles, and more. Or inquire at the information desk on the baggage claim level for suggestions about how to get around.

i **Since Intercontinental is one of Continental Airlines' hubs, you can often find last-minute weekend getaway flights between Houston and locations around the country, as well as South America, for as little as $119 round-trip. Visit www.continental.com and go to "Deals & Offers" to check out the current deals.**

Airlines Serving Hobby Airport

Airline	Phone Number	Web Site
AirTran Airways	(800) 247-8726	www.airtran.com
American Airlines	(800) 433-7300	www.aa.com
Delta Air Lines	(800) 221-1212	www.delta.com
JetBlue Airways	(800) 538-2583	www.jetblue.com
Southwest Airlines	(800) 435-9792	www.southwest.com

i **Picking someone up at the airport? Avoid the hassle of circling the terminal by parking in the free passenger pickup waiting lot at either Intercontinental or Hobby. Just remind your guest to call and let you know when he or she has arrived.**

Car Rental

Eight national rental car agencies serve Houston's two airports. Most rental car agencies have additional drop-off and pickup locations around the city, although these don't typically have as many cars for rent—and often close earlier—than the airport locations.

To rent a car at Hobby, head down to the baggage claim level and find the booth for your preferred agency. Once you pay, an agent will send you outside to catch a shuttle to the appropriate pickup lot.

At Intercontinental, the eight rental companies share a consolidated rental car facility, located about five minutes from the terminals. Just follow the rental car signs and head outside after picking up your bags in baggage claim. Then hop on one of the white and maroon buses marked RENTAL CAR SHUTTLE and take a free five-minute ride to the facility, where you'll find

i **Save yourself a headache and rent a GPS system at the car rental agency. You don't want to be stuck consulting a map while you drive down the jam-packed freeways here.**

your agency's office and car lot. If you're dropping off a rental car at the airport, give yourself an extra 15 minutes or so to leave the car.

i **If you're 60 or older, don't be coy about your age. Cab drivers give a 10 percent discount to senior passengers.**

Taxis and Limousines

City ordinances require Houston cabbies to charge $2.50 for the first 2/11 mile and 17 cents for each additional 1/11 mile. (That translates to $4 for the first mile and $1.87 for each additional mile.) The meters calculate waiting at a rate of 33 cents per minute. There's an additional $1.00 surcharge for all trips that start between 8 p.m. and 6 a.m.

Those 1/11 miles can add up quickly so Houston cab drivers charge a zone rate for trips to and from the airport. Most cab drivers will also run the meter and charge you the metered fare if it is less than the flat rate. Gratuity is not included in the zone rates, which are listed in a sidebar.

If you're traveling back to the airport or you need a cab or limo to get around town, call to reserve your ride. Although there are plenty of cabs in Houston, you won't typically see them in droves like you would in, say, New York City. On the following page are the phone numbers and Web sites for several taxi, town car, and limo companies. In many cases, you can make a reservation online, as well as over the phone.

Rental Car Agencies
Serving Intercontinental and Hobby Airports

Agency	Phone Number	Web Site
Alamo	(888) 826-6893	www.alamo.com
Avis	(281) 443-5800	www.avis.com
Budget	(281) 449-0145	www.budget.com
Dollar Car Rental	(866) 434-2226	www.dollar.com
Enterprise	(281) 230-8200	www.enterprise.com
Hertz	(281) 209-6700	www.hertz.com
National	(888) 826-6890	www.nationalcar.com
Thrifty Car Rental	(877) 283-0898	www.thrifty.com

A1 TRANSPORTATION TAXI, LIMO & TOWN CAR SERVICE
(866) 416-1975
www.a1transportationtaxi.com

AFC CORPORATE TRANSPORTATION
(713) 988-5466
www.afchouston.com

LIBERTY CAB
(713) 695-6700
www.libertycab.net

RIVER OAKS LIMO & TRANSPORTATION
(832) 203-7622
www.riveroakslimo.com

TAXIS FIESTA
(713) 225-2666
www.taxisfiesta.com

UNITED CAB
(713) 224-4445
www.unitedcab.com

YELLOW CAB TAXI
(713) 236-1111
www.yellowcabhouston.com

YELLOW CAB TOWNE CAR SERVICE
(713) 236-8877
www.yellowcabhouston.com

i Take advantage of what's known as "Six in the City." Every cab ride that starts and ends downtown costs a flat rate of $6.

Airport Shuttles

If you don't want to shell out money for a cab, limo, or rental car, there are a few alternatives for getting to and from the airport and around Houston:

SuperShuttle's blue and yellow vans provide ground transportation to and from Intercontinental and Hobby Airports. SuperShuttle offers a shared-ride service, which takes longer to get to your destination than a cab. The company also offers a more expensive Exclusive Ride Service. Prices vary, but shared rides usually cost between $20 and $30 with an advance reservation; Exclusive Ride Service costs about $75. Discounts are available for groups and round-trip purchases. Catch a ride on SuperShuttle by going to the company's desk in the baggage claim area or save a few dollars by making reservations in advance at (800) 258-3826 or www.supershuttle.com.

Houston's bus service, **METRO**, offers a nonstop shuttle between Intercontinental and downtown. The 30-minute trip costs $15 one-way or $30 round-trip. The shuttle leaves every 30 minutes. Downtown pickup is available at the Airport Direct Passenger Plaza at 1900 Main St. The shuttle runs from downtown to the airport

Taxi Zone Rates

To/From Intercontinental Airport

Zone	Rate
North Houston, 610 North	$38.00
Downtown	$44.50
Galleria, Greenway Plaza, Medical Center, Memorial, River Oaks	$51.00
Reliant Center	$55.00
Hobby Airport	$62.00
West Memorial, Bear Creek	$69.00
Ellington Airport, Westside	$74.50
NASA, Space Center Houston	$88.50
Kingwood	$28.50
Willowbrook	$35.00

To/From Hobby Airport

Zone	Rate
Medical Center, Ellington Field, Southeast Houston	$27.00
Downtown	$22.00
The Heights, Greenway Plaza	$33.00
Galleria, North Loop	$46.00
Bellaire, Town & Country	$52.00
Dairy Ashford	$59.50
TX 6	$68.50
Intercontinental Airport, Greenspoint	$60.50
NASA, Space Center Houston	$31.50
Kingwood	$73.00
Willowbrook	$67.50

every day from 5:30 a.m. to 8:00 p.m. and from Intercontinental to downtown from 6:10 a.m. to 8:40 p.m. To take the shuttle from the airport to downtown, look for the METRO AIRPORT DIRECT sign in the baggage claim area. For more information, call (713) 635-4000 or visit www.ridemetro.org.

Some hotels—especially those near the airport—offer complimentary shuttle service for their guests. Call ahead to find out if yours does. Hotels farther away from the airport don't usually provide service to and from the airport, but they might provide service to attractions and restaurants within a 3-mile radius.

i The Fannin South Park & Ride lot charges a daily parking rate of $2.50.

BY TRAIN AND BUS

Amtrak

The Houston Amtrak station is located on the northwestern edge of downtown at 902 Washington Ave., just off I-45. The station provides service on the Sunset Route, which extends from Los Angeles to New Orleans, with stops in San Antonio and other locations on the southern border of Arizona, New Mexico, California, and Louisiana. The full-service station is very clean and has an indoor waiting area. Those traveling with heavy luggage can get free baggage assistance and check bags here. Free short-term and long-term parking is available; there is also a taxi stand. The station is fully wheelchair accessible. For a schedule or to purchase tickets, call (800) 872-7245 or go online to www.amtrak.com.

i Make sure you have a paid ticket while standing on the METRORail platform. These are paid-fare zones, so you can receive a class C misdemeanor and a fine of up to $500 for waiting on the platform sans ticket.

Greyhound

There are six Greyhound stations in Houston, plus a few more in the exurbs, including Conroe, Humble, Katy, and Texas City. The main Houston Greyhound station is located a few miles north of downtown at 2121 South Main St.; the ticket counter and station here are open 24 hours. Other locations are based in North, Northwest, Southeast, and Southwest Houston, though these are not typically open all night. Greyhound buses also stop at the Amtrak station, listed above, but there are no bus ticketing or baggage facilities at that location. Greyhound Bus Line information, including addresses of additional Houston stations, is available by calling (800) 231-2222 or (713) 759-6565, or by visiting www.greyhound.com.

BY FERRY

If you're spending time east of Houston in the Baytown area, you may need to take the Lynchburg Ferry. It takes Houstonians, visitors, and their cars across the Houston Ship Channel so they can get to and from Houston. One of the fleet's two ferries departs every 5 to 10 minutes from 4:30 a.m. to 8:15 p.m. Just drive onto the ferry at 1001 South Lynchburg Rd. in Baytown, and set sail for a free 7- to 10-minute trip to the other side. The ferries hold 12 cars at a time. Call (281) 424-3521 for more information.

BY PUBLIC TRANSPORTATION

Houston's public transportation options—though improving—aren't nearly as abundant or efficient as those in other large cities like New York, Chicago, and San Francisco. The Metropolitan Transit Authority, better known as METRO, runs the city's public transportation, which includes bus service and a new light-rail system.

METRO buses run all over Harris County and most routes travel on local streets, with stops every other block or so. Coupled with Houston traffic, this can make for some very slow travel if you have far to go, especially if you need to switch buses. To speed up their commute, some people ride their bikes for part of the way and then board a bus with the bike to travel longer distances. If you take your bike on a bus, be aware that the bus driver is not permitted to help you maneuver and lock up your bike.

Those who don't want to drive long distances to work or don't want to hassle with parking can take advantage of METRO's Park & Ride service, which allows commuters to park their cars for free at a designated Park & Ride location and take the bus to work. There are 26 Park & Ride lots in Harris County. Prices to ride the Park & Ride buses vary depending on where you are traveling, but you will pay somewhere between $2.00 and $4.50. Discounts are available for seniors.

Houston's METRORail system, which just opened in 2004, provides service between downtown, the Museum District, Hermann Park, Rice University, the Houston Zoo, and Reliant Park. Five more rail lines will open in 2012, making it even easier to get around the downtown area. Riding from one end of the existing red line to the other takes 30 minutes. The METRORail begins running at 4:30 a.m. on weekdays and at 5:30 a.m. on weekends. The train runs until 11:40 p.m. Monday through Thursday, until 2:15 a.m. Friday and Saturday, and until 12:45 a.m. Sunday.

i For METRORail and METRO bus routes, Park & Ride locations, or schedule information, call (713) 635-4000 or visit www.ridemetro.org. METRORail and local METRO bus fare costs $1.25 (60 cents for seniors) per trip. This includes free transfers for up to two hours after you board your first bus or train. You may pay for a ride on a METRO bus in cash or using a Q Card ride pass, which can be purchased at retailers around the city, including Valero gas stations and Fiesta, Randalls, and Kroger grocery stores. METRORail riders must have a Q Card or a METRORail ticket, which can be purchased from the ticket vending machines located on all the rail platforms. Although you will not be asked for your ticket when you board the train, an officer may come onboard to make sure you have one. A complete list of retailers that sell Q Cards can be found on the METRO Web site.

HOUSTON HISTORY

Like many U.S. cities founded in the first half of the 1800s, Houston's story begins with some entrepreneurs heading west hoping to strike it rich. In August 1836, just four months after Texas revolutionaries had defeated the Mexican army and won Texas its independence, two entrepreneurial brothers arrived in Texas, looking to establish a port city. Their names were Augustus Chapman Allen and John Kirby Allen.

The Allen brothers, who hailed from New York City, wanted to build a city where a stream called the Buffalo Bayou met the San Jacinto River—not far from where Texas revolutionaries had won the decisive Battle of San Jacinto a few months earlier. When they couldn't strike a deal to buy this fertile land, the Allen brothers journeyed a little farther west, following the Buffalo Bayou to the spot where it merges with White Oak Bayou. Since the duo wanted to build a port city, they sought a place where other countries and parties could come to trade and the narrow bayou seemed to provide ample space for the ships of those days to enter the city and turn around. The Allens decided to build their city in this spot, now dubbed Allen's Landing. They purchased about 6,600 acres of land for $9,000.

Simply discovering an ideal place for a city wasn't enough, of course. The Allens, being the real estate developers that they were, needed people to pay them to live on the land. On August 30, 1836, the brothers placed an ad in the Texas newspaper *Telegraph and Texas Register,* inviting people to purchase lots in their new town for relatively low prices. The ad promised abundant timber and grassland in the coastal plains town. It also declared that the new town would become the "great interior commercial emporium of Texas." In case this wasn't enough to lure people to the new city, the Allens also suggested that ships from New York and New Orleans could sail up Buffalo Bayou to the city, which boasted cool breezes. This last part, as any Houstonian can tell you, bordered on false advertising. Houston is hot and humid most of the year.

The brothers' ad referred to the new city as the "Town of Houston." The name Houston was already familiar to many Texans. The city's namesake—General Sam Houston—had led the Texas revolutionaries to victory and helped Texas become an independent nation in April 1836. General Houston's army—Texians, they were called—had been defeated at the Alamo in San Antonio on March 6, and that defeat and the "Remember the Alamo!" battle cry it inspired had led many colonialists to join the Texas revolutionaries. Six weeks later, on April 21, 1836, Houston and his army snuck up on the Mexican army as it took a siesta at San Jacinto, an area just southeast of what is now Houston. In less than 20 minutes, General Houston and his army captured the Mexican president and general Antonio López de Santa Anna and captured or killed hundreds of other Mexicans. Within three weeks, Santa Anna signed peace treaties agreeing to Mexico's pullout of what is now Texas. Sam Houston, meanwhile, became a national hero and got a city named after him. While the Allen brothers' sales skills convinced 12 people to move to their new city as of January 1, 1837, having the general's name attached couldn't have hurt either.

THE CAPITAL YEARS

The Allen brothers had big visions for their little town, so they convinced the still-new Texas Congress and then-Texas president Sam Houston to move the Republic of Texas capital from nearby Columbia to Houston. On May 1, 1837, the Texas Congress met in Houston for the first time. One month later, on June 5, 1837, the congress granted the incorporation of the City of Houston. James S. Holman, an agent who worked for the Allen Brothers' Houston Town Company, was named the city's first mayor. Shortly after becoming an incorporated city, Houston was named the county seat of Harrisburg County. The county was renamed Harris County in 1839.

Houston's tenure as the capital of Texas was short-lived. When Mirabeau B. Lamar became Texas's second president in 1839, he had the capital moved two hours northwest to Austin, which is the capital today. Still, the Houston's founders kept pushing forward. In 1840 Houston established a chamber of commerce to promote shipping and trade along the Buffalo Bayou. Shortly thereafter, Mayor John Andrews and the city aldermen established the Port of Houston Authority, which oversaw the regulation of slips, wharves, and roads of neighboring Buffalo Bayou and White Oak Bayou.

Houston was renamed the capital only briefly in 1842. Three years later, in 1845, the Republic of Texas was annexed by the United States, becoming the 28th state to join the Union. For the moment, Houston's future looked dreary. Some residents weren't thrilled about becoming U.S. citizens; some worried about the new state's financial situation. To make matters worse, a deadly yellow fever and cholera outbreak hit the Midwest and the port city wasn't producing the kind of trade the Allen Brothers had envisioned. This may have been partly because Houston lost its credibility when it ceased being the capital and it didn't help that the Buffalo Bayou wasn't nearly as easy to navigate as the city's founders had thought or hoped. In fact, when Francis R. Lubbock rode the first steamship to Houston in 1837, he lamented that the branches that filled Buffalo Bayou made it nearly impossible to see the town. To make matters worse, frequent rainstorms created so much mud that it was nearly impossible to reach the city by land.

> **i** The site of the Texas army's victory at San Jacinto is now marked with a towering monument and museum that are open to the public. Find out about visiting the San Jacinto Battleground State Historic Site on page 118 of the "Attractions" chapter.

Despite these problems, most Houstonians stuck around. Like so many Americans in those days, they held out hope—in this case, hope that the city would eventually become a trading hot spot, just as the Allen brothers had envisioned.

BIRTH OF THE RAILROADS

Houston's early settlers soon got their wish. Thanks in part to the new chamber of commerce and the port authority, business began picking up in the city, with frame buildings popping up around what is now the downtown area. In 1842 the Texas legislature authorized the city to clean up the Buffalo Bayou to make it easier for ships to navigate. The chamber of commerce, meanwhile, began a channel improvement project that would result in repeated attempts to widen Buffalo Bayou so that ships could get in and out more easily.

The waterways are just one part of Houston's story during those early years. Recognizing that people had to be able to get around—and move agriculture and other goods—if Houston was to become a major city, the chamber of commerce helped develop the state's first railroad—Buffalo Bayou, Brazos & Colorado Railroad. The chamber also established Texas's first telegraph line. The railroad, which began providing service in 1853, was only the second railroad west of the Mississippi River and the first part of what is now the Southern Pacific Railroad. Other railroads followed and, within a few years, Houston's railroads were connected with those of Galveston—the area immediately on the Gulf Coast, about 50 miles southeast of downtown. Houston railroads were also connected with other rails in the state, earning Houston the nickname "city where 17 railroads meet the sea." The new railroads shipped out agricultural products and lumber from East Texas's piney woods; they brought in cotton from nearby plantations.

All of this shipping activity inspired optimism and confidence in Houstonians and Texans. Streets were paved with shells, Buffalo Bayou was dredged deeper, and the population and the local economy were growing. The city suffered a big blow in 1859, when a fire raged through it, destroying many homes and businesses. Still, with the railroads in place, the city continued trading.

THE CIVIL WAR YEARS

Two years after that devastating fire, the people of Texas voted to secede from the Union and Governor Sam Houston was forced out of office for refusing to join the Confederacy. The Union blockaded the Texas coastline at the beginning of the war and took control of nearby Galveston in October 1862. Three months later, on January 1, 1863, Confederate general John Magruder surprised Union troops with a quick offensive that allowed the Confederacy to reclaim Galveston. Magruder used Houston to get his troops organized for the Battle of Galveston, which was waged both on land and at sea. No fighting ever took place on Houston soil, though.

January 1, 1863, also happened to be the day that President Abraham Lincoln's Emancipation Proclamation was supposed to take effect. But Houston's railroads and telegraphs weren't sufficient to get the word out that the slaves were freed—certainly not when Texas was under Confederate control. Not until June 19, 1865, did the news spread that slaves in Texas were emancipated. That's the day that Union general Gordon Granger and some 2,000 federal troops arrived in Galveston to reclaim Texas and announce the slaves' liberation. Slaves throughout Galveston—and soon Houston—celebrated in the streets. The date of Granger's arrival and proclamation

became known as Juneteenth and continues to be celebrated in Texas, 28 other states, and Washington, D.C. today.

The Texas economy suffered greatly when the Civil War ended in 1865, and Houston suffered another yellow fever outbreak two years later. But all of the activity going on in the fledgling city might have made it seem otherwise. New brick buildings were cropping up, more streets were paved with shells, and in 1876 public schools opened for children ages 8 to 14. There were so many railroads traveling through the city that, by 1890, Houston was regarded as Texas's biggest railroad hub.

Buffalo Bayou was also undergoing further development. In 1869 civic leaders established the Houston Ship Channel Company, which was tasked with digging a channel and dredging Buffalo Bayou deeper. As always, the hope was that ships could travel through and turn around more easily. During the last decade of the 19th century, the rest of the world finally got access to the Port of Houston. But the endless efforts to develop Buffalo Bayou still weren't enough to unseat the older and more easily accessible Port of Galveston as the state's most bustling port.

PORT DOMINANCE

The Port of Houston's struggle to match the traffic of Port of Galveston came to an abrupt end when a hurricane struck Galveston in September 1900. Known as the Hurricane of 1900, the devastating storm killed an estimated 8,000 people and destroyed millions of dollars' worth of property and infrastructure. Galveston worked to rebuild its port, but the storm's fierceness had done damage that no amount of rebuilding could fix: The hurricane highlighted that inland ports are far better protected than those along the Gulf Coast. Houston soon became Texas's leader in trade and industry.

This development wasn't lost on the rest of the country. Between 1900 and 1910, the city's population doubled to 78,000, and in 1902 President Theodore Roosevelt appropriated $1 million to develop the Port of Houston and make it into a deep-water port, allowing bigger ships to visit the area. Congress soon allocated millions more on the condition that Harris County taxpayers pay for the other half of the construction of a 25-foot channel. In November 1914, after seven years of digging, President Woodrow Wilson pressed a button at the White House, remotely firing a mortar gun and officially opening the Port of Houston to shipping and marine commerce. That port, located on the east side of Houston, is now home to the Houston Ship Channel.

OIL BOOM

At the same time that Houston was making its name as a major national and international port, the city was also staking out another claim to economic prosperity: oil. In 1901 oil was discovered on a salt-dome formation at Spindletop, located east of Houston near Beaumont, Texas. This wasn't just any oil, mind you. The first geyser, produced after salt-dome formation expert Anthony F. Lucas had drilled in the area, blew oil more than 100 feet high. The geyser took nine days to cap; it flowed close to 100,000 barrels a day. With that, land prices in the area jumped and major oil companies and entrepreneurs moved in to find places to drill. When they did strike gold, they built refining units, pipelines, and storage facilities around the area. Everyone wanted to get a piece of the petroleum pie, and Houston's economy reaped the benefits.

The fact that the discovery of oil at Spindletop coincided with the opening of the ship channel was particularly fortuitous. Now the city had another asset to export—an asset that everyone around the world wanted and needed as automobiles and airplanes were becoming more common. It was also an asset that would become crucial in two world wars.

AIDING THE WAR EFFORT

Trains and ships helped shape much of Houston's early history, so it seems only fitting that airplanes also played a role here. In 1917, shortly before World War I began, the United States government purchased nearly 1,300 acres in southeast Houston to build an air base. Ellington Field, as it was named, served as a flight-training base during World War I. About 5,000 men and 250 aircraft were assigned to the base over the course of the war.

The government ordered the closure of Ellington Field in 1923, but the Texas National Guard decided to base the 111th Observation Squadron there. The facilities at Ellington Field were becoming quickly outdated, though, and within a few years, the National Guard transferred the squadron to newer facilities at the municipal airport (now known as William P. Hobby Airport). The military subsequently leased Ellington Field to local farmers, who used the then-overgrown fields as pasture.

Shortly before the United States became involved in World War II, it became apparent that Ellington Field would be needed by the military once again. Houston had become a leader in the petrochemical industry and many petrochemical refineries and manufacturing plants had been constructed along the ship channel to build and fuel new ships to aid the war effort. These refineries and plants, U.S. representative Albert Thomas argued, needed military protection, and Ellington Field was the most convenient place to base this protection.

Ellington Field was quickly expanded and used to provide advanced training for bomber pilots and house the United States Army Air Corps' bombardier school, which was soon replaced with a navigation school. More than five dozen women in the Women's Army Corps were also stationed at Ellington Field, which became a reserve air base once the war ended.

POSTWAR GROWTH AND DIVERSIFICATION

During World War II, tonnage levels had been decreased and shipping had been halted in the Houston Ship Channel, but the petrochemical industry, steel manufacturing, shipbuilding, and explosives factories had helped sustain Houston's economy. Once the war was over, though, there was no use for the wartime factories. With tonnage levels back at their normal levels and shipping resumed, Houston's economy became port driven again. Now, however, the city was diversifying its offerings, with the energy industry becoming a huge asset. The city had developed natural gas, and the Houston-based Texas Eastern Transmission Corporation had laid pipes that could transport gas northward to heat homes during the winter. Just as people up north were getting their winter heat, people down south were introduced to a modern amenity called air-conditioning—an amenity that Houstonians can't imagine living without today. When air-conditioning became available in the 1950s, many companies moved to Houston, which by then was considered the home of the energy sector.

Houston's postwar diversification also extended to medicine. In 1945 the M.D. Anderson Foundation founded the Texas Medical Center, positioning the city to become an international leader in medicine and research. As the Texas Medical Center grew in the years that followed, people from around the world visited Houston to seek treatment for cancer, heart disease, and countless other ailments from some of the world's leading doctors.

SPACE CITY LIFTS OFF

In 1963 the **National Aeronautics and Space Administration** (NASA) opened its Manned Spacecraft Center 30 miles south of Houston. Renamed the Lyndon B. Johnson Space Center in 1973, the NASA field installation made the aerospace industry an essential component of Houston's economy and earned the city the nickname "Space City." As the Mission Control Center for human space flights and the home base for U.S. astronauts, the Johnson Space Center employed more than 5,000 people during its early days. (Today, the Johnson Space Center employs more than 19,000 people.) These weren't the only jobs NASA brought to town. More than

100 companies followed NASA to Houston in the 1960s and 1970s.

The Johnson Space Center wasn't the only exciting addition to Houston in the 1960s. In 1965 the Astrodome opened. As the world's first indoor domed sports stadium, the Astrodome was nicknamed "Eighth Wonder of the World." From the beginning, the 9.5-acre Astrodome was home to the Houston Astros baseball team. Named the Colt .45s when they joined Major League Baseball and came to Houston in 1962, the Astros adopted a new name, which—like the Astrodome's name—paid homage to Houston's new role in the space industry. The Astros played their first season at the Astrodome on green-painted dirt and dead grass before Astroturf was installed in 1966. Notably, Mickey Mantle hit the first home run at the Astrodome during an April 9, 1965, preseason game between the Astros and the New York Yankees. In 1968 the Houston Oilers—a charter member of the American Football League in 1960—made their home at the Astrodome, too. In the years that followed, the Astrodome would host a variety of events, including the 1989 NBA All-Star Game, the 1992 Republican National Convention, the annual Houston Livestock Show and Rodeo, University of Houston football games, bowl games, the 1971 Final Four, and many conventions.

BOOMTOWN

For years after World War II, Houston experienced tremendous population growth—and not just because people were having babies. After the war, Houston doubled in size when the city annexed unincorporated areas into the city limits. While the city would continue to annex other unincorporated areas over the years, the population grew throughout the late 1970s, in part, because the economy in the Midwest's rust-belt states had collapsed. Many Midwesterners saw this as a sign that it was time to jump ship, abandon the harsh winters, and head to where the jobs were. The Arab oil embargo had created plenty of job opportunities in the oil sector, luring many of these Midwesterners to Houston.

"HOUSTON, WE HAVE A PROBLEM"

The 1980s weren't a great time for Houston. In 1983 Hurricane Alicia—a category-3 storm—hit Galveston and Houston. The storm killed 21 people and caused $2.6 billion in damage, making it Texas's first billion-dollar storm. Alicia caused close to two-dozen tornadoes and a major oil spill in nearby Texas City. It also blew windows out of many office buildings and stores.

Houston's population boom also came to an abrupt halt during the 1980s. Falling oil prices mid-decade spelled layoffs and fewer job openings in the oil sector. Some people who worked in the oil business left the industry or even the city.

The explosion of the space shuttle *Challenger* in 1986 didn't help matters. For several years thereafter, the entire aerospace industry was in disarray, as government officials and the public questioned the safety and future of human space flight. Financial cuts and ill perceptions of the aerospace industry hurt Houston at a time when a recession was already putting pressure on the economy.

BASKETBALL, BUSHES, AND THE EARLY 1990S

At the end of the 1980s and during the early 1990s, Houston gained some positive PR and a little economic boost when the city showed its hospitality. In 1989 the NBA hosted its annual All-Star Game at the Astrodome, with 44,735 people in attendance. The following year, then-president and Houston resident George H. W. Bush hosted international financial leaders at the 16th annual G-7 Summit, which was held at Rice University. Two years later, the GOP held its Republican National Convention at the Astrodome, where the convention renominated Bush and his vice president, Dan Quayle. After the duo lost the general election to Bill Clinton and Al Gore, Bush and First Lady Barbara Bush moved to Houston, where they are often seen at sporting events today.

CLUTCH CITY

For many years Houston sports fans had a chip on their shoulders: None of Houston's major sports teams had ever won a national title. They'd come close a few times: The Astros had put up a good fight in the National League Championship Series in 1986 and the Rockets had made it to the NBA Finals in 1981 and 1986. But Houston didn't get a world championship until June 22, 1994, when the Houston Rockets basketball team defeated the New York Knicks in game seven of the NBA Finals. Reaching this point hadn't been easy. In the second round of the playoffs against the Phoenix Suns, the Rockets had blown leads and lost their first two games. A giant headline on the front page of the *Houston Chronicle* had declared Houston "Choke City," a reminder of the many times that Houston's basketball, football, and baseball teams had come close to a big win, only to choke. Yet the 1994 Rockets team, led by now–Hall of Famer Hakeem Olajuwon, showed tenacity and came back to beat Phoenix in seven games, rallying the city around them. After they won the next two series—and the city's first championship—the *Chronicle* ran a front-page headline that read "Clutch City." With that, the city had a new nickname, and the team had a new rallying cry. National commentators didn't pick—or even seem to want—the Rockets to win it all. But this team had done it in the most unfathomable way and 1 million Houstonians gladly celebrated the Rockets in their victory parade that summer. The following year the Rockets made a trade to bring native son Clyde Drexler home to play for the team and did it all over again: They blew the first two games against Phoenix in the second round before going on to win the city's second major championship—and raise a new rallying cry: "Double Clutch."

STADIUM MANIA AND THE DOWNTOWN REVITALIZATION

While the Rockets' success gave Houstonians a taste of victory and the city's other sports teams something to aspire to, their victories were also a prelude to some tough years ahead. In 1997 the owner of the Houston Oilers moved the football team to Tennessee, leaving Houstonians with no one team to root for. (Cheering for the nearby Dallas Cowboys is unthinkable.) As part of an effort to convince the NFL to award Houston an expansion team, the city and Houston Livestock Show and Rodeo officials proposed building a new stadium. In October 1999 the NFL awarded Houston an expansion team and the 2004 Super Bowl, to be held in the new stadium. Named Reliant Stadium, the new arena would sit next door to the Astrodome and have the NFL's first retractable roof. The new team would be named the Houston Texans. They played their first game at Reliant Stadium on September 8, 2002, upsetting the cross-state rival Dallas Cowboys in a game that remains a treasured piece of Houston sports history. As an indicator of how much Houstonians love their new football franchise, the Texans have sold out every single game—this, despite having never gone to the playoffs as of the 2008 season.

Houston's new football franchise wasn't the only team in town to get a new stadium. In 2000 the Houston Astros moved downtown to the new Enron Field. The following year, the Houston-based energy company Enron collapsed, mired in scandal and inflated profits in the second-largest bankruptcy ever. Needless to say, the Enron name was no longer fit for the city's baseball stadium. In 2002 Houston-based Minute Maid acquired the naming rights and renamed the stadium Minute Maid Park.

The following year the Houston Rockets and the Houston Aeros hockey team moved downtown to the Toyota Center. The new downtown stadiums commanded the attention of their home teams' respective leagues, with Minute Maid Park named the site of the 2004 MLB All-Star Game and the Toyota Center named the site of the 2006 NBA All-Star Game. The Astros also earned local and national attention in 2005, when they went to the World Series for the first time in the franchise's 45-year history. Although the team got swept by the Chicago White Sox, Houstonians were more joyful than distraught over the team's loss: They had finally gotten a taste of life near the top of Major League Baseball.

Building Minute Maid Park and the Toyota Center downtown was an essential part of the city's effort to give the center of Houston a much-needed makeover. In addition to the new stadiums, the city has built a light rail, making it easier for Houstonians to travel between downtown and some of the city's biggest attractions, including Hermann Park and Reliant Stadium. Several blocks worth of concrete have been turned into an enchanting park called Discovery Green. The redevelopment has also led to the opening of many new restaurants, hotels, and lofts and luxury apartments downtown.

STORMY WEATHER

Tropical Storm Allison

During the first decade of the 21st century, Houston dealt with more than its fair share of storms. In 2001 Tropical Storm Allison dumped more than 37 inches of rain on some parts of the city, causing severe flooding and teaching many Houstonians the importance of flood insurance. Twenty people were killed, and the city suffered billions of dollars' worth of damage.

Hurricane Katrina

Four years later, in 2005, Houston provided shelter for 150,000 people who fled Hurricane Katrina. About 25,000 Louisianans who had been staying at the Superdome in New Orleans were put up at the Astrodome; many others stayed at other buildings in the Reliant Center complex. Events at the Astrodome were canceled for the rest of the year, even though the evacuees moved out of the Astrodome and into local apartments or the neighboring Reliant Arena by mid-September. Many young Katrina evacuees enrolled in schools around the city, as many families decided to stay in Houston permanently; others moved back to Louisiana or elsewhere in the region.

Hurricane Rita

With the Katrina evacuees serving as a fresh reminder of the damage wreaked by the most recent Gulf Coast storm, Houstonians fretted when

(Q) Close-up

Important Dates in Houston History

1836: Texas wins its independence from Mexico; Houston is founded by the Allen Brothers.

1837: Houston is incorporated and named the capital of Texas and the county seat of Harrisburg County.

1839: Harrisburg County is renamed Harris County; Texas capital is moved to Austin.

1840: Houston Chamber of Commerce is established.

1845: Texas is annexed by the United States.

1853: Buffalo Bayou, Brazos & Colorado Railroad begins providing service, becoming Texas's first railroad.

1859: A major fire destroys many Houston homes and businesses.

1861: Texas secedes from the Union.

1862: The Union takes control of Galveston.

1863: Confederate general John Magruder and his troops reclaim Galveston in the Battle of Galveston.

1865: Union general Gordon Granger arrives in Galveston and announces slaves' liberation.

1869: The Houston Ship Channel Company is established.

1876: Houston public schools are established.

1900: Hurricane of 1900 hits Galveston, killing 8,000.

1901: Oil is discovered at Spindletop.

1902: President Theodore Roosevelt appropriates $1 million to make the Port of Houston a deep-water port.

1914: The Port of Houston opens.

1917: Ellington Field opens as a flight-training base for the military.

1930: Houston is the most populous city in Texas.

1945: The Texas Medical Center is founded.

1963: NASA opens the Manned Spacecraft Center, 30 miles southeast of Houston.

the category-5 storm Hurricane Rita was expected to strike the Houston area. About 2.5 million Houstonians evacuated in anticipation of the storm's landfall in late September 2005, marking the largest urban evacuation in U.S. history. The freeways were so congested that the two-and-a-half-hour drive to San Antonio took Houston evacuees up to 20 hours. In the end Rita did little damage to Houston, but schools were closed for days after the storm so evacuees could return home without causing the same sort of traffic build-up that they had caused during their exodus.

Hurricane Ike

On September 13, 2008, Hurricane Ike hit Galveston Island before rolling into Houston. Ike was only a category-2 storm by the time it stuck the Texas coast, but high winds, subsequent rain and flooding in parts of the city, and the passage of the storm's eye right over the city made Ike the third most destructive hurricane to ever hit the United States. Mandatory evacuations were ordered in Galveston, where residents were warned that they would "face certain death." Thousands defied these orders, though, and

1965: The Astrodome opens.

1973: The Manned Spacecraft Center is renamed Lyndon B. Johnson Space Center.

1983: Hurricane Alicia strikes Galveston and the Greater Houston area.

1986: Space shuttle *Challenger* explodes, hindering Houston's aerospace industry; the Astrodome hosts the MLB All-Star Game.

1989: The NBA All-Star Game is played at the Astrodome.

1990: Houston hosts the 16th G-7 Summit.

1992: Houston hosts the Republican National Convention.

1994 and 1995: Houston Rockets basketball team wins its first two NBA championships—the city's first professional sports championships.

1997: Houston elects its first black mayor, Lee Brown; Houston's football team, the Oilers, moves to Tennessee, leaving the city without a pro football team.

2000: The Houston Astros baseball team leaves the Astrodome and moves downtown to Enron Field.

2001: Hurricane Allison kills 20 people and floods Houston after more than 37 inches of rain fall on parts of the city; Houston-based Enron collapses.

2002: Enron Field is renamed Astros Park, then renamed Minute Maid Park; Houston's new pro football franchise, the Houston Texans, play their inaugural season and christen the new Reliant Stadium.

2003: The Houston Rockets basketball team and Houston Aeros hockey team move downtown to the Toyota Center.

2004: Super Bowl XXXVIII is played at Reliant Stadium; the MLB All-Star Game is played at Minute Maid Park.

2005: 150,000 Hurricane Katrina evacuees flee to Houston in August; in September 2.5 million Houstonians evacuate to avoid the impending landfall of Hurricane Rita; the Houston Astros play in their first World Series.

2006: The NBA All-Star Game is played at the Toyota Center.

2008: Hurricane Ike hits Galveston and Houston.

many paid the price with their lives. Thousands more Galvestonians and others in low-lying areas surrounding Houston lost their homes. Although fewer lives were lost in the City of Houston, the damage was still devastating. Many areas of the city didn't have power for two or even three weeks, preventing most schools from reopening for nearly two weeks after the storm. The high winds, flooding, fallen stoplights, and falling trees damaged or destroyed thousands of homes and businesses, many of which were put out of business or are still rebuilding today. The wind broke windows throughout downtown office buildings, including the JPMorgan Chase building—the city's tallest building—and tore huge holes in the roof at Reliant Stadium, the home of the Houston Texans football team, forcing the team to delay one game and play the rest of the season with an open roof. Yet while the damage seemed never ending at the time, the city has largely recovered, with most of the damage being repaired in Houston proper within a matter of weeks, or in some cases, a few months. In some ways the storm provided an opportunity for Houstonians to demonstrate their hospitality and bond with their neighbors. Many Houstonians who had air-conditioning or didn't sustain damage opened their homes to those who did and gave their time and resources to help their community. In Galveston and outlying areas closer to the coast, however, the rebuilding process has not happened quite as quickly, in part because the city's oceanfront was hit with the highest of tides, which swept away or flooded homes, possessions, and businesses.

DIVERSIFICATION AND TODAY'S ECONOMY

After the 1980s recession, Houston learned its lesson and diversified its economy, relying less on the petroleum industry and focusing more on the aerospace, health-care and biotechnology, technology, and education industries. At the same time the city has remained a big player on the international scene, serving as a major trading port between North and South America (particularly in the NAFTA era) and as a major hub for flights to Latin and South America, as well as Asia and Europe. Tourism and conventions also benefit the local economy: More than 31 million people visited the greater Houston area in 2007 and in 2008 the city hosted some 256 conventions, events, and shows, bringing in more than $550 million.

The fact that Houston has not allowed a single industry to define it has served the city well, even in the aftermath of Hurricane Ike and during the recession that began in 2008. While Houston has not been immune to layoffs or declining housing prices, it has fared better than most of the country. The city was recently identified as one of the best places to find a job, due in part to Houston's large, recession-proof health-care/biotechnology sector, as well as the city's role in education, technology, and international trade.

ACCOMMODATIONS

So you need a place to stay in Houston. Good news: You've got choices—lots of them. There are more than 60,000 hotel rooms in the Greater Houston area, not to mention RV parks, hostels, and chic bed-and-breakfasts. The vast majority of accommodations here are hotels and most—but certainly not all—are chains, many of which have multiple locations around the Greater Houston area. This chapter highlights some of the most centrally located accommodations. Additional locations can be found by consulting the phone book or visiting the Web site of your preferred hotel chain.

Accommodations here span a range of prices and bells and whistles. Most hotels include free cable, local phone calls, and some sort of shuttle service. About half throw in free high-speed Internet, others charge a daily or per-stay fee to get online. A few—including a couple of extended-stay hotels—have kitchens inside the rooms and some include breakfast in the cost of your visit. Parking is available at all hotels, although many—particularly those in the Galleria, Medical Center, and downtown—charge anywhere from $6 to $25 to park your car each night. If you're traveling with family, consider staying at one of the hotels with suites or request a connecting room, which many hotels offer. Just about all hotels here are wheelchair accessible. Several accommodate guests' four-legged friends; one hotel even has special doggie beds. Some pet-friendly hotels charge an extra fee for your furry friends to spend the night, but many don't. Several hotels in Houston are smoke-free facilities; these have been identified as such in the listings that follow.

There are a number of voguish hotels that cost upwards of $300 a night, but the majority of hotels here charge between $100 and $200 a night for a room. RV parks and hostels—as well as hotels located outside of high-traffic areas like downtown and the Galleria—charge significantly less. Prices are typically cheaper if you make reservations at least three weeks in advance. Many hotels offer Internet-only deals on their Web sites; these often beat the deals you'd get by making your reservation over the phone.

WHERE TO STAY

If you plan to see a bit Houston—and reading this book suggests you do—you'd be wise to stay in the Galleria area or downtown. Both of these areas are centrally located and offer easy access to restaurants, shopping, and anyplace you might want to go inside the Loop. The Galleria hotels are just a 15-minute drive from Reliant Park, downtown, the Texas Medical Center, the Museum District, and Hermann Park. Downtown hotels are even closer to these locations and within walking distance of the George R. Brown Convention Center, Discovery Green, Fortune 500 companies, Minute Maid Park, the Toyota Center, and the Theater District.

If you prefer something a little more off-the-beaten path, you've still got some good options. There are a range of accommodations in the Montrose and Museum District area, and there are RV parks along South Loop 610, just minutes from Reliant Center and the Texas Medical Center. If you're in town for the Houston Livestock Show and Rodeo, a Houston Texans football game, the Texas Bowl, or some other event at Reliant Center, you might want to stay at one of the hotels in the Medical Center or the West Loop.

This chapter presents a sampling of the accommodations in the Houston area, organized by neighborhood. This is by no means a comprehensive list of Houston accommodations but it should give you many options—and save you the hassle of Web site–hopping to find a place to rest your head.

Price Code

$................... under $100
$$ ....$100 to $199
$$$ ....$200 to $299
$$$$.................over $299

Prices are based on a one-night stay in one standard room. Please note: In a few cases, this chapter includes price ranges, such as $$–$$$. This typically means that there are some rooms available in the lower price bracket but many options—particularly suites—cost more. The price ranges listed here are based on May 2009 rates. Hotel rates often change and may be higher during the holidays or other peak times like during the Houston Livestock Show and Rodeo in late February and March. Rates here do not include the Houston hotel tax, which is 17 percent.

Downtown

ALDEN HOTEL $$$$
1117 Prairie St.
(832) 200-8800
www.aldenhotels.com
Guests at the Alden Hotel bask in luxury throughout their stay. Each of the 97 suites—not to mention the rest of the hotel—is decorated in a chic contemporary style. The beds here are covered with 400-thread-count, Egyptian-cotton sheets and down pillows and comforters. Other highlights include the requisite high-speed Internet, a free DVD and CD collection to use with the 42-inch plasma TV in each room, plush terry cloth robes, a 24-hour gym, and 24-hour room

service. Free shuttle service is offered within a 3-mile radius of the hotel. During your stay, be sure to dine at Alden's restaurant, *17, and the hip lounge, a+ bar and grille. You'll enjoy unique cocktails, an extensive wine list, and five-star American cuisine.

ATHENS HOTEL SUITES $$
1308 Clay St. at Caroline Street
(713) 739-1960
www.rainbowinnandstudios.com
With just 23 suites, Athens Hotel Suites looks and feels like a European hotel. Each suite has a washer and dryer, as well as a kitchenette with a full-size refrigerator, microwave, oven, and coffeepot. Cable, Internet, breakfast, and maid service are also included. Depending on your needs and price range, you can choose from executive, deluxe, and standard suites. Athens Hotel Suites is conveniently located in the heart of downtown, within walking distance of the George R. Brown Convention Center, the Theater District, the Toyota Center, City Hall, Minute Maid Park, and the METRORail.

BEST WESTERN DOWNTOWN $$
915 W. Dallas
(713) 571-7733
www.bwdowntown.com
Located on the west side of downtown, Best Western Downtown caters to guests who want few frills and don't want to shell out a lot of money. Guests who stay in one of the 75 suites here enjoy free parking, high-speed Internet, cable, and a hot breakfast, as well as use of the exercise room and Jacuzzi. This is a good place for professionals to stay or meet: In addition to a business center, the Best Western has a boardroom that seats 10. The hotel doesn't have any smoking rooms. It also offers free shuttle service to and from downtown.

COMFORT INN DOWNTOWN $
5820 Katy Fwy.
(713) 869-9211
www.choicehotels.com

 Make your reservation online to get lower room rates at the Alden Hotel.

Located just a couple minutes from the Downtown Aquarium and all of Houston's other downtown attractions, the Comfort Inn Downtown offers a good location for a fraction of the price of most downtown hotels. The 90 rooms here include standard Comfort Inn amenities like free continental breakfast, free local calls, free high-speed Internet, and daily newspaper delivery. There's also an outdoor pool. Some rooms have microwaves and refrigerators; laundry facilities are available onsite.

DOUBLETREE HOUSTON DOWNTOWN $$
400 Dallas St.
(713) 759-0202
http://doubletree1.hilton.com
When location matters, the Doubletree Houston Downtown delivers. This newly renovated hotel is located within walking distance of many big downtown firms and attractions, including the Theater District, Sam Houston Park, Minute Maid Park, the Toyota Center, the Downtown Aquarium, and the METRORail. The hotel is also connected to the downtown tunnel system, making it easy to get around. (Learn more about the tunnel system on page 115.) The Doubletree Houston Downtown has 350 guest rooms—some of which are large rooms, others are full suites. Every room and suite includes the Doubletree's signature Sweet Dreams beds and high-speed Internet; most also offer great views of Sam Houston Park or the downtown skyline. The hotel has a fitness center. Pets are permitted.

FOUR SEASONS DOWNTOWN $$$$
1300 Lamar St.
(713) 650-1300
www.fourseasons.com/houston
The 20 floors of the Four Seasons are home to 404 luxurious guest rooms, including 12 suites. Every room comes with the usual Four Seasons amenities—cushy beds, flat-screen TVs, CD/DVD players, wireless Internet, terry cloth robes, and twice-daily housekeeping service. When you leave your room, you've got options galore—a visit to the spa, fitness center, pool and hot tub, or the award-winning Italian restaurant Quattro.

Younger guests enjoy nightly milk and cookies, kid-size robes, and welcome bags. Babysitting is also available.

HILTON AMERICAS—HOUSTON $$$
1600 Lamar
(713) 739-8000
www.hilton.com
With 1,203 guest rooms, Hilton Americas—Houston is the largest convention hotel in the area. It's even connected to the George R. Brown Convention Center, making it the perfect place to stay if you're in town for a trade show or other convention. The hotel, which opened at the end of 2003, has two presidential suites, two chairman suites, and 36 one-bedroom and two-bedroom suites. Many rooms offer striking views of downtown and Discovery Green, an enchanting park and activity hub that is just across the street. Guests enjoy the amenities and great beds for which the Hilton is known, plus a heated pool; the Skyline Spa & Health Club; three bars and lounges; the hotel restaurant, Spencer's for Steaks and Chops; and high-speed Internet throughout the hotel. The hotel is located within walking distance of Minute Maid Park, the Toyota Center, the METRORail, and some great restaurants. Pets are permitted.

i Texas resident? Request the Texas Resident Package—aka a big discount on your room at the Hilton Americas—Houston.

HOLIDAY INN EXPRESS $$
1810 Bell St.
(713) 652-9400
www.hiexpress.com
Located just a few blocks from the George R. Brown Convention Center, Discovery Green, Minute Maid Park, Toyota Center, and tons of restaurants, the Holiday Inn Express offers a prime downtown location at an affordable price. Since the hotel just opened in 2001, the 114 rooms here are in great shape. Like other Holiday Inn Expresses, this one offers a free breakfast buffet, high-speed Internet and cable, and daily

housekeeping. There's also a business center, a whirlpool, and a small workout room.

HOTEL ICON $$$$
220 Main St.
(713) 224-4266
www.hotelicon.com

Hotel ICON offers one-of-a-kind accommodations, which helps explain why so many celebrities stay here. Located in the 1911 Union National Bank building, this "it" hotel features neoclassical architecture blended with intrepid contemporary designs. The 12-floor hotel has 135 guest rooms, including nine suites. Guests can take advantage of the luxury spa, oversized personal safes, a 24-hour fitness center, free Wi-Fi, and a first-class fitness center. The hotel is also home to Voice, one of the city's hottest new American restaurants, which you can learn more about on page 45 of the "Restaurants" chapter. Hotel ICON offers free car service, but it's within walking distance of major corporations' headquarters, Minute Maid Park, the Toyota Center, George R. Brown Convention Center, and the Theater District. Hotel ICON is also conveniently located on the METRORail line.

HYATT REGENCY $$$
1200 Louisiana St.
(713) 654-1234
www.hyattregencyhouston.com

Beauty and location are the hallmarks of this 30-floor atrium hotel. The 977 rooms at this Hyatt Regency location feature contemporary designs and great views of downtown. Every room includes Portico bath products, high-speed Internet, the Hyatt's trademark Hyatt Grand Beds, and 24-hour fitness center access. Imperial, presidential, and VIP grande suites are available. The Hyatt Regency is also home to Shula's Steakhouse and the people-watching hot spot, LobbiBar. The hotel is located within walking distance of Sam Houston Park, City Hall, the Theater District, dozens of restaurants and Fortune 500 companies, and Houston's baseball and basketball stadiums.

INN AT THE BALLPARK $$
1520 Texas Ave. at Crawford Street
(713) 228-1520
www.innattheballpark.com

Located just across from Minute Maid Park, this 208-room luxury hotel offers big-city amenities while allowing guests plenty of personal space for relaxing or working. Inn at the Ballpark is owned by the Landry restaurant family, which also owns the nearby Downtown Aquarium. Guests can take advantage of in-room spa services, evening turndown, 24-hour room service, free coffee, AVEDA bath products, free Wi-Fi and transportation, and safe deposit boxes. Suites are available starting at $300 for those who want even more space. When you're ready to leave your room, relax in the four-story bar and lounge or enjoy a fancy dinner at Vic & Anthony's Steakhouse, which you can learn more about on page 70 of the "Restaurants" chapter.

THE LANCASTER $$
701 Texas Ave.
(713) 228-9500
www.thelancaster.com

When you want intimacy and luxury, stay at the Lancaster, which *Condé Nast Traveler* called "one of the best places to stay in the world." With just 84 rooms and nine suites, the Lancaster enables its staff to focus on doing what they do best—catering to guests' every need and keeping the vases in the lobby filled with beautiful fresh-cut flowers. Every room offers a European feel with brass door knockers, marble vanities, and four-post wooden beds covered with high-end bedding, as well as in-room massage service. There's also free Wi-Fi and free town car service to local attractions. Bistro Lancaster offers 24-hour room service and dine-in options for those in the mood for everything from osso bucco to pan-seared crab cakes.

MAGNOLIA HOTEL $$
1100 Texas Ave.
(888) 915-1110
www.magnoliahotelhouston.com

Long gone are this building's days as the home of the *Houston Post-Dispatch* and as the headquarters for Shell Oil Company. Named Houston's best hotel by TripAdvisor.com, Magnolia Hotel epitomizes luxury, from the velvet curtains in each of the 314 guest rooms and suites to the rooftop pool and Jacuzzi. Guests enjoy free breakfast each morning and free domestic beer, house wine, and soft drinks in Magnolia's swanky lounges each evening. Other perks include a 24-hour fitness center, free Wi-Fi, car service, a bedtime cookie buffet, and a billiards room. Magnolia Hotel is just a few blocks from Fortune 500 companies' headquarters, Minute Maid Park, Discovery Green, the George R. Brown Convention Center, and the Toyota Center.

Galleria

CANDLEWOOD EXTENDED STAY $
4900 Loop Central Dr.
(888) 299-2208
www.candlewoodsuites.com
Located just half a mile south of the Galleria, the Candlewood Extended Stay is a popular choice for those in town for a few weeks, as well as those traveling on a budget. The 122 rooms and 24 suites here all include a full kitchen and access to the DVD and CD library. Housekeepers tidy up the rooms once a week. There's also a small workout room. Pets under 80 pounds are permitted for a fee of $75 for one to six nights and $150 for seven nights or more. On-site parking is free.

DOUBLETREE GUEST SUITES $$
5353 Westheimer Rd.
(713) 961-9000
http://doubletree1.hilton.com
Doubletree Guest Suites sits just a block from the Galleria and its 350-plus fine shopping and dining options, making this a great place to stay if you're planning to do some serious shopping or just want to stay in a central location. The 380 rooms here include a number of large suites, which are perfect for stays with the family. The hotel features all of the usual Doubletree amenities—great beds, great chocolate chip cookies,

Wi-Fi, and sophisticated decor. Every room also includes a microwave and a minirefrigerator and many rooms include a 32-inch TV. Sunbathers and swimmers can take advantage of the outdoor pool and whirlpool spa. Pets are permitted.

HILTON HOUSTON POST OAK $$
2001 Post Oak Blvd.
(713) 961-9300
www1.hilton.com
Located within walking distance of the Galleria, Hilton Houston Post Oak offers guests convenience and the Hilton amenities they've come to expect. The 448 guest rooms here include minibars, safes, high-speed Internet, and cushy bedding. The hotel also offers 24-hour room service, a business center, and a fitness center, as well as a British-style pub and a casual American restaurant called the Promenade. Complimentary shuttle service is available within a 3-mile radius of the hotel. Pets are permitted.

HOMESTEAD HOUSTON $
2300 W. Loop South
(713) 960-9660
www.homesteadhotels.com
The newly renovated rooms at Homestead Houston cater to those who are in town for a few weeks, as well as those looking for an inexpensive place to stay for a night or two. The studios and suites here include full kitchens, complete with utensils and cookware. There are also on-site laundry facilities. Wireless Internet costs $4.99 for the course of your stay. Pets are permitted for $25 per day. Van transportation is offered within a 3-mile radius.

HOTEL DEREK $$-$$$
2525 W. Loop South
(713) 961-3000
www.hotelderek.com
Hotel Derek is "designed to impress," according to its marketing materials, and at that the hotel succeeds. This is one of the most sophisticated hotels in Houston, featuring 314 contemporary guest rooms and great service. Guests enjoy high-

speed Internet, complimentary overnight shoe shine, a 24-hour fitness center, daily newspaper delivery, and free shuttle service within a 3-mile radius. The hotel is located across the street from the Galleria, providing easy access to some of the city's best shopping and restaurants.

INTERCONTINENTAL HOTEL $$–$$$$
2222 W. Loop South
(877) 270-1390
www.ichotelsgroup.com

Guests at this luxurious Galleria-area hotel enjoy countless amenities, including access to the business center, a full-service gym, same-day dry cleaning and laundry service, live entertainment, and use of the whirlpool and outdoor pool. Each of the 485 guest rooms and 13 suites includes cable and satellite TV, morning newspaper delivery, a coffee and tea maker, and plush bathrobes. High-speed Internet costs an additional $10.95 per day. Guests who don't want to venture down the street to the Galleria can dine on French and Spanish delicacies at the aptly named The Restaurant, or enjoy a martini and tapas at The Bar.

MARIOTT HOUSTON WEST LOOP $$$
1750 W. Loop South
(713) 960-0111
www.marriott.com

With its 14 meeting rooms, the Marriott Houston West Loop is a popular spot for businesspeople. The 13-floor, smoke-free hotel has 300 guest rooms, including two suites. Each room includes lavish down bedding, cable, and coffee and tea. Wireless Internet is an extra $12.95 per day. The on-site Alexander Restaurant serves Southwestern fare and the Fairway Lounge serves American dishes. Exercise options include an indoor atrium pool and a fitness center. The hotel is near the Galleria shopping area, as well as the running and biking trails of Memorial Park.

OMNI HOUSTON HOTEL $$
4 Riverway
(713) 871-8181
www.omnihotels.com

The Omni Houston Hotel offers luxurious Galleria-area accommodations at a reasonable price. There are 378 newly renovated guest rooms here, including 33 suites. Most offer great views of Houston or the hotel's two outdoor swimming pools. Every room includes an ample sitting area decorated with traditional decor, as well as amenities such as marble baths, plush robes, nightly turndown service, free Wi-Fi, and daily newspaper delivery. Guests can also get pampered at Mokara Spa and Cerón Salon or dine at Noe, an award-winning restaurant that serves eclectic American dishes. Special kid-friendly amenities are available. The Omni is about a three-minute drive from the Galleria.

SHERATON SUITES HOUSTON $$
2400 W. Loop South
(713) 586-2444
www.sheratonsuiteshouston.com

The Sheraton Suites is just a 2-block walk from the Galleria mall and restaurants. The hotel has 281 spacious suites, all of which come with free high-speed Internet, plush bathrobes and slippers, and two flat-screen televisions. Professionals have easy access to fax machines and copiers here, too. There's an Omaha Steakhouse on-site but there are plenty of better restaurants nearby. See the "Restaurants" chapter for suggestions.

THE ST. REGIS HOUSTON $$$
1919 Briar Oaks Lane
(713) 840-7600
www.starwoodhotels.com

Up until 10 years ago, the St. Regis was the Ritz-Carlton. Despite the name change, guests can still expect the same luxurious accommodations and great service, not to mention a convenient location smack-dab in between the Galleria and the exclusive River Oaks neighborhood. Owned by Starwood Hotels, the St. Regis has 232 spacious rooms and suites, which feature floor-to-ceiling windows, high-speed Internet, safes, and top-of-the-line linens. The hotel, which is known for its butler service, offers 24-hour room service, a fitness center, twice-daily turndown service, and a spa. Dining is available in the Zagat-rated Remington Restaurant, which features live music on Friday and Saturday nights. There's also an intimate wine room and an afternoon tearoom. Dogs are welcome.

THE WESTIN GALLERIA HOUSTON $$$
5060 W. Alabama
(713) 960-8100
www.starwoodhotels.com

A popular spot for meetings, weddings, and bar and bat mitzvah parties, the Westin Galleria is connected to the Galleria mall. The 487 rooms and 23 suites here all include Starwood Hotels' signature Heavenly bedding, coffeemakers with Starbucks coffee, and bathrobes. You can even request a special Heavenly Bed for your dog. High-speed Internet is available for a fee. Those in need of a workout can exercise in the gym or jog along nearby running paths. The hotel offers a running map with a 3-mile and a 5-mile route. Children's programming and babysitting are also available.

WESTIN OAKS $$$
5011 Westheimer at Post Oak
(713) 960-8100
www.starwoodhotels.com

Yes, there are two Westins at the Galleria, and yes, both of them are connected to the mall. They are not the same hotel, though: If you reserve a room at the Westin Galleria, they won't be able to find your name over at the Westin Oaks. Rooms at Westin Oaks are slightly pricier than those at the Westin Galleria, but the 406 rooms and nine suites here offer basically the same perks and accommodations—the Heavenly bedding, a gym, dog beds, babysitting service, and children's programming. There are also Jacuzzis in many of the rooms at this location.

Greenway Plaza

RENAISSANCE HOUSTON HOTEL
GREENWAY PLAZA $-$$
6 Greenway Plaza East
(713) 629-1200
www.marriott.com

Centrally located off US 59, this Marriott-owned hotel is just minutes from River Oaks, Montrose, West University, Rice University, the Museum District, and the Texas Medical Center. The airy rooms here are decorated with contemporary furniture and bold colors. The floor-to-ceiling windows give many of the 379 guest rooms and nine spacious suites some great views of the downtown skyline. Every room includes cable and bathrobes. High-speed Internet access is available for $12.95 a day. This is a smoke-free hotel.

Medical Center

BEST WESTERN MEDICAL CENTER $$
6700 S. Main St.
(713) 522-2811
www.bestwesterntexas.com

When you need to be near a relative or friend in the hospital, this Best Western is a good option. The hotel is located within walking distance of Baylor Clinic, Scurlock Tower, Smith Tower, Methodist Hospital, and Texas Children's Hospital, and just a short drive from M.D. Anderson Hospital, VA Hospital, and St. Luke's Hospital. The rooms are typical Best Western with frills including free high-speed Internet access, free hot breakfast, and a microwave and satellite TV in every room. There's also an indoor pool and exercise room. The hotel's 125 rooms and suites include 25 wheelchair-accessible suites. This is a nonsmoking hotel. Free shuttle service is available to and from the Texas Medical Center hospitals.

HILTON HOUSTON PLAZA/
MEDICAL CENTER $$
6633 Travis St.
(713) 313-4000
www1.hilton.com

This stylish Medical Center hotel is home to 141 luxurious suites and 42 deluxe guest rooms, each of which has a wet bar, lush bedding, cable, and panoramic views of the city. High-speed Internet access is available for a fee. Fitness buffs can take advantage of the outdoor pool and private running track. The Hilton Houston Plaza/Medical Center is located near all of the Texas Medical

Center hospitals and just minutes from Rice University, Hermann Park, Reliant Center, and the Museum District. Free shuttle service is available to the area hospitals and medical facilities. This is a nonsmoking hotel.

HOLIDAY INN $$
6800 S. Main St.
(713) 528-7744
www.holidayinn.com

There are 287 guest rooms and 215 suites at this Holiday Inn, which is located within walking distance of Scurlock Tower, Smith Tower, Baylor Clinic, Methodist Hospital, and Texas Children's Hospital and is just a short drive from Rice University, Hermann Park, and other Medical Center hospitals and facilities. Free high-speed Internet access and cable is available in all the rooms; the suites include full kitchens with cookware and utensils. The hotel recently renovated its fitness center, which includes top-notch cardio equipment and weights. Free shuttle service is available with 24-hour notice.

Memorial

**THE HOUSTONIAN HOTEL,
CLUB & SPA** $$$-$$$$
111 N. Post Oak Lane
(713) 680-2626
www.houstonian.com

Houston is full of luxury hotels, but none is quite like the Houstonian. Located just five minutes from the Galleria and practically across the street from Memorial Park, this lavish hotel sits on 18 wooded acres, some of which are used for running and walking trails. This makes for a tranquil setting, no matter which room you stay in. All 289 of the elegantly decorated guest rooms feature floor-to-ceiling views of the wooded scenery and vibrantly colored landscaping, high-speed Internet, safes, and terry cloth robes. Guests can swim in the pool and gaze at the waterfalls or get their hair and nails done or get a massage at Trellis, The Spa. Every guest also enjoys free access to the Houstonian Fitness Club, which is widely considered one of the country's best private gyms.

Several dining options are available including the Gazebo by the pool and American cuisine with a Mediterranean twist at Olivette.

Montrose

MODERN B&B $$-$$$
4003 Hazard
(713) 279-6367
www.modernbb.com

Think bed-and-breakfasts are rustic digs? Think again. Modern B&B lives up to its name, blending Houston's cosmopolitan style with the cozy feel of a bed-and-breakfast. Housed in a contemporary four-story building, Modern B&B has eight guest rooms, each of which features lively contemporary decor and art. Guests have access to free Wi-Fi, cable, a guest kitchen, exercise equipment, a guest office, and a hip, high-ceilinged gathering area filled with modern furniture, books, and a fireplace. A hot organic breakfast is also included in your stay. The B&B is conveniently located in the heart of Montrose, giving guests easy access to the Museum District, Hermann Park, Rice University, Upper Kirby, the Medical District, West University, and some of the city's best restaurants.

Museum District

HOTEL ZAZA $$-$$$
5701 Main St.
(713) 526-1991
www.hotelzaza.com/houston

Located in the heart of the Museum District just a block from Hermann Park and the Museum of Natural Science, Hotel ZaZa has been described as one of the 10 best business hotels in the world by *Forbes*. ZaZa is a good place to stay for business, but it's an even better place to stay for pleasure. Located in what was previously the Warwick Hotel, ZaZa caters to the young, hip, and wealthy with a style all its own. The hotel indulges guests with fluffy bedding, plasma TVs, leopard-print carpets, plush robes, and exquisite views. The hotel's more than 300 guest rooms include several Concept Suites, which are decorated with themes ranging from Casa Blanca (Moroccan-inspired decor) to "Houston, We Have a Problem" (contemporary icy blue and gray decor that is reminiscent of the moon). A popular draw here is the Monarch Restaurant & Lounge, which serves breakfast and brunch; cocktails, like the Moulin Rouge and the Blue Mojito; salads; sushi; and stylishly presented entrees. Even though many of the dishes are fancy fish and steak fare, Monarch also serves burgers, sandwiches, and fries. The Monarch offers bottle service, giving guests access to a long list of fine wines.

HOUSTON INTERNATIONAL HOSTEL $
5302 Crawford St.
(713) 523-1009
www.houstonhostel.com
Houston International Hostel sits right in the heart of the Museum District, just a short walk from Hermann Park and Rice University. If you've stayed in a hostel before, you should know what to expect: Several bunk beds packed into a room, a communal kitchen, and a common room. There are also lockers to store your stuff in, three bathrooms with hot showers, a laundry room, and a few computers. The place isn't anything fancy, but it's tidy and the beds are comfortable. Plus, at $15 a night, a stay here is dirt cheap. Like most other hostels, Houston International Hostel has mandatory lockout hours from 10 a.m. to 5 p.m. and midnight to 8 a.m., so you've got to find somewhere else to hang out during the day and return before midnight. The office here is only open from 8 to 10 a.m. and 5 to 11 p.m. each day, so call to make your reservations accordingly.

South Loop
HAMPTON INN & SUITES, MEDICAL CENTER/RELIANT PARK $$
1715 Old Spanish Trail at Fannin
(713) 797-0040
www.hamptoninn.com
Attending an event at Reliant Center or spending some time at the Texas Medical Center? The Hampton Inn & Suites is a conveniently located option that's not too hard on the wallet. The 120 hotel rooms here include the Hampton

Inn's Cloud Nine luxury bedding and free high-speed Internet; some also include microwaves and refrigerators. Other perks include a business center, swimming pool, fitness center, and free hot breakfast.

LAKE VIEW RV RESORT $
11991 S. Main St.
(713) 723-0973
www.lakeviewrvresort.com
Park your RV at this highly rated resort and stay in one of the fully furnished cabins or park models. Rentals are available by the day, week, or month. Guests can take advantage of free barbecue and picnic areas, propane, a walking track, a pool and Jacuzzi, fitness and recreation rooms, free high-speed Internet, and even a fishing lake. There's also daily maid service. Pets aren't allowed.

i Because Houston is such a diverse city, most hotels have staff members who speak several different languages, including Spanish. If you need someone to translate for you or a companion, inquire at the front desk.

SOUTH MAIN RV PARK $
10100 S. Main
(713) 667-0120
www.smrvpark.com
Located at the intersection of South Main and I-610, the South Main RV Park is just a mile from Reliant Center (home of the Houston Texans and the Houston Livestock Show and Rodeo), 2.5 miles from the Texas Medical Center, and 7 miles from downtown. There are some shaded areas at this securely gated, well-maintained RV camp. Amenities include 20/30/50 amps, concrete patios, paved streets, free local phone calls and wireless Internet, cable TV, and laundry facilities. The park is managed on-site. Save yourself the headache of driving your RV in Houston traffic by taking the park's free shuttle service to the Medical Center and nearby shopping areas.

RESTAURANTS

Ask 10 Houstonians what their favorite Houston restaurant is, and you are likely to get 10—probably more, like 30 or 40—different answers. A difference in taste will partly explain why you get so many different answers, but so will the sheer number of great restaurants in this city. The cuisine here rivals that of cities like New York, Chicago, and Los Angeles in quality, quantity, and diversity.

The city's thousands of restaurants cover every kind of cuisine you could want: American, Greek, Spanish tapas, Middle Eastern, Italian, steak, pizza, Southern and Cajun, vegetarian, hot dogs and burgers, every kind of Asian food imaginable, sandwiches and bagels, breakfast and brunch fare, Texas barbecue, seafood straight from the Gulf of Mexico, and, of course, Tex-Mex—that is, Mexican food with a Texas twist. Those looking for a fun place to socialize, cap off a great meal, or satisfy their sweet tooth will also enjoy the many fantastic dessert and coffee shops here.

With so many restaurants in Houston, it's impossible to list all of the great ones in the space of a chapter. In the pages that follow, you'll find some of the best and most popular restaurants here. The chapter is organized to make it as easy as possible for you to find the kind of food you want in the neighborhood in which you want to dine. Restaurants (as well as dessert options and coffee shops) are organized by cuisine, then broken down by neighborhood within each cuisine. Many restaurants have multiple locations. Additional locations that are in central areas are listed here; consult the phone book or the restaurant Web site to find locations in other areas.

The restaurants listed span from highly expensive to dirt cheap, although the majority fall somewhere in between. Most Houston restaurants offer at least a few vegetarian options; those that don't—with the exception of steak houses—have been identified as such in these pages. There are plenty of places to dine with children; the barbecue, burger, and hot dog restaurants are particularly good candidates for family dining. Most restaurants are open seven days a week for lunch and dinner and many serve brunch. Those that are closed on certain days or for certain meals have been flagged accordingly. It can't hurt to call ahead to double-check a restaurant's hours, though, as these often change.

When choosing a place to eat, keep in mind that the restaurant landscape is constantly changing. By the time you read this book, some of the restaurants listed may have moved or gone out of business so it's a good idea to call ahead before your visit.

Popular restaurants—which is to say, just about every restaurant listed in this chapter—tend to fill up on Friday and Saturday nights and holidays. Many fill up on weekdays as well. Pricier restaurants tend to take reservations so call ahead to get a table wherever possible.

Price Code

The following prices are based on a meal for two, without drinks, appetizers, desserts, or tip. Prices are also based on averages only and assume guests eat at least one pricier meat entree.

$ . . . . under $16
$$ . . . . $16 to $30
$$$ . . . . $31 to $50
$$$$ . . . . over $50

AMERICAN AND ECLECTIC

Downtown

THE GROVE AND
THE TREEHOUSE $$$–$$$$
1611 Lamar
(713) 337-7321
www.thegrovehouston.com
www.treehousehouston.com

Since opening in 2008, **The Grove** has become one of Houston's hottest restaurants and its location deserves at least a little of the credit. Tucked on the south end of Discovery Green, this urbane restaurant makes ecofriendly dining chic. Glass, wood, and steel comprise the contemporary design, giving the restaurant an earthy feel. The Grove maintains its own herb and tomato garden, uses lots of recycled materials, and recycles and composts just about everything used—or, in some cases, not used—in the restaurant. The Grove, which serves both lunch and dinner, describes its food as "American Rustic." For lunch that means epicurean delights, like wood-grilled vegetable skewers, skirt steak, ceviche, a fried-oyster BLT, and a lamb burger topped with goat cheese. The longer dinner menu includes big and small plate options, as well as a tasting menu. Dinner options are similar to the lunch fare and include a range of veggie, chicken, fish, steak, burger, and salad options. Save room for one of the desserts—perhaps the Texas pecan and brown butter cake topped with vanilla ice cream, a strawberry rhubarb turnover with homemade crème fraîche, flan made with local goat milk, or a chocolate espresso torte with candied kumquats and cinnamon anglaise. The Grove offers an extensive selection of beer, wine, liquor, and specialty drinks, including Champagne Mangos Cosmos, mojitos, ginger margaritas, and Summers in Bombay, which was featured in *GQ*. Avoid a wait by calling ahead or going online to make reservations. The Grove is open seven days a week.

If you're looking for a lighter and more leisurely meal outdoors, head up to the **Treehouse** on the second floor. With both indoor and outdoor seating, The Grove's sister restaurant offers a one-of-a-kind view of downtown and a chance to look out on Discovery Green as the oak trees sway around you. The Treehouse menu includes tapas-size plates of cold dishes, like cauliflower and fennel, hominy cakes with olive tapenade, calamari bruschetta, and pulled chicken tapas. Many people come here for the drink selection, which includes wine, sangria, mojitos, tequila flights, and specialties like pomegranate screwdrivers and ginger margaritas. The Treehouse opens at 4 p.m. Thursday through Sunday. It is closed Monday through Wednesday. Reservations aren't accepted.

i Heading to the theater after dinner at The Grove? Order off The Grove's pre-theater dinner menu, which includes a starter, an entree, and a dessert for $35 per person.

VOICE RESTAURANT AND LOUNGE $$$$
Hotel ICON
220 Main St.
(832) 667-4470
www.hotelicon.com/voice-restaurant

Voice epitomizes fine dining. The beautifully decorated restaurant is located downtown inside Hotel ICON, which is listed in the "Accommodations" chapter of this book. It's not just the restaurant and lounge's appearance (or the cowhide-backed barstools) that count here; chef Michael Kramer also places considerable emphasis on the presentation of the food, which includes plenty of seafood, lamb, duck, chicken, and beef options. Everything is made and embellished with produce from local farmers' markets, but vegetarians don't have many options, aside from salads and appetizers. Those who dine in the lounge have their pick of cheese options, crab cakes, and fish and chips made with tuna tartare. The restaurant also serves breakfast. The attire here is dressy. Make a reservation online or by phone.

Galleria

RESTAURANT RDG + BAR ANNIE $$-$$$$
1800 Post Oak Blvd., at Ambassador Way
(713) 840-1111
www.rdgbarannie.com
Up until the summer of 2009, Restaurant RDG + Bar Annie was known as Café Annie and located across the street at Post Oak and Westheimer. The new location, which is divided into two dining areas, is even swankier than the last. Downstairs in the BLVD Lounge you can drink cocktails and eat hors d'oeuvres while sitting on one of the cushy sofas. Upstairs you can dine in either the RDG Grill Room, which serves steaks, seafood, and some of the city's finest Southwestern dishes, or Bar Annie, which serves less-fancy fare like burgers and onion rings in a more laid-back setting. The old Café Annie used to be the kind of place you dressed up to visit; it's A-OK to leave your suit at home when dining at the new incarnation.

The Heights

BENJY'S $$$
5922 Washington Ave.
(713) 868-1131
www.benjys.com
See the Benjy's description in the "West University," section below.

MAX'S WINE DIVE $$$
4720 Washington Ave.
(713) 880-8737
www.maxswinedive.com
If you've never eaten fried chicken or nachos with wine, Max's Wine Dive beckons you to change your ways. Named one of the "Hot 10" wine bars in the country by *Bon Appetit*, this popular spot serves fried chicken, Kobe burgers, nachos, salads, and boatloads of great wine. The jukebox here plays all day long. Max's is open until midnight Sunday through Wednesday and 2 a.m. Thursday through Saturday. Call ahead for reservations.

Memorial

BARNABY'S CAFÉ $$
5750 Woodway Dr.
(713) 266-0046
www.barnabyscafe.com
See the Barnaby's Café description in the "Montrose" section.

SMOOTHIE ISLAND JUICE BAR & GRILL $$
5709 Woodway, at Bering
(713) 334-4036
www.islandgrillhouston.com
Don't be fooled by the name of this casual restaurant: Smoothie Island serves smoothies—good ones, at that—but the menu also includes a hodgepodge of burgers, pasta, salads, sandwiches, and pitas stuffed with everything from grilled chicken and feta to falafel and hummus. There are quite a few vegetarian options on the menu, as well as some kiddie options. The service is great. There is some outdoor seating.

Midtown

BARNABY'S CAFÉ $$
414 W. Gray
(713) 522-8898
www.barnabyscafe.com
See the Barnaby's Café description in the "Montrose" section below. Breakfast is served at this location on Saturday and Sunday mornings.

Montrose

BABA YEGA $$
2607 Grant St., at Missouri
(713) 522-0042
www.babayega.com
Since opening in 1975, Baba Yega has fit right in to its quirky Montrose neighborhood. The restaurant occupies a charming house that was recently expanded. The menu is filled with healthy options like smoked turkey sandwiches topped with brie, grilled trout, a veggie club, and lots of other vegetarian options. On Tuesday nights, you can design your own pasta dish. Visit for Sunday brunch and get your fill of eggs, meat, veggies, brown rice, and lox and bagels for $18.95.

BARNABY'S CAFÉ $$

604 Fairview St.
(713) 522-0106
www.barnabyscafe.com

This funky, bold-hued restaurant dishes up good sandwiches and burgers (including a meatless one), as well as an eclectic mix of baby back ribs, meatloaf, General Tso's Chicken, lasagna, and burritos. Complete your meal with some of Barnaby's tasty homemade brownies and cookies. You'll find lots of dog decor here—maybe even a few dogs sitting at their humans' feet. That's because the restaurant is named after the owner's childhood sheepdog, Barnaby, so dogs are considered special guests here. Head next door to **Baby Barnaby's** (602 Fairview; 713-522-4229) for breakfast or brunch seven days a week. The breakfast dishes cover the basics—eggs, pancakes, waffles, bacon. Barnaby's Café has three additional locations in Memorial, River Oaks, and Midtown; the Montrose location is the original restaurant.

MARK'S AMERICAN CUISINE $$$$

1658 Westheimer Rd.
(713) 523-3800
www.marks1658.com

If you think dining in an old church can't be romantic, you have probably never eaten at Mark's American Cuisine. Diners at this renovated 1920s church sit under gold ceilings and among handpainted deco walls. You might even get to eat in the old choir loft, whose exquisite decor gives it a bit of European allure. Most of the artfully presented dishes at this oft-noisy restaurant revolve around beef, seafood, or chicken. Mark's uses only the freshest ingredients so the menus are seasonal. The specials even change throughout the day, depending on what has just arrived from suppliers or just been prepared in the kitchen. Ask the knowledgeable staff for wine suggestions; they've got countless bottles to choose from and will help you find one that pairs perfectly with your meal. Mark's serves lunch and dinner, although lunch is only served on weekdays.

River Oaks

BACKSTREET CAFÉ $$$

1103 S. Shepherd Dr.
(713) 521-2239
www.backstreetcafe.net

Backstreet Café gets its charm partly from its location inside a 1930s house, partly from its lovely patio and garden, and partly from the food. The menu is filled with sophisticated comfort foods—dishes like red corn chicken enchiladas, jalapeño fettucine, grilled rib eye with mashed potatoes, and chicken milanesa served with green bean salad and bacon mac and cheese. On the weekends from 11 a.m. to 3 p.m., the Backstreet Café serves brunch dishes like migas, breakfast pizza, and crawfish grits cakes and eggs.

BARNABY'S CAFÉ $$

1701 S. Shepherd
(713) 520-5131
www.barnabyscafe.com

See the Barnaby's Café description in the "Montrose" section above. Breakfast is served at this location Tuesday through Sunday mornings.

Upper Kirby

HOBBIT CAFÉ $$

2243 Richmond Ave.
(713) 526-5460

In its early years the Hobbit Café catered primarily to vegetarians and health nuts. To a large degree this is still the case but now there are plenty of nonvegetarian options like chicken salad and burgers made with beef. Still, the soy or black bean burgers remain popular. The menu also includes sandwiches, wraps, Mexican dishes, and homemade juices. Visit for brunch—and the requisite mimosas—on the weekends. True to the restaurant's name, the decor and many of the dishes' names show some *Lord of the Rings* inspiration.

RUGGLES GREEN $$

2311 W. Alabama
(713) 533-0777
www.rugglesgreen.com

Ruggles Green is Houston's first certified "green" restaurant, which means everything is made with organic, all-natural, hormone-free, preservative-free products. Taste is also a huge priority. The menu includes burgers of the meat, veggie, and turkey varieties; grilled panini; soups; salads; pizza; and pasta. Among the sides are butternut squash, carmelized sweet plantains, and sweet potato fries. There's also a kids' menu with old favorites like burgers, chicken tenders, mac and cheese, and grilled cheese. Ruggles Green offers a selection of organic wines and gluten-free beers. It also offers free Wi-Fi.

West University/Rice Village

BENJY'S   **$$$**
2424 Dunstan, at Kelvin
(713) 522-7655
www.benjys.com

This posh restaurant/lounge serves well-presented, eclectic dishes like nut-crusted salmon salad, pistachio-crusted goat cheesecakes, margarita surf and turf, and sweet potato risotto with brussel sprouts, as well as a good espresso tres leches. Many people flock here for brunch on Sunday. No matter when you plan to visit, call ahead to make reservations. This small place fills up quickly. For a reprieve from the noise, order a drink from the lounge and sit on the patio upstairs. The restaurant recently opened a second location in the Heights, although the service, lack of brunch, and ambience have left many Benjy's loyalists disappointed. See the Benjy's listing in "The Heights" section for the address and phone number.

RUGGLES CAFÉ BAKERY   **$$–$$$**
2365 Rice Blvd.
(713) 520-6662
www.rugglescafebakery.com

Part bakery, part restaurant, Ruggles serves fresh food that's made to order. Entrees here range from shrimp tacos to a turkey Reuben to a spicy black bean burger to the warm-baked, Texas–goat cheese salad. Top your meal off with one of Ruggles' beautiful, mouth-watering desserts

like the tres leches, the Strawberry Bomb (angel food cake topped with mascarpone, whipped cream, and fresh strawberries), or the fresh fruit tart. When the weather's nice, dine or sip a cup of tea on the patio.

ASIAN

Alief

KIM SON   **$$**
10603 Bellaire Blvd.
(281) 575-0140
www.kimson.com

See the Kim Son description in the "Downtown" section below.

KOREA GARDEN GRILLE   **$$–$$$**
11360 Bellaire Blvd.
(281) 568-0008

Fill up on your favorite Korean dishes at Korea Garden Grille, Houston's first all-you-can-eat Korean barbecue restaurant. The servers will grill your choice of meat for you while you pick your sides from the never-ending buffet. Korea Garden Grille is BYOB, so bring your own beer or wine. The lunch buffet is $13.95; the dinner buffet is $18.95. Kids under five eat free. Korea Garden Grille is closed on Wednesday.

Dairy Ashford

NIT NOI THAI   **$$**
1005 Dairy Ashford
(281) 496-9200
www.nitnoithai.com

See the Nit Noi Thai description in the "Memorial" section. This location is closed on Sunday.

Downtown

KIM SON   **$$**
2001 Jefferson St.
(713) 222-2461
www.kimson.com

This family-owned Vietnamese and Chinese food restaurant is practically a Houston empire at this point. Today Kim Son has four restaurants, three banquet halls, and kiosks scattered throughout the city. While part of the restaurant's success can be attributed to the Vietnamese community, the food also deserves a lot of the credit. The menu is an overwhelming 13 pages long, with highlights including Vietnamese crepes, black-peppered soft-shell crabs, noodle salad, and spring rolls. Both the Southwest Freeway location and the flagship downtown restaurant—which is home to a koi pond—serve lunch and dinner from the menu. The Alief location has menu options but it places more focus on the overwhelmingly large buffet, which is decent but not great. The buffet options range from sushi to fried rice to pork, chicken, and tofu dishes. Both the Alief and Stafford locations serve what is widely considered the best dim sum in town. See the Kim Son listings in the "Alief" and "Stafford" sections for addresses and phone numbers.

i Avoid a long wait at Kim Son's downtown location by calling ahead to make a reservation.

Galleria/Uptown

INDIA'S $$
5704 Richmond Ave.
(713) 266-0131
www.indiasrestauranthouston.com
Among the best Indian restaurants in town, India's serves up some great curries, tikkas, kebabs, masalas, and a large selection of naans. One of the biggest draws here is the lunch buffet. It's not quite as large as some Indian buffets, but it still offers plenty of options for carnivores and vegetarians alike. The buffet costs about $15 per person.

NIT NOI THAI $$
4703 Richmond Ave.
(713) 621-6088
www.nitnoithai.com
See the Nit Noi Thai description in the "Memorial" section.

UPTOWN SUSHI $$$
1131–14 Uptown Park Blvd.
(713) 871-1200
www.uptown-sushi.com
Don't be surprised if you walk into Uptown Sushi and think you're in Manhattan. This trendy Asian fusion and sushi restaurant is the sort of spot you might expect Carrie Bradshaw to frequent. Uptown Sushi is the place to see and be seen—and eat fresh sushi. The menu consists of Asian fusion dishes like wasabi caviar tuna, lobster tempura, and eggroll prawns, as well as unusual sushi rolls like the Bahama Breeze, which includes onion ring and peppercorn tuna topped with lobster salad mix, cilantro, wonton skin, and spicy miso dressing. And don't worry if you prefer sushi staples: There are plenty of commonplace rolls and sashimi options on the menu as well. The bar offers the requisite sake and wine, as well as more than a dozen specialty martinis, like the Belgium White Chocolate Martini and the Key Lime Pie Martini.

Memorial

NIT NOI THAI $$
6395 Woodway Dr., at Voss
(713) 789-1711
www.nitnoithai.com
Since opening in Rice Village in 1987, Nit Noi Thai has expanded to several locations around the city. Each restaurant serves Nit Noi's special sauce, which is made fresh each morning at this location. The extensive menu offers plenty of choices, including some delicious pad thai, spring rolls, and curry dishes. Portions are large, so sharing is a good idea. Service can be slow at this location. Nit Noi has temporarily closed its Rice Village location for construction, but there are plans to reopen in the near future.

Midtown

NIT NOI THAI $$
2020 Louisiana
(713) 652-5855
www.nitnoithai.com
See the Nit Noi Thai description in the "Memorial" section above.

Montrose

INDIKA $$$

516 Westheimer Rd.
(713) 524-2170
www.indikausa.com

Creative takes on traditional Indian ingredients and dishes have won this Indian fusion restaurant praise from foodie bibles like the *Zagat Survey* and *Gourmet*. Local ingredients are used to make the dishes here. The menu changes seasonally; recent dishes include roasted eggplant stuffed with paneer and cashews and slow-cooked spiced lamb shank with an onion, mushroom, and tomato masala. Indika serves brunch on Sunday, with dishes like chickpea crepes and grilled chicken naan sandwiches with spinach, goat cheese, and mango chutney. There's a shorter menu for those who eat at the bar. Indika often fills up, so call ahead or make reservations online. It is closed Monday.

i Want to learn to make your own Indian food? Take a cooking class from Indika chef-owner Anita Jaisinghani. Visit Indika's Web site (www.indikausa .com) to learn more.

NIDDA THAI CUISINE $$

1226 Westheimer Rd.
(713) 522-8895
www.niddathai.com

You'll be hard-pressed to find someone who doesn't like Nidda Thai Cuisine. This popular Montrose restaurant is known for its curries and coconut Tom Kha Gai soup. The Chu Chee Eggplant—battered and topped with red curry sauce—is also a big hit. Visit during lunch and get a full meal with your choice of tofu or chicken for $6.95.

North Houston/FM 1960

NIT NOI THAI $$

850 FM 1960 West off I-45
(281) 444-7650
www.nitnoithai.com

See the Nit Noi Thai description in the "Memorial" section. This location is closed on Sunday.

River Oaks/Highland Village

KIRAN'S $$$$

4100 Westheimer Rd.
(713) 960-8472
www.kiranshouston.com

Lavish decor and quality food make Kiran's a popular Indian restaurant among those willing to part with a decent chunk of money. The restaurant serves traditional tikis, vindaloos, saags, and samosas, as well as unique dishes like Onion Bhaji (vidalia with chickpea flour and spinach) and paneer wraps made with naan and vindaloo aioli. Kiran's has an extensive wine list, and the wait-staff can help you find one to drink with those hard-to-pair Indian flavors. Don't be surprised if chef-owner and namesake Kiran stops by your table to chat. The restaurant is closed for lunch on Saturday and for lunch and dinner on Sunday.

Sharpstown/Chinatown

FU FU CAFÉ $

9889 Bellaire Blvd., at Corporate Drive
(713) 981-8818

Some of Houston's best Chinese noodles and soups can be found at Fu Fu Café, where you can have your soup served in a bowl or in a dumpling. There are plenty of nonsoup dishes like green beans with pork, as well as a long list of pan-fried dumpling options. The restaurant tends to be packed, so show up early for lunch or dinner, or expect a wait. Fu Fu Café is open until 2 a.m. Sunday through Thursday and 4 a.m. on Friday and Saturday.

Stafford

KIM SON $$

12750 Southwest Fwy.
(281) 242-3500
www.kimson.com

See the Kim Son description in the "Downtown" section.

Sugar Land

MADRAS PAVILION
16260 Kensington
(281) 491-3672
www.madraspavilion.us
See the Madras Pavilion description in the "Upper Kirby/Greenway" section below.

Upper Kirby/Greenway

AKA SUSHI HOUSE $$
2390 W. Alabama St.
(713) 807-7895
www.akasushi.net
Aka Sushi House may sit in a strip center, but it doesn't feel that way once you step inside amid the classy red and black decor. The menu at this sushi bar includes some great rolls, such as the signature Nautilus Roll, the Tsunami Roll (shrimp tempura, grilled eel, crab, and mango), and the Crater Roll (baked roll with crab meat and baked scallops). Some rolls are discounted during happy hour Monday through Friday and all day on Sunday. Be sure to try the miso soup with clams.

BLUE FISH HOUSE $$
2241 Richmond Ave.
(713) 529-3100
www.bluefishhouse.com
This recently renovated sushi bar serves Pan-Asian fare and very fresh sushi in a casual atmosphere. It's got plenty of vegetarian options, including the U Pick It Tofu, where the chef mixes tofu and vegetables with your choice of sauces, like Japanese curry, spicy lime, and hot balsamic. U Pick It options are also available for chicken, beef, pork, and a variety of fishes. Visit during lunch for some really cheap—and filling—options. Blue Fish House is closed Sunday.

MADRAS PAVILION $$
3910 Kirby
(713) 521-2617
www.madraspavilion.us
Madras Pavilion has locations across Texas and the surrounding states but the chain started right here in Houston. This is one of the few restaurants in town that serves South Indian food, in addition to the standard North Indian cuisine. The popular lunch buffet includes a constantly changing array of dishes, with an abundance of vegetarian options. Every buffet order costs $10.81 and comes with a dosa—a giant South Indian rice crepe filled with potatoes, spices, and other tasty treats. The dinner menu includes affordable specials and some options for kids. All of the food served at this location is kosher; the food at the Sugar Land location is not.

OISHII $$
3764 Richmond Ave.
(713) 621-8628
www.oishiihouston.com
This hole-in-the-wall may not have the best decor in town, but the sushi is good for the price. A 32-piece sashimi boat will run you $29.95. There are also plenty of nonfish options for those who aren't big on sushi. The place tends to fill up around 6:30 in the evening, so show up early to avoid a wait. Oishii also offers free Wi-Fi.

Westchase

PHO ONE $–$$
11148 Westheimer Rd., at Wilcrest
(713) 917-0351
If you're in the mood for Vietnamese noodles, check out Pho One. They serve some of the best pho noodle soup and bahn mi in town. The menu includes plenty of vegetarian options. The service here is great, too.

THAI CHOICE $$
11161 Westheimer Rd.
(713) 780-8323
The ambience at Thai Choice leaves something to be desired, but that's a small sacrifice to make for the flavorful curries and homemade sauces. The expansive menu includes a large vegetarian selection.

West University

ORIGINAL MORNINGSIDE THAI $$
6710 Morningside Dr.
(713) 661-4400
www.morningsidethai.com
Don't be put off by the relatively empty parking lot at Morningside Thai. Those who have discovered this little restaurant love the flavorful dishes, especially curries like the pineapple shrimp curry. The lunch specials range from $7.45 to $9.45. It is closed Sunday.

The Woodlands

NIT NOI THAI $$
6700 Woodland Pkwy.
(281) 367-3355
www.nitnoithai.com
See the Nit Noi Thai description in the "Memorial" section.

BARBECUE

Downtown

PAPPAS BAR-B-Q $$
1217 Pierce, at San Jacinto
(713) 659-1245
www.pappasbbq.com
Pappas Bar-B-Q is owned by the Pappas restaurant family, which also owns steak, seafood, and Tex-Mex restaurants around Houston and elsewhere in Texas. This local chain may not serve the best barbecue in town, but it is one of the most popular restaurants of its ilk. The Texas-style barbecue here is lean and slowly smoked, and it's a big hit when served on top of baked potatoes. There are lots of chicken and turkey options for those who don't want beef or pork. Portions are Texas-size here. There are 18 Pappas Bar-B-Q locations in the Greater Houston area, most of them in outlying areas. Visit the Web site or consult the white pages to find the location nearest you.

i Stuck downtown with no time to grab lunch? Call Pappas Bar-B-Q's downtown delivery line (713-759-0039) and get barbecue brought right to you.

Memorial

GOODE COMPANY TEXAS BARBEQUE $$
8911 Katy Fwy.
(713) 464-1901
www.goodecompany.com
You'll find some of the best barbecue in town at Goode Company Texas Barbeque. All of the duck and pork ribs, sausage, pepper chicken, and brisket are slowly smoked over mesquite. Among the most popular dishes is the huge brisket sandwich. The food is served cafeteria-style. Be sure to try the jalapeño cheese bread and the pecan pie, both of which are made by Goode Company. The restaurant has additional locations in Northwest Houston and in West University.

Montrose

DEMERIS $$
2911 S. Shepherd
(713) 529-7326
www.demeris.com
Since 1964, the Demeris family has been synonymous with barbecue. This Houston staple serves beef, ribs, sausage, ham, turkey, and chicken, as well as burgers, fajitas, and salad. If you're dining in a group or have a big appetite and can't decide on just one meat, order the barbecue dinner, which includes two sides and your choice of one to four meats.

Northwest Houston

GOODE COMPANY TEXAS BARBEQUE $$
20102 Northwest Fwy.
(832) 678-3562
www.goodecompany.com
See the Good Company Texas Barbeque description in the "Memorial" section above.

West University

GOODE COMPANY TEXAS BARBEQUE $$
5109 Kirby Dr.
(713) 522-2530
www.goodecompany.com
See the Good Company Texas Barbeque description in the "Memorial" section above.

BREAKFAST/BRUNCH

Galleria

FOUNTAINVIEW CAFÉ $
1842 Fountain View Dr.
(713) 785-9060
The Fountain View Café is a cafe in name but like a diner, it serves greasy breakfast food and sandwiches from morning until afternoon. Visit on the weekend and you're likely to have to wait in a long line to order and find a seat.

Memorial

THE BUFFALO GRILLE $
1301 S. Voss Rd., at Woodway
(713) 784-3663
www.thebuffalogrille.com
The Buffalo Grille serves breakfast, lunch, and dinner, but breakfast is the real reason to come here. The long menu includes a long list of egg options—huevos rancheros, *migas,* and omelets among them—as well as French toast and pancakes. You'll also get your choice of hash browns or grits. There's some outdoor seating, but it can be tough to come by on weekends, when there's typically a line out the door.

i If you sit outside at Buffalo Grille, avoid sitting directly under the trees. The resident birds often mistake these tables for a bathroom.

Midtown

THE BREAKFAST KLUB $
3711 Travis St., at Alabama
(713) 528-8561
www.thebreakfastklub.com
"If breakfast is the most important meal of the day, why not have it twice?" That's the motto of the Breakfast Klub, which serves some of the best breakfast in town until 2 p.m., six days a week. Frankly, it'd be tough to eat breakfast here twice a day: There's almost always a line to get a table, and most of the food is covered in gravy and/or fried. Signature dishes include the catfish and

grits as well as the wings and waffle platter. The Breakfast Klub even offers breakfast sandwiches as well as its own version of Green Eggs and Ham, complete with spinach, chives, and bell peppers. Don't want breakfast food? The Breakfast Klub dishes up several lunch sandwiches and salads—except on Saturday, when the restaurant only serves breakfast. It is closed Sunday.

i Avoid a long wait by visiting the Breakfast Klub during the week.

West University

THE BUFFALO GRILLE $
3116 Bissonnet, at Buffalo Speedway
(713) 661-3663
www.thebuffalogrille.com
See the Buffalo Grille description in the "Memorial" section on this page.

BURGERS AND HOT DOGS

Bellaire

BECKS PRIME $$
708 Meyerland Plaza
(713) 667-4076
www.becksprime.com
See the Becks Prime description in the "Upper Kirby" section.

Downtown

JAMES CONEY ISLAND $
815 Dallas St.
(713) 652-3819
www.jamesconeyisland.com
Ask any Houstonian where to find the best hot dog in town and you'll probably get the same answer over and over: James Coney Island. When it opened in 1923, James Coney Island was a two-brother-run hot dog stand; today it has expanded to nearly two-dozen locations around the Greater Houston area. In addition to several different hot dogs, the menu includes burgers, corn dogs, chicken strips, and some delicious chili. There's

almost always a line at lunchtime, but it tends to move quickly. The downtown, Galleria, Memorial, Meyerland, and Upper Kirby locations are listed in this section; visit the Web site or consult the white pages to find additional locations.

 Kids eat free at James Coney Island on Wednesday.

Galleria

JAMES CONEY ISLAND $
5745 Westheimer Rd.
(713) 785-9333
www.jamesconeyisland.com
See the James Coney Island description in the "Downtown" section on the previous page.

PAPPAS BURGER $$
5815 Westheimer Rd., at Bering
(713) 975-6082
www.pappasburger.com
With several big-screen TVs, Pappas Burger is a great place to cheer on your favorite team while eating a big half-pound burger or indulging in a little chicken fried steak or fried catfish. If you prefer something less greasy, you've got options here, including a grilled tuna niçoise salad, a grilled portobello sandwich, and a Cajun catfish sandwich. This family-friendly joint also has a kids' menu.

SOUTHWELL'S HAMBURGER GRILL $
5860 San Felipe St.
(713) 789-4972
Southwell's Hamburger Grill isn't anything fancy, but the burgers are solid—and cheap. You can even swap the meat patty on any burger for a veggie patty. Southwell's also offers chicken and salad options, as well as some tasty milk shakes. Be sure to try the waffle fries. Southwell's has additional locations in Memorial and West University, near the Medical Center.

Memorial

BECKS PRIME $$
Memorial City Mall
514 Memorial City Mall
(713) 463-4486
www.becksprime.com
See the Becks Prime description in the "Upper Kirby" section below.

JAMES CONEY ISLAND $
701 Town & Country
(713) 973-9143
www.jamesconeyisland.com
See the James Coney Island description in the "Downtown" section above.

SOUTHWELL'S HAMBURGER GRILL $
8800 Katy Fwy., at Echo Lane and Gaylord.
(713) 464-5268
See the Southwell's Hamburger Grill description in the "Galleria" section above.

Meyerland

JAMES CONEY ISLAND $
530 Meyerland Plaza
(713) 664-4900
www.jamesconeyisland.com
See the James Coney Island description in the "Downtown" section above.

Upper Kirby

BECKS PRIME $$
2902 Kirby Dr.
(713) 524-7085
www.becksprime.com
This local chain uses only the freshest meat, which makes for some of the best burgers in town. Other hits here include the grilled ahi tuna sandwich, the baked potatoes, the fries, and the thick milkshakes. Most of the food here wouldn't please your cardiologist, but it's just one meal, right? Sit outside at one of the picnic tables and enjoy the shade. Becks Prime has 11 locations around the city. The Memorial City and Bellaire

locations are listed in this chapter. Visit the Web site or consult the white pages to find additional locations.

JAMES CONEY ISLAND $

3607 S. Shepherd Dr.
(713) 524-7400
www.jamesconeyisland.com
See the James Coney Island description in the "Downtown" section.

West University

GOODE COMPANY TAQUERIA & HAMBURGERS $$-$$$

4902 Kirby Dr.
(713) 520-9153
www.goodecompany.com
This laid-back restaurant is a good place to go with the kids or when everyone can't agree on what they want to eat. The menu includes mesquite-grilled burger and mesquite-grilled chicken options, hot dogs, kid's dishes, salads, enchiladas, and tacos that can be topped with salsa at the condiment bar. Also popular are the chocolate cinnamon shakes and the homemade desserts. On weekends Goode Company Taqueria & Hamburgers serves breakfast favorites like pecan waffles, huevos con chorizo, and eggs served with everything from catfish to quail.

SOUTHWELL'S HAMBURGER GRILL $

2252 West Holcombe Blvd.
(713) 664-4959
See the Southwell's Hamburger Grill description in the "Galleria" section.

CAJUN, SOUL, AND SOUTHERN

Downtown

RAJIN CAJUN $$

930 Main St., T-230 (in the tunnel)
(713) 571-2422
www.ragin-cajun.com
See the Rajin Cajun description in the "Upper Kirby/Greenway" section on this page.

TREEBEARDS $-$$

315 Travis, on Market Square
(713) 228-2622
www.treebeards.com
Long before the downtown revitalization ushered in new restaurants and entertainment (not to mention new stadiums and a light rail), there was Treebeards. Since 1978, this downtown staple has been a popular spot to lunch on Southern and Cajun dishes, like duck and seafood gumbo, jerk chicken, chicken-fried steak, pot roast, vegetarian red beans and rice, cheese grits, corn bread dressing, and mustard greens. In addition to the downtown Market Square location, Treebeards has locations downtown at the Cloister at Christ Church Cathedral (1117 Texas Ave.; 713-229-8248) and in the downtown tunnels at 1100 Louisiana (713-752-2601). There's also a take-out location in the tunnels at 801 Louisiana (713-224-6677). All locations are open Monday through Friday from 11 a.m. to 2 p.m.

i If you crave Cajun and Creole food, try breakfast or lunch at the Breakfast Klub, located in Midtown and listed in the "Breakfast/Brunch" section of this chapter.

Memorial

RAJIN CAJUN $$

9600 Westheimer
(832) 251-7171
www.ragin-cajun.com
See the Rajin Cajun description in the "Upper Kirby/Greenway" section below.

South Central Houston

FRENCHY'S CHICKEN $

3919 Scott, at Wheeler
(713) 748-2233
www.frenchyschicken.com
Cajun and Creole influences rule at this local fast-food chain, which serves what many call

the best fried chicken in town. Sides include dirty rice, collard greens, corn muffins, and bread pudding. There's often a wait. Bring cash; they're not big on credit card transactions at Frenchy's. The flagship location is near the University of Houston; Frenchy's has several more locations around town. Consult the white pages to find additional ones.

Sugar Land

RAJIN CAJUN $$
16100 Kensington
(281) 277-0704
www.ragin-cajun.com
See the Rajin Cajun description in the "Upper Kirby/Greenway" section.

Upper Kirby/Greenway

RAJIN CAJUN $$
4302 Richmond Ave.
(713) 623-6321
www.ragin-cajun.com
The crawfish, oysters, and fried shrimp are always good at this casual joint, which is owned by Houston's famed restaurant family, the Mandolas. The family-style seating, HDTVs airing sports events, and good food make this the kind of place that you come for dinner and stick around for a couple of hours. Rajin Cajin also offers free Wi-Fi. Locations in Memorial, downtown, and Sugar Land are listed in this section.

COFFEE SHOPS

The Heights

ONION CREEK COFFEE HOUSE $-$$
3106 White Oak Blvd., between Studewood and Heights Boulevard
(713) 880-0706
www.onioncreekcafe.com
Onion Creek Coffee House is a fun place to grab a cup of coffee during the day or hang out with friends in the evening. There are several couches and tables, as well as an outdoor patio. Some come for the coffee or the alcohol; others come

for the occasional live music or to munch on a sandwich, burger, salad, pizza, or panini. Onion Creek Coffee House also serves breakfast every morning. If you plan to order food, be prepared to wait. The kitchen is small and this popular coffee shop usually has several orders in the queue. It is open seven days a week from 6:30 a.m. to 2 a.m.

Montrose

AGORA $
1712 Westheimer Rd.
(713) 526-7212
www.agorahouston.com
This Greek-inspired coffeehouse is a little on the quirky side but that's part of the reason that the *Houston Press* has named it the city's best coffee shop several times in the past few years. There are plenty of tables—upstairs and down—for those who want to drink a cup of coffee, read Agora's free periodicals, and use the free Wi-Fi. Those hanging out in groups can make use of the couches or sit on the patio. Agora serves beer, wine, port, coffee, and then some. Check out the replicas of ancient art on the walls. If you're lucky, you might see some live belly dancing here. It is open daily from 9 a.m. to 2 a.m.

BRASIL $-$$
2604 Dunlavy St.
(713) 528-1993
This funky coffee shop is a great place to unwind after a long day or catch up with friends. In addition to the requisite coffee, tea, and Italian sodas, Brasil serves wine and beer, pizza, and sandwiches. Local musicians often play here and it can get loud. Patio seating is available.

DIRK'S COFFEE $
4005 Montrose Blvd.
(713) 526-1319
www.dirkscoffee.com
Formerly known as Diedrich's, Dirk's makes some strong coffee and espresso. This location is a great place to people watch or, if you prefer, play board games. Beware, though, if you plan to work

on your laptop here: You won't find Wi-Fi or any power outlets to plug your power cord into.

EMPIRE CAFÉ $-$$
1732 Westheimer Rd.
(713) 528-5282
www.empirecafe.net
More hip than your neighborhood Starbucks, the Empire Café is a great place to grab a cup of coffee—or wine, beer, or a mixed drink—with a friend. In addition to the many alcoholic and nonalcoholic drink options here, Empire serves breakfast and dinner dishes, such as pasta, panini, and a handful of chicken and veggie dishes. Visit on Monday night to take advantage of Empire's buy-one-get-one-free desserts, which include an array of cakes. There's tons of outdoor seating.

Rice Village/West University
SALENTO $-$$
2407 Rice Blvd.
(713) 528-7478
Good music, free Wi-Fi, a solid food menu, and a good selection of wine, beer, and coffee drinks make Salento the kind of coffee shop where people linger. Salento uses only single origin and medium dark roast coffee, which makes for some high-quality coffee.

DELIS, BAGELS, AND SANDWICHES

Conroe
KATZ'S EXPRESS $$
19075 I-45 North (exit 77)
(936) 321-1880
www.ilovekatzs.com
See the Katz's Deli listing in the "Montrose" section.

Downtown
ANTONE'S $
801 Capitol, at Travis Street
(713) 224-4679

Antone's sandwich shop caters to those who need to grab a sandwich to go. You'll find tons of already packaged sandwiches here, as well as made-to-order po'boys and Mediterranean treats like stuffed grape leaves and baklava. Antone's sandwiches may not be the very best in town, but with options like a slice of Gouda on your sandwich, they're definitely among the most original. There are several locations around town; the West University and Galleria locations are listed in this section. Check the phone book for additional locations.

BROWN BAG DELI $
810 Capitol
(713) 224-7000
www.thebrownbagdeli.net
If you've eaten at a Which Wich?, you're familiar with the Brown Bag Deli concept: You grab a brown bag, check off the kind of bread, meat, cheese, and toppings you want, and hand the bag to the resident sandwich maker, who then makes you a huge sandwich. The meat options include turkey, ham, roast beef, and salami; nonmeat options include egg salad, tuna with pecans, pimento cheese, and PB&J. Everything here is fresh and the bread—jalapeño cheese bread included—is homemade. Choose from potato chips, chocolate chip cookies, rice crispy treats, and sides, like red potato salad and fresh fruit if you want something more. Brown Bag Deli has additional locations in Montrose, West University, and Northwest Houston.

Fondren Southwest
NEW YORK BAGEL & COFFEE SHOP $
9720–4 Hillcroft St.
(713) 723-8650
Tasty breakfast options abound at New York Bagel & Coffee Shop. This kosher deli and bakery serves everything from corned beef hash sandwiches to eggs with crispy homefries to whitefish, gefilte fish, and challah. The best reason to come here, though, is the bagels, which you can buy by the dozen at the connected bakery. They're big, fluffy, and—if you get there at the right time—hot.

Galleria

ANTONE'S $
5000 Westheimer, at Post Oak
(713) 877-1222
See the Antone's description in the "Downtown" section on the previous page.

KENNY & ZIGGY'S $$$
2327 Post Oak Blvd.
(713) 871-8883
www.kennyandziggys.com
Looking for a nice Jewish deli? Head directly to Kenny & Ziggy's. This popular New York–style delicatessen has a menu with more than 200 items, many of which have witty names like "Fiddler on the Roof of Your Mouth" (a triple-decker sandwich with corned beef and pastrami) and "Luck Be a Latke" (brisket sandwiched between two potato pancakes). The menu includes all of the standard Jewish and New York–deli fare—lox and bagels, blintzes, matzo brei, potato pancakes, whitefish, and pickled herring among them. For those who prefer something else, there are eggs, burgers, sandwiches, salads, schnitzels, Philly cheesesteaks, and meatballs. Kenny & Ziggy's also serves some mighty big desserts, including chocolate-dipped macaroons, cheesecake, Boston cream cake, an array of pies, and a Belgian waffle topped with three—yes, three—scoops of ice cream, hot fudge, caramel sauce, whipped cream, and cherries. The restaurant cures and pickles all of the meat and bakes all of its own bread. Want some whitefish, rye bread, or a cheesecake for the house (or hotel)? Kenny & Ziggy's will gladly pack it up for you. It also caters. Kenny & Ziggy's is open seven days a week for breakfast, lunch, and dinner. Breakfast is served until 11 a.m. on weekdays and until 2 p.m. on weekends and holidays. The place is particularly crowded on Saturday and Sunday mornings so arrive early or plan to wait in line.

Memorial

STONE MILL BAKERS $$
1415 Voss, at San Felipe
(713) 349-0077
www.stonemillbakers.com

It's no secret why there's a long line at Stone Mill Bakers during lunchtime: This sandwich shop and bakery serves up some great sandwiches on homemade breads. The bread selection changes daily, but there are always several options to choose from, ranging from rye and multigrain to cranberry, corn bread, and challah. Try the whole wheat Dakota bread, which includes sunflower seeds, pumpkin seeds, sesame seeds, and millet. The sandwiches here are big so consider saving half or sharing. Stone Mill also serves homemade cookies and soups. There's a second location in River Oaks; see the listing in this section for the address and phone number.

Montrose

BROWN BAG DELI $
2038 Westheimer Rd.
(713) 807-9191
www.thebrownbagdeli.net
See the Brown Bag Deli description in the "Downtown" section.

THE HOT BAGEL $
2009 S. Shepherd Dr.
(713) 520-0340
www.hotbagelshop.bravehost.com
The Hot Bagel is a bit of a dive, but the bagels more than make up for the surroundings. The shop serves 26 flavors of bagels, which range from the expected sesame, poppy, and everything bagel to less mainstream flavors, like sea salt, sun-dried tomato, and cinnamon apple. All of these can be topped with about 10 different flavors of cream cheese, including fat-free, lox, and honey walnut varieties. Deli sandwiches are also available. This long-standing Houston establishment often has a line out the door on weekend mornings so show up early, or be prepared for a short wait.

KATZ'S DELI $$
616 Westheimer Rd.
(713) 521-3838
www.ilovekatzs.com
Katz's isn't the best deli in town, but it is certainly good—and open 24 hours, 7 days a week.

The extensive menu includes half-pound deli sandwiches and 26 specialty sandwiches, including Meat Loaf Mania, Grilled Salmon Hero, and Yankee Pot Roast. Any sandwich can be made on Katz's homemade rye, challah (braided egg bread), French, or whole wheat bread. The restaurant also serves a hodgepodge of American entrees like fried chicken, pasta, and salad, as well as traditional Jewish dishes like matzo ball soup, potato pancakes, bagels and lox, and kugel. Among the biggest draws are the fried pickles and the breakfast dishes, which are served all day. There's a full bar here. Katz's has a second location with a less-extensive menu—and no late-night hours—in Conroe.

KRAFTS'MEN BAKING $$
4100 Montrose Blvd.
(713) 524-3737
(713) 524-3737 (sandwich pickup orders)
www.kraftsmenbaking.com
If you believe that great bread makes for great sandwiches, visit Krafts'men Baking, one of the city's premier bakeries. Located inside an ivy-covered building next door to the Black Labrador, Krafts'men Baking has a salad and sandwich menu sure to please. The highlights include the Effin' Good Sandwich with turkey, salami, red onion, and provolone on a croissant and the Cold Fish, which combines smoked salmon, cucumbers, arugula, and caper dill mascarpone cheese on Krafts'men's homemade *biologique* (organic) bread. Also tempting are Krafts'men's rather large sticky cinnamon rolls made from day-old croissants, tasty zucchini bread, and baguettes that taste like they were made in a little French bakery half a world away. For a peaceful reprieve on a nice day, bring a book and sit outside.

PAULIE'S $$
1834 Westheimer Rd.
(713) 807-7271
www.pauliescookies.com
This neighborhood restaurant is worth a cross-town trip. The exposed brick walls and the art on the walls create a cozy atmosphere in which to eat and drink lemonade, beer, or wine. Paulie's

has a great selection of salads, soups, and sandwiches, ranging from Italian hoagies to grilled-shrimp BLTs, meatball sandwiches, and grilled portobello sandwiches topped with red bell peppers and goat cheese. It also serves panini, pasta, pizza, and other entrees, as well as desserts ranging from cannoli to some of the prettiest decorated sugar cookies in town. Paulie's is open for lunch and dinner. It is closed Sunday.

> **i** Stop by Paulie's at lunchtime to pick up a box lunch. For $9.00 to $11.50, you'll get a sandwich, pasta and fruit salad, a cookie, and bottled water.

Northwest Houston

BROWN BAG DELI $
13169 Northwest Fwy.
(713) 690-8600
www.thebrownbagdeli.net
See the Brown Bag Deli description in the "Downtown" section.

River Oaks

STONE MILL BAKERS $$
2518 Kirby, at Westheimer
(713) 524-6600
www.stonemillbakers.com
See the Stone Mill Bakers description in the "Memorial" section.

TINY BOXWOODS CAFÉ & ESPRESSO BAR $$
3600 W. Alabama
(713) 622-4244
www.thompsonhanson.com
Breakfast, brunch, dinner, lunch—Tiny Boxwoods does it all. Located at the Thompson & Hanson nursery (listed on page 198), this chic restaurant and espresso bar is lined with large windows, allowing diners to feel like they're eating amid the flowers and plants just outside. The short menu consists of French-inspired salads, cheese plates, pizzas, and sandwiches made with fresh

ingredients and, in more than a couple cases, topped with goat cheese and pesto. Breakfast options include croissants, quiche, bread and jam, and hard-boiled eggs. Tiny Boxwoods serves breakfast, lunch, and afternoon snacks from Monday through Saturday and brunch on Sunday. Dinner is served Wednesday through Saturday. Times vary by day and meal so call ahead to make sure the cafe will be open during your visit. The espresso bar is open daily.

West University/Rice Village

ANTONE'S $
2424 Dunstan Rd.
(713) 521-2883
See the Antone's description in the "Downtown" section.

BROWN BAG DELI $
2540 Amherst
(713) 520-6100
www.thebrownbagdeli.net
See the Brown Bag Deli description in the "Downtown" section.

KAHN'S DELI $$
2429 Rice Blvd.
(713) 529-2891
www.kahnsdeli.com
Kahn's Deli has been recognized by just about all of the big restaurant raters—Zagat, AOL City Guide, and Citysearch. The reason? The sandwiches. They include pastrami, roast beef, corned beef, tuna melts, chicken salad, and three different kinds of Reubens. Kahn's also makes some one-of-a-kinders like the Soho (smoked turkey breast with melted cheese, cranberry sauce, lettuce, and tomato on wheat bread) and the Village Special (chargrilled chicken and vegetables, olive tapenade, and sun-dried tomato pesto on ciabatta bread). You'll find lox and bagels here, too, along with breakfast options ranging from challah French toast to eggs to wraps. Kahn's Deli is open for breakfast and lunch every day.

i The sandwiches at Kahn's Deli are huge so consider sharing if you're dining with someone else.

DESSERT

Braeswood

MOELLER'S BAKERY $-$$
4201 Bellaire Blvd.
(713) 667-0983
This Houston bakery mainstay makes cookies, petit fours, orange rolls, almond logs, danishes, and cakes galore. They might not look like anything you'd see on a Food Network show, like *Ace of Cakes*, but they more than make up for it in taste.

THREE BROTHERS BAKERY $-$$
4036 S. Braeswood Blvd.
(713) 666-2253
www.3brothersbakery.com
This kosher bakery has provided the sweets for thousands of local Jewish events. Three Brothers makes cookies, pastries, and some creative sheet cakes—some even feature the face of the person of honor! They also make bagels and Jewish-baked goods like challah and, for Purim, hamantaschen. You can find sugar-free desserts here. There are several locations around town; the Braeswood shop is the main location. Consult the white pages for additional stores.

Galleria/Uptown Park

BERRIPOP $
1101–08 Uptown Park Blvd.
(713) 965-9949
www.berripop.com
Cheery colors decorate this popular yogurt shop—and, if you like, your yogurt. More tart than sweet, the frozen yogurt here comes in unusual—yet delicious—flavors like black cherry, green tea, and raspberry pomegranate. Toppings range from fresh fruit, like mango, pomegranate, and blackberries to sugary cereals like Cap'n

Crunch. There's a second location in the Upper Kirby area; see the listing in this section. Berripop also offers free Wi-Fi.

CRAVE CUPCAKES $
1151-06 Uptown Park Blvd.
(713) 622-7283
www.cravecupcakes.com

One of Houston's hottest dessert crazes is Crave Cupcakes, a bakery that sells nothing but—you guessed it—cupcakes. The cupcakes sold at this large airy bakery aren't the colorful sort of things with sprinkles that you're used to, though. These elegant-looking cupcakes come in flavors such as candy bar, banana, cranberry orange, nutella, and white chocolate macadamia nut. Crave even sells breakfast cupcakes. To ensure the cupcakes stay fresh, Crave's staff bakes small batches. There's little seating inside since most customers come here to buy cupcakes by the dozen for parties or to take home, but there are two wooden benches right outside, as well as a couple of benches under the trees outside the Starbucks a few doors down. Single cupcakes cost $3.25; one-dozen costs $36. Local delivery and nationwide shipping are available.

DESSERT GALLERY BAKERY AND
CAFE $–$$
1616 Post Oak Blvd.
(713) 622-0007
www.dessertgallery.com

There are desserts and then there are Dessert Gallery desserts—delicacies so decadent that you should break your diet for a bite or two. Chocoholics will find plenty of options here, from the ultrarich Turtle Candy Cake to the flourless Everyone's Favorite Mousse Cake to the Chocolate Concorde Cake. Also worthy of a taste are the many nonchocolate offerings, including the heavenly Lemon Vacherin, which pairs meringue with lemon mousse; the Toffee-licious Cake; and the French Vanilla Cake. Cakes are available by the slice or whole. Other dessert options include chocolate-covered Oreo truffles, gourmet cupcakes, and seasonal treats. Dessert Gallery also

makes sandwiches and salads. Sit in one of the Dessert Gallery's plush chairs and play a board game while you savor your dessert and a cup of coffee or Italian soda. Or sit outside and watch the cars drive past. Dessert Gallery makes wedding cakes and sells gift baskets. It even delivers. The Dessert Gallery has additional locations in Upper Kirby and Sugar Land; addresses are listed in this section.

HOUSE OF PIES $
6142 Westheimer Rd.
(713) 782-1290
www.houseofpies.com

With its diner atmosphere, House of Pies is something of a dive. But this hot spot serves great pies (and other diner food) 24/7, making it a perennial favorite, especially among students and other nocturnal types. Diabetics, take note: House of Pies makes sugar-free pies. There's a second location in Upper Kirby, listed in this section.

SWIRLL ITALIAN YOGURT $
5000 Westheimer Rd.
(713) 552-0863
www.swirlls.com

The bright orange and green decor at Swirll is a giveaway that this isn't your typical yogurt shop. Here you can serve yourself a dozen different flavors of frozen yogurt—pomegranate, green apple, cookies and cream, and country vanilla included. Top yours with fresh fruit, Fruity Pebbles, or mochi, then savor the taste and ambience while sitting in a big comfy orange chair. You can even bring your laptop and use the free Wi-Fi. Swirll has additional locations in Midtown, Sugar Land, and Rice Village; they're listed in this section accordingly.

Midtown

SWIRLL ITALIAN YOGURT $
1944A W. Gray
(713) 523-4888
www.swirlls.com

See the Swirll Italian Yogurt description in the "Galleria/Uptown Park" section above.

River Oaks

THE CHOCOLATE BAR $–$$
1835 W. Alabama
(713) 520-8599
www.theoriginalchocolatebar.com

Chocolate in the shapes of tools. Chocolate and orange ice cream. Brownie lollipops. Chocolate-topped tres leches. These are just a few of the chocolate treats available at the Chocolate Bar where, as the slogan suggests, "Every hour is happy hour." In addition to a variety of chocolate cakes and cookies, this chocoholic's heaven sells more than a dozen flavors of ice cream—just about all of them incorporating chocolate in some way. There's plenty of seating if you want to dine in. The Chocolate Bar has a second location in Rice Village, located three doors down from Candylicious, a sweet tooth's heaven without the chocolate. It's no coincidence that there's also a Candylicious next door to the Chocolate Bar's River Oaks location: These sweet shops share the same owners.

GELATO BLU $
5710 Memorial Dr.
(713) 880-5900
www.gelatoblu.com

Eat some of the best gelato in town in this very blue little shop. Flavors range from standard gelato fare, like pistachio, to Orange Push Up. Gelato Blu even serves gelato shakes. Nongelato options include smoothies, coffee, and sandwiches.

Sugar Land

DESSERT GALLERY $–$$
2260 Lone Star Dr.
(713) 797-8000
www.dessertgallery.com

See the Dessert Gallery description in the "Galleria/Uptown Park" section.

SWIRLL ITALIAN YOGURT $
15955 City Walk
(832) 414-3995
www.swirlls.com

See the Swirll Italian Yogurt description in the "Galleria/Uptown Park" section.

Upper Kirby

BERRIPOP $
3825 Richmond
(713) 960-1940
www.berripop.com

See the Berripop description in the "Galleria/Uptown Park" section.

DESSERT GALLERY $–$$
3200 Kirby Dr.
(713) 522-9999
www.dessertgallery.com

See the Dessert Gallery description in the "Galleria/Uptown Park" section.

HOUSE OF PIES $
3112 Kirby Dr.
(713) 528-3816
www.houseofpies.com

See the House of Pies description in the "Galleria/Uptown Park" section.

West University/Rice Village

THE CHOCOLATE BAR $–$$
2521 University Blvd.
(713) 520-8888
www.theoriginalchocolatebar.com

See the Chocolate Bar description in the "River Oaks" section above.

SWIRLL ITALIAN YOGURT $
2531 University Blvd.
www.swirlls.com
(713) 526-7947

See the Swirll Italian Yogurt description in the "Galleria/Uptown Park" section.

EUROPEAN ECLECTIC

Upper Kirby/Greenway Plaza

TONY'S $$$$
3755 Richmond Ave.
(713) 622-6778
www.tonyshouston.com

After making its home on Post Oak Boulevard for more than 30 years, Tony's moved to its current Greenway Plaza location in 2005. With that move came $5 million in renovations—and the same great service, first-class dishes, and incredible wine selection that Houstonians have come to expect from owner Tony Vallone. The new location is something of a museum: Decorating the airy restaurant are works of art by the likes of Robert Rauschenberg and Texas sculptor Jesús Moroles. The menu is equally worthy of a museum—of the culinary variety. The chef uses the freshest ingredients to make meticulously presented dishes, like the crab-meat tower, lobster bisque, slow-roasted sea bass, crisp roast duckling, truffled macaroni and cheese, and 30-day aged Snake River Kobe beef. If you've got any dietary restrictions, the chef can usually accommodate them. For rehearsal dinners, birthdays, business meetings, and other special events, Tony's private rooms seat anywhere from 8 to 100 people. Dress is formal attire. Call ahead to make reservations.

GREEK/MEDITERRANEAN

Galleria

YIA YIA MARY'S $$$
4747 San Felipe
(713) 840-8665
www.yiayiamarys.com

When you walk up to the counter to order at this Pappas-owned restaurant, you might feel overwhelmed by all of the options. But rest assured: Just about everything here—from the moussaka to the Greek salad to the pita to the souvlaki—is worth a try. If you can't decide on something or don't want to spend a lot of money, order a few

mesas (appetizers) like the baked feta, roasted eggplant dip, and spanakopita. There's a line to order at lunch, but it tends to move quickly.

Montrose

NIKO NIKO'S $$
2520 Montrose
(713) 528-0966
www.nikonikos.com

Whether you want stuffed grape leaves, Greek meatball gyros, or pita bread with falafel and hummus, you will find some of the best in town at Niko Niko's. This Montrose mainstay has recently expanded to accommodate even more customers. Service is pretty quick, although you may have to wait in line to order and look around for a table if you visit during a peak time. This is a good place to bring kids: The menu is extensive, with plenty of kid options. The restaurant's nothing fancy, and you'll eat off paper plates.

i Get your fill of authentic Greek food at the Greek Festival in October. Find out more on page 165 of the "Annual Events" chapter.

ITALIAN

Downtown

MIA BELLA $$
320 Main St.
(713) 237-0505
www.miabellatrattoria.com

This charming restaurant serves Italian dishes with a contemporary flair. The extensive menu includes delectable pasta dishes like Papardelle al Modo Mio (sautéed artichoke hearts, mushrooms, goat cheese, and toasted pine nuts with fresh tomato basil olive oil), seafood lasagna, thin-crust pizza and calzones, and numerous beef and chicken options accompanied by sides like herbed couscous, basil risotto, and roasted leeks. On Sunday Mia Bella offers brunch—and bottomless Bellinis. Portions here are large, and the service is solid. Ask the servers to help you pair one of Mia Bella's many wines with your meal. There's a second location in Upper Kirby; the address and phone number are listed in this section.

Galleria

GROTTO $$$
4715 Westheimer, at West Loop 610 South
(713) 622-3663
www.grottorestaurants.com
Although it's owned by Landry's Restaurants and in a relatively new location, Grotto continues to be one of the most popular upscale Italian spots in town. Bold-colored murals and plates line the walls, giving the noisy restaurant a festive atmosphere. Choose from one of the many savory pizza, pasta, meat, chicken, or seafood dishes, or pick a few selections from the antipasto bar. Save room for one of the sinfully rich Italian pastries or cakes and consider sampling one of Grotto's many Italian wines. Call ahead to make reservations, especially if you're visiting on a weekend evening. The restaurant has a second location in the Woodlands; see the listing below for the address and phone number.

LA VISTA $$$
1936 Fountain View Dr.
(713) 787-9899
www.fatbutter.com
La Vista's slogan is "Where it's all good," which speaks to the quality of the food as much as to the laid-back atmosphere. Dishes here aren't traditional Italian, but they cover the usual Italian food groups—pasta, pizza, meat, chicken, and seafood. The food here often embodies unique flavors. There's a pork tenderloin dish, for instance, that's crusted with cinnamon, coffee, and cumin; there's also a pizza topped with mushrooms, Asiago cheese, sweet sugar, caramelized onions, and sage. La Vista has quite a bit of patio seating, complete with a view of the parking lot. La Vista doesn't take reservations, so there's often a wait. The restaurant is BYOB, with a $7 corkage fee. La Vista has a second location in Memorial, which is listed in this section.

The Heights

PINK'S PIZZA $$
1403 Heights Blvd.
(713) 864-7465
www.pinkspizza.com
Thin-crust pizza plus fresh premium ingredients make for some mighty good pizza here. Most of the pizzas at Pink's are a bit unusual. The Freshetta, for instance, has garlic, feta, spinach, sun-dried tomatoes, bacon, marinated chicken, and fresh tomatoes; the Luigi combines Canadian bacon, Gorgonzola, mozzarella, portobello mushroom, apple, roasted garlic, pesto sauce, and sun-dried tomato. If you can't find a pizza that appeals to you, just name your own toppings. Twelve-inch pizzas cost $16.99; the 16-inch costs $20.99. Standard cheese pizzas cost less. Grinders, Philly cheesesteaks, and other sandwiches and pasta dishes are also available. Pink's delivers for free.

STAR PIZZA II $$
77 Harvard, at Washington
(713) 869-1241
www.starpizza.net
See the Star Pizza description in the "Upper Kirby" section.

Medical Center

TREVISIO $$$
6550 Bertner
(713) 749-0400
www.trevisiorestaurant.com
Located at the top of the John P. McGovern Texas Medical Center Commons Building, Trevisio offers world-class dining in the Texas Medical Center. A water wall stands at the restaurant's entrance, hinting at the simple yet sophisticated decor and food that is yet to come. Dishes here include the likes of shellfish soup with arugula and saffron tomato broth, four-cheese pizza, and tortellini stuffed with smoked duck and ricotta, dried cherries, and toasted pistacchio bianco sauce. There are also plenty of beef, veal, and seafood options.

Save room for the exquisitely presented Godiva cheesecake. On a cool night, sit outside on the patio and take in some great views of the area.

Memorial

ANTONIO'S FLYING PIZZA $$
2920 Hillcroft St.
(713) 783-6080
www.antonios.com

Food at this popular family restaurant doesn't come out five minutes after you order it, but that's because everything here is prepared fresh. That includes the pizzas, which are made with hand-tossed dough. Dishes here are classic Italian, spanning the range of pastas, calzones, panini, veal, chicken, and seafood entrees you might expect. The decor here could use a little updating, but Antonio's is well maintained. The restaurant is located slightly south of Memorial toward the Galleria. It is closed Sunday and Monday.

i While you wait for your food at Antonio's, take the kids to the front of the restaurant to watch the chefs toss the pizza dough; the chef might even offer your little ones a little ball of dough of their own.

CARRABBA'S ITALIAN GRILL $$$
1399 S. Voss, at Woodway
(713) 468-0868
www.carrabbas.com

See the Carrabba's Italian Grill description in the "Upper Kirby" section.

CIRO'S ITALIAN GRILL $$
9755 Katy Fwy., at Bunker Hill
(713) 467-9336
www.ciros.com

Ciro's serves Italian food done right: The dishes here tend to be simple and include pizzas made in a wood-burning oven, pasta, soup, and entrees like eggplant parmigiana and veal scallopini. While the dishes here are quite large, the pastas

and salads are available in smaller sizes. Ciro's also caters to those watching their weight with healthy "Great Taste: No Waist" dishes. Whether you're dieting or not, be sure to try the bread and ask your server to bring you refills so you don't spoil your meal!

LA VISTA $$$
1936 Fountain View Dr.
(713) 787-9899
www.fatbutter.com

See the La Vista description in the "Galleria" section.

PRONTO CUCININO $$
791 Town & Country Blvd.
(713) 467-8646

See the Pronto Cucinino description in the "Midtown" section below.

Midtown

DAMIAN'S CUCINA ITALIANA $$$
3011 Smith, between Elgin and Tuam
(713) 522-0439
www.damians.com

Couples wanting a romantic evening often seek refuge in the quiet yet elegant atmosphere of Damian's. From the murals on the wall to a menu filled with dishes like spaghetti Bolognese, Damian's is one of the most authentic Italian restaurants in town. The menu includes flavorful pasta dishes aplenty, as well as veal, fish, chicken, and the requisite minestrone soup and antipasti. Damian's is owned by Bubba Butera and Frankie Mandola, whose family members run several great restaurants in Houston and Austin. Call ahead to make a reservation. Damian's is closed on Sunday.

MIA BELLA $$
2006 Lexington
(713) 528-2428
www.miabellatrattoria.com

See the Mia Bella description in the "Downtown" section.

PRONTO CUCININO $$

1401 Montrose
(713) 528-8646
www.pronto-2-go.com

A newcomer to the acclaimed Mandola restaurant family, Pronto serves classic Italian dishes that Houstonians have come to expect from the owners. The menu consists largely of pasta, chicken, salad, and fish dishes; Pronto also serves panini and pizza squares. Unlike most of the other Mandola restaurants, this one caters to the take-out crowd as well as people who have no problem walking up to the counter to order their meal. Pronto has a location on the border of West University and Braeswood, as wells as a new one in Memorial at the Town & Country Village shopping center.

VINCENT'S, NINO'S, GRAPPINO DI NINO $$$

2701 W. Dallas (Vincent's)
(713) 528-4313

2817 W. Dallas (Nino's)
713) 522-5120

West Dallas at Eberhardt (Grappino Di Nino)
(713) 522-5120
www.ninos-vincents.com

The Mandola family has three restaurants located next door to each other on West Dallas: Vincent's, Nino's, and Grappino di Nino. All three serve basically the same menu, which includes a range of pastas, wooden-oven baked pizzas, salads, meat, and fish. Vincent's restaurant is known for its rotisserie-cooked chicken. There's also an extensive wine selection. It's a good idea to call ahead for reservations, although you can always head to one of the other two if you can't get a table at the restaurant of your choosing. Nino's is slightly dressier than the other two restaurants, which are casual. That said, you won't usually find people wearing tank tops, shorts, and tennis shoes at any of the restaurants.

Montrose

LA STRADA $$$

322 Westheimer
(713) 523-1014
www.lastradahouston.com

High ceilings, bold-colored walls, and funky light fixtures are only part of La Strada's charm. Many of the artfully served dishes here have a culinary twist. This makes for delicious entrees like the angel hair pasta with a goat cheese medallion tossed in asparagus, wild mushroom ravioli, and a corn-crusted fish of the day topped with roasted ancho-chipotle sauce. On Saturday from 12 to 4 p.m. and Sunday from 11 a.m. to 6 p.m., La Strada serves what many consider the best brunch—and mimosas—in town.

Upper Kirby

CARRABBA'S ITALIAN GRILL $$$

3115 Kirby Dr.
(713) 522-3131
www.carrabbas.com

There's a good chance that you've eaten at Carrabba's before since the restaurant has more than 200 locations in 27 states. But you probably haven't been to the original restaurant, which is located right here in Houston and, like the Memorial location, is still operated by the Carrabba family. The food here may not be the best Italian in town, but it's still pretty good. The menu is filled with pasta, steaks and chops, pizza, and soups and salads. There are also a number of specialty dishes, like the Stuffed Shrimp Mandola (shrimp stuffed and baked with Italian-style crab dressing) and Chicken Bryan Texas (grilled chicken topped with goat cheese, sun-dried tomatoes, and basil butter).

STAR PIZZA $$

2111 Norfolk St.
(713) 523-0800
www.starpizza.net

Star Pizza is frequently mentioned among the city's best pizza places. You can opt for thin or deep-dish crust for any of the pizzas here, which include mainstream toppings made of fresh ingredients. Whole wheat crust is also available. Those who don't want pizza have plenty of salads, pastas, salads, and sandwiches to choose from. Service can take a while if you order a pizza since each one is made fresh and comes out of the oven hot. Delivery is available to nearby locations. Star Pizza has a second location (aptly named Star Pizza II) in the Heights, which is listed in this section.

West University

PREGO $$$
2520 Amherst St.
(713) 529-2420
www.prego-houston.com

This sister restaurant to the Backstreet Café and Hugo's is modeled after the neighborhood trattorias found in Italy. Elegant yet contemporary, Prego has received countless awards and write-ups in magazines ranging from *Bon Appetit* to *Money Magazine*. The reason? Chef John Watt uses the freshest ingredients to produce unique flavors and dishes, such as polenta-crusted oysters, roasted red pepper and poblano cream soup with crème fraîche, pumpkin seed–crusted red snapper, and stone-oven pizzas made with whole milk mozzarella. You'll also find a tempting selection of risottos, chicken, meat, vegetarian, and eclectic pasta dishes, as well as some mouthwatering desserts. Prego has an extensive wine selection. Diners here tend to dress up a little, so leave the jeans, shorts, and flip-flops at home. It's a good idea to call ahead for reservations.

PRONTO CUCININO $$
3191 W. Holcombe Blvd.
(713) 592-8646
www.pronto-2-go.com

See the Pronto Cucino description in the "Midtown" section.

The Woodlands

GROTTO $$$
9595 6 Pines
(281) 419-4252
www.grottorestaurants.com

See the Grotto description in the "Galleria" section.

LATIN AMERICAN

Galleria

AMÉRICAS $$$$
1800 Post Oak Blvd.,
between San Felipe and Westheimer
(713) 961-1492
www.cordua.com

From the moment you enter Américas, you'll understand why this restaurant is so special. Chicago architect Jordan Mozer designed it to resemble South America, with an exquisite mosaic tree, walls resembling Machu Picchu, and handblown glass chandeliers that look like flowers. The food itself is also great, with many options borrowed from sister restaurant Churrasco's. The steaks and seafood are big draws, as are the appetizers, which include things like corn-smoked crab fingers with herbed yuca polenta and jalapeño lime sauce, ceviche served in a pineapple, and empanadas. There's also a prix-fixe option for those willing to spend a little more. Every meal comes with some of Américas' bottomless plantain chips and sauces. The wine menu and mixed-drink options here are also great. Free valet parking is available. Call ahead for reservations. The attire is dressy. There's a second location in the Woodlands; see the listing in this section. This location is closed Sunday; the Woodlands location is open seven days a week.

River Oaks

CHURRASCO'S $$$$
2055 Westheimer Rd.
(713) 527-8300
www.churrascos.com

For 20 years Churrasco's has set the benchmark for Latin American food in Houston. Owned by the Cordúa family of restaurants, this is a sister restaurant to the Amazón Grill, Artista in the Hobby Center for the Performing Arts, and Américas. The elegantly decorated Churrasco's tends to feel intimate even when it is crowded. Every meal starts with some of the restaurant's signature plantain chips and chimichurri sauces. The restaurant is perhaps best known for its eponymous Churrasco—a charcoal-grilled center-cut beef tenderloin steak. Other hits include plantain-crusted chicken and shrimp, the empanadas, and the yucca fries. If you're looking for a nonmeat option, try the Cubana—a rich, black-bean soup served in a sourdough bread bowl lined with a unique cheese sauce. Although it is listed on the soup menu, the Cubana is more than enough for an entire meal. Whatever you order, save room for a few bites of the tres leches, which is one of the best desserts you'll find in this city. Churrasco's has an extensive wine collection with lots of great Chilean bottles. Call ahead to make reservations. The attire is dressy. Complimentary valet parking is available.

Westchase

CHURRASCO'S   **$$$$**
9705 Westheimer
(713) 952-1988
www.churrascos.com
See the Churrasco's description in the "River Oaks" section.

West University

AMAZÓN GRILL   **$$**
5114 Kirby Dr.
(713) 522-5888
www.cordua.com
This sister restaurant to the fancier Churrasco's and Américas serves up great Latin fusion fare in a casual, family-friendly setting. The restaurant operates self-serve style: You walk up to order your meal, then grab your own drinks and, if you want, a salad. The menu includes chicken and beef options, burgers, wraps, sandwiches, salads, and seafood, as well as the Cordúa restaurant family's signature plantain chips. Among the sides are some great sweet potato and yucca fries. There's a separate kids menu, which includes cotton candy with every meal. Kids also love the s'mores, which you make right at your table. Sit outside on the patio when the weather's nice.

i   Visit Amazón Grill Monday through Friday from 4 to 7 p.m. for $2 drinks—sangria, *mojitos,* and margaritas among them—and free snacks.

The Woodlands

AMÉRICAS   **$$$$**
21 Waterway Ave.
(281) 367-1492
www.cordua.com
See the Américas description in the "Galleria" section above. This location is open on Sunday.

MIDDLE EASTERN

Bellaire

FADI'S MEDITERRANEAN GRILL   **$**
4738 Beechnut
(713) 666-4644
www.fadiscuisine.com
To love Mediterranean food is to love Fadi's. This popular Mediterranean restaurant operates cafeteria-style, albeit with more upscale decor than you'll find at most cafeterias. Entrees—which include sandwich, platter, and sampler options with falafel, kebabs, and/or shawarma—come with your choice of fresh sides like balsamic mushrooms, cilantro zucchini, pomegranate eggplant, hummus, or tabouli. Every meal comes with all the warm pita bread you can stack on your plate. Serving sizes are large but lunch-size portions are offered for some items at lunchtime. There's a second location between the Galleria and Memorial areas, listed below.

Galleria

FADI'S MEDITERRANEAN GRILL   **$**
8383 Westheimer Rd.
(713) 532-0666
www.fadiscuisine.com
See the Fadi's Mediterranean Grill description in the "Bellaire" section above.

Memorial

EMPIRE TURKISH GRILL   **$$**

12448 Memorial Dr.,
between Gessner and Benignus
(713) 827-7475
www.empiretrgrill.com

The decor at the Empire Turkish Grill isn't particularly contemporary, but this doesn't tend to bother diners, who come for the peaceful atmosphere and the food. Big winners here include the *baba ghanoush* (mashed and seasoned eggplant), kebabs, and tomato sauce–topped cabbage rolls that are stuffed with ground lamb, rice, and herbs. The restaurant also caters to indecisive types with combination appetizer platters that feature five to seven appetizers of your choosing.

PUB FOOD

Montrose

THE BLACK LABRADOR   **$$**

4100 Montrose Blvd., at Richmond
(713) 529-1199
www.blacklabradorpub.com

You don't have to leave Houston to feel like you're in London. This popular pub plays the part, from the red British-style phone booth outside to the authentic pub atmosphere inside the ivy-clad brick walls. A fountain and a life-size chess set help provide the ambience for those who dine outside beneath the trees. The Black Lab's extensive menu includes a mix of burgers, soups, salads, quesadillas, zucchini crab cakes, mussels, and traditional pub fare, such as shepherd's pie, bangers and mash, and fish and chips. There's also a proper beer selection. It is open seven days a week for lunch and dinner and for brunch on Sunday.

SEAFOOD

Galleria

PAPPADEAUX SEAFOOD KITCHEN   **$$$**

6015 Westheimer Rd.
(713) 782-6310
www.pappadeaux.com

See the Pappadeaux Seafood Kitchen description in the "Upper Kirby" section.

i Dining downtown? Consider eating at the Downtown Aquarium's seafood restaurant, which offers a unique ambience and some well-presented dishes. See page 112 of the "Attractions" chapter for more information.

Memorial

DENIS' SEAFOOD HOUSE   **$$$**

9777 Katy Fwy., at Bunker Hill
(713) 464-6900

This sophisticated Memorial seafood restaurant does seafood your way. The best way to order here is to select one of the fish of the day listed on the chalkboard and then tell your server how you want it cooked—blackened, sautéed, or grilled. Other options include gumbo, crab, and boiled crawfish. Although the food is good and the decor is striking, Denis' Seafood House is a bit on the pricey side.

GOODE COMPANY SEAFOOD   **$$$**

10211 Katy Fwy.
(713) 464-7933
www.goodecompany.com

See the Goode Company Texas Seafood description in the "West University" section.

Montrose

PAPPAS SEAFOOD HOUSE   **$$$**

3001 S. Shepherd Dr., at Alabama
(713) 522-4595
www.pappasseafood.com

This Pappas restaurant serves all things seafood—étouffée, gumbo, blackened and grilled fish, boiled crawfish, oysters, and lobster—with plenty of fried, blackened, and grilled options. You'll also find Pappas' Famous Greek Salad here, topped with crabmeat or shrimp if you like. All the seafood is flown in daily. Portions are huge. Pappas Seafood House has seven locations around the Houston area; visit the Web site or consult the white pages to find additional locations.

River Oaks

**TONY MANDOLA'S GULF
COAST KITCHEN**   **$$$**
1962 W. Gray
(713) 528-3474
www.tonymandolas.com

The fresh seafood here may come from the Gulf Coast, but much of the culinary inspiration comes from Tony Mandola's Italian roots, as well as New Orleans–style cooking. Smoked corn and crab chowder, Cajun coleslaw, a crawfish po'boy, and shrimp and crabmeat spaghetti are just a few of the dishes you can choose from at this bistro. You'll also find an extensive wine list, as well as an eclectic martini selection that includes a Cajun Martini. Tony Mandola's is open for dinner seven days a week and for lunch Monday through Saturday. Call ahead to make a reservation for lunch or dinner.

Upper Kirby

PAPPADEAUX SEAFOOD KITCHEN   **$$$**
2410 Richmond Ave., at Kirby
(713) 527-9137
www.pappadeaux.com

One of the city's most popular seafood restaurants, Pappadeaux offers an extensive menu filled with grilled and fried seafood options, some Cajun-flavored fishes, lobster, crab, and even a blackened shrimp, and crawfish fondeaux (fondue). All of the fish are flown in daily. Visit during lunchtime and order off of the slightly cheaper lunch menu. There's often a wait to be seated, especially on the weekends, so call ahead to make reservations. Pappadeaux has another location at the Galleria (listed in this section), as well as locations at the Reliant Center (where the Houston Texans play football) and at William P. Hobby Airport.

West University

GOODE COMPANY TEXAS SEAFOOD   **$$$**
2621 Westpark Dr.
(713) 523-7154
www.goodecompany.com

Goode Company Texas Seafood serves up seafood with some Gulf Coast flair. That means you'll find gumbo, étouffée, shrimp creole, and mesquite-grilled seafood on the menu. You'll also find solid po'boys here, along with handmade shrimp and crabmeat tamales and seafood empanadas. Sides include Southern favorites like fried green tomatoes and hush puppies. The restaurant is a little more upscale than many seafood restaurants, but it's still laid-back. There's a second location in Memorial, which is listed in this section.

STEAK HOUSES

Downtown

VIC & ANTHONY'S STEAKHOUSE   **$$$$**
1510 Texas Ave.
(713) 228-1111
www.vicandanthonys.com

This swanky restaurant is one of the city's newest steak houses, and it's already one of the most popular. Built in the Craftsman style, Vic & Anthony's features huge stained-glass chandeliers and high-class ambience. The restaurant, which is owned by Landry's, sits across from Minute Maid Park, where the Houston Astros play baseball. The big draw here, of course, is the steak, but the iceberg wedge salad, crab cakes and oysters, and seafood dishes also get high marks. Ask your server for wine suggestions from the extensive wine list. Call in advance for reservations and dress nicely.

Galleria

PAPPAS BROS. STEAKHOUSE   **$$$$**
5839 Westheimer, at Bering
(713) 780-7352
www.pappasbros.com

The dark paneling and leather booths here are a good indicator that Pappas Bros. Steakhouse is—like other Pappas restaurants—the real deal. The menu includes plenty of steak options: filet mignon, rib eye, strip steak, peppercorn, veal steak, porterhouse, and lamb chops. There are also some great seafood options (lobster tail, anyone?) and appetizers ranging from caviar to house-cured salmon and bacon-wrapped scallops. Call ahead for reservations and get dressed up.

Memorial

BRENNER'S $$$$
10911 Katy Fwy., at Wilcrest
(713) 465-2901
www.brennerssteakhouse.com
Many people consider Brenner's the best steak house in Houston. For more than 70 years, this upscale spot has been a popular place to celebrate birthdays, anniversaries, and other milestones. Menu options here include the requisite filet mignon, rib eye, and strip steaks, as well as plenty of fish and chicken options—all exquisitely presented. Among the biggest nonsteak hits here are the crunchy German potatoes, the apple strudel, and when the chef makes it, the chocolate soufflé. With more than 200 bottles of wine, Brenner's offers a wine selection that lays claim to consecutive Awards of Excellence from *Wine Spectator* magazine. Brenner's also serves brunch. The attire is dressy. Make reservations online or by phone. Brenner's has a beautiful second location on Buffalo Bayou in River Oaks; see the "River Oaks" section for the address and phone number.

SALTGRASS $$$
8943 Katy Fwy., between Campbell and Voss
(713) 461-6111
www.saltgrass.com
Saltgrass isn't the city's best steak house, but it's a popular choice for those dining on a budget or with children. The menu includes certified Angus beef steaks and burgers, as well as what Saltgrass calls "Ranch Hand Favorites," like chicken-fried steak and baby back ribs. Be sure to get your fill of the Shiner Bock Beer Bread. There's often a line to get in on Friday and Saturday evenings so show up early to avoid a long wait. Saltgrass has more than a dozen locations around the Houston area;

visit the Web site or consult the white pages to find the one nearest you.

TASTE OF TEXAS $$$
10505 Katy Fwy.
(713) 932-6901
www.tasteoftexas.com
If you're dining with children or don't want to get dressed up to eat a steak, check out the Taste of Texas. You might feel like you've left the big city when you walk into the restaurant, which features lots of Texas and ranch decor. Pick your own steak cut at the butcher shop, then grab some salad, cheese, and bread from the famed salad bar. Those who don't want steak have plenty of alternatives, such as burgers, chicken, and steak sandwiches, a tenderloin salad, jumbo grilled shrimp, pecan-crusted chicken, and a veggie platter.

River Oaks

BRENNER'S ON THE BAYOU $$$$
1 Birdsall St., off Memorial near Bayou Bend
(713) 868-4444
www.brennersonthebayou.com
See the Brenner's on the Bayou description in the "Memorial" section.

TAPAS

Sugar Land

MI LUNA $$
2298 Texas Dr.
(281) 277-8272
www.mi-luna.com
See the Mi Luna description in the "West University/Rice Village" section.

West University/Rice Village

MI LUNA $$
2441 University Blvd.
(713) 520-5025
www.mi-luna.com

This brightly colored, festive restaurant and bar brings a little bit of Spain to Houston. Mi Luna offers a long list of tapas—appetizers—that include plenty of vegetarian and meat options, both hot and cold. The pizzas and paella are also worth trying. Typically two to three appetizers per person should be enough food, making this a very affordable dining option. Get the full Spanish experience by ordering one of Mi Luna's Spanish wines, or some sangria. On weekdays, happy hour lasts from 3 to 7 p.m., giving you plenty of time to get your fill of $5 margaritas and $3 sangria. There's live Latin, flamenco, merengue, or salsa music from Wednesday through Saturday evenings. Visit Mi Luna for Sunday brunch, where you'll enjoy omelets, seafood, homemade desserts, and bottomless sangria and mimosas. It is closed Sunday evenings. The restaurant now has a second location in Sugar Land, listed in this section.

TEX-MEX

Bellaire/Meyerland

ESCALANTE'S $$
590 Meyerland Plaza
(713) 663-7080
See the Escalante's description in the "Memorial" section.

PICO'S MEX-MEX $$$
5941 Bellaire Blvd.
(713) 662-8383
www.picos.net
If you prefer traditional Mexican fare to the "Texanized" version you find at many restaurants here, try Pico's Mex-Mex. Since 1984, this charming hole-in-the-wall has been serving what it calls Mex-Mex food—meats cooked in banana leaves, mole, pickled red onions, queso made with Chihuahua cheese and topped with chorizo. There are also more traditional Tex-Mex options like enchiladas, fajitas, and tacos, as well as the requisite—and requisitely good—margaritas. While there's lots of meat on the menu, vegetarians

have options, too. The casual atmosphere makes this a good spot for families.

Downtown
GUADALAJARA DEL CENTRO $$$
1201 San Jacinto
(713) 650-0101
www.guadalajarahacienda.com
See the Guadalajara Hacienda description in the "Memorial" section below.

IRMA'S $$$
22 N. Chenevert
(713) 222-0767
This small, family-run Mexican restaurant has long been a staple for city government employees and other downtown workers, although the quality of food and service has been inconsistent in the last few years. There's no menu at Irma's, so you have to ask the waitstaff what is being served. Among the more popular dishes are enchiladas, fajitas, and pork chops with ancho chile sauce. The fresh-squeezed lemonade is also popular. Most entrees, though relatively small, run at least $15.

The Heights
EL TIEMPO $$$
5602 Washington Ave.
(713) 681-3645
www.eltiempocantina.com
El Tiempo has a sacred place in Houston Tex-Mex culture: It is owned by the grandson of Mama Ninfa, the woman who brought us the popular Ninfa's restaurants (listed on page 76). The rather pricey menu includes all the standard Tex-Mex fare—enchiladas, chalupas, tacos, flautas, quesadillas, salads, fajitas, steak, and seafood. Among the most notable dishes is the Cañonball—an avocado stuffed with shrimp, lathered in melted cheese, then breaded and fried. You'll find some of the city's best margaritas here—and quite a bit of noise. El Tiempo has additional locations in River Oaks and Upper Kirby. It is open seven days a week but hours vary by location and by day, so call ahead.

Memorial

ESCALANTE'S $$$

www.escalantes.net

12821 Kimberley Lane, in Town and Country shopping center

(713) 467-5577

6582 Woodway, at Voss

(713) 461-5400

Bright funky decor and an extensive menu make Escalante's a great place to eat Tex-Mex, whether on a date, with friends, or with children. The menu includes some great fajitas, enchiladas, and fish tacos, as well as some great ceviche and Pat's Mexico City Salad topped with shrimp, pine nuts, walnuts, and a goat cheese medallion. No matter what you order, you can choose healthy options. Mexican rice, for instance, can be replaced with the vegetarian cilantro rice, and you can choose white, wheat, or corn tortillas for any dish. You can also choose from pinto, charro, or some of Escalante's tasty fat-free refried black beans. Believe it or not, you can even request baked chips instead of the deliciously fattening chips the waitstaff typically serve. Lunch and Sunday brunch specials are available. Service tends to be pretty quick, but you might have to wait up to 45 minutes to get a table on Friday and Saturday nights. Escalante's doesn't take reservations, unfortunately, but you can munch on some chips and sip a margarita at the bar while you wait. Escalante's has two locations in Memorial, as well as additional locations in Bellaire/Meyerland, Sugar Land, and River Oaks' Highland Village shopping center. See the corresponding sections for those locations' addresses.

GUADALAJARA HACIENDA $$$

9799 Katy Fwy., at Bunker Hill

(713) 461-5300

www.guadalajarahacienda.com

A popular place to dine with family or large groups, Guadalajara boasts a Hacienda-style atmosphere and solid Tex-Mex fare. The menu at this noisy restaurant includes the expected enchiladas, fajitas, and taco dishes, as well as some more unique dishes like Camarones Paci-fico (bacon-wrapped jumbo shrimp stuffed with cheese and jalapeños), South Texas Quail, and Costillas Fronteras (fire-braised baby back ribs slathered with raspberry chipotle barbecue sauce). The only real vegetarian options here include cheese (or jalapeño cheese) enchiladas and salad. Guadalajara often fills up on weekend evenings so show up early or plan to wait at the bar. There are additional locations in Upper Kirby, downtown, and The Woodlands; see the corresponding listings in this section.

PAPPASITO'S CANTINA $$$

10409 I-10 W. Sam Houston Tollway

(713) 468-1913

www.pappasitos.com

Consistently named one of the best Tex-Mex restaurants in the city, Pappasito's Cantina is another member of the Pappas restaurant family. Although you'll now find Pappasito's as far away as Georgia, the chain started right here in Houston. Pappasito's isn't a good place to go to for intimate conversation; the place is noisy and packed with people who come for the margaritas, chips, salsa, fajitas, and an endless array of Tex-Mex dishes. There aren't many vegetarian options here; even the cheese enchiladas have meat in the sauce. Portions are big and there's usually a wait, but that doesn't keep people away. Pappasito's has 13 locations around the city, including locations at both airports. The Upper Kirby location—dubbed Little Pappasito's—is listed in this section; visit the Web site or consult the white pages to find additional locations.

Midtown

TACOS A GO-GO $

3704 Main St.

(713) 807-8226

www.tacosagogo.com

Got a late night or early morning craving for a breakfast taco? This funky Midtown joint is the place to, well, a go-go. Name the ingredients for your breakfast tacos, or choose from huevos rancheros, *migas*, salads, and a full range of tacos—fish tacos included—available on corn,

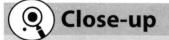 **Close-up**

An Insider's Guide to Tex-Mex

If you're eating Tex-Mex or Mexican food for the first time, you may see some unfamiliar items on the menu. Here's a glossary of some names you're likely to see:

Antojitos: Appetizers or tapas

Botanas: Appetizers

Breakfast taco: Eggs, cheese, and sometimes meat, peppers, or potatoes wrapped in a tortilla; topped with salsa

Cabrito: Young goat, typically very tender

Camarones: Shrimp

Cerveza: Beer

Chalupa: Flat, crispy shell topped with chicken, pork, lettuce, tomatoes, cheese, and/or salsa

Chilaquiles: Fried corn tortillas topped with salsa or mole, cheese, and scrambled or fried eggs

Chili con carne: Chili with meat

Chile rellenos: Stuffed peppers

Chorizo: Spicy pork sausage

Codorniz a las Brazas: Grilled quail

Costillas de Cerdo al Carbon: Pork ribs

Empanadas (pronounced emp-uh-nah-duhs): Pastry stuffed with ground-up vegetables and meats

Enchilada: Tortilla wrapped around a hot filling, such as cheese, beef, spinach, or chicken and lathered with a sauce

Ensalada: Salad

flour, whole wheat, or crispy tortillas. If you're not counting calories—and who can at a Tex-Mex joint?—order a side of chips with your choice of salsa, queso, or some of the best guacamole in town. Tacos a Go-Go is open daily and until 2 a.m. on Friday and Saturday.

Montrose

HUGO'S $$$
1600 Westheimer Rd., at Mandell Street
(713) 524-7744
www.hugosrestaurant.net
Much of the food at this acclaimed restaurant—pronounced "ew-goes"—is distinctively *not* Tex-Mex. Dishes feature flavors and ingredients found in more central and southern regions of Mexico, including Oaxaca, Campeche, and Puebla. That means you'll find things on the menu like pan de cazón (chile-bathed tortillas layered with black beans and grilled shark), sopesitos (three masa pancakes topped with duck with mole poblano and served with pork cracklings in salsa verde), and cabrito (roasted goat meat pulled from the bone). Less adventurous types, rest assured: The menu also includes more standard Mexican fare such as enchiladas, tamales, and chile rellenos, as well as seasonal twists on these dishes. There are plenty of vegetarian options as well. Hugo's award-winning sommelier will help pair your meal with the perfect glass of wine or try one

Fajitas (pronounced fuh-heat-uhs): Grilled strips of steak or chicken eaten in a flour tortilla; usually served with pico de gallo, cheese, and sour cream on the side

Frijoles refritos: Refried beans

Guacamole: Chopped avocado dip peppered with herbs, chopped onions, and chiles

Huevos rancheros: Fried eggs with a tomato-chile sauce

Margarita: Mixed drink made with tequila and lime, served in a salted glass; sometimes includes other flavors such as mango or strawberry

Migas: Eggs scrambled with cheese and corn tortilla strips or chips

Mole (pronounced mo-lay): Sauce made of unsweetened chocolate, nuts, and spices; served on top of enchiladas

Mollejas al Ajillo: Sautéed sweetbreads with garlic, Guajillo, and olive oil, typically served with tortillas to make tacos

Pico de gallo: Hot salsa made with tomatoes, onions, chiles, and cilantro

Quesadilla (pronounced kay-suh-dee-yuh): Two tortillas with cheese between them, served baked

Queso: Cheese dip, often made with Mexican cheese, sometimes includes peppers

Queso con carne: Cheese dip with meat

Salsa verde: Green salsa made with green chiles, garlic, cilantro, and tomatillos; often used on top of enchiladas or for dipping tortilla chips

Sopapilla: Fried pastry topped with honey

Tamale: Corn dough filled with pork, chicken, or vegetables and rolled in a corn husk; served steamed, sometimes with a chile sauce

Tortilla (pronounced tor-tee-yuh): A flat round bread, usually made of corn, flour, or whole wheat; used to make enchiladas and to accompany dishes such as fajitas and *migas*

Tostada: Fried tortilla

of the best margaritas in town. Whatever you order, save room for some tres leches, churros, or hot chocolate. The restaurant serves brunch on Sunday. Hugo's is a little nicer than most Mexican restaurants so guests tend to shy away from flip-flops and shorts. Call ahead to make a reservation; even weeknights are fairly busy here.

River Oaks

EL TIEMPO   **$$$**

1308 Montrose Blvd.

(713) 807-8996

www.eltiempocantina.com

See the El Tiempo description in the "Heights" section.

ESCALANTE'S   **$$$**

4053 Westheimer Rd., in Highland Village

(713) 623-4200

www.escalantes.net

See the Escalante's description in the "Memorial" section.

TACO MILAGRO RESTAURANT & BEACH BAR   **$$**

2555 Kirby, at Westheimer

(713) 522-1999

www.taco-milagro.com

Taco Milagro doesn't have the best Tex-Mex in town but the atmosphere, margaritas, and long list of top-shelf tequilas keep people coming back.

There's often live music and salsa dancing; those who prefer a quieter atmosphere—or the chance to people watch—can find seating on the patio. The food is standard Tex-Mex fare—hard and soft tacos, fajitas, tamales, burritos, and enchiladas, including the less-standard veggie sweet potato and spinach enchiladas. Taco Milagro is open at 11 a.m. daily and stays open until 1 a.m. on Thursday and midnight on Friday and Saturday.

Second Ward

NINFA'S ON NAVIGATION $$$
2704 Navigation Blvd.
(713) 228-1175
www.ninfas.com

You're likely to see several Ninfa's restaurants when you drive around Houston, but if you're going to eat at one, make it Ninfa's on Navigation, which lies just east of downtown. Back in 1973 a woman known to Houstonians as Mama Ninfa opened a little hole-in-the-wall here and popularized Tex-Mex. Mama Ninfa and her family no longer own the restaurant, but many people still love the food at this location, whose decor has gotten a makeover. Chef Alex Padilla, a former line cook under Mama Ninfa, serves up enchiladas, handmade tamales, salads, and a variety of tacos—including some with redfish and chipotle mayo. The fajitas are among the most popular dishes, and the margaritas have more than a few fans. Ninfa's on Navigation tends to fill up quickly so plan to wait.

Sugar Land

ESCALANTE'S $$$
15933 City Walk
(281) 242-1100
See the Escalante's description in the "Memorial" section.

LUPE TORTILLA MEXICAN
RESTAURANT $$$
15801 Southwest Fwy., at TX 6 and TX 59
(281) 298-5274
www.lupetortilla.com

See the Lupe Tortilla Mexican Retaurant description in the "Upper Kirby" section below.

Upper Kirby

EL TIEMPO $$$
3130 Richmond,
between Buffalo Speedway and Kirby
(713) 807-1600
www.eltiempocantina.com
See the El Tiempo description in the "Heights" section.

GUADALAJARA MEXICAN BAR & GRILL $$$
2925 Southwest Fwy., at Kirby
(713) 942-0772
www.guadalajarahacienda.com
See the Guadalajara Hacienda description in the "Memorial" section.

LITTLE PAPPASITO'S $$$
2356 Richmond Ave., at Kirby
(713) 520-5066
www.pappasitos.com
See the Pappasito's Cantina description in the "Memorial" section.

LUPE TORTILLA MEXICAN
RESTAURANT $$$
2414 Southwest Fwy., near Kirby
(713) 522-4420
www.lupetortilla.com

Lupe Tortilla is nothing fancy but many people consider it the best Tex-Mex restaurant in town. The menu includes standard Tex-Mex fare, made with the freshest ingredients and (where appropriate) served with handmade tortillas. This is a great place to take young children: The restaurant has a sandbox, as well as a kid-friendly soft drink bar. Be prepared to wait; it often takes up to an hour to get seated here. Lupe Tortilla has seven locations around Houston. The locations in Sugar Land and the Woodlands are listed here; visit the Web site or consult the white pages for additional locations.

The Woodlands

GUADALAJARA HACIENDA $$$
27885 I-45 North
(281) 362-0774
www.guadalajarahacienda.com
See the Guadalajara Hacienda description in the "Memorial" section.

**LUPE TORTILLA MEXICAN
RESTAURANT** $$$
19437 I-45 South
(281) 298-5274
www.lupetortilla.com
See the Lupe Tortilla Mexican Retaurant description in the "Upper Kirby" section.

VEGAN/VEGETARIAN

River Oaks/Highland Village

PEPPER TREE VEGGIE CUISINE $$
3821 Richmond, at Weslayan
(713) 621-9488
www.peppertreeveggiecuisine.com
This popular vegetarian restaurant features a variety of East Asian dishes, with some Western variation. The menu includes dishes like French tofu fries, sesame vegan chicken, General Tso's vegan chicken, sweet and sour vegan fish sticks, and tofu ball spaghetti with tomato sauce. About 95 percent of the items on the menu are vegan and there's no MSG in the food here. If you can't decide what to eat, opt for the buffet, which features about 18 hot dishes, fresh salad, dumplings, spring rolls, egg rolls, and vegan desserts. The buffet costs just $9.99 on weekdays from 11 a.m. to 2 p.m. and $13.85 all day on Saturday and Sunday. Pepper Tree is closed on Monday.

i Find out about some of the hottest restaurants and bars in town by subscribing to *Houston Tidbits'* e-newsletter at http://houston.gotidbits.com.

Upper Kirby

FIELD OF GREENS $$
2320 W. Alabama, between Kirby and Greenbriar
(713) 533-0029
www.fieldofgreenscuisine.com
Health nuts and vegetarians sing the praises of Field of Greens. The restaurant uses largely organic products and has a number of raw food and microbiotic offerings. The menu is largely comprised of healthy vegetarian fare like a barbecue soy chicken patty, a falafel burger, vegetarian fish tacos, and eggplant parmesan. There are also a few nonvegetarian options, like the grilled salmon burger. Many of the dishes here are vegan (or can be made vegan), and low-carb and low-fat options abound. The restaurant is BYOB; there's no corkage fee. Vegan brunch is served on Saturday and Sunday from 10:30 a.m. to 3:30 p.m.

NIGHTLIFE

What's there to see and do in the evenings and wee hours of the morning in Houston? Quite a bit. Scattered around the city—particularly in Montrose, Midtown, downtown, and the Heights—are bars, pubs, and lounges that range from chic to dive, from beer to wine to absinthe, and from quiet to deafening. Those who like to dance can get their fix at posh dance clubs that play hip-hop and salsa, authentic country-and-western bars, and several bars that cater to the gay and lesbian community. If you prefer to kick back and listen to some live music, check out one of the city's many live music venues. You'll find everything from tiny holes-in-the-wall to sophisticated jazz clubs to sports arenas rocking on Bruce Springsteen's latest tour. Many local restaurants also feature a lounge atmosphere and, in some cases, live music. If this appeals to you, take a closer look at the "Restaurants" chapter and try Max's Wine Dive (page 46), Taco Milagro (page 76), the Treehouse (page 45), Uptown Sushi (page 49), Benjy's (page 48), the Black Labrador (page 69), or Mi Luna (page 71). While you're checking out the "Restaurants" chapter, take note of coffee shops such as Agora, Brasil, Empire Café, and Onion Creek Coffee House—all listed there starting on page 56. Many of these coffee shops feature live entertainment, and all of them serve alcohol in the evening.

Prefer to avoid the crowded bar and lounge atmosphere? You might enjoy visiting a comedy club, attending a reading by a famous author, or taking in a movie at one of the city's unusual theaters. Or you might prefer to cheer on one of the city's sports teams or watch a theater performance. You can learn more about these sorts of options in the "Spectator Sports" and "Performing Arts" chapters, respectively.

There are far too many bars, clubs, and music venues to list here, so this chapter offers up some of the city's most popular nightlife options. Before you head out, take note: Most of the bars and clubs in this chapter require guests to be 21 or older, with a valid ID. The legal drinking age in Texas is 21, and most clubs and bars don't let in anyone who is younger. Often Houston clubs and bars charge a cover of anywhere from a couple dollars up to $10 or even $20. This does not include drinks or food; it merely gets you in the door. Bars often have higher cover charges on weekends and for special events. Many bars offer happy hour specials, although the hours, days, and discounts vary. For live music venues, it's always a good idea to purchase your tickets early. Many events—especially those featuring big acts—sell out. Tickets can be purchased at the venue, on the venue's Web site, or by phone, unless indicated otherwise.

Bars, lounges, and pubs in Houston typically close by 2 a.m. on the weekends and earlier during the week. Hours and days do change sometimes, though, so it's a good idea to call ahead.

BARS, PUBS, AND LOUNGES

Downtown

EIGHTEEN TWENTY BAR
1820 Franklin Ave.
(713) 224-5535

Popular among the 20-something crowd, Eighteen Twenty Bar has a full bar with reasonably priced drinks, a jukebox, and a popular photo booth. There's plenty of seating, as well as ample space for standing around. Visit on the first and last Friday of the month and pay $15 to play all the arcade games you want next door at Joystix, a huge video game retail shop, from 9 p.m. to 2 a.m.

LA CARAFE
813 Congress St.
(713) 229-9399
www.owlnet.rice.edu/~hans320/projects/lacarafe

La Carafe isn't like other wine bars in Houston. For one thing, it's located in a 160-plus-year-old building that has some ghost stories of its own. For another, it's rumored to be the city's oldest bar. It also happens to be a dive. All this seems to make Houstonians love it even more. You'll find a decent selection of wines and beers here, along with some creaky seats and an outdoor patio. Bring cash because La Carafe doesn't take plastic.

The Heights
BIG STAR BAR
1005 W. 19th St.
(281) 501-9560
www.bigstarbar.com

Big Star Bar is a good place to get a cheap drink or shoot some billiards. The bartenders serve cold beer and specialty drinks named after semi-famous people like Fonzi. Other quirky attractions at this dive bar include an outdoor fire pit (seriously), Hula-hooping, a jukebox, and an occasional DJ.

COVA
5555 Washington Ave.
(713) 868-3366
www.covawines.com

During the day, Cova is a wine retail shop; after 5 p.m., it transforms into a relaxed wine bar, serving wine, tapas, and cheese platters. The original location is in West University; see the listing in this section. Visit either location Monday through Wednesday from 4 to 7 p.m. to take advantage of the $5 happy hour menu. On Sunday evenings, the Heights location features live jazz.

i Want to sound like you know what you're talking about when it comes to wine? Take a wine class through Cova. Visit the Web site or call for more information.

Midtown
13 CELSIUS
3000 Caroline St.
(713) 529-8466
www.13celsius.com

Named for the optimal temperature at which to store wine, 13 Celsius is one of the city's best wine bars. The sommeliers here know their wines and will help you navigate the impressive list of wines and handcrafted beers, as well as the selection of fine cheeses, meats, and fresh espresso. Almost as impressive as the wine and beer choices is the setting itself: 13 Celsius makes its home in a 1927 Mediterranean-style building intended to pay homage to European wine bars and bistros. When the weather is nice, sit outside in the courtyard. If you like your wine, purchase a bottle at retail price to take home. 13 Celsius opens at 4 p.m. every day and stays open until midnight from Sunday through Wednesday and until 2 a.m. Thursday through Saturday.

Montrose
ABSINTHE BRASSERIE
609 Richmond Ave.
(713) 528-7575
www.absinthelounge.com

This classy bar is the place to go if you need to satisfy your absinthe fix. You'll find half-a-dozen absinthe cocktails here, as well as beer, wine, and mixed drinks like mint juleps, *mojitos*, sangria, and martinis. Absinthe Brasserie also has a short menu of appetizers, pizzas, and panini. The place can get loud and busy in the evenings.

i Absinthe Brasserie isn't marked on the outside, so be on the lookout for gothic double doors.

BOHEME CAFÉ & WINE BAR

307 Fairview St.

(713) 529-1099

www.barboheme.com

Housed in a revamped historic building, Boheme Café & Wine Bar offers some great ambience. A garden with stone Zimbabwean sculptures surrounds the building while a stucco accent wall and antique light fixtures help liven up the inside. Boheme serves wine; beer; liquor; mixed drinks, like sangria, frozen *mojitos,* and the popular pinot noir martini; coffee; and a few small food items. Visit on Sunday and Monday for all-day happy hour. Boheme is open from 8 a.m. to 12 a.m. on Sunday and Monday and from 8 a.m. to 2 a.m. the rest of the week. It also offers free Wi-Fi.

SO VINO WINE BAR & BISTRO

507 Westheimer Rd.

(713) 524-1000

www.sovinowines.com

This ambient wine bar features a very long list of great wines, many of which hail from the Southern Hemisphere. If wine's not your thing, worry not: So Vino has a full bar with premium liquors. Complement your drink with a snack like truffle popcorn or edamame, or if you prefer, an entre— like risotto, mussels, or shiraz-braised spare ribs.

 Visit So Vino on Monday night and get half off any bottle under $100.

WEST ALABAMA ICE HOUSE

1919 W. Alabama, at Hazard

(713) 528-6874

www.myspace.com/thewaih

Like other ice houses around Texas, the West Alabama Ice House isn't air-conditioned. But that's okay with many Houstonians who come to this dive for the ice cold beer and conversation. The limited seating here includes some stools and a picnic table.

River Oaks

DOWNING STREET PUB

2549 Kirby, at Westheimer

(713) 523-2291

www.downingstreetpub.com

Discriminating drinkers and cigar smokers can be found sitting on the leather couches at Downing Street Pub. This popular spot has nearly 100 single malt scotches to choose from, as well as extensive wine and beer menus. If you want to smoke a cigar, this is the place to do it. Downing Street's 400-square-foot humidor holds some of the country's finest cigars. There's also a limited food menu here for those who want a snack.

MARFRELESS

2006 Pedent, at McDuffie behind

River Oaks Theatre

(713) 528-0083

www.marfreless.net

This speakeasy isn't easy to find; there's no sign on the outside so you have to know to look for the blue door. The relatively quiet atmosphere and lounge-style seating make Marfreless a good place to go with a small group. The bartenders mix some good drinks, too. Head upstairs and you're likely to find couples getting, uh, cozy.

Second Ward

THE CORKSCREW

1919 Washington, near Sawyer

(713) 864-9463

www.houstoncorkscrew.com

Located just west of downtown in the Second Ward, this popular wine bar and date spot offers a rotating selection of more than 250 wines. The Corkscrew's menu includes short descriptions of each wine, making the seemingly overwhelming decision of what to order slightly easier. The dimly lit place can get loud, especially on Monday nights when there's live acoustic music and on Thursday, which is Karaoke Night. The Corkscrew also offers free Wi-Fi.

Upper Kirby/Greenway

OPORTO CAFÉ
3833 Richmond Ave.
(713) 621-1114
www.oporto.us
Inspired by European "gastro bars," Oporto Café features more than 50 wines by the glass, many of which come from Spain, Italy, and Portugal. You'll also find the city's largest selection of Portuguese ports here, along with mixed drinks such as *mojitos,* sangria, and caipirinha. Enjoy hot and cold tapas while you sit at the bar or at one of the tables in this narrow cafe. On Thursday Oporto features live flamenco music. It also offers free Wi-Fi.

West University

COVA
5555 Washington Ave.
(713) 868-3366
www.covawines.com
See the "Heights" listing in this section.

THE GINGER MAN
5607 Morningside
(713) 526-2770
www.houston.gingermanpub.com
The Ginger Man has several locations around Texas and a few on the East Coast, but this Rice Village location is the original. This pub serves a long list of specialty beers in an unpretentious setting, making it a popular hangout for Rice University and med school students. Sip your beer on the patio when the weather's nice.

COMEDY CLUBS

Midtown

LAFF STOP
526 Waugh Dr.
(713) 524-2333
www.laffstop.com
Laff Stop is Houston's premiere comedy club. Each week a different comic takes the stage on Thursday (one show), Friday (two shows), and Saturday night (three shows). Recent acts include "Mr. Las Vegas" Ron Kenney and frequent sitcom guest star Clinton Jackson. The crowd tends to really get into the shows, which makes for a good time. There's a two-item minimum purchase requirement; you can order food and drinks at your table or order from the bar if you show up early. Visit on Wednesday for Open Mic Night, where some successful comics have gotten their start. Open Mic Night begins at 7:30 p.m. Show up an hour early if you want to perform.

i Make defensive driving more bearable by taking one of the Laff Stop's defensive driving classes. Visit the Web site or call for more information.

COUNTRY-AND-WESTERN DANCING

Midtown

WHISKEY CREEK
2905 Travis St., at Taum
(281) 989-8658
www.whiskeycreekhouston.com
The big dance floor at this upscale country-and-western bar tends to fill up. Most of the time, you'll hear top-40 country and some Texas music, but the DJs occasionally mix things up with a little hip-hop or pop. Whiskey barrel tables and photos of Wild West outlaws like Billy the Kid and Buffalo Bill add to the Western aura here. While the bar has a definite country vibe, you won't be out of place if you show up sans boots, denim, and hat. Visit on Thursday, when there's no cover for ladies ($6 for men) and beer and shooters are just $3. Whiskey Creek is closed Sunday through Wednesday.

River Oaks

BLANCO'S BAR & GRILL
3406 W. Alabama, at Buffalo Speedway
(713) 439-0072
www.houstonredneck.com/blancos.html
If you've got your cowboy or cowgirl boots on and are ready to two-step, head over to Blanco's.

Frequently named the city's best country bar by the *Houston Press,* Blanco's showcases what it calls "live authentic Texas music," as well as some jukebox tunes. That means you'll hear plenty of bluegrass, zydeco, country of all strands, Americana rockabilly, honky-tonk, and oldies. The crowd here is a diverse mix of couples and singles—young and old—in search of a dance partner. Blanco's is closed to the public on Saturday and Sunday.

DANCE CLUBS

Galleria/Uptown Park

BELVEDERE
1131–01 Uptown Park, off Post Oak
(713) 552-9271
www.belvedereinfo.com
This swanky bar is one of those places people go to see and be seen. Many come here just to grab a drink but it's hard to ignore the music, which plays most days from 4 p.m. to 2 a.m. The DJs spin a mix of '80s and '90s dance tunes, salsa, merengue, hip-hop, Spanish and Arabic rock, and then some. On Wednesday from 4 p.m. to 2 a.m., Belvedere plays remixes of current pop and dance tunes. Thursday night features a mix of Latin and house beats, and Friday features hip-hop remixes. Be sure to dress up and leave your Converse at home; otherwise, you're likely to be turned away at the door.

Midtown

UNION BAR LOUNGE
2708 Bagby St.
(281) 974-1916
www.unionbarhouston.com
Union Bar Lounge is a cross between a chic lounge and a sports bar. There are several large-screen TVs around the lounge. Sometimes sporting events are on, other times music videos. Union Bar Lounge often features live music and on weekends the DJ gets everybody on their feet and dancing.

Montrose

NUMBERS NIGHT CLUB
300 Westheimer Rd.
(713) 526-6551
www.numbersnightclub.com
Numbers has been around for years and it's no less of a dive now than it was 15 years ago. Filthy bathrooms and floors don't keep people from coming here to dance, though. Numbers often hosts lives shows and the DJs play a mix of dance tunes that gets big crowds on the floor. Thursday nights feature what the club calls Bangin' Electric Dance Beats—loud new music, attractive dancers., and the city's longest running Electro (electronic music) show. The crowd here tends to be fairly young since Numbers is one of the few dance clubs in the city that lets in guests under 21.

SCOTT GERTNER'S SKYBAR & GRILLE
3400 Montrose Blvd.
(713) 520-9688
www.myspace.com/scottgertnersskybar
Known simply as Skybar among locals, this popular dance bar is owned by jazz musician and Grammy nominee Scott Gertner, who often plays here with his band. Between the live music and the mixes played by the DJs, Skybar offers plenty of excuses to dance all week long. Thursday night is Salsa Night—and Ladies' Night, which means ladies get in for free. Don't want to dance? Skybar offers plenty of alternatives: Hang out at the bars, which offer champagne, martinis, wine, and *mojitos.* Or you can take in a great view of the city from two spacious terraces. If the city view doesn't excite you, head to the west terrace to watch a movie on a 103-inch screen.

GAY AND LESBIAN BARS

Montrose

CHANCES LESBIAN BAR
1102 and 1/2 Westheimer Rd.
(713) 523-7217
www.chancesbar.com
Chances is the only bar in town that caters specifically to lesbians every night. You'll find

a little of everything here—live music and DJs, karaoke, go-go girls, a martini bar, pool tables, a mechanical bull, and special events like a recent *L Word* viewing party. One of the biggest draws, of course, is the music: Those who want to kick up their heels and do the Texas two-step can dance to the country music in the room nicknamed the Barn, while those who prefer to groove to hip-hop and pop can get down in the G-Spot.

METEOR

2306 Genesee St.
(713) 521-0123
www.meteorhouston.com
One of the city's classiest gay bars, Meteor offers guests comfortable seating options, good drinks, and great pop and dance music videos. The DJ knows how to fill up the dance floor; in fact, it's not unusual to see people dancing on the tables here. Those who need a break from dancing often hang out on the patio. Visit between 4 and 9 p.m. Wednesday through Sunday for half-price happy hour. Smoking is off-limits inside Meteor.

SOUTH BEACH

810 Pacific St.
(713) 529-7623
www.southbeachthenightclub.com
A huge dance floor, really loud music played by DJs, and black lights make South Beach a very popular spot to dance and flirt. The club attracts a very diverse clientele, with people of all races, ages, and sexual orientations hanging out here on any given night. For those who don't want to dance, the front lounge, several bars, and the patio are popular alternatives. Among the weekly events here: Cheap Drink Night (Wed), Latin Night (Thurs), and the Super Sunday Drag Show. There's typically a cover charge between $10 and $20, depending on the night.

LITERARY READINGS

If you're an avid reader and/or writer, don't miss the poetry and prose readings held in Houston throughout the year. Some of the most renowned readings are hosted by **Inprint.** Each year this local literary organization holds its Brown Reading Series, which brings several great writers to the city between September and April. The authors read from their work, get interviewed on stage by Houston Public Radio's cultural programming director St. John Flynn, and sign copies of their books. The readings are held at different venues around the city, primarily in the Theater District. Recent authors include Ha Jin, Ann Patchett, Richard Price, and Charles Simic. Individual tickets cost $5 and can be purchased through the Inprint Web site (www.inprint houston.org); season tickets are also available. Inprint also hosts readings on the lawn at Discovery Green. Learn more about these events, as well as workshops and children's readings put on by Inprint online or by calling (713) 521-2026.

The **University of Houston's Graduate Program in Creative Writing** also hosts public readings by distinguished faculty, students, and guests. Learn about upcoming readings and other literary events online at www.class.uh.edu/cwp or by calling the program at (713) 743-2255.

i Find out about upcoming readings and other fun events around the city by visiting the blog www.houstonist.com.

LIVE MUSIC

Downtown

THE RED CAT JAZZ CAFÉ

924 Congress St.
(713) 226-7870
www.redcatjazzcafe.com
This bar and lounge features live jazz—sometimes even during lunchtime—in a hip environment reminiscent of the French Quarter. The Red Cat Jazz Café serves mixed drinks, as well as a small selection of wine and beer. Those who want to drink without the noise can sit upstairs in the lounge. If you're hungry, feast on New Orleans–inspired dishes like gumbo, blackened chicken, and okra Creole.

SAMBUCA JAZZ CAFE
909 Texas, at Travis
(713) 224-5299
www.sambucarestaurant.com

Although Sambuca is a dinner club, many people prefer the music to the food. Live bands and musicians play here every night. Much of the time, as the name suggests, jazz is the featured genre, but on any given night you might hear top 40, classic rock, Latin, or soul. Among the bar's offerings are a long list of specialty cocktails like the Pomtini, Bull's Eye (Belvedere and Red Bull), and the Maker's Manhattan. Visit the Web site to find out about upcoming performances, then reserve your table online.

TOYOTA CENTER
1510 Polk St.
(866) 446-8849 (box office)
www.houstontoyotacenter.com

When it's not being used for Houston Rockets basketball or Houston Aeros hockey games, the Toyota Center hosts big concerts. Recent acts have included Bruce Springsteen, Eric Clapton, Pink, and Green Day. Parking is available for $15 in the Tundra parking garage next door to the Toyota Center, but you can often find available parking on nearby side streets. Purchase tickets by visiting or calling the Toyota Center box office or visiting the Toyota Center Web site.

VERIZON WIRELESS THEATER
520 Texas St.
(713) 230-1666
www.verizonwirelesstheater.com

This midsize concert venue boasts good sound quality and an opportunity to see big-name acts up close. Recent performers at Verizon Wireless Theater include James Taylor, the Killers, Deftones, Chris Isaak, and the Indigo Girls. There's reserved seating as well as standing-room-only space. Call or visit the Web site to purchase tickets. Don't wait until the last minute because many shows sell out. Valet parking is available but there's often a line. If you don't want to wait, park in the Theater District Parking Garage across the street at the intersection of Smith and Texas.

Midtown
THE CONTINENTAL CLUB
3700 Main St.
(713) 529-9899
www.continentalclub.com/houston.html

Like the Continental Club in Austin, this Midtown joint offers an intimate atmosphere for seeing live music, much of it local. On any given night, you might see a cover band, blues, rockabilly, or ska. There's some space for dancing, as well as a patio for relaxing. On Wicked Wednesday the Continental Club features burlesque shows between set changes.

i Got the munchies? The Continental Club's neighbor, Tacos A Go-Go (713-807-8226), will usually deliver some of their breakfast tacos to bar guests.

Montrose
CÉZANNE
4100 Montrose Blvd., at Richmond
(713) 522-9621
www.blacklabradorpub.com/cezanne_
about.html

Located above the Black Labrador pub (page 69), Cézanne is an intimate piano bar featuring performances by some of the best jazz musicians from Houston, New York, and San Francisco. Just how intimate, you ask? There are just 40 seats in this classy wood-paneled bar so expect to get close and personal with your fellow guests as you sip one of Cézanne's renowned martinis. There's a $10 cover and a one-drink minimum. It is only open on Friday and Saturday evenings.

North Houston
JAVAJAZZ COFFEEHOUSE
16300 Kuykendahl
(832) 295-5077
www.javajazzcoffeehouse.com

Located up north on FM 1960, JavaJazz Coffeehouse is Houston's version of the legendary New York club CBGB. The club tends to feature rising emo and punk groups like Say Anything, the Plain White T's, and Drop Dead Gorgeous. JavaJazz doesn't serve alcohol. Purchase tickets in advance on the Web site.

Upper Kirby

GOODE'S ARMADILLO PALACE
5015 Kirby, at Barlett
(713) 526-9700
www.thearmadillopalace.com
Goode's Armadillo Palace offers a down-home, Texas-style drinking, dining, and evening entertainment experience. This member of the Goode restaurant family features shuffleboard, dominos, and billiards, as well as a lineup of Texas musicians. Sit on the patio and throw back a few cold beers or sample some whiskey at the whiskey bar. When you get hungry, order your choice of Southern delights—wings, fried chicken, or venison chili, to name a few.

McGONIGEL'S MUCKY DUCK
2425 Norfolk
(713) 528-5999
www.mcgonigels.com
Widely considered one of the city's best small live-music venues, McGonigel's Mucky Duck features live music just about every night of the year. Most musicians who perform at this Irish-themed bar hail from Texas; recent acts include Trish Murphy and Joe Ely. On Monday nights, the Mucky Duck hosts an open-mic night, which attracts everyone from poets to comedians. This weekly event is free, but most other shows require tickets, which can be purchased in advance on the Web site. The only alcohol served here is beer, wine, and champagne. Step out on the outdoor patio when you need a smoke or a reprieve from the noise.

i Pick up a free copy of the *Houston Press* at a local newsstand to find out about upcoming shows in the area.

The Woodlands

CYNTHIA WOODS MITCHELL PAVILION
2005 Lake Robbins Dr., The Woodlands
(281) 363-3300
www.woodlandscenter.org

Located north of Houston in The Woodlands, the Cynthia Woods Mitchell Pavilion hosts some of the city's biggest concerts and performing arts events amid lush grass and towering pine trees. Throughout the year, this outdoor amphitheater features big acts, like the Dave Matthews Band, Kenny Chesney, and Styx. The Houston Symphony and Houston Ballet also perform here on occasion. General admission seating is available on the lawn; those who want to be closer to the action or to avoid the heat and rain can pay more to sit in the covered amphitheater. Tickets can be purchased through Ticketmaster (www.ticketmaster.com or 800-745-3000) or at the box office. Take note, though: Tickets do not go on sale at the box office until five hours after they have gone on sale at Ticketmaster. Paid parking is available in lots around the pavilion. Parking prices vary but aren't usually more than $15. Be sure to bring some cash for parking and wear comfortable shoes. Most of the parking lots are a bit of a hike from the amphitheater.

i Concerts at the Cynthia Woods Mitchell Pavilion are generally held rain or shine, so bring some rain gear if there's rain in the forecast.

MOVIE THEATERS

There are dozens of movie theaters in the Houston area. Many of these are your standard AMC, Cinemark, or Edwards fare, but the city is also home to several unique movie theaters, which are listed below. Showtimes for all local theaters can be found on their respective Web sites, in the *Houston Chronicle,* or online at www.movies.yahoo.com or www.fandango.com. Movie tickets tend to run around $10 for adults as of May 2009; most theaters offer discounts for children and seniors. Some offer student discounts with a valid ID.

Downtown

ANGELIKA FILM CENTER
510 Texas Ave., at Smith Street
(713) 225-1470
www.angelikafilmcenter.com

This modern theater is the place to see independent and foreign-language films—the kind of movies that might screen at the Sundance Film Festival. Angelika usually shows a few popular films, such as *Slumdog Millionaire* and *Angels and Demons*, too. The theaters are fairly small and although they're not as swanky as, say, a Tinseltown theater, they are clean and comfortable. Angelika is located in Bayou Place, a downtown dining and entertainment complex with a Hard Rock Cafe, Slick Willies Billiard's, restaurants, and a few bars. Parking is free at Angelika, but it's a bit of a hassle. You have to pay $7 in cash to park in the Theater District Garage at Smith and Texas, then take your receipt to the Angelika ticket counter, where you'll be reimbursed.

Katy

ALAMO DRAFTHOUSE
531 South Mason Rd., in Mason Park
Shopping Center
(281) 920-9266
www.drafthouse.com/mason

See the "West Houston" listing in this section.

Memorial

EDWARDS HOUSTON MARQ*E
STADIUM 23 & IMAX
7620 Katy Fwy.
(713) 263-7843

For the most part, the Edwards Marq*e Stadium 23 is a pretty standard theater with lots of screens. What makes this theater unique is its IMAX screen—the largest such screen in Houston. The IMAX screen here is typically used for big action movies like *Spiderman* and *Star Trek*. Tickets to IMAX shows tend to run about $4 more than tickets to the regular shows.

STUDIO MOVIE GRILL CITYCENTRE
805 Town and Country Lane
(713) 461-4449
www.studiomoviegrill.com/townand
country.html

Forget about eating popcorn at the movies. At the new Studio Movie Grill CityCentre in Town & Country Village's CityCentre complex, you can watch movies while you drink and dine at a table. Purchase your ticket to the movie outside, then order your food and drinks before or during the movie. A server will bring your order right to your table. The menu includes burgers, chicken, quesadillas, beer, wine, and salads; there's also a kids' menu. Most movies that play here are blockbusters (or wannabe blockbusters) like *X-Men Origins: Wolverine, Next Day Air,* and *Ghosts of Girlfriends Past.*

River Oaks

RIVER OAKS THEATRE
2009 West Gray
(713) 850-0217
www.landmarktheatres.com

This old art deco–style theater has been a staple of Houston's independent and foreign-language film scene since 1939. The River Oaks Theatre, which could use some repairs, screens just a handful of movies a day. Some are big flicks like *The Terminator;* others are more obscure films like Cary Joji Fukunaga's *Sin Nombre.* Visit at midnight on Friday or Saturday night to see older favorites like *Eternal Sunshine of the Spotless Mind, Fear and Loathing in Las Vegas,* and *The Rocky Horror Picture Show.*

West Houston

ALAMO DRAFTHOUSE
West Oaks Mall #429
Westheimer Road at TX 6
(281) 920-9268
www.drafthouse.com/westoaks

After visiting the Alamo Drafthouse once or twice, you may never want to see a movie anywhere else. Like the newer Studio Movie Grill CityCentre, the Alamo Drafthouse serves dinner and drinks in the theater while you watch a movie. The Alamo's menu is filled with burgers (including a good veggie burger), nachos, salads, and pizzas, greasy appetizers, beer, wine, and sangria. While many people come here to see blockbuster movies, some of the Alamo's biggest draws are special events, such as special midnight showings of new movies, marathon screenings of old TV series like *Twin Peaks,* and season-finale watch parties for shows like *LOST* and *24.* The Alamo sometimes even serves thematic food and drinks to complement the featured movie. (Think White Russians for the *Big Lebowski.*) There's now a second location in Katy. See the listing in this section for that location's address and phone number.

i Got kids? For the first matinee of any Tuesday showing at the Alamo Drafthouse, parents can bring their little ones to see the flick, and no one will complain about crying.

AURORA PICTURE SHOW
800 Aurora St.
(713) 868-2101
www.aurorapictureshow.org
Located inside a church dating back to 1924, this nonprofit cinema screens short films and videos made by noncommercial artists. Aurora Picture Show also hosts a number of filmmakers, videographers, and curators who come to talk about their work. The small theater seats only 100; screenings are sometimes held at other locations around the city. Tickets cost just $6 for most screenings; special events may cost a little more.

PERFORMING ARTS

When it comes to Houston's cultural scene, the performing arts play a starring role. Only five cities in the country have resident professional companies in ballet, opera, theater, and symphony—and Houston is one of them. Nine acclaimed performing arts organizations—as well as some touring groups—perform downtown in the Theater District, a 17-block area that's only second to Manhattan when it comes to the number of theater seats in a concentrated downtown area. While the Theater District is home to some of the biggest acts in town, it is hardly the only place to see the performing arts here. Houston is home to many smaller community and professional theaters, as well as Miller Outdoor Theatre in Hermann Park.

OVERVIEW

In this chapter, you'll find a sampling of Houston's performing arts offerings, which are just about as diverse as they come. We've got everything from puppet shows to ballet to theater to Broadway musicals to opera to chamber music to symphony to contemporary music in the classical spirit. Many of the theaters here also offer special performances for children and families; a few of the best theaters for kids can be found in the "Kidstuff" chapter.

Because there are so many performing arts organizations and venues around the city, it is impossible to include them all here. Considered some of the best in their respective genres, the groups listed in this chapter tend to attract large audiences. In most cases, this chapter highlights performing arts companies, some of which have their own theaters and others that "borrow" venues. In a couple of cases, specific venues are highlighted since their setting and the breadth of events they host make them attractions in themselves.

In addition to the live-music options listed here, many clubs and other venues around the city feature live music and big-ticket concerts throughout the year. Check out the "Nightlife" chapter to learn about the live-music scene here.

Ticket prices for performances vary quite a bit. Shows in the Theater District tend to be the priciest, although most theaters offer special prices for students, seniors, children, and groups of 10 or more. Tickets to performances on Friday and Saturday evenings typically cost more than those for weeknights and weekend matinees. In most cases tickets can be purchased by calling or visiting the theater box office or visiting the theater's Web site. Tickets at theaters outside the Theater District tend to be fairly inexpensive (or, in the case of Miller Outdoor Theatre, free); tickets for performances at these venues are often only available by calling or visiting the box office. Price ranges listed here are based on 2008–2009 season ticket costs. Keep in mind that theaters often raise ticket prices from one year to the next, so you might have to pay a little more than expected. All ticket prices listed are for individual tickets; season tickets are also available for most local performing arts companies.

Performance days and times vary. Some venues and groups only offer weekend evening and matinee shows; many have a few weeknight performances. Most theaters—especially those

i Find out about the latest offbeat performing and visual arts events in Houston by visiting the Fresh Arts Coalition's Web site (www.fresharts.org). This arts collaborative highlights the work and upcoming events of 25 of the city's best independent arts groups.

in the Theater District—host shows from September to May or June, then take a couple of months off for the summer. Check the Web site or call the box office to find out about upcoming shows. Schedules are often released as much as six months to a year in advance. Tickets for acclaimed performances, as well as seasonal shows, can be tough to nab at the last minute, so order yours as far in advance as possible.

Phone numbers listed here are for the box office, which, in most cases, is located at the theater. Exceptions include the addresses of both the theater and box office. All venues listed here are wheelchair accessible and many offer assisted-listening devices. Inquire at the box office for additional information.

Theater District venues are identified as such. Parking for these venues is available in nine Theater District parking garages, which are scattered around this 17-block section of downtown. Parking in these garages costs $7, payable upon entry, on Saturday, Sunday, city holidays, and after 5 p.m. Monday through Friday. The cost for parking at other times is based on an hourly rate. Find the garage closest to the theater you're visiting on the downtown map (page vii). Tunnels running between the downtown theaters and garages provide protection from the weather. Parking at other theaters around the city is typically free and available on-site. Exceptions are included in the listings that follow.

BALLET

HOUSTON BALLET
Wortham Theater (Theater District)
501 Texas Ave., at Smith Street
(713) 227-2787
www.houstonballet.org
The Houston Ballet is the country's fourth-largest professional ballet group. Led by artistic director Stanton Welch, the ballet's 54 dancers put on more than 70 performances of about 10 different ballets each year. Each season's shows feature ballets ranging from an adaptation of the five-act opera *Manon* to classics, like *Swan Lake* and *Sleeping Beauty*. In December the Houston Ballet puts

on more than 30 performances of *The Nutcracker*, many of which are offered at discounted prices to make the ballet accessible to more Houstonians, especially children who love the magical holiday performance. The Houston Ballet occasionally holds shows at Miller Outdoor Theatre (page 93). While these performances are free, they require advance tickets for seats in the covered area. In addition to local performances, the Houston Ballet tours to other cities around the United States, Canada, and Europe. The Houston Ballet also has choreographed productions with the Boston Ballet, the National Ballet of Canada, and others.

Houston Ballet Foundation, which runs the ballet, operates a ballet academy, which currently trains about 300 dancers, ranging from 4 to 60 years of age. More than half of the Houston Ballet's dancers are former academy students.

Tickets to the Houston Ballet are available through the box office and range from about $30 to $104, depending on where you sit and when you attend a performance.

ℹ️ Get a sneak peak of the upcoming theater season, a backstage tour, and a chance to meet some of Houston's best ballerinas, musicians, and actors by attending the free Theater District Open House, held each August. This daylong, family-friendly event takes place at the main Theater District venues—Alley Theatre, Jones Hall, Wortham Center, and Hobby Center. Learn more by calling (713) 658-8938 or going online to www.houstontheaterdistrict.org.

MUSIC

DA CAMERA OF HOUSTON
Lillie Cullen Theater at Wortham Center
(Theater District)
501 Texas, at Smith Street (theater)
1427 Branard St. (box office)
(713) 524-5050
www.dacamera.com
Since 1987, Da Camera has brought Houstonians an assortment of musical styles and sounds,

including chamber music and jazz performances by some of the world's best musicians. Many Da Camera concerts connect music with other art forms. Some performances, for instance, have combined dance and chamber music. Others, like Da Camera's Music and Literary Imagination programs, have paired music with the stories of literary giants like Franz Kafka and Thomas Mann. This innovative programming has won Da Camera national and international attention, as the organization's shows have often gone on tour. Da Camera puts on about 17 performances each year; there is typically only one performance of each show. Although Da Camera makes its home at the Cullen Theater in the Theater District's Wortham Center, events are often held at other venues around town, including the Menil Collection and the Rothko Chapel, which you can learn about in the "Museums" chapter. Admission to jazz concerts ranges from $30 to $50; classical concert tickets cost $25 to $45, and tickets to concerts held at the Menil Collection cost $35. Students and adults over 60 get in for half price. Tickets can be purchased online, over the phone, or by visiting the box office. Tickets go on sale at the theater at 6:30 p.m. on the night of the performance.

FOUNDATION FOR MODERN MUSIC
1915 Commonwealth
(713) 529-3928
www.modernmusic.org
Classical music lovers, take note: The Foundation for Modern Music features contemporary music written in the classical tradition by living American composers such as Yoko Ono, Johnson Reagon, and Jerome Kitzke. The featured composers often attend the performances, which are held at locations such as the Rothko Chapel and Stages Repertory Theatre. The River Oaks–based

i Love classical music? Tune into Houston Public Radio/KUHF on 88.7 FM. KUHF plays far more classical music than most public radio stations—and it gives airtime to local composers and performers, who also help run the station.

foundation also holds an annual competition for teenage composers. Ticket prices vary based on the event and venue.

HOUSTON FRIENDS OF MUSIC
Rice University
Stude Concert Hall
6100 Main St.
(713) 348-5400
www.houstonfriendsofmusic.org
For close to 50 years, Houston Friends of Music has been collaborating with Rice University's Shepherd School of Music to bring outstanding chamber music to Houston. Each year the Houston Friends of Music board of directors sifts through more than 100 applications from international performing groups who want to be considered for one of the nine performances scheduled for the upcoming season. Shows are held at Stude Concert Hall on the Rice University campus once or twice a month during the school year. Individual tickets cost $46 to $67 for adults, $36 to $56 for seniors 65 and older, and $18 to $23 for students with an ID.

HOUSTON SYMPHONY
Jones Hall (Theater District)
615 Louisiana St., at Capitol Street
Zilkha Hall at the Hobby Center for the Performing Arts (Theater District)
800 Bagby St.
(713) 224-7575
www.houstonsymphony.org
One of the country's oldest performing arts organizations, the internationally acclaimed Houston Symphony is comprised of 90 full-time musicians. Each year some 350,000 people come out to listen to the Houston Symphony's concerts. Some come for one (or more) of the 18 classical concerts, which have featured the likes of Beethoven's Violin Concerto and Brahms's First. Others come for the nine pops concerts, which have featured rockapella, Broadway tunes, and songs from Billy Joel. Each season the symphony also features special events, ranging from talks about different musicians to performances by world-renowned musicians like Yo-Yo Ma.

On four Saturday mornings each year, the Houston Symphony hosts the Weatherford Family Concerts, which are geared toward kids ages 4 to 11. These concerts showcase music from favorite children's movies and stories, like *Aladdin*. Before and after each concert, you'll find entertainment and fun activities for the kids in the theater lobby. Season tickets to the Weatherford series are $54 for adults and $28 for children. The symphony also offers special concerts for schools and hosts concerto and orchestral competitions for students and young adults ages 16 to 29.

Ticket prices vary for different events but generally range from $27 to $107. Most concerts are held at Jones Hall; some smaller events are held at the Hobby Center's Zilkha Hall. Both venues are located downtown in the Theater District.

OPERA

HOUSTON GRAND OPERA
Wortham Center
550 Prairie
(713) 228-6737
www.houstongrandopera.org
The Houston Grand Opera—also known as HGO—is one of the world's most acclaimed opera companies. Each year HGO puts on six operas—some classics like *Rigoletto* and *Tosca*, others debut operas like André Previn's *Brief Encounter*. Since 1973, HGO has commissioned and produced dozens of new operas, 38 of which made their world debut in Houston. This innovation—not to mention the accompanying artistic stylings—has won the HGO two Grammy Awards, two Emmy Awards, a Tony Award, and a Grand Prix du Disques. No other opera company in the world has won all four of these prestigious awards.

HGO also trains aspiring operatic performers in the Houston Grand Opera Studio Program. Each year 8 to 12 students are selected to participate in the rigorous nine-month to three-year program, wherein they take classes in voice, acting, languages, stage movement, and diction from some of HGO's finest professionals. Students also receive individual coaching to prepare for careers in opera.

HGO always uses supertitles, even for operas performed in English. The company puts on about five performances of each opera. Ticket prices vary, depending on the day and time, but typically range from about $35 to $125.

> **i** Got season tickets but can't make a show? Most theaters allow season ticket holders to exchange their tickets for another performance date or time.

PUPPETRY

BOBBINDOCTRIN PUPPET THEATRE
1601 Vermont, Ste. 150
(713) 259-1304
www.bobbindoctrin.org
If you think puppets are for kids, you've probably never been to Bobbindoctrin Puppet Theatre. Since 1995, Bobbindoctrin has been putting on puppet shows that use a combination of rod, shadow, hand, tabletop, and string puppetry and elaborate puppets. Sometimes shows even incorporate masks. The shows here are a combination of newer scripts and original ones written by local playwrights, and few are kid friendly. All participating artists hail from the Houston area. Previous shows include *Ivan the Fool*, based on Leo Tolstoy's short story; *Oh, Lenin!* an adaptation of a nonsensical poem by Kornei Chukovski; and sillier titles such as *Got Brains?* and *Sea Monkeys*. During the winter holiday season, Bobbindoctrin produces a puppet festival, featuring a series of short puppet shows. Shows are often held at nightclubs and museums around the city. Ticket prices vary based on the event and venue.

THEATER

ALLEY THEATRE
615 Texas Ave. (Theater District)
(713) 220-5700
www.alleytheatre.org
For more than 60 years, the Alley Theatre has been the heart and soul of Houston theater. Each year thousands of Houstonians come to see this Tony Award–winning company perform a gamut

of new, rediscovered, classic, and musical plays. Recent shows include *Cyrano de Bergerac, The Man Who Came to Dinner, Rock 'n' Roll,* and *The Farnsworth Invention,* written by *The West Wing* creator Aaron Sorkin. The Alley even coproduced and premiered *Jekyll & Hyde* in 1990—seven years before the hit show opened on Broadway.

As part of its commitment to youth and the future of theater, the Alley Theatre offers summer camps for kids in grades 2 through 12, leads theater workshops at local schools, and offers low-cost student matinee performances for school groups.

The Alley puts on 11 productions every year, including *A Christmas Carol.* There are several performances of each show. Ticket prices typically range from about $40 to $67, depending on the day and time. For some shows, the Alley offers "Cheap Thrill" tickets—$21 tickets for Sunday and Tuesday evening performances.

BROADWAY ACROSS AMERICA
Hobby Center
800 Bagby St. (Theater District)
(713) 622-7469
www.broadwayacrossamerica.com/houston
There's no need to travel to Manhattan to see the most talked about Broadway shows anymore. Each year Broadway Across America brings five touring Broadway musicals to Houston's Hobby Center for the Performing Arts. These shows include some new hits like *Avenue Q, Spamalot, The Lion King, Jersey Boys,* and *Wicked,* as well as classics like *The Wizard of Oz* and *Mary Poppins.* While some shows are far better than others, there are at least a couple serious crowd-pleasers each season. Tickets can be hard to come by for the shows that have received the most acclaim on Broadway, so it's a good idea to order tickets in advance. Tickets are sold through Ticketmaster and can be purchased by phone, at the Hobby Center box office, or online. Prices range from $32 to $78 for weekday evenings and weekend matinees, and from $33.55 to $83.55 for weekend evenings. These prices do not include the $5.50 per ticket surcharge.

i Dine at Artista, located on the second floor of the Hobby Center, before taking in a show at the Hobby Center. This sister restaurant of Churrasco's and Américas (listed in the "Restaurants" chapter) dishes up artsy decor and some of the best—and best-looking—Latin food around. Make reservations online at www.cordua.com or by calling (713) 278-4782.

COUNTRY PLAYHOUSE
12802 Queensbury Lane
(713) 467-4497
www.countryplayhouse.org
Since opening in 1956, the Country Playhouse has moved several times, but one thing remains constant about the oldest community theater in town: It champions quality in everything from well-known plays to first-run plays. All the plays here are performed by locals who audition and work hard to get their role just right. Many are performed on the Cerwinske Stage, which seats up to 225 people. Recent shows include *The Best Little Whorehouse of Texas, The Best Christmas Pageant Ever,* and *Lend Me a Tenor.* The Black Box Lab, which previously functioned as a rehearsal space, features rehearsed readings of scripts written by locals. Many of these scripts go on to become full productions. These readings, dubbed "New Plays by Houstonians," are held on Sunday evenings and are free to the public. Tickets to most other performances are $12.

Country Playhouse is located in the Town & Country Village shopping center in Memorial. There's not always someone at the theater to answer the phone, so the easiest way to purchase tickets is to order them online or purchase them at the theater up to two hours before the show.

i Attending a Sunday matinee or weeknight show in the Theater District? Arrive about a half hour early and you should be able to find free parking on the street.

Close-up

Society for the Performing Arts

Houston may be best known for all of the performances put on (and written) by local artists, but these aren't the only shows in town. Each year the city also hosts a number of traveling shows. Credit for these events is due, in part, to the Society for the Performing Arts (various locations, 713-227-4772, www.spahouston.org).

Each year, the Society for the Performing Arts—aka SPA—brings some of the best national and international theater, dance, and music artists and companies to town. The selection is always diverse, ranging from orchestras to solo vocalists to gospel choirs to Broadway tunes. And that's just a sample of the music selection. The SPA also brings to town ballet groups, contemporary dance groups, operas, jazz, theater performances, and guest speakers who are experts in the performing arts. Recent seasons have brought the likes of the Salzburg Chamber Soloists, the bluegrass band Cherryholmes, the Aspen Santa Fe Ballet, and the Virsky Ukrainian National Dance Company. The SPA also offers a Family Fun Series, which features popular kids' acts like the musical group Hot Peas N' Butter. Tickets to events in the Family Fun Series are half price for kids.

Most events are held at Theater District venues such as Jones Hall (listed under the "Houston Symphony") and the Wortham Center (listed under the "Houston Grand Opera"). The full SPA season includes about 17 events, and subscribers can create their own subscription of four or more events. Single ticket prices vary, depending on the event and venue, but most range from about $27 to $47.

MAIN STREET THEATER
2540 Times Blvd. (Rice Village)
4617 Montrose Blvd. (Museum District)
(713) 524-6706
www.mainstreettheater.com

When the Main Street Theater entered the local theater scene in the 1970s, its founders sought to entertain Houstonians with more provocative plays and musicals and give more professional thespians training and a stage to show off their skills. More than 30 years later, the Main Street Theater continues to do both of these things—for children and adult audiences alike. Recent shows on the adult-oriented MainStage include *The Light in the Piazza, Urinetown,* the world premiere of . . . *and L.A. Is Burning,* and touring shows like *A Midsummer Night's Dream.* Main Street Theater also offers a great selection of plays for children, as well as children's acting classes. See the "Kidstuff" chapter to learn more about these offerings.

Tickets for MainStage events range from $20 to $36, depending on the day and time. Tickets for adults 65 and over cost between $14 and

$30; students can get tickets for $10 to $26. As part of its commitment to making theater accessible to people of all income levels, Main Street Theater offers "Pay-What-You-Can" performances on the first Sunday after opening night. On three specified days prior to opening night, the theater offers sneak previews for $10.

Main Street Theater has two locations—one in Rice Village, the other in the Chelsea Market shopping center in the Museum District. The box office is at the Rice Village location. Call the box office or check the Web site to find out where your desired performance is being held.

MILLER OUTDOOR THEATRE
100 Concert Dr., in Hermann Park
(281) 373-3386
www.milleroutdoortheatre.com

Who said theatergoing had to be an indoor affair? Each year, from March to October, thousands of Houstonians head to Hermann Park's Miller Outdoor Theatre to watch a cornucopia of music, dance, theater, and even film events. The shows

⊙ Close-up

Uniquely Houston and the Performing Arts

Houston is home to dozens of nonprofit performing arts group, but not all of them have a theater or the resources that their Theater District counterparts do. To help some of the city's best emerging music, theater, and dance groups develop a following, the Hobby Center for the Performing Arts launched Uniquely Houston (713-315-2525, www.thehobbycenter.org). This program provides participating groups with technical, operational, and marketing support. It also gives them a Theater District venue—Zilkha Hall at the Hobby Center—for practicing and performing. The more than one dozen groups that participate in Uniquely Houston represent a variety of cultures and ethnicities and reflect the true diversity of the city's performing arts offerings. Below are brief descriptions and, where applicable, the Web sites and phone numbers of the participating programs. Tickets to events can be purchased by calling the Hobby Center or visiting its box office. Prices vary, but are typically pretty low.

ARS LYRICA HOUSTON
www.arslyricahouston.org

Ars Lyrica Houston plays Baroque music—think Handel and Bach—using period instruments. It has put on everything from staged dramas to chamber music programs.

CANTARE HOUSTON
(713) 724-9648
www.cantarehoustonsingers.org

This chorus of lively professional singers performs choral music spanning five centuries and a number of countries and cultures. In addition to performing classics, Cantare commissions new choral works.

COLOMBIAN FOLKLORIC BALLET
www.cfb-usa.org

The Colombian Folkloric Ballet performs ballets, as well as dances from other Latin American countries whose dance forms aren't well represented in Houston. The touring group brings in ballet masters and choreographers from Colombia to help stage the annual folkloric performance of *Colombia, a Land of Contrasts*.

HOUSTON CHAMBER SYMPHONY
(713) 523-0776
www.houstonchambersymphony.org

This chamber symphony plays a diverse array of concerts featuring music by everyone from Mozart and Bach to 20th-century composers like Dmitri Shostakovich and Paul Hindemith. The Houston Chamber Symphony also debuts the concerts of many living composers.

HOUSTON EBONY OPERA GUILD
(713) 335-3800
www.houstonebonymusic.org

Houston Ebony Opera Guild highlights the work of black choral and opera singers through performances of classic and new operas, as well as concerts composed by black Americans.

MAGGINI STRING ENSEMBLE
www.maggini.org

Comprised solely of string instruments, this youthful orchestra plays classical, contemporary, and popular tunes.

are put on by a number of local performing arts groups, including the Houston Metropolitan Dance Company, Express Children's Theatre, Theater Under the Stars, the Houston Ballet, the Houston Symphony, Houston Grand Opera, Stages Repertory Theatre, and Miller Theatre Advisory Board. Many of the shows are geared

specifically toward young children, with recent productions including *The Three Little Pigs* and *Aladdin*. Two of the biggest highlights here are the Fourth of July celebration, which features the Houston Symphony playing Tchaikovsky's *1812 Overture*, followed by a 16-cannon salute and a fireworks display, and the Shakespeare Festi-

MASQUERADE THEATRE
(713) 861-7045
www.masqueradetheatre.com

This musical theater company only employs actors and actresses from Houston. They perform a number of older and newer classics such as *Evita, The Producers,* and *The Music Man.*

MUSIQA
(713) 524-5678
www.musiqahouston.org

Musiqa is a small ensemble of composers and music professors from Rice University's Shepherd School of Music and the University of Houston's Moores School of Music. The group seeks to make contemporary classical music fun and engaging for people who might not normally listen to the genre. Musiqa plays four concerts at Zilkha Hall each year, as well as concerts for families, at schools, at the Menil Collection, and the Contemporary Arts Museum Houston (the latter two of which are listed in the "Museums" chapter).

PROJECT DIVISI
(832) 607-7352
www.projectdivisi.org

This 24-piece string orchestra makes classical music exciting by juxtaposing the work of contemporary composers like Benjamin Britten with that of old masters like Tchaikovsky and Bach. Recent concerts include Crossroads of America and Behind the Iron Curtain.

PSOPHONIA DANCE COMPANY
(713) 802-1181
www.psophonia.com

Psophonia is one of Houston's leading modern dance companies. The group performs artistically distinctive dances onstage and seeks to engage at-risk children through in-school visits and special performances.

SAMSKRITI SOCIETY FOR INDIAN PERFORMING ARTS
(281) 265-2787
www.samskritihouston.org

Samskriti celebrates Indian culture through an array of cultural dance, theater, and music performances.

SANDRA ORGAN DANCE COMPANY
(713) 225-0677
www.organdance.org

This modern ballet company blends neoclassic ballet with more contemporary dance forms and moves. The use of popular music, as well as the shows' universal themes, helps engage diverse audiences.

UNITED NATIONS INTERNATIONAL CHOIR
(713) 667-7044
www.unahouston.org/unachoir

The 80 singers in this choir represent a variety of cultural, racial, ethnic, and socioeconomic backgrounds. They sing music from around the world in their original languages.

VIRTUOSI OF HOUSTON
(713) 807-0888
www.virtuosiofhouston.org

Virtuosi is the country's only youth chamber orchestra. The company seeks to mold Houston's most talented young musicians into professionals and prepare them to go on to attend the best conservatories. Virtuosi plays two concerts at the Hobby Center each year.

val, which features several performances of two Shakespeare plays each August. More information about these two events can be found in the "Annual Events" chapter.

While many bring picnic baskets and blankets to watch the show from the amphitheater's grassy hill, more than 1,500 attendees—including those in wheelchairs—have the chance to sit in covered seating at Miller Outdoor Theatre. Since admission is always free, these seats are available on a first-come, first-served basis. Parking spaces—not to mention the best covered and lawn seats—tend to fill up quickly at Miller Outdoor Theatre, so try to arrive at least a half hour early. Visit the Web site to download the complete schedule for the current or upcoming season.

STAGES REPERTORY THEATRE
Houston Center for the Arts
3201 Allen Pkwy.
(713) 527-0123
www.stagestheatre.com

The *New York Times*, the *Wall Street Journal*, *Vogue*, and *Variety* have a few things in common but here's one you probably don't know: They have all covered Stages Repertory Theatre for its innovative theatrical productions. Since it opened in a basement of a downtown brewery in 1978, Stages has been committed to producing brave new plays and offering groundbreaking revisions on literary, dramatic, and musical classics. Each year Stages puts on six shows. Recent shows include Stages artistic director Ted Swindley's international hit musical *Always . . . Patsy Cline* and the 2007 Pulitzer Prize–winning drama *Rabbit Hole.*

Adults aren't the only ones treated to pioneering works at Stages. Through what it calls EarlyStages, the company offers whimsical yet professional performances geared toward families and school groups. The EarlyStages repertoire includes new presentations of old folktales and multicultural tales, as well as original plays and musicals. Recently EarlyStages put on the wacky musical *Panto Cinderella.*

Ticket prices vary, although they tend to run between $20 and $30, depending on the day, time, and show. Season tickets cost just $150. During performances, free parking is available in the Houston Center for the Arts parking lot on the south side of the building.

THEATER UNDER THE STARS
Hobby Center
800 Bagby St. (Theater District)
(713) 558-8887
www.tuts.com

Theater Under the Stars is Houston's musical theater company, and it is considered a gem on the national and international musical scene. Since launching in 1968, Theater Under the Stars—aka TUTS—has produced more than 300 musicals, many of them national and international premieres. Musicals that TUTS has debuted include *Jekyll & Hyde* (in collaboration with the Alley Theatre and the 5th Avenue Theatre of Seattle), *Annie Warbucks, Zorro: The Musical, Scrooge, Mame,* and the Tony Award–winning redux of *Carousel.* TUTS also offers its own rendition of new and old musicals ranging from *Rent* to *Les Misérables* to *Legally Blonde.*

TUTS trains aspiring young actors through its Humphreys School of Musical Theatre, which holds summer camps for kids ages four and up. The Humphreys School also offers two distinct training tracks year-round. The Studio program helps students who are new to theater, as well as professionals seeking to take their work up a notch to develop their rhythm and enhance their skills. The Academy program trains students who intend to become professional actors in dance, acting, improvisation, scene study, directing, or voice. Students must audition to participate in the highly selective Academy program.

TUTS typically puts on about a half-dozen shows at the Hobby Center each year; the company or the Humphreys School typically puts on a show at Miller Outdoor Theatre each summer as well. Each show runs for about two weeks, with several matinee and evening performances during that period. Tickets typically range from to $26 to $75, depending on the showtime and day. Purchase tickets online or at the Hobby Center box office.

i **Opt for seating in the center sections. Get a side seat and you might end up with a lousy view.**

MUSEUMS

If you're still struggling to shed the image of Texans as boot-wearing, funny-talking folks, a visit to the local museums will remind you that this city is truly cosmopolitan. Among Houston's finest gems are its more than two-dozen museums. The Museum of Fine Arts Houston is one of the largest art museums in the country, and the Menil Collection holds one of the most noteworthy collections of art assembled during the 20th century. There are also art museums dedicated to craft, contemporary art, photography, and decorative arts—not to mention the Rothko Chapel and the Byzantine Fresco Chapel Museum, which explore the role of art in religion.

In addition to its many art museums, Houston touts one-of-a-kind museums dedicated to history, culture, and science. Aside from the renowned Houston Museum of Natural Science, most of the museums in this category aren't the sort of history and science museums you might expect. Here you can learn about the funeral industry at the National Museum of Funeral History, the homes of some of the city's first residents at the Heritage Society in Sam Houston Park, hatred at the Holocaust Museum, Houston, how tornadoes form at the John C. Freeman Weather Museum, and how your body operates at the Health Museum. Many of these museums are the first and only ones of their kind in the country.

Houston is also home to a wonderful children's museum, which you can learn about on page 174 of the "Kidstuff" chapter. History buffs should check out the "Attractions" chapter as well, where you'll learn about the San Jacinto Battleground State Historic Site and Space Center Houston, each of which features plenty of artifacts and films sure to whet almost any appetite for history.

i Look for the brown street signs while walking or driving through the Museum District. These will point you toward some of the larger museums in the vicinity, including most of the ones mentioned in this chapter.

OVERVIEW

This chapter highlights the best of the city's museums, many of which are located in the Museum District. This area surrounding Hermann Park and Montrose is home to some 18 museums. Several of these are within walking distance of one another. A map of the Museum District can be found on page viii. All Houston museums have some degree of parking, although it is limited in some cases. You may find it easier to take the METRORail to the Museum District stop and walk, if you plan to visit a couple of museums.

Most museums are closed at least one day, if not two, each week. These closure days are included in the descriptions below. Some museums have seasonal hours, so it is a good idea to consult the individual museums' Web sites to double-check this information and find out about special events and exhibits, which are added throughout the year.

Because so many of Houston's museums are free, it is possible to get a hefty dose of culture without paying a penny. That said, some museums do charge admission fees, which generally range from about $5 to $15. Most take a dollar or two off the price of admission for seniors, children, and students.

If you plan to visit multiple museums and attractions in Houston, you can save some money—and avoid ticket lines—by purchasing a Houston CityPass for $34. The pass will get you into the Houston Museum of Natural Science, either the Museum of Fine Arts Houston or the Children's Museum of Houston, either the Health Museum or the George Ranch Historical Park, and Space Center Houston, the Downtown Aquarium, and the Houston Zoo. Houston CityPasses can be purchased online at www.citypass.com, or at the ticket desk of any of the aforementioned locations. The pass is only good for nine days after your first use, though, so use it quickly and often.

Most museums host special fund-raisers and educational programs throughout the year. To learn about upcoming events at Houston's museums, visit the museums' Web sites. Alternatively, you can find out about upcoming exhibits in the *Houston Press* (www.houstonpress.com), the *Village Voice*–owned alternative newsweekly, or the *Houston Chronicle* (www.chron.com).

All museums are wheelchair accessible unless indicated otherwise.

Price Code

$.....................under $5
$$ ....$5 to $10
$$$ .... over $10

ART MUSEUMS

BYZANTINE FRESCO CHAPEL
MUSEUM   FREE
4011 Yupon St.,
at Branard Street in the Museum District
(713) 525-9400
www.menil.org/visit/byzantine.php
One of the newest members of the Houston museum scene, the Byzantine Fresco Chapel Museum is infused with several centuries of history. This 4,000-square-foot museum features the Western Hemisphere's largest intact Byzantine frescoes, including an apse and a dome. These Christianity-themed frescoes date back to the 13th century. After thieves stole the frescoes from their original chapel in Turkish-occupied Cyprus in the 1980s and attempted to sell them, the Houston-based Menil Foundation lawfully acquired the religious works from the Church of Cyprus. At the instruction of art collector and Menil Foundation benefactor Dominique de Menil, the frescoes were restored. De Menil's son, architect François de Menil, then designed a chapel to house the frescoes and return them to their original spiritual function. Today visitors to the Byzantine Fresco Chapel Museum can meditate in a highly contemporary building as they look at the meticulous fresco images that hung in a Cyprus chapel more than 700 years ago. Admission is free and free parking is available along the street or in a lot located at 1515 West Alabama St., about 2 blocks north of the chapel. The Byzantine Fresco Chapel Museum is closed on Monday and Tuesday.

CONTEMPORARY ARTS MUSEUM
HOUSTON   FREE
5216 Montrose Blvd., at Bissonnet, just
kitty-corner from the Museum of Fine Arts
Houston in the Museum District
(713) 284-8250
www.camh.org
The Contemporary Arts Museum Houston makes its home in one of the Museum District's most distinctive buildings. Designed by renowned architect Gunnar Birkerts, the stainless steel building almost appears to be two-dimensional from the street. Inside, though, visitors discover volume and depth aplenty. The museum has no permanent collections; instead, it hosts traveling exhibits and organizes thematic exhibits, showcasing some of the most cutting-edge 20th- and 21st-century art from Texas, the United States, and abroad. Exhibits here encompass a variety of media, including video, and test the boundaries of art. Occasionally you might see an exhibit that makes you question its validity as art, but far more often than not, the work here is impressive. Recent exhibits have explored the imagery surrounding puppets and showcased the work of local teenagers. During each exhibit, the museum

hosts several corresponding gallery talks that offer a variety of critical (and insightful) views about the work on display. Check the museum Web site for upcoming lectures and events. While you're at the museum, be sure to check out the gift shop. In addition to some fun toys, books, gifts, and home decor, you'll find some unusual jewelry.

Museum admission is always free. Parking can be tough to come by. During the week, free parking is typically available at the church across the street. There is also limited parking on side streets in the area. The Contemporary Arts Museum Houston is closed Monday.

ℹ️ **Learn about some of the Museum District's most important sites—including the Museum of Fine Arts Houston, the Holocaust Museum Houston, the Health Museum, the Houston Museum of Natural Science, and the Children's Museum of Houston—by taking an audio tour as you walk and ride the METRORail through the neighborhood. The two-hour tour is narrated by former local news anchor Shara Fryer. A detailed map, along with the audio tour, can be downloaded for free from www.audisseyguides.com/houston/museum district. You can start the 2-mile tour, produced by Audissey Guides, either at Monument Au Fantome in Discovery Green (downtown) or at the Museum District Light Rail Station.**

FOTOFEST   **FREE**
1113 Vine St., just north of I-10 and
east of North Main Street
(713) 223-5522
www.fotofest.org
FotoFest is best known for the huge photography festival and conference it puts on in even-numbered years. (See page 158 of the "Annual Events" chapter for information about the festival.) But between the festivals, FotoFest hosts a number of interbiennial exhibits and events. These exhibits reflect the pulse of contemporary photography by showcasing some of the most talented contemporary photographers

from Texas, the United States, and around the globe. Many of the exhibits here are curated in collaboration with the Houston Center for Photography.

Fotofest also sponsors the awe-inspiring Literacy Through Photography program, which teaches more than 1,500 local primary and secondary school students to express themselves using photography and writing. The program culminates each May with FotoFence, a special exhibit of participating students' work.

Fotofest offers free guided tours for all exhibits and most exhibits also feature special talks with the artists and curators. Some of these talks are held at other Houston museums and cultural centers, so be sure to check the Web site for information about upcoming talks. Fotofest interbiennial events and exhibits are free and open to the public. On-site parking is available for free.

HOUSTON CENTER FOR
CONTEMPORARY CRAFT   **FREE**
4848 Main St., at Rosedale Street, 2 blocks
south of US 59 in the Museum District
(713) 529-4848
www.crafthouston.org
The Houston Center for Contemporary Craft might not look that impressive or well kept from the outside but inside you'll find some of the most intriguing exhibits in town. Located in the Museum District just a block from Lawndale Art Center, the center showcases objects made from fiber, metal, clay, glass, and wood. These handmade objects might not all seem like art but as each exhibit demonstrates, the making and design of crafts is an intensive process, one with a long and constantly evolving history. Although the center exhibits the work of crafters from around the world, Texas crafters tend to get quite a bit of show time here. The center only opened in 2001, however, so as it evolves, its focus might change. In 2009 the center held its first curated invitational exhibit, which looked at the human body in a variety of media, including glass, quilts, silver, wire, wood, sculpture, and more. The center's gift shop—the Asher Gallery—feels like an additional exhibit. In the Asher Gallery, you'll find

meticulously crafted pieces in a variety of media from established and emerging crafters from around the world.

Admission is free and free parking is available on the street and in a wheelchair-accessible lot behind the museum on Travis Street. The center is closed Monday.

HOUSTON CENTER FOR PHOTOGRAPHY   FREE
1441 W. Alabama, at Mulberry Street, 1 block south of Westheimer in the Museum District
(713) 529-4755
www.hcponline.org

Since opening in 1981, the Houston Center for Photography—also known as HCP—has displayed the work of some 3,200 photographers and educated thousands more. The HCP does not have a permanent collection, but it is constantly exhibiting timely and culturally significant photography and photojournalism produced by established and emerging photographers. Recent exhibits have looked at how conflict in the Middle East affects life in the United States, as well as 60 years of photos produced by Magnum Photos, the world's most acclaimed photography cooperative. The HCP often features the work of some of the area's most promising high school–age photographers. One of the biggest draws of the year is the annual Print Auction Exhibition, a free-to-attend auction of prints donated by some of the world's finest photographers.

HCP is the only organization in the South or the Southwest that provides year-round programming focused on photography and other relevant visual arts. This programming includes photography classes catering to everyone from beginners, who need help figuring out the basics of their digital cameras, to pros, who want to keep up with the latest technology. More than 200 classes are offered each year, and they fill up quickly. Check the Web site for upcoming courses and sign up early. Students and HCP members also have access to the center's state-of-the-art digital darkroom, which touts top-notch film scanners, printers, and iMacs loaded with Adobe Creative Suite. The center also has a great library filled with more than 2,000 photography tomes.

Each year the center's outreach programs enable underserved high school students and young cancer patients at M.D. Anderson Cancer Center—among others—to represent their plights through imagery. The HCP often exhibits the photographs produced through these outreach programs.

Admission is free. Parking is available on the street and in the free HCP parking lot. The center is closed Monday and Tuesday.

i Many Houston museums have designated times when admission is free. To find out the latest admission-free days and times for museums in the Museum District, visit www.houstonmuseumdistrict .org. The Web site also highlights area resources, volunteer opportunities, and upcoming Museum District events.

LAWNDALE ART CENTER   FREE
4912 Main St., between Portland and Rosedale Streets in the Museum District
(713) 528-5858
www.lawndaleartcenter.org

Houston's museums are filled with the works of great regional, national, and international artists, but only the Lawndale Art Center is dedicated to showcasing the work of Houston artists. The center, located in an art deco–style building just a block from the Houston Center for Contemporary Craft, houses four galleries, which offer a combined 20-plus exhibits each year. Informal talks with the curators and artists accompany many of these exhibits.

The center also hosts a number of special events, the biggest of which is Dia de los Muertos (Day of the Dead) in early November. To commemorate those who have died, the center offers sugar skull decoration and papier-mâché skeleton workshops, a silent auction, and classical music and dance performances.

Another big draw is the annual 20th Century Modern Market, held each April. Art dealers from around the country come to the center to sell ceramics, glass, metal, textiles, furniture, clothes, and other high-quality designs produced during the 20th century.

Admission to Lawndale Art Center is always free, but there is a charge for admission to Modern Market events. Parking is available on the street and in the center parking lot. The center is closed Sunday.

THE MENIL COLLECTION   FREE
1515 Sul Ross St., between Mulberry and Mandell Streets in the Museum District
(713) 525-9400
www.menil.org

One of the most significant private art collections assembled during the 20th century can be found in Houston. Known as the Menil Collection, this gem of a museum houses some 15,000 works of art—paintings, sculptures, photographs, prints, and rare books—that span from antiquity to the Byzantine and medieval eras to African and Oceanic tribes on up to the 20th century. The collection, amassed by John and Dominique de Menil, also includes some of the world's finest examples of surrealism (think Max Ernst and René Magritte), cubism (think Henri Matisse and Pablo Picasso), and pop art by the likes of Jasper Johns and Andy Warhol. The Menil Collection recently expanded its permanent collection of drawings. In early 2008 the museum launched the Menil Drawing Institute and Study Center, which collects, exhibits, and studies modernist drawings by the likes of Paul Cézanne, Picasso, Paul Klee, Mark Rothko, and Jackson Pollock.

To say the Menil Collection is more than a museum would be an understatement. The main museum building is located on Sul Ross Street in the Museum District, but the houses and buildings along several blocks surrounding the Sul Ross Street building are also owned by the Menil Foundation. Almost all of these buildings share a rich gray color. Some are offices of the museum or other arts organizations; many are private homes. A couple—the Cy Twombly Gallery and Richmond Hall—showcase single-artist exhibits. Also located in the Menil neighborhood are the Byzantine Fresco Chapel Museum and the Rothko Chapel, each of which are owned by the Menil Collection and are worthy of their own write-ups in this chapter.

The Menil Collection holds special events throughout the year; most of these are found at the main building on Sul Ross Street. On the first Sunday of each month, the Artist's Eye series features a local artist talking about his or her favorite (or most inspiring) work from the collection. Museum members also have the chance to attend special talks with artists and curators throughout the year. Also popular is the Menil/Rice Lecture Series held at nearby Rice University throughout the year. All of the lectures relate to a theme found in the museum's permanent collection.

Admission is free for all Menil Collection exhibits—those held at the main museum as well as those held at the other Menil sites. Guests may park for free behind the Menil Collection on West Alabama Street between Mulberry and Mandell Streets. The Menil Collection is closed Monday and Tuesday.

MUSEUM OF FINE ARTS HOUSTON $–$$
Caroline Wiess Law Building
1001 Bissonnet St., between Montrose and Main Streets in the Museum District

Audrey Jones Beck Building
5601 Main St., on the corner of Bissonnet and Main Streets in the Museum District
(713) 639-7300
www.mfah.org

With more than 57,000 works of art in its permanent collection and 300,000 square feet dedicated to exhibiting this work, the Museum of Fine Arts Houston is one of the country's largest art museums. MFAH, as the museum is often called, consists of two main buildings—the Caroline Wiess Law Building and the new Audrey Jones Beck Building. The MFAH practically qualifies as an empire when you add the Lillie and Hugh Roy Cullen Sculpture Garden, some 18 acres of public gardens, the Glassell School of Art, and two houses devoted to decorative arts.

The Caroline Wiess Law Building, located on Bissonnet, is the museum's original building. It dates back to 1924, when William Ward Watkin designed the building in the neoclassical style. Between the late 1950s and mid-1970s, renowned architect Ludwig Mies van der Rohe designed two additions—Cullinan Hall and Brown Pavilion—in the international style. Today the Law Building is where much of the city's artistic action is found: Film buffs and inquisitive minds love to watch classic and contemporary flicks in the Brown Auditorium Theatre, while art historians research in the Hirsche Library, one of the country's leading art-research facilities. Of course most people head to the Law Building for the art exhibits. Inside its large airy galleries, the MFAH displays most of its 20th- and 21st-century pieces and hosts internationally acclaimed exhibits spanning centuries, continents, and media. Also on display are some of the museum's impressive multicultural holdings, including art from Asia, sub-Saharan Africa, and the Pacific Islands, as well as the world's most renowned collection of gold objects.

In 2000 the MFAH expanded with the opening of the Audrey Jones Beck Building, located just a few steps east of the Law Building on the corner of Bissonnet and Main Streets. The first major museum designed by Pritzker Prize–winning architect Rafael Moneo, the museum features large lanternlike skylights in the roof, bringing natural light to many of the building's galleries. Inside are exquisite American art, prints, drawings, photographs, a very high-ceilinged sculpture court, and a good number of special exhibits. There's no need to go outside to travel between the Beck and Law Buildings; their respective lower levels are connected by a tunnel lined with James Turrell's neon-colored light installation, *The Light Inside*.

Learn about the MFAH's permanent collection, special exhibits, art history, and specific works or artists by taking one of several free tours geared toward adults; participation is free with paid admission or a museum membership. A special tour is also offered for guests with Alzheimer's and their caretakers. Depending on which tour you take, these close-up looks at the museum last

from 20 minutes to an hour. Tours are not offered in September.

On Sunday the museum offers Sunday Storytime—free tours for kids ages four to eight. School tours are offered on select weekdays. Reservations aren't required for any of the adult tours or Sunday Storytime.

Before leaving the museum's main campus, be sure to walk through the Lillie and Hugh Roy Cullen Sculpture Garden, located at the corner of Montrose Boulevard and Bissonnet Street. With more than 20 sculptures and other works from 19th- and 20th-century artists like Henri Matisse and Auguste Rodin, this serene garden is the perfect place to contemplate or daydream. The garden is open daily, and entry is always free.

A museum ticket gets you into both the Beck and Law Buildings. Admission is $7 for adults and $3.50 for seniors 65 and up, children ages 6 to 18, and college students with a valid ID. Museum members, Glassell students, and kids five and under get in free. The MFAH is also included on the Houston CityPass.

There is plenty of parking available in the area. Two free lots are located on Main Street at Bissonnet and Main Street at Oakdale. Additional parking can be found on side streets around the museum and in a parking lot across the street from the entrance. There's also a hard-to-miss four-story parking garage just east of the museum on Binz Street: You'll know you have found the garage when you see the big yellow arrow standing in the grass outside the entrance. Parking here costs $3.

The Museum of Fine Arts Houston is closed on Monday, excluding Monday holidays such as Memorial Day and Labor Day. The museum is also closed on Christmas and Thanksgiving.

Don't worry about packing a sack lunch or filling your bag with snacks to keep your stomach from growling during your visit to the Museum of Fine Arts Houston. Café Express, located on the lower level of the Beck Building, serves up some tasty sandwiches, soups, and salads.

Close-up

Glassell School of Art

Just a block north of the Museum of Fine Arts Houston's main campus is the Glassell School of Art (5101 Montrose Blvd., a block and a half north of Bissonnet, just past Berthea Street; 713-639-7500).

This is the MFAH's teaching arm, and classes are offered through two separate schools. Adults take classes through the Studio School for Adults, while young children and teenagers take classes in the Junior School, the country's only museum school that focuses on art education for kids. Both Glassell schools offer classes in media ranging from jewelry design to photography to painting to printmaking to art history. Many parents send their children to the Junior School to take classes during spring break and summer vacation. Although tuition can be pricey, Glassell does award tuition scholarships to nearly 200 students each year.

Further demonstrating Glassell's commitment to making art education accessible to the community are the school's outreach programs. Each year Glassell's Community Bridge Programs offer free workshops at hospitals and community centers to give underserved populations and ill Houstonians of all ages the chance to try their hand at a variety of artistic media.

Glassell also touts the prestigious Core Artist-in-Residence Program, which provides recent art school graduates space and funding to work on their projects for nine months, as well as access to the school's state-of-the-art facilities. The work of the Core artists is often exhibited at Glassell. Other exhibits showcase the works of thought-provoking contemporary artists from around the country. No matter whose work appears in these exhibits, they are held together by one common strand: They all encourage visitors to reconsider the boundaries of art and look at contemporary art from new perspectives. Glassell exhibits are free and parking is available on-site for no charge.

Visit the Museum of Fine Arts Houston Web site (www.mfah.org) for information about upcoming exhibits and classes at Glassell.

MUSEUM OF FINE ARTS HOUSTON— BAYOU BEND $$

1 Westcott St., at Memorial Dr., just east of Memorial Park Golf Course
(713) 639-7750
www.mfah.org/bayoubend

The Museum of Fine Arts Houston (MFAH) showcases one of the most extensive collections of American decor at the former home of a woman named Ima Hogg, the daughter of former Texas governor James S. Hogg. Don't let the former resident's name fool you: The Bayou Bend Collection and Gardens command a long list of superlatives—and favorable ones, at that.

Built in the late 1920s for Ima and her two brothers, the Hogg manse features 28 different rooms, every one of them taking visitors back to another period in American history. Each room is filled with American furniture, ceramics, silver, and wall decor spanning from 1620 to 1870. There are thousands of pieces throughout the house.

For many the most enchanting aspect of the MFAH's Bayou Bend site is the gardens surrounding the home. Hogg didn't want to just look at the gardens from indoors; she wanted to live and entertain in them so she planted dozens of flowers, plants, and trees while leaving plenty of green space. Hogg also refused to cut down many of the trees and wild green thickets that comprised an integral part of Bayou Bend. Both the gardens and woodlands remain in place today, providing a relaxing oasis of color for visitors and passersby alike.

Admission is $10 for adults and $8.50 for college students and seniors 65 and up. Children 10 to 17 get in for $5. Admission includes a guided tour or an audio tour. Reservations are required for guided tours. MFAH members get $2 off the price of tickets.

Kids under 10 are not permitted on guided house tours; they can take self-guided audio tours of the house, however.

Admission to the garden—which includes a self-guided audio tour—is $3 for adults and free for kids nine and under.

Free parking is available in a public lot on Westcott Street.

RIENZI $$
1406 Kirby Dr., in River Oaks, just east of River Oaks Country Club
(713) 639-7800
www.mfah.org/rienzi

In 1999 the Museum of Fine Arts Houston expanded its decorative arts holdings with the acquisition of Rienzi, also known as the Center for European Decorative Arts. Rienzi consists of an exquisite house, vibrant gardens, and fine European decor dating back several centuries. Houston philanthropists Carroll Sterling Masterson and Harris Masterson III donated the River Oaks home and the collection to the MFAH when they died in the 1990s. Inside the home is an extensive display of European ceramics dating back to the early 1800s, English portraits, religious paintings from Spain and Italy, Worcester porcelain, and one-of-a-kind pieces of European furniture. The elaborate house sits on 4.4 acres, much of which are filled with gardens—some formal, others filled with native plants such as ferns. Depending on the season, visitors can enjoy dozens of different blooms, thanks to the Garden Club of Houston, which now maintains the gardens.

Guided tours of the house and the gardens are available. Call in advance to make reservations, which are required on weekdays and recommended on weekends. Admission, which includes the cost of the tour and parking, is $6 for adults and $4 for museum members, seniors 65 and up, college students, and kids 12 to 18 years old. Kids under 12 get in free. On Sunday admission is $5 for individuals of all ages, $10

for families of two to four people, and $15 for families of five to six. Admission to the gardens is free. Limited free parking is available on side streets around Rienzi for those who don't take a tour; those who do get free parking on-site. Rienzi is closed Monday and Tuesday.

i **Want to buy some great art? There are dozens of Houston art galleries where you can stock your personal art collection. Many of these represent artists whose work is showcased at some of the world's most prestigious art festivals and exhibits, including the Carnegie International, the Whitney Biennial, and Venice Biennale. Some of the best galleries, including a few in the prestigious Gallery Row (www .galleryrowhouston.com), are listed in the "Shopping" chapter.**

THE ROTHKO CHAPEL FREE
1409 Sul Ross St., between Yupon and Mulberry Streets about 5 blocks west of Montrose Boulevard
(713) 524-9839
www.rothkochapel.org

After visiting some of Europe's great churches in the 1950s, Menil Collection benefactors John and Dominique de Menil wanted to develop a Houston worship space that would showcase great art. They later enlisted architect Philip Johnson to create a chapel to house the paintings of artist Mark Rothko. The octagon-shaped chapel opened in 1969. Inside the nonsectarian worship space hang 14 enormous Rothko paintings. Wooden benches can be used for resting, contemplation, or prayer. The tranquility of the space leads families of all faiths to use the Rothko Chapel for weddings and other religious ceremonies; the chapel also hosts music and spiritual events, as well as guest speakers whose work focuses on social justice and environmentalism.

The Rothko Chapel is open every day of the year. Admission is free, but donations are encouraged. Free parking is available on Yupon and Sul Ross Streets. Wheelchair access is located at the north end of the chapel on Sul Ross Street.

(Q) Close-up

Project Row Houses

Plenty of museums in Houston will give you the chance to appreciate some great art, but few show you the power of art to change lives and communities. That's the job of Project Row Houses, some 40 houses and other properties spanning 6 blocks in the Third Ward, just southeast of downtown and east of the Texas Medical Center. The organization grew out of a longing among black artists in the Third Ward to use art and creativity to revitalize their poor neighborhood. Seven of these remodeled row houses have been transformed into artist studios and exhibit spaces. Although the exhibits showcase the work of artists from around the world, themes are always relevant to the Third Ward and the challenges and joys that its predominately black residents face. Outside the exhibit spaces are plenty of colorful murals and smiling faces—evidence of Project Row Houses' profound impact on a community that was dilapidated when the organization launched in 1993.

As part of Project Row Houses' commitment to the community, the organization awards free studio space to three local artists each year. They give back to the community by participating in artist talks and exhibits and leading classes. The organization also sponsors an arts-in-education program, which enables local schoolchildren to work with local artists to discover their inner artist—or hone talents that have already been discovered. Programs are offered after school and in the summer in media such as photography, painting, creative writing, ceramics, music, and dance. There is even a program geared toward helping struggling students with their homework. The fees for these programs are determined on a sliding scale based on the income of participating children's families. Project Row Houses also offers residential space to poor single mothers who are trying to finish school and launch a career.

Call or stop into Project Row Houses headquarters at 2521 Holman (between St. Charles and Live Oak Streets in the Third Ward; 713-526-7662; www.projectrowhouses.org) to find out about current exhibits and other programming. Admission to Project Row Houses exhibits and artist talks is currently free, though donations are requested. The organization is considering charging for group visits in the future. Parking can be found on the streets surrounding the main office. Project Row Houses is closed Monday and Tuesday.

HISTORY, CULTURE, AND SCIENCE MUSEUMS

THE HEALTH MUSEUM $$
1515 Hermann Dr., between LaBranch and Crawford Streets, just east of the Hermann Park Golf Course in the Museum District
(713) 521-1515
www.thehealthmuseum.org

With a long history of providing some of the world's best health care and health-care education at the Texas Medical Center, it's only fitting that Houston has one of the country's only museums devoted to health. For 21 years Houston celebrated its commitment to health and medicine at the Houston Museum of Natural Science

in what was known as the Museum of Medical Science. But since medicine is such a big part of the city's economy and identity, members of the medical and science community—including Dr. John P. McGovern—lobbied hard for a museum devoted to health and medicine. In 1996 Houston finally got its Health Museum, which was dedicated to McGovern five years later, shortly before his death.

With a variety of interactive exhibits and activities designed to help visitors better understand their bodies, the Health Museum is one of the city's can't-miss attractions—and a place sure to entertain visitors of all ages. You: The Exhibit lets museumgoers see their internal organs in real time using a body scanner. You can also explore how living in Houston affects the body and how living elsewhere might affect your body differently. Or discover the importance of keeping arteries unclogged, the brain challenged, and bones exercised when you walk through an enormous human body in the Amazing Body Pavilion. The McGovern 4D Theater shows films about the body—complete with real scents, rain, lightning, and, of course, surround sound. In the Challenge Gallery, you can test your reflexes, play Dance Dance Revolution, and try your hands (and brain) at puzzles and games. The museum also features a variety of special exhibits throughout the year. The Health Museum is a member institution of the Texas Medical Center, so the museum often collaborates with the Medical Center to host special events and family-friendly activities.

Admission costs $8 for adults and $6 for kids ages 3 to 12 and seniors 65 and up. Museum members get in free. The museum is also included on the Houston CityPass. Parking is available in the museum parking lot for $3 with the purchase of an admission ticket. Metered parking is also available along the streets surrounding the museum. The Health Museum is closed Monday.

ℹ️ Get a breath of fresh air—it's good for you—by heading out to the Sensory Garden, where you can smell the flowers and sit on a bench before heading back into the sometimes-noisy Health Museum.

THE HERITAGE SOCIETY AT
SAM HOUSTON PARK   FREE TO $$
Sam Houston Park in downtown Houston
1100 Bagby, between McKinney Street and
Allen Parkway
(713) 655-1912
www.heritagesociety.org
Downtown Houston isn't all skyscrapers and tunnels. Kitty-corner from City Hall at the northwest edge of downtown is Sam Houston Park, a beautifully landscaped park that is now home to eight carefully restored homes and a church that date

back to the 1800s and early 1900s. Thanks to the Heritage Society, visitors can tour these buildings, each of which has played a distinctive role in Houston's history.

The park came to life in 1900 when Houston mayor Sam Brashier purchased the Kellum-Noble House and land—which then was considered the edge of town—and turned the area into Sam Houston Park. The oldest brick house in Houston, the Kellum-Noble House was built in 1847 and became home to one of the city's first private schools. A brick kiln and a sawmill were also operated on the Kellum-Noble property. When the house faced demolition in 1954, locals formed the Heritage Foundation to save it. The Kellum-Noble House is the only restored building in Sam Houston Park that remains at its original site.

The seven other homes and St. John Church, which German farmers built in northwest Harris County in 1891, have been moved into the park from other locations around the city and Harris County. Among the most notable properties in the park are Yates House, 4th Ward Cottage, Nichols-Rice-Cherry House, Pillot House, and the Old Place. Yates House was built in Houston's Fourth Ward by former slave, education advocate, and religious leader Rev. Jack Yates in 1870, just five years after he was freed. Predating the Yates House is 4th Ward Cottage, the oldest known "workingman house" in Houston and a part of Houston's black "Freedman's Town" neighborhood, where blacks lived, worked, and played in the years following the signing of the Emancipation Proclamation. The Greek Revival–style Nichols-Rice-Cherry House was owned by William Marsh Rice, whose estate gets credit for the establishment of Rice University. One of the city's first

ℹ️ Bring your cell phone and dial a designated phone number in front of each of five selected homes to get the SparkNotes version of their history if you don't have time for a full guided tour. It won't cost you anything more than cell phone minutes.

(Q) Close-up

Orange Show Center for Visionary Art Eyeopener Tours

Around Houston, the Orange Show Center for Visionary Art is best known for putting on the annual Art Car Parade (see page 161 of the "Annual Events" chapter). The rest of the year, the Orange Show Center celebrates other whimsical forms of art, such as mural art, a renovated Beer Can House at 222 Malone St., and the Orange Show Monument, a 3,000-square-foot outdoor monument built out of mannequins, wagon wheels, tiles, tractor seats, and other found art.

Several times each year the Orange Show Center offers an inside look at other unusual art, architecture, homes, and gardens on Eyeopener Tours. Some tours focus on Houston neighborhoods such as the Heights; many visit other parts of Texas. Once a year, the Orange Show Center takes lovers of eccentric art to other parts of the country. Past trips visited Wisconsin, Iowa, Minnesota, New Mexico, Ohio, Louisiana, the Carolinas, and Mexico. Whether the tour takes place in town or out, participants are in for some unexpected culture and art as they explore public art displays, found art, artists' studios, intriguing architecture and music, and tasty meals. The idea is to show participants art they might never journey to see—or might never notice. Tours around Houston last a few hours and cost $40 for Orange Show Center members and $60 for nonmembers. Trips outside the city last as long as five or six days and vary in price. New tours are added all the time so check the Web site often. Sign up quickly since space is limited. The Orange Show Center is located at 2402 Munger St., 1 block south of the Gulf Freeway (713-926-6368; www.orangeshow.org/eyeopener.html).

attached kitchens lies in the Victorian-era Pillot House, which has been undergoing renovation after experiencing significant flood damage from Tropical Storm Allison in 2001. A true log cabin, the Old Place dates back to 1823 and is believed to be the oldest building in Harris County. Along with to the period artifacts found in each building, the Heritage Society Museum, located at the corner of Bagby Street and Lamar Street, displays hundreds of antique phonographs, textiles, tools, silver, toys, and decorative works.

In addition to maintaining these historic properties and artifacts, the Heritage Society has made itself a hub of local culture. On the third Thursday of each month, the free Hill/Finger Noontime Lecture Series introduces Houstonians to local artists, historians, and preservationists. Each fall the Heritage Society sponsors special workshops for Texas history teachers. Elementary school students and scout groups from across the city tour the houses each year, and many local organizations and businesses host events

at Sam Houston Park throughout the year. Some couples even get married at the park.

Admission to the Heritage Society Museum is free. To see the insides of the houses and church, you'll have to take a guided tour, which lasts about an hour and 15 minutes and offers kids the chance to churn butter at the Duncan Store. Guided tours are free for guests 18 and under, $8 for adults over 18, and $6 for seniors 65 and up. Free parking is available off Allen Parkway going into downtown. The parking lot is behind a big white brick building—the Kellum-Noble House. The museum is closed Monday.

HOLOCAUST MUSEUM HOUSTON   FREE
5401 Caroline St., about 1 block northeast of Binz Street and 3 blocks southeast of Main Street in the Museum District
(713) 942-8000
www.hmh.org

The Holocaust Museum Houston is the kind of museum that can change lives. Although the museum's exhibits revolve around the Holocaust, the museum's goal is to make visitors think about hatred and intolerance more broadly.

The Holocaust Museum's permanent exhibit, dubbed Bearing Witness: A Community Remembers, highlights the stories of Houston residents who survived the Holocaust. Using artifacts, photographs, and written explanations, this exhibit follows the lives of these survivors before the Holocaust, during Hitler's rise to power, and during their time in concentration camps. Bearing Witness concludes with a film in which local survivors share their stories. Rotating art and photography exhibits complement many of the struggles and themes highlighted in Bearing Witness. Also on permanent display are two examples of the types of vehicles used to carry Holocaust victims and survivors. The 1942 World War II railcar is like those used to take millions of Jews and other outcasts to the concentration camps, and a newly acquired 1942 Danish rescue boat is identical to those used to save more than 7,200 Jews from death.

Those who need time to reflect after viewing the exhibits can visit the Lack Family Memorial Room, a reflection room with a Wall of Remembrance, a Wall of Tears, and a Wall of Hope, as well as a Memorial Wall where survivors can honor friends and relatives lost in the Holocaust. Meditative types can step outside the Memorial Room and into the Eric Alexander Garden of Hope, a small but beautiful garden that celebrates the memory of the children killed by the Nazis.

Students, teachers, researchers, and other inquiring minds who want to learn more about the Holocaust can use the Boniuk Library and Resource Center, which houses more than 4,000 books and 300 videos about World War II, the Holocaust, religion, and anti-Semitism. There are

> **i** Check out the National Museum of Funeral History's Web site (www .nmfh.org) to see online-only exhibits and enjoy special Web accompaniments to the exhibits hosted at the museum.

also thousands of original photographs, journals, letters, and other artifacts available for viewing in the archives.

Admission to the museum is free and those who visit on weekend afternoons can also take a docent-led tour. Free parking is available in lots beside the museum's Caroline Street entrance and alongside the building on Calumet Street. Parking is also available along the streets around the museum. The museum is open seven days a week.

HOUSTON MUSEUM OF NATURAL SCIENCE $$$
1 Hermann Circle Dr., between Caroline and San Jacinto Streets in Hermann Park just east of Main Street and Fannin Street
(713) 639-4629
www.hmns.org

The Houston Museum of Natural Science is one of those museums that you could tour for a day or two and still not see everything. Here you'll find permanent exhibits spanning astronomy and space, oil and energy, chemistry, paleontology, shells, Texas wildlife, dinosaurs, and rare gems and minerals. The museum hosts two or three special exhibits at any given time. Recent ones featured the famous Lucy fossil, gave visitors the chance to try their hand at forensic science, and showcased gifts designed for, given to, and used by Tibet's Dalai Lamas over the past nine centuries.

In addition to these exhibits, the Houston Museum of Natural Science is home to several learning centers, whose exhibits and activities are not included in the cost of general admission. The Burke Baker Planetarium offers the chance to identify constellations, watch science-themed movies, and listen to music. If you want to feel like you're on an adventure outside the museum, check out one of several IMAX films about nature in the Wortham Theater. Most IMAX films are screened just once or twice a day, so check the schedule online or by calling (713) 639-4629 before your visit to make sure you can make it to the show you want to see. IMAX movies often sell out so purchase tickets and line up early to get a good seat.

One of the museum's biggest draws is the Cockrell Butterfly Center and the Brown Hall of Entomology, where majestic butterflies flutter around, sip nectar, and rest inside a simulated tropical rain forest—complete with a 50-foot waterfall and exotic plants—designed just for them. Brown Hall, which is located in the butterfly center, is filled with even more live insects and spiders, including walking sticks, cockroaches, and tarantulas. If you feel inspired after watching these creatures, head over to the "Insects and Us" section, where you can learn how to build your own butterfly garden, ward off mosquitoes (an essential skill in Houston), and keep bees. Young children can also play with insect-themed toys and read insect-themed books. Parents, beware: Strollers aren't allowed in the Cockrell Butterfly Center. Butterflies sometimes pay visits to the humans down below, so you can probably imagine why strollers are a no-go.

The Houston Museum of Natural Science has two satellite educational campuses. The Woodlands Xploration Station, located just north of Houston, features 13 dinosaur skeletons, live frogs, as well as exhibits on minerals and gems. About an hour south of the city, in Fort Bend County's Brazos Bend State Park, is the George Observatory, which boasts three domed telescopes. Among them is the 36-inch Gueymard Research Telescope, one of the country's largest telescopes available for public viewing. The George Observatory is also home to the Challenger Learning Center, which teaches visitors about space exploration and science through simulated missions. Both the Woodlands Xploration Station and the George Observatory are a bit of a drive for many Houstonians, so the two campuses cater largely to school and scout groups. See the museum's Web site for additional information on these two sites.

Admission to the main campus's exhibits is $15 for adults and $9 for college students, seniors 62 and up, and children ages 3 to 11. Members get in free. The museum is also included on the Houston CityPass. Admission to the Cockrell Butterfly Center, Burke Baker Planetarium, and Wortham Theater IMAX movies requires the purchase of additional tickets, which cost $8 for the butterfly center, $7 for the planetarium, and $10 for an IMAX movie. Seniors, students, and children under 11 pay $6 to see the butterflies, $6 to visit the planetarium, and $8 to see an IMAX movie. A McDonald's is located inside the museum for hungry tikes and adults in need of refueling.

Paid parking is available in the museum garage on Caroline Street; museum members pay $5 and nonmembers who show their museum ticket stub pay $10. If you don't have a ticket, you'll be charged $20. Limited parking is available on the streets around the museum. The METRO-Rail stops at the "Museum District" stop, just 3 blocks from the museum. The Houston Museum of Natural Science is open seven days a week.

ℹ️ **Heard about some hot new exhibit you want to see? Tickets for new exhibits often sell out days or even weeks in advance so buy yours early, especially for the Museum of Fine Arts Houston and the Houston Museum of Natural Science.**

JOHN C. FREEMAN WEATHER MUSEUM $–$$
5104 Caroline St., between Southmore Boulevard and Palm Street, 3 blocks east of Main Street in the Museum District
(713) 529-3076
www.weathermuseum.org
If you're an aspiring meteorologist (or the parent of one) or you want to understand how those hurricanes form in the Gulf of Mexico, head to the John C. Freeman Weather Museum. This small Houston institution is the country's only museum dedicated to weather. It was founded in 2006 and is run by meteorologists from the Weather Research Center, a Houston-based non-profit organization devoted to educating the public about weather and weather safety. The

museum is particularly popular among children, who get a kick out of the many hands-on activities. There are opportunities to record your own weather broadcast in a simulated studio, touch a simulated tornado vortex in the Tornado Chamber, and watch meteorologists perform experiments in the Weather Wizard Corner. You can even trace the history of meteorology and learn how tornadoes form and how to track hurricanes using satellite images of Hurricanes Katrina and Rita. Throughout the year, the Weather Museum also offers kids the chance to learn more about the weather at weather camps.

Self-guided tours of the museum are $5 for adults, $3 for students and seniors, and free for kids under three. Guided tours cost $8 for adults and $5 for students, teachers, and seniors. Guided tours last an hour to an hour-and-a-half and must be booked in advance by phone. Parking is available on the streets around the museum. The museum is closed Sunday.

NATIONAL MUSEUM OF FUNERAL
HISTORY $$
**415 Barren Springs Dr., at Ella Boulevard,
just west of I-45 and George Bush
Intercontinental Airport and east of
Kuykendahl Road in north Houston
(281) 876-3063
www.nmfh.org**
The National Museum of Funeral History, located

in north Houston, is true to its slogan: "Any Day Above Ground is a Good One." This museum has the potential to be depressing, but most guests describe the exhibits as interesting and unexpected. Founded by Houston funeral director Robert L. Waltrip in 1992, the museum traces the funeral industry's long history with a recreated 1900s casket factory that features artifacts from actual casket factories. Also on display are different caskets used around the world and information about the burials of public figures, such as President John F. Kennedy. The museum hosts special exhibits and honors leading funeral and cemetery industry icons in the National Museum of Funeral History Hall of Fame. Perhaps the most amusing—yes, amusing—permanent exhibit here is the over-the-top fantasy coffins created by Ghanaian sculptor Kane Quaye. These coffins resemble animals such as fish, lobsters, and roosters, as well as material objects such as airplanes and cars.

Admission is $10 for adults, $9 for seniors and veterans, $7 for kids 3 to 12, and free for kids under 3. Visitors can park for free in the museum parking lot. The museum is open seven days a week.

i   **You can take your camera into just about every museum in town but keep the flash off and the fancy equipment at home to stay on the guards' good side.**

ATTRACTIONS

While Houston's museums should be at the top of your list of places to visit, these are far from the only sites to include on your must-see list. Houston is also home to historical houses, a magnificent aquarium, one of the country's best zoos, Space Center Houston, the pivotal battleground of the Texas Revolution, and an unusual tunnel system that's ripe for exploring. And that's just a few of the highlights. In this chapter, you'll learn about some more places you must visit in order to get the real Houston experience and, as it happens, places that don't fit neatly into other chapters. Several of these locales—City Hall, the Houston Tunnel System, the Heritage Society at Sam Houston Park, and Downtown Aquarium—are located downtown. Others like the Kemah Boardwalk and San Jacinto Battleground State Historic Site aren't technically located in Houston, even though they are among the most definitive Houston attractions. Only one—Williams Tower and Water Wall—is in the Galleria area. Nevertheless, all of these attractions—few as they might seem—are definitively Houston. You'll find nothing quite like them, even elsewhere in Texas. For that reason, among others, the attractions in this chapter are the places you shouldn't miss if you want to get a real taste of my hometown.

A few of the attractions in Houston are free, but most cost somewhere between $5 and $15, although these prices are subject to change and do not include sales tax. Typically there are discounts for children and guests over 65. If you plan to see several attractions plus a museum or two, you can avoid ticket lines and save money by purchasing a Houston CityPass. This $34 pass will get you into the Houston Museum of Natural Science, three popular attractions—Space Center Houston, the Downtown Aquarium, and the Houston Zoo—as well as either the Museum of Fine Arts Houston or the Children's Museum of Houston and either the George Ranch Historical Park or the Health Museum. Houston CityPasses can be purchased online at www.citypass.com, or at the ticket desk of any of the above locations. Just be sure to use the pass within nine days of your first use. After that, it is good for nothing more than a memento.

Most of the attractions listed here are open seven days a week, although hours often vary depending on the season. To be on the safe side, call ahead to make sure your attraction of choice will be open when you plan to visit.

Free parking is typically available on-site for attractions that aren't located downtown. A couple of downtown attractions have their own parking lots; others do not. For these attractions, the easiest place to park is typically in one of the Theater District parking garages, which can be identified from the street by the lavender, aqua, and black Theater District Parking signs. These garages are spread out around the downtown theaters; the most convenient garages for each attraction have been identified in the individual write-ups below. The parking fee ranges from free for 10 minutes up to $9 for three hours or more. Parking for special events and on weekends and holidays is $7, payable upon entry. A map with the parking garages can be found on page vii of this book.

Price Code

```
$...................... $5 to $8
$$ .................... $9 to $12
$$$ ................... over $12
```

DOWNTOWN AQUARIUM $–$$$

410 Bagby St., at Memorial Drive
(713) 223-3474
www.aquariumrestaurants.com/downtown
aquariumhouston

Houston's Downtown Aquarium is the kind of place that is just as popular for dates as it is for school field trips, birthday parties, and business conferences. This local hot spot is home to eight one-of-a-kind "adventure exhibits," a couple of which pay homage to the Gulf of Mexico region. The Louisiana Swamp exhibit, for instance, celebrates Texas's eastern neighbor with recreated Gulf Coast marshes and bayous that introduce you to some of the state's slimier residents—alligator snapping turtles, crayfish, spotted gar, and some good ol' dwarf alligators. The Gulf of Mexico exhibit, meanwhile, offers a look at the nurse sharks, snapper, and other aquatic creatures that live around the gulf's offshore rigs. Also not to be missed are the aquarium's more international exhibits, which include a sunken temple that showcases a 20-foot tiger reticulated python and other species from a lost Mayan civilization, as well as the white tigers—yes, *tigers*—that strut around the replicated ruins of an ancient Indian temple. Fans of sharks and those looking to transform their fear into admiration will enjoy the aquarium's shark offerings: A ride on the CP Huntington train will take you through the Shark Voyage exhibit, where you can gaze at zebra sharks, blacktips, and sandtigers as they swim in a 200,000-gallon habitat, while Discovery Rig's shark nursery offers a close-up look at baby bamboo sharks and shark eggs.

When all of the marine biology lessons start wearing you or the kids out, head outdoors to play the aquarium's carnival-style games, ride on a carousel comprised of plastic alligators, or take in some of the best views of the Houston skyline on the Diving Bell Ferris. If you're hungry, stop in at the Aquarium restaurant, where you will dine surrounded by a 150,000-gallon aquarium. Seafood, of course, comprises a large portion of the menu here, but don't worry if you are uneasy about eating fish while you watch their brethren swim. There are also plenty of salad, pasta, burger, and steak options. The food is much better than you might expect since the aquarium is owned by Landry's Restaurants, a solid national seafood chain that began in nearby Katy. Entrees range from about $9 for a burger to $32 for seafood and steak platters. Kids' meals are $5.99 and include typical kiddie fare with underwater names like Coral Reef Chicken, Barracuda Burgers, and Surfer's Mac & Cheese. If you're traveling sans kids and still aren't ready to leave—or are looking to kill time while waiting for a table—visit the Dive Lounge, where you'll find the usual beers and thematically named martinis and specialty drinks like the Redfish Rita, a margarita with cranberry juice.

In addition to the standard admission offerings, the aquarium features a number of special offerings, including school and scout trips. The aquarium's ballroom is a popular spot for conferences, weddings, bar and bat mitzvah parties, and other special events. Plus, inquisitive children can participate in the Marine Biologist for a Day and Zoologist for a Day programs, overnight adventures, and a weeklong Sea Safari Camp during the summer. Camps range from $49.95 for a day to $200 for a week. The aquarium also hosts children's birthday parties, which range from $28 per child for admission, dinner, cake, a few rides, and a group photo, on up to $79.95 per child for a slumber party, complete with nighttime snacks, T-shirts, and breakfast.

Admission to the aquarium is $6.25 for kids ages 2 to 12, $9.25 for adults, and $8.25 for seniors 65 and up. Kids under 2 get in free. Don't

i Call in advance to make reservations to dine at the Aquarium restaurant on Friday and Saturday nights. Otherwise, you may have to ride the carousel or tour the exhibits for more than an hour before a table opens up.

be fooled by the prices, though. A trip to the aquarium can add up quickly. Rides—including the Shark Voyage—aren't included in general admission, so you'll wind up paying $2.99 to $4.99 per ride. If you plan to make a day of it, go ahead and shell out $15.99 per person for an All-Day Adventure Pass, which allows you to see all of the exhibits and ride as many rides as you want. The All-Day Adventure Pass costs the same price, regardless of the guest's age.

Parking is available for $6 in a lot on-site; valet parking is available in front of the aquarium for $8.

GEORGE RANCH HISTORICAL PARK $$
10215 FM 762, Richmond
(281) 343-0218
www.georgeranch.org
If Houston the urban metropolis isn't quite what you expected Texas to be, take a trip to George Ranch Historical Park. Although the park's Richmond location is only about 30 minutes southwest of downtown Houston, it seems like a world away. This 23,000-acre working ranch was the home of Henry and Nancy Jones and three generations of their descendants. Founded in 1824, the ranch predates Texas's independence from Mexico.

Tours of each of the four generations' spacious homes put this 185-year history into perspective: The oldest of these, the Henry and Nancy Jones Homestead, features outdoor kitchens, activities like weaving and corn grinding, and crops that you can help harvest. At Polly and William Ryon's post–Civil War home, learn how the ranch expanded after the war and swap stories with a charming actor playing the part of Colonel William Ryon. The Davis Mansion, which dates back to the 1890s, sheds light on the work of sharecroppers and blacksmiths and features an old chuck wagon, a railroad car, and a longhorn pen. Built in the 1930s and inhabited by A. P. and Mamie George, the George Ranch House blends the past with the present as the resident cowboys rope, sort, and tend cattle before sending them off to one of the country's last remaining cattle dipping vats to rid them of fleas and ticks.

George Ranch is also home to an authentic general store, actors clad in old-timey garb, plenty of livestock, and burgers and sandwiches at the Dinner Belle Cafe. The park is situated around a mile-long loop and visitors can either walk from site to site, or get chauffeured from one stop to the next in a tractor-drawn tram.

Sometimes George Ranch serves up special meals. Every Saturday barbecue or pork is offered for lunch in one of the houses. On the third Wednesday evening of each month, an eight-course candlelight dinner is served in the Ryon Prairie Home, along with a helping of "back in my day" stories told by costumed waitstaff who aren't nearly as old as the stories they tell. Call the park in advance to make reservations for these special meals.

George Ranch Historical Park can be accessed from Houston by taking US 59 South and exiting at Grand Parkway/TX 99. Take a left at Crab River Road/FM 2759; the well-marked ranch is about 6 miles down the road. Admission is $9 for adults and $5 for kids ages 5 to 15. Children 4 and under get in for free. The park is open Tuesday through Saturday.

i George Ranch Historical Park is all about keeping things authentic, so many of the buildings aren't air-conditioned. Dress accordingly and be sure to wear comfortable shoes that you won't mind getting muddy, especially if it has rained in the days leading up to your visit.

THE HERITAGE SOCIETY AT
SAM HOUSTON PARK FREE–$
1100 Bagby, between McKinney Street and Allen Parkway
(713) 655-1912
www.heritagesociety.org
Downtown Houston isn't all skyscrapers and tunnels. Kitty-corner from City Hall at the northwest edge of downtown is Sam Houston Park, a beautifully landscaped park that is now home to eight carefully restored homes and a church that date back to the 1800s and early 1900s. Thanks to the

Heritage Society, visitors can tour these buildings, each of which has played a distinctive role in Houston's history.

The park came to life in 1900 when Houston mayor Sam Brashier purchased the Kellum-Noble House and land—which then was considered the edge of town—and turned the area into Sam Houston Park. The oldest brick house in Houston, the Kellum-Noble House was built in 1847 and became home to one of the city's first private schools. A brick kiln and a sawmill were also operated on the Kellum-Noble property. When the house faced demolition in 1954, locals formed the Heritage Foundation to save it. The Kellum-Noble House is the only restored building in Sam Houston Park that remains at its original site.

The seven other homes and St. John Church, which German farmers built in northwest Harris County in 1891, have been moved into the park from other locations around the city and Harris County. Among the most notable properties in the park are Yates House, 4th Ward Cottage, Nichols-Rice-Cherry House, Pillot House, and the Old Place. Yates House was built in Houston's Fourth Ward by former slave, education advocate, and religious leader Rev. Jack Yates in 1870, just five years after he was freed. Predating the Yates House is 4th Ward Cottage, the oldest known "workingman house" in Houston and a part of Houston's black "Freedman's Town" neighborhood, where blacks lived, worked, and played in the years following the signing of the Emancipation Proclamation. The Greek Revival–style Nichols-Rice-Cherry House was owned by William Marsh Rice, whose estate gets credit for the establishment of Rice University. One of the city's first attached kitchens lies in the Victorian-era Pillot House, which has been undergoing renovation after experiencing significant flood damage from Tropical Storm Allison in 2001. A true log cabin, the Old Place dates back to 1823, and is believed to be the oldest building in Harris County. In addition to the period artifacts found in each building, the Heritage Society Museum, located at the corner of Bagby Street and Lamar Street, displays hundreds of antique phonographs, textiles, tools, silver, toys, and decorative works.

In addition to maintaining these historic properties and artifacts, the Heritage Society has made itself a hub of local culture. On the third Thursday of each month, the free Hill/Finger Noontime Lecture Series introduces Houstonians to local artists, historians, and preservationists. Each fall the Heritage Society sponsors special workshops for Texas history teachers. Elementary school students and scout groups from across the city tour the houses each year, and many local organizations and businesses host events at Sam Houston Park throughout the year. Some couples even get married at the park.

Admission to the Heritage Society Museum is free. To see inside the houses and church, you'll have to take a guided tour, which lasts about an hour and 15 minutes and offers kids the chance to churn butter at the Duncan Store. Guided tours are free for guests 18 and under, $8 for adults over 18, and $6 for seniors 65 and up. Free parking is available off Allen Parkway going into downtown. The parking lot is behind a big white brick building—the Kellum-Noble House.

i **Visit the City of Houston Visitors Center on the first floor of City Hall to get directions and advice on where to go and what to see. You can also get help and suggestions by calling the center at (800) 4-HOUSTON.**

HOUSTON CITY HALL FREE
901 Bagby St.
Reflection pool and main entrance located on Smith Street between McKinney Street and Walker Street
(832) 393-0943
www.houstontx.gov/cao/cityhalltours.html
At just 11 stories tall, Houston's City Hall may look small and insignificant compared to the towering buildings nearby. But don't be fooled: This symbol of Houston government is a spectacular building—one that was criticized for being "ultramodern" when it was designed by Austin architect Joseph Finger in the late 1930s. It was

also criticized for having private showers for each city council member, as well as a private elevator for the mayor, which some speculate may still be in use.

One of the first air-conditioned office buildings, the art deco–style structure has largely outlasted early criticism and made its way into the National Register of Historic Places. City Hall is faceted with Texas Cordova limestone, and the lobby walls are lined with marble. Aluminum medallions of legendary "lawgivers" like Thomas Jefferson, Moses, and Julius Caesar sit above the building's main entryways. Lining the ceiling of the first floor lobby is a bold-colored, gold-leafed mural featuring—among other things—the Western Hemisphere, with Houston at its center.

Sitting above City Hall's main front entrance is a stone sculpture with two men taming a wild horse. It is said to depict people teaming up to govern the world around them. This entrance opens onto a large reflecting pool in Martha Hermann Square, where festivals, concerts, and protests are frequently held. Each December the square is also inhabited by a large menorah and Christmas tree, which are lit for Hanukkah and Christmas, respectively. No matter the holiday season, a light at the top of City Hall lights up every evening, letting theatergoers know if they are running late.

City Hall lies in the heart of the downtown Civic Center, which also includes the City Hall Annex, George R. Brown Convention Center, Sam Houston Park, the Houston Public Library's main branch, Wortham Theater, the Hobby Center, Jones Hall, and Tranquility Park. All of these are located downtown within a few blocks of City Hall.

Free tours of City Hall offer a peek at the city council chambers, the Mayor's Proclamation Room, council offices, and the rotunda and reflection pool, and chance to watch a documentary about Houston in the visitors bureau. Touring City Hall requires planning ahead, though. Free tours for individuals are only offered on the fourth Thursday afternoon of each month; groups of 10 to 40 people can tour City Hall on the second Monday morning of each month and

on the fourth Thursday afternoon. Registration for tours ends at noon two weeks—yes, two weeks—before the scheduled tour. If there aren't enough people signed up for the tour at that point, City Hall may nix the tour altogether. Likewise, if more than 40 people are signed up, you will have to wait until the next tour date. Tours meet in the City Hall Annex, located behind City Hall at 900 Bagby St.

City Hall parking is available in several nearby Theater District garages, including two located at Rusk Street at Bagby Street, one at Walker at Bagby Street, and one at Capitol Street and Smith. Signs inside the garages will direct you to City Hall and the City Hall Annex.

i If you want to relax, reflect, or just let the kids run around during your visit to City Hall, pack a picnic lunch and eat on one of the benches around the reflection pool in Martha Hermann Square or across the street at Tranquility Park.

HOUSTON TUNNEL SYSTEM   **FREE**
Entrances located inside buildings throughout downtown
www.houstontx.gov/abouthouston/ exploringtunnels.html

Houston might not have a subway system, but that doesn't keep Houstonians who work and play downtown from spending time underground. About 20 feet below the streets of downtown Houston are 6 miles worth of tunnels, most of which are interconnected. Inspired by New York City's Rockefeller Center, these air-conditioned tunnels link hotels, office buildings, banks, theaters, and City Hall. The tunnel system—or the tunnels, as locals call them—is often credited with giving people a reprieve from the heat, rain, and humidity as they walk through downtown. This, no doubt, rings true, but the tunnels have also had a commercial dimension since the beginning.

Entrepreneur Will Horwitz built the first tunnels in the 1930s because he was going to have to excavate the basements of three movie theaters he was building downtown. He figured he might as well build tunnels to connect the theaters, which have since been replaced by the Houston Club and JPMorgan Chase, both on Capitol Street. Being the entertainment entrepreneur that he was, Horwitz also opened an arcade and a wine tavern in the tunnels. The tavern and the arcade are now gone, but the tunnels are filled with shops, restaurants, dry cleaners, eyeglass stores, salons, barber shops, printing shops, florists, and just about every other service or shop a busy professional might need. The tunnel system, which connects some 95 city blocks today, also links with a number of skywalks and connects most of the major buildings. The Harris County courts, jails, and other legal facilities—all located in northern downtown from Franklin Street on the north to Preston on the South—have their own tunnel system, which does not connect to the other downtown tunnels. The Toyota Center, the Downtown Aquarium, Minute Maid Park, and the George R. Brown Convention Center are not on the tunnel system.

The tunnels can be accessed from street-level stairs, elevators, or escalators inside any building that is part of the tunnel system. Street access is also available at Wells Fargo Plaza, located on Louisiana Street between McKinney and Lamar. Check out the downtown map on page vii to see where the tunnels lie and what buildings they connect.

The tunnels are only open on weekdays until 6 p.m. The exceptions are the tunnels connecting Wortham Theater Center, Bayou Place, Jones Plaza, Jones Hall, and the Alley Theatre, which are also open before, during, and immediately after theater performances.

i During your visit to the tunnel system, stop in at the JPMorgan Chase Tower, the city's tallest building. Ride the elevator to the Sky Lobby on the 60th floor, where you can see two colorful sculptures by Spanish artist Joan Miró and check out the city from the highest public viewpoint.

i While you're downtown, stop by Allen's Landing at 1001 Commerce St. and Main. Often referred to as Houston's "Plymouth Rock," this is the spot where August C. and John K. Allen landed at Houston and laid claim to it in 1836.

HOUSTON ZOO $–$$
6200 Golf Course Dr., at North MacGregor Dr.
(713) 533-6500
www.houstonzoo.org

Located in the Museum District amid the lush grass of Hermann Park, the Houston Zoo is home to more than 4,500 animals representing more than 900 species. In addition to the usual suspects, the conservation-minded zoo is home to many rare breeds, including an adorable red panda named Toby and a young sifaka family. The 55-acre zoo is also the only zoo in the state to have a giant eland exhibit and one of just 14 worldwide to have a leucistic American alligator exhibit. The Texas Wetlands exhibit features some local amphibians, and the Pheasant Run offers a fun place for children to watch pheasants interact. But perhaps the most popular spot is the John P. McGovern Children's Zoo, where children can touch and pet sheep and goats, play on the playground, ride a wildlife carousel, and check out different animal habitats.

As part of its commitment to educate and entertain the public, the zoo hosts more than two dozen "Meet the Keeper" talks each day. During these kid-friendly talks, zookeepers from different sections of the zoo tell guests about the animals they work with and, in some cases, offer hands-on demonstrations. Find out about upcoming talks online at www.houstonzoo.org/chats.

The zoo offers many other hands-on programs for visitors to learn more about the animals. On Tuesday and Thursday mornings at 9:15, parents can get some exercise and learn about the animals as they push their newborn to 30-month-old children through a section of the zoo. Dubbed Wild Wheels, the hour-long stroll concludes in the children's zoo, where the kids can pet and play with the animals. Wild Wheels i Get in for free when you visit the zoo on Martin Luther King Jr. Day, Presidents' Day, Columbus Day, the day after Thanksgiving, or New Year's Day. Beware, though: Free admission and closed schools make for some big crowds.

costs $7 per child; parents get in for the regular cost of admission. Also popular among the younger set are the New Beginnings programs, held on Wednesday and Saturday mornings. During these hour-long sessions, kids learn about animals through songs, games, stories, and the occasional hands-on demonstration. Classes cost $20 per child and require advance registration, available online.

General admission is free for infants, $6 for kids ages 2 to 11, $10 for ages 12 to 64, and $6 for seniors 65 and up. The zoo is open every day except Christmas and stops admitting visitors one hour before closing each evening. During daylight saving time (from Mar to Nov), the zoo is open from 9 a.m. to 7 p.m., and during Central Standard Time (from Nov to Mar), it is open from 9 a.m. to 6 p.m.

Free parking is available in a lot on Golf Course Drive, but spots fill up quickly in the summer and on weekends and holidays. Paid parking can be found near the Houston Museum of Natural Science or at Memorial Hermann Medical Plaza at 6400 Fannin St. If you don't have a car or don't want to mess with parking, take the METRORail to the Memorial Hermann Hospital/Houston Zoo stop.

i Enjoy a free audio tour of the zoo by downloading MP3s about some of the exhibits at www.houstonzoo.org/map.asp. Then turn on your iPod, Zune, or other MP3 player and learn about the animals as you walk from exhibit to exhibit.

KEMAH BOARDWALK $$$
217 Kipp Ave., Kemah
(877) 285-3624
www.kemahboardwalk.com

Located in the Bay Area town of Kemah about 30 miles south of downtown, the Kemah Boardwalk is where many Houston families and young couples head when they want to escape the city (or the suburbs) for an afternoon or evening. With dining options aplenty, amusement park games and rides, souvenir shops, occasional live music, and tranquil views of Galveston Bay, this entertainment district offers something for just about everyone. Kemah suffered significant damage from Hurricane Ike, but by March 2009, just about everything was up and running again.

All of the restaurants here are owned by Landry's, the popular seafood chain that launched in nearby Katy in the 1980s before going national. This makes for some good dining options—and variety, too. Currently there are about 10 restaurants—plus two coffee shops—at the Kemah Boardwalk, and they range from the kid-friendly Pizza Oven, Joe's Crab Shack, and Saltgrass Steak House to the chic Red Sushi to fine dining options like the Chart House steak house. Classic seafood and some of the best views of Galveston Bay can be found at Landry's Seafood House, while good margaritas and decent Tex-Mex can be found at the noisy Cadillac Bar. The Downtown Aquarium seafood restaurant also has a second location at Kemah.

Around the restaurants are several souvenir shops with T-shirts and trinkets. The Stingray Reef allows children to watch—and touch—stingrays as they swim past. Perhaps the biggest draw is the amusement park. Little ones enjoy riding the two-story carousel, the Kemah Train, and the Balloon Wheel, while older kids—and kids at heart—get a thrill from scream-inducing rides such as the Broadway Bullet roller coaster and the quick-falling Drop Zone. An all-day ride pass costs $16.99 for guests under 48 inches tall and $18.99 for guests 48 inches and taller. Individual rides cost between $3.00 and $4.75.

Even more thrills can be found onboard the *Boardwalk Beast,* an open-deck speedboat that is painted to look like a shark, albeit a rainbow-hued one. This 25-minute ride speeds out into Galveston Bay at 40 miles an hour and almost no one gets off the boat dry. But between the music, views, and other entertainment, it's hard to complain. Those who ride the *Boardwalk Beast* in the evening enjoy a slower ride—and alcoholic and nonalcoholic drink options. Tickets for the *Boardwalk Beast* can be purchased on site. They cost $12 for adults and $9 for kids 12 and under.

To reach Kemah, take the South Loop to TX 225 East, then take TX 146 South to Bayport Boulevard. Take a left at 6th Street and another left at Bradford Street. Free parking is available on-site; during the weekend and holidays, however, there's a $7 fee to park in the lots closest to the boardwalk.

i Learn about Houston's most notable landmarks (and a few well-kept secrets) by taking one of the Greater Houston Preservation Alliance's walking tours on the fourth Sunday of the month. The docent-led tours cost $10 per person. Find out about upcoming tours by calling (713) 216-5000 or visiting www.ghpa.org/tours.

SAINT ARNOLD BREWING COMPANY $
2000 Lyons Ave.
(713) 686-9494
www.saintarnold.com

Beer aficionados, this one's for you: Saint Arnold Brewing Company is Texas's oldest craft brewery. Named for the patron saint of brewing, Saint Arnold of Metz, Saint Arnold Brewing Company was opened by two Rice University alums in 1994. Today the brewery makes several ales, an IPA, a wheat beer, seasonal pilsners, bocks, ales, and stouts. Saint Arnold also makes its own root beer. Each Saturday shortly before 1 p.m., hundreds of Houstonians young and old line up at Saint Arnold to learn about the brewery and its beers—and sample them. Admission costs $5 in cash, which includes a tall shooter glass that can be filled with several large samples during your visit. Many people bring small kids here so don't stress about getting a babysitter. It's also A-OK to bring a pizza or other food to lunch on before the tour. Saint Arnold Brewing Company used to be located in an old warehouse in northwest

Houston; at the time this book went to press, the brewery was planning to move to an old three-story brick building just north of downtown in the fall of 2009. The address included here is for the new brewery; call ahead to make sure Saint Arnold has actually moved before visiting in the fall of 2009. The tour starts at 1 p.m. but show up early since the line to get in is always long.

i Bring your own large beer mug to Saint Arnold Brewing Company to get larger samples.

SAN JACINTO BATTLEGROUND
STATE HISTORIC SITE $-$$
3527 Battleground Rd., La Porte
Battleship *Texas*: (281) 479-2431
www.battleshiptexas.org

San Jacinto Museum of History:
(281) 479-2421
www.sanjacinto-museum.org

Home to the San Jacinto Museum of History, the San Jacinto Monument, and the battleship *Texas*, the San Jacinto Battleground State Historic Site is a war history buff's dream come true. While San Antonio's Alamo may be Texas's most recognizable battle site to non-Texans, the San Jacinto Battleground is every bit as important. It helped put Houston on the map by landing the city's namesake—General Sam Houston—a spot in history books. This site is where General Houston and his Texas revolutionaries surprised Mexico's general Antonio López de Santa Anna and his army on April 21, 1836, and took control of their camp in a mere 18 minutes. The Texans' victory in what became known as the Battle of San Jacinto led to Texas's independence from Mexico and the state's annexation by the United States.

That battle is now commemorated by the San Jacinto Monument, which is billed as the world's tallest monument tower. Built in the art-deco style, the 570-foot monument shaft is topped with a 34-foot, 220-ton star made of concrete, stone, and steel. Inside the monument is the San

Jacinto Museum of History, which is chock-full of artifacts that span Texas's long history before, during, and after the Battle of San Jacinto. Among the artifacts on display are Sam Houston's personal dictionary, Mayan art, arrowheads, and manuscripts from New Spain, Texas, the United States, and Mexico. The museum is open from 9 a.m. to 6 p.m. daily. In the Jesse H. Jones Theatre for Texas Studies, you can also watch a film about the Battle of San Jacinto. The film is screened every hour on the hour from 10 a.m. to 6 p.m. Tickets cost $3.50 for children 11 and younger, $4.00 for seniors 65 and older, and $4.50 for adults.

To get the lay of the battleground, take a 500-foot elevator ride to the observation deck near the top of the monument. Not only does the observation deck offer a great view of the battleground below, but its high-powered binoculars also offer some of the best views of Houston and the Houston Ship Channel. Admission costs $3.00 for children 11 and younger, $3.50 for seniors 65 and up, and $4.00 for adults.

If you still haven't gotten your war history fix after all of this, pay a visit to the battleship *Texas*, which is permanently affixed to the Buffalo Bayou and the Houston Ship Channel. Although the *Texas* is anchored by the battleground, its place in history dates back to World Wars I and II, not the Texas Revolution. The *Texas* was extremely powerful in her day: She was the first U.S. battleship to mount aircraft guns, the first to launch an aircraft, and the first recipient of a commercial radar. Today visitors can walk around the deck, test out unloaded antiaircraft guns, and see the infirmary, living quarters, mess areas, and other sections of the restored battleship. Admission to the *Texas* costs $10 for ages 13 and up and $5 for seniors 65 and up. Kids 12 and under get in free.

Held each April around the Battle of San Jacinto's anniversary, the San Jacinto Festival and Battle Reenactment features old-timey craft demonstrations, live music and entertainment, arts and crafts for the kids, food and art that give a nod to the Texas of yore, and, fittingly, an elaborate battle reenactment—the largest in the Lone Star State. Festival admission is free.

The battleground site is just a few miles south of Houston along the Houston Ship Channel. To reach the battleground site, drive south on the aptly named Sam Houston Tollway/Beltway 8 and cross the Houston Ship Channel. Then exit TX 225 East/Texas Independence Highway and take the road to La Porte. Exit at Battleground Road and take a left. Stay in the left lane when the road separates into two, and continue through the park's stone gates. Free parking is available on-site.

The Texas Parks and Wildlife Department charges $1 per person to enter the battleground site. There is no additional charge for admission to the San Jacinto Museum of History or the battleship *Texas*. The site is open every day except Thanksgiving, Christmas Eve Day, and Christmas Day.

i After your visit to San Jacinto Battleground State Historic Site, take a free—if at times industrial-scented—ride on the Lynchburg Ferry, which stops less than a mile from the battleground site. Just drive northeast on Battleground Road/TX 134, and you'll run into the ferry stop. Learn more in the "Getting Here, Getting Around" chapter on page 15.

SPACE CENTER HOUSTON $$$
1601 NASA Pkwy.
(281) 244-2100
www.spacecenter.org

If you only have time to visit one attraction in Houston, make sure it's Space Center Houston, the official visitors center of NASA's Lyndon B. Johnson Space Center. The space center's 100-building complex is where all U.S. astronauts train. It is also the home of NASA's Mission Control, which coordinates and tracks all of the United States' human spaceflight and directs all space shuttle missions and International Space Station activities.

Space Center Houston offers dozens of hands-on and informational exhibits and activities tracing the history of spaceflight. A film in the Space Center Theater traces the evolution of aerospace technology and equipment and highlights the challenges that astronauts encounter. In the Blast Off Theater, you'll feel like you are traveling in space as large monitors air live updates about current shuttle missions and simulated shuttle exhaust blows into the room. The Feel of Space exhibit lets you see for yourself how astronauts shower, eat, and live in outer space, and the Kids Space Place lets kids practice flying a space shuttle. Also not to be missed are exhibits featuring old spacesuits, artifacts, and space shuttle hardware. Get the scoop on what you're looking at in each exhibit by taking an Astronaut Audio Tour. These digital tours are narrated by astronaut greats like John Glenn, Gene Cernan, Alan Bean, Gene Kranz, Shannon Lucid, Eileen Collins, and Barry Corbin; different versions are available for kids.

Want a close-up look at the Johnson Space Center's day-to-day operations? Participate in the Level Nine Tour. This four- to five-hour tour will take you inside Mission Control and give you a close-up look at the space vehicle mock-up area, as well as the Space Environment Simulation Lab and the Neutral Buoyancy Lab where the astronauts train. You'll even get to eat lunch in the cafeteria where astronauts and NASA employees eat. Be sure to purchase tickets for a Level Nine Tour in advance online. The tours are offered Monday through Friday, but only 12 people are allowed on each one. Tour tickets cost a hefty $84.95 each, and kids under 14 are not allowed on the tour.

During the summer, spring break, and other school holidays, Space Center Houston hosts daylong, half-day, and weeklong day camps and scout camps where kids can participate in hands-on activities and check out some special space exhibits. The space center also hosts a weeklong Space Camp throughout the year for students ages 15 to 18. Space Camp participants attend presentations by NASA personnel and undertake a NASA-like project while operating within a true-to-life NASA budget, potential cuts and all.

General admission to Space Center Houston costs $19.95 for adults, $18.95 for seniors 65 and older, and $15.95 for kids 4 to 11. Save $3 off each general admission ticket by purchasing and printing your tickets online before your visit.

Space Center Houston is located about 25 miles south of downtown near Clear Lake. To get there, take I-45 South toward Galveston, then take exit 25 for NASA Parkway/TX 1. Drive east and follow the signs for the Johnson Space Center.

i NASA Parkway was previously named NASA Road 1, and some maps and GPS systems don't account for the name change.

WILLIAMS TOWER AND WATER WALL   FREE
2800 Post Oak Blvd.
(713) 526-6461
www.property-website.com/pws/sites/4/live
It may be only the third tallest building in town, but the Williams Tower is one of the most recognizable buildings in Houston. Known as the Transco Tower up until 1999, the Galleria-area tower is visible from points all over the city on clear days, giving it a leg up on the 75-story JPMorgan Chase building and the 71-floor Wells Fargo Plaza—the city's first- and second-tallest buildings, which blend in among the towering structures that comprise the downtown skyline. On clear nights, a light at the top of the tower beams nearly 40 miles. Visitors used to be able to look out onto the city from the observation deck on the 51st floor, but security-related concerns have led to the permanent closure of the observation deck. Today the biggest draw *inside* the Williams Tower is the building's art gallery, which features special exhibits of contemporary artists. Located on the first floor, the gallery is open to the public on weekdays. Gallery admission is free.

By far the most popular attraction at the Williams Tower is the Water Wall, a semicircular fountain that sits amid 188 heritage live oak trees on the tower's south side. The wall is 64 feet tall, with one foot for each floor of the Williams Tower. Plenty of picnickers, young families, tourists, and restless teenagers enjoy the Water Wall, but this spot is perhaps most popular among romantics:

i Take a guided two-hour tour along Buffalo Bayou Parkway to learn about the history of downtown Houston and its architecture. The Architecture Center Houston offers tours on the first Saturday morning of the month, weather permitting. Tours cost $15. Call the Architecture Center Houston (713-520-0155) or visit www.aia houston.org for more information.

Plenty of couples have shared their first kiss or gotten engaged or married near the wall, small water droplets splashing on their faces. Water flows down the wall every day from 8 a.m. to 9 p.m., although it has been known to shut off as early as 6 p.m. on occasion.

Located near the intersection of Loop 610 and US 59, Williams Tower and Water Wall is just a block away from the Galleria. To access the tower and Water Wall from Loop 610, exit at Westheimer Road and head west. Then take a left on South Post Oak. Williams Tower will be on the right, just after you pass West Alabama Street and before you hit Hidalgo Street. Parking is available in the Williams Tower parking garage located on West Alabama Street. During the day, parking costs $2 to $12, depending on how long you stick around. Free parking is available in the garage—as well as on surrounding streets—on weekends and after 6 p.m. on weekdays.

PARKS

With so many miles of freeways and roads, Houston can sometimes look like a concrete jungle. But this city is also home to countless acres of parks and greenery. Today the Houston Parks and Recreation Department maintains some 350 parks, as well as more than 200 esplanades and other green spaces. And that's not even all of the area parks: Just southwest of Houston is a major state park, Brazos Bend State Park, and around the city are more than 50 parks operated by Harris County.

With so many parks, Houstonians and visitors have a wealth of opportunities. Want to bike at a velodrome? There's a park for that. Want to practice shooting before the next hunting season or go camping? There are parks where you can do those things, too. There are even several skate parks, which you can learn about in the "Recreation" chapter. With a number of parks located along Buffalo Bayou, there are also opportunities to canoe, kayak, or fish in the middle of the city. There's plenty of standard fare, too: picnic areas, playgrounds, basketball and tennis courts, soccer and baseball fields, off-leash dog areas, and shaded trails for hiking, biking, walking, and running. Nature lovers can also get their fill of wildlife watching at Brazos Bend State Park and the Houston Arboretum & Nature Center in Memorial Park.

The parks here aren't just for solo visits or small gatherings, though: Some of the city's parks—especially Hermann Park and Discovery Green—bring Houstonians and visitors together for festivals and special events throughout the year. Groups also use the parks for special family or neighborhood events, weddings, company picnics, and sports tournaments on park fields. Organized events like these require a permit, so contact the Houston Parks and Recreation Department (713-865-4500) if you're planning a sizeable gathering.

The majority of parks in Houston are smaller neighborhood parks, which you'll find sprinkled throughout the city. Most have publicly accessible playgrounds and some also have pools, tennis and basketball courts, and soccer or baseball fields. Although the playgrounds and other open areas are typically open to the public, pools, athletic courts, and fields are often available only to neighborhood residents or groups who have reserved the area in advance.

Because there are so many parks in Houston, it's impossible to list and describe them all. The parks in this chapter are among the city's biggest, best, and most visited. With the exception of Brazos Bend State Park, all are located in Houston proper. For a complete list of Houston-area parks, visit the Web sites of the Houston Parks and Recreation Department (www.houstonparks.org), Harris County (www.pct3.hctx.net), and the Buffalo Bayou Conservancy (www.buffalobayou.org). Maps of the listed parks can be downloaded from their corresponding Web sites. Parking is typically free at area parks, though you may have to shell out a few quarters—or dollars—to park during special events or when visiting busy urban parks like Discovery Green and Hermann Park.

BRAZOS BEND STATE PARK
21901 FM 762, Needville
(979) 553-5102
www.tpwd.state.tx.us

Located about 30 miles southwest of Houston in Needville, Brazos Bend State Park is a big hit among outdoor enthusiasts. Opened by the state in 1984, this 5,000-acre oasis runs along the Brazos River, which was used to transport cotton and for other commerce in the 1800s. The park's history appears to date back much further, though: Artifacts found here suggest that people have been coming to Brazos Bend State Park for thousands of years.

Today Brazos Bend's campsites make it a popular place to go camping. The park's Brazos River location makes for plenty of fishing opportunities—as well as occasional alligator and freshwater snake sightings. The expansive park is also lined with wooded hiking and biking trails, including the Creekfield Lake Nature Trail, where you can see and learn about different wetlands creatures from a number of interpretive panels. Each weekend the park offers free guided hikes. Visit the Nature Center at the park to participate in an upcoming hike. While you're there, be sure to check out the Habits and Niches display, where you can touch and learn more about some of the local wildlife.

General admission to the park is $5 for visitors 13 and older. Kids 12 and under get in free. Camping fees range from $12 to $25 per night for individuals and families, depending on how primitive the campsite is.

ℹ️ If you're looking for a fun date night or a family adventure, head to Brazos Bend State Park on Saturday from 3 to 10 p.m. That's when the Houston Museum of Natural Science–owned George Observatory is open for stargazing. The observatory owns one of the largest publicly accessible domed telescopes, which makes for some unbelievable views of the sky.

BUFFALO BAYOU PARK AND ELEANOR TINSLEY PARK
18–3600 Allen Pkwy. and Memorial Dr., from Shepherd Drive to Bagby Street
www.buffalobayou.org/parks.html

Nearly 125 acres of greenbelt and bayou water along Allen Parkway comprise Buffalo Bayou Park. With the park approaching downtown, Buffalo Bayou Park offers magnificent views of the city's skyline, as well as leisure opportunities aplenty. Many Houstonians run or walk along this greenbelt's trails, which include a number of stretching stations. Quite a bit of public art decorates the park—most notably in the Buffalo Bayou Artpark, which displays public art from the community. Buffalo Bayou flows through the middle of Buffalo Bayou Park, enabling visitors to canoe or kayak from one of the park's two canoe launches to other locations on the bayou, including downtown's Sesquicentennial Park. (One canoe launch is located on the park's north side; the other is on the south end in Eleanor Tinsley Park, discussed below.)

Canoe and Kayak Rentals

Canoes and kayaks are not available for rent at Buffalo Bayou Park. However, canoes and kayaks can be rented by calling one of the following companies:

REI
7538 Westheimer Rd.
(713) 353-2582
www.rei.com

ACK Canoesport
5822 Bissonnet
(713) 660-7000
www.austinkayak.com

Learn more about ACK Canoesport and other sporting goods shops in the area in the "Shopping" chapter.

Other park highlights include the Jim Mozola Memorial Disc Golf Course on the park's northside and a section for dogs and their owners to play (see the "Dog Parks" Close-up on page 131 of this chapter). A Mayan-inspired Police Officers' Memorial is also located in the park, although this pyramid structure isn't easily accessible from most parts of the park. The easiest way to reach the memorial is to park in the parking lot at 2400 Memorial Drive.

On the south side of Buffalo Bayou Park lies Eleanor Tinsley Park, the site of the city's annual 4th of July Freedom Over Texas fireworks show. (Learn more about this extravaganza in the "Annual Events" chapter.) The rest of the year, families visit Eleanor Tinsley Park to play on the playground, admire the Gus Wortham Fountain, take their dogs to the dog park, and check out the Mexican free-tailed bat colony living under the Waugh Bridge, located at Waugh Street between Allen Parkway and Memorial Drive. Each evening around sunset, the bats emerge en masse from the bridge, assuming the temperature is above 50 and the sky is neither cloudy nor foggy. The best glimpses of this amazing sight are available from the sidewalk on the bridge or the north bayou bank, just east of the bridge in Buffalo Bayou Park.

i For an up-close look at where the bats live and an enchanting view of the bats in flight, take a bat boat tour on the Buffalo Bayou Partnership's pontoon boat. Trips are typically offered on the second Friday evening of the month. Visit www .buffalobayou.org or call (713) 752-0314 for information on upcoming bat boat tours.

CULLEN PARK

19008 Saums Rd., just north of I-10
www.houstontx.gov/parks/cullenpark.html
Located on Houston's west side just east of Katy, Cullen Park sits in Addicks Reservoir, an open flood-zone space used to retain storm water and prevent flooding. The 9,200-acre park rarely floods, though, and is filled with recreational opportunities. Here you'll find the requisite picnic areas with barbecue grills, as well as more than 8 miles of hiking and biking trails. Depending on the season, you might see armadillos, deer, and snakes along the trails. Some of the snakes here can be venomous so be sure to watch where you step and keep your eyes on young children. Although the trails take you past beautiful oak trees, a cemetery, and flora, they are not always the prettiest in town. Sometimes the weeds along the trail are overgrown or trash lines the area. There are also baseball and soccer fields, as well as a water playground, where kids can run beneath misting flowers to cool off. Archers can practice using their bow and arrows at the archery range on the park's east side at 13751 Clay Rd.

Most notably, Cullen Park is home to Alkek Velodrome, a 333-meter outdoor cement track for cyclists. There are just 19 velodromes in the country, and people who use them are serious cyclists. So keep the little ones away because cyclists here won't be looking out for them.

i Lock your car and leave valuables at home when you visit Cullen Park. Thieves have been known to spoil parkgoers' fun by breaking into their vehicles.

DISCOVERY GREEN

**Downtown between McKinney and Lamar, 1 block east of Austin at La Branch Street
(713) 400-7336
www.discoverygreen.com**
Discovery Green just opened in 2008, but it is already one of the most popular spots in town. This 12-acre downtown park is the brainchild of Houston mayor Bill White and the Discovery Green Conservancy, who wanted to convert a space comprised largely of parking lots into urban green space that would serve as a recreational hub for Houstonians. After looking at urban parks in other big cities, they found that visitors to urban parks come for both the tranquility and the recreational opportunities.

These features, it turns out, are exactly what Houstonians and visitors seek when they come to Discovery Green. The park is across the street from the always-busy George R. Brown Convention Center and the Hilton Americas—Houston Hotel and just a few blocks from Minute Maid Park, the Toyota Center, and more than a couple towering buildings. But the hustle and bustle of the city feels distant when you step into Discovery Green. Maybe it's the sight of the 100-year-old oak trees, the lush grass, and the gardens filled with native plants. Or maybe it's the sight of children and adults navigating their rented remote-controlled sailboats along Kinder Lake.

Discovery Green is loved for more than its trees, grass, gardens, and lake, of course. Children want to come here to play on the playground, run through Gateway Fountain as its jets cycle on and off, play with remote-controlled sailboats, and ice-skate on the Ice at Discovery Green during the winter holiday season. (See the write-up on the Ice at Discovery Green in the "Annual Events" chapter for more information.) Dogs love to come here to socialize and frolic in the Kinder Large Dog Run and Harriet and Joe Foster Dog Runs. Adults love to come to Discovery Green to run along the half-mile McNair Foundation jogging trail, admire the contemporary art installations, or play recreational games like chess and bocce, which can be checked out for free from the whimsically decorated Art Carts around the park. Those who stay awhile often bring along a picnic or grab a drink or dinner at The Grove restaurant overlooking the park or at the more casual Treehouse. (More information about The Grove and the Treehouse can be found on page 45 of the "Restaurants" chapter.)

Discovery Green is also a popular site for special events and festivals such as the Menu of Menus Extravaganza, preparade events for the Art Car Parade, and the Houston International Jazz Festival—all of which are covered in the "Annual Events" chapter. On Saturday Discovery Green is home to the Downtown Green Market, a co-op and farmers' market that offers organic, locally grown produce and which is described in detail on page 196 of the "Shopping" chapter.

Yoga and pilates classes, youth writing workshops, and bike repair workshops are regularly offered at the park as well. The park also hosts film screenings, concerts, and theater events at the Anheuser-Busch Stage and Fondren Foundation Performance Space. Most, but not all, events held at Discovery Green are free. Visit the Web site to learn about upcoming events and pricing.

There is quite a bit of metered parking around Discovery Green, but if you visit the park during the summer, for special events, or on the weekend, you may have trouble finding a space. Additional parking is available in the Convention District Parking garage at 1002 Avenida de las Americas, the Hilton Americas–Houston garage at 1600 Lamar, and the Houston Center garage at 1200 McKinney St. Prices vary depending on the garage, day of the week, and whether there are any special events going on.

GEORGE BUSH PARK
16756 Westheimer Pkwy.
www.pct3.hctx.net

George Bush Park is the largest park run and owned by Harris County. Before being renamed in honor of the 41st U.S. president and Houston resident George H. W. Bush in 1997, it was named Cullen-Barker Park. Located in the far western part of the city, the park occupies about half of the 13,500-acre Barker Reservoir, which was built in the 1940s to control flooding. Here you will find a playground that includes activities for children with physical limitations, two large soccer fields, and six baseball fields, only two of which are available for public use. In addition, gun enthusiasts can practice their shot at the American Shooting Center, while airplane aficionados can fly model airplanes in the Dick Scobee Memorial Flying Fields, named after the commander of the space shuttle *Challenger*, which disintegrated just after launching in 1986. Also inside the park, on the south end of Westheimer Parkway, is Millie Bush Dog Park, a spacious off-leash area named after George and Barbara Bush's now-deceased springer spaniel. See the Close-up box, "Dog Parks," in this chapter for more information on Millie Bush Dog Park.

Miles of biking, running, and even equestrian trails also fill the park and many of these run along the Buffalo Bayou or smaller swamps and bodies of water, where visitors can go fishing. The trails are popular among runners, as well as cyclists, who find them easy to navigate. Although the park has trees here and there, shade is scarce, making this a hot place to spend time during the summer.

HERMANN PARK
Fannin Street between North McGregor and Hermann Drive
(713) 524-5876
www.hermannpark.org

Since opening in 1914, Hermann Park has been one of the city's most popular recreational destinations. Not only is the park a great place to jog, golf, nap, or just enjoy a pretty day, but it is also home to three of the city's biggest attractions—the Houston Zoo, the Houston Museum of Natural Science, and Miller Outdoor Theatre, which holds free events throughout the year. More information on Miller Outdoor Theatre can be found in the "Performing Arts" chapter, and special events held at the theater can be found in the "Annual Events" chapter. For information about the Houston Museum of Natural Science, see the "Museum" chapter, and the Houston Zoo can be found in the "Attractions" chapter.

Visitors who enter the park from Fannin onto Hermann Drive are greeted by a giant statue of Sam Houston. To the left is the Houston Museum of Natural Science and, a little farther down, the Houston Garden Center, which is surrounded by more than 2,500 rosebushes. To the right is the bulk of the park, which includes about 2 miles worth of well-shaded trails for walking and jogging, as well as Miller Outdoor Theatre, the Houston Zoo, and the Hermann Park Golf Course. See the "Recreation" chapter for information on the Hermann Park Golf Course.

These are just some of this beloved park's highlights. The 445-acre park is also home to McGovern Lake, where children can feed the ducks, birders can watch for migratory birds, and families and couples can ride in four-seat paddleboats, which can be rented from the Hermann Park Boathouse across from the zoo for $8 per half hour. Children 12 and under and adults 65 and over—yes, you read that right—can also partake in some catch-and-release fishing here, although guests ages 65 to 70 must have a Texas fishing license. See the Web site or call for more information on fishing in the park.

The Hermann Park Railroad—a red, open-air train that has been beloved by generations of children and their parents—journeys around one of the three islands at McGovern Lake. The kid-size train runs from 10 a.m. to 5:30 p.m. on weekdays and 10 a.m. to 6 p.m. on weekends. Rides cost $2.75 per person. Located on the lake's north shore are shaded picnic area and fountains that little visitors love to run through.

Directly north of McGovern Lake is the 740-foot-long Mary Gibbs and Jesse H. Jones Reflection Pool, which is also visible from the Sam Houston statue at the park's entrance. Lined with large oak trees, the reflection pool is a soothing place to take a walk, picnic, and of course, reflect. Just west of the reflection pool is the park's simple yet elegant Japanese Garden, which has a few shaded paths for meditating or cooling off. Each April the garden is the site of the Japan Festival, a two-day event celebrating all things Japanese. More information on this event can be found in the "Annual Events" chapter.

East of McGovern Lake is the Buddy Carruth Playground for All Children, a fun place to have a birthday party or just run off some extra energy. Most of the equipment on the playground, as its name suggests, is designed for use by children of all physical abilities, including those confined to wheelchairs. While visiting the park, children often enjoy visiting Bayou Parkland, which offers special educational programs for kids throughout the year. Learn more by calling the park.

Visit the Hermann Park Web site to download a map of the park. The centrally located park is right across the street from Rice University and within walking distance of the Texas Medical Center and the Museum District. Hermann Park can also be easily accessed by taking the METRORail to the Hermann Park/Rice U station. Free parking is available in several lots around the park. Free lots are located in front of the Houston Zoo, at the Bayou Parkland Pavilion, at the Houston Garden Center, near Miller Outdoor Theatre, and at the golf course clubhouse at the corner of Almeda and MacGregor Streets. The Houston Museum of Natural Science also has a publicly accessible pay-for-parking garage on Caroline Street, although this can get pricey if you're not visiting the museum. Museum members park for $5 and nonmembers who show their museum ticket stub pay $10. Those without a ticket pay $20.

LAKE HOUSTON WILDERNESS PARK
22031 Baptist Encampment Rd., New Caney
www.houstontx.gov/parks/lakehouston
park.html

Located northeast of the city in New Caney, Lake Houston Wilderness Park offers plenty of outdoor opportunities on and around the human-made Lake Houston. The park, which was previously operated by the state, became the City of Houston's property in 2006. The city continues to develop and expand the park's offerings, which include close to 5,000 acres of forest and 12 miles of trails for hiking and biking. The pine- and cypress-shaded trails offer opportunities to bird-watch, take some nature photos, and ride horses, although you'll have to bring your own horse to do the latter. It's common to see snakes along the trail so be sure to watch your feet. Those who want to better understand what they see in the park should visit the Nature Center, which features four rooms that teach visitors about different ecosystems, amphibians, invertebrates, reptiles, and butterflies. The park also offers opportunities to canoe, kayak, and fish for bass, crappie, and catfish in the stocked lake. There are many boats in the lake although the lake's boating entry points are not located in the park. See page 142 of the "Recreation" chapter for additional information about water activities on Lake Houston.

Among of the park's biggest draws are its camping opportunities. Lake Houston Wilderness Park is the only city-owned and operated park where visitors can camp, and for this reason, it attracts a number of scout groups throughout the year. Campsites here cater to everyone from primitive campers to city slickers who need their A/C and refrigerator. Want to pitch a tent? You can do just that in one of the park's campsites, where you'll also have access to fire rings, picnic tables, and lantern lights. Or do you prefer to sleep in bunk beds? If so, stay in one of the park's lodges or cottages, which range from primitive to air-conditioned and heated spaces with kitchens and bathrooms. There are even campsites for campers who bring their horses to the park. Camping fees range from $4 per night per person for one of the primitive campsites to $160 per night, plus a one-time cleaning fee of $75, for a group of up to 26 people to sleep in the air-conditioned Lazy Creek Cottage. Individual rooms and beds are not available in the lodges and cottages. Camping fees do not include the $3 park admission fee that all visitors must pay upon entry.

> **i** Celebrate Houston's parks by participating in the Park to Park Run, held each February. The event includes several races—a 5-mile run and wheelchair race from Discovery Green to Hermann Park, a 2-mile walk for families, and a 1K kids' fun run, all of which are held at Hermann Park. Learn more about the Park to Park Run in the "Annual Events" chapter.

MEMORIAL PARK
6501 Memorial Dr., at the southeastern
intersection of I-10 and Loop 610
(713) 863-8403
www.memorialparkconservancy.org

Thanks to its wooded trails and a central location just east of Memorial and west of downtown, Memorial Park is one of the most popular places to run in the city. In total there are more than 30 miles of trails here, but the most popular trail is the 2.9-mile Seymour Lieberman Exercise Trail made of crushed granite and packed earth. To maximize jogger safety and make running possible for those who work past sundown, the trail is lighted and includes several exercise stations, restrooms, and water fountains—including some for the many dogs who come here with their humans. There is also a 0.25-mile asphalt-timing track where runners can practice their speed for upcoming races. The rest of the trails are largely used for hiking, in-line and roller-skating, biking, and even horseback riding. Some of these trails are more challenging than others, which makes the park an attractive place for everyone from mountain bikers and others trying to build leg muscles to more leisurely riders and hikers. Some of the most scenic trails can be found along the Buffalo Bayou, which comprises the park's southern border. No matter which trail you travel, you're likely to find some lizards, raccoons, and other native plant and animal life.

The recreational possibilities at Memorial Park extend far beyond its trails. Located just off the Seymour Lieberman Exercise Trail at 1500 Memorial Loop is the Memorial Park Tennis Center, where visitors can practice their serve on 18 courts or a practice wall, take lessons, and participate in tournaments and tennis leagues. Golfers, meanwhile, can play at the Memorial Park Golf Course (1001 Memorial Loop Dr. East), a 250-acre, 18-hole course that attracts more than 60,000 people each year. The park is also home to a sand volleyball court, baseball fields, a croquet field, picnic facilities aplenty, and a playground. Those who prefer to get in shape indoors can work out at the Memorial Park Fitness Center, located in the park at 6402 Arnott. Daily and monthly memberships are available. Next door to the fitness center, swimmers can swim in the 33-meter outdoor pool, which is free and open to the public from Memorial Day to Labor Day. Additional information about the tennis center, golf course, and fitness center can be found in the "Recreation" chapter.

Nature lovers and children also visit the park to learn about nature and wildlife. In addition to the creatures and plants found on the trails around the park, Memorial Park is home to the Houston Arboretum & Nature Center, a beautiful nature reserve whose 5 miles of nature trails are filled with forest, wetland, pond, and meadow habitats filled with native plants and animals. Learn more about the arboretum, which is located on the park's western edge at 4501 Woodway Dr., on page 172 of the "Kidstuff" chapter.

A number of events are held at Memorial Park throughout the year. The most notable of these is the Bayou City Art Festival, which takes place here each March.

Located on what was once Camp Logan, Memorial Park is dedicated to the memory of U.S. soldiers who died in World War I. Visit the park Web site to download maps of the park. Free parking is available in several lots around the park.

ℹ️ **Between the winding trails and the density of trees, it is tough for pedestrians and cyclists to see others coming along Memorial Park's trails. Yell "RIDER!" if you're riding your bike and approaching a curve, so that other visitors can get out of your way.**

SAM HOUSTON PARK
1100 Bagby, between McKinney Street and Allen Parkway
(713) 655-1912
www.houstontx.gov/parks
Sam Houston Park is the city's oldest park. Located on the northwest edge of downtown, the 20-acre park was established in 1899 at the request of Mayor Sam Brashier. The park lies on land where, in 1847, Nathaniel Kellum built what is now the oldest surviving house in Houston. Since 1954, the park has been largely known as the site of several Victorian homes and other historic buildings. Many Houstonians visit Sam Houston Park to learn about the city's early history at the Heritage Society, which you can learn more about on page 113 of the "Attractions" chapter.

However, the park's close proximity to City Hall as well as its substantial green space, gardens, trails, and charming lily pond also make it a popular spot for picnicking or throwing a Frisbee. Many festivals and events are also held in Sam Houston Park throughout the year. Among the festivals held here are the Houston International Festival in April, Art Car Parade VIPit Party in May, the Bayou City Art Festival in October, and Via

(Q) Close-up

Armand Bayou Nature Center

The country's largest urban wildlife refuge is located just southeast of Houston in Pasadena. Named after Gulf Coast wilderness conservationist Armand Yramategui, Armand Bayou Nature Center may not be a park in name, but it offers many of the attractions and activities that make other local parks popular, including canoeing, hiking, and even pontoon boat cruises. These are among the ways that visitors—which include a large number of student groups—can learn about different wildlife and the ecosystems in which they live. Hike along the Martyn, Karankawa, Marsh, Prairie, or Lady Bird Trails, where you'll learn about the forest, prairie, marsh, and natural bayou habitats that were once abundant in the Houston area. Or walk along the center's boardwalk, where you can explore exquisite butterfly gardens and a farm site inhabited by about one-dozen European families during the mid-1800s. Once a month near the full moon, the nature center offers moonlit (and flashlight-lit) walks through the woods in search of owls, as well as additional evening walks to look at nighttime creatures, such as raccoons and possums. On one Friday a month, the center offers Prairie Night Rides—hayride tours that offer a glimpse at armadillos, rabbits, deer, and other nocturnal creatures. These special activities cost an additional $8 for visitors six and older. Guests under 18 must be accompanied by an adult. Reservations are required, so call ahead.

Throughout the year, the park offers educational programming for local students and scout groups and hosts birthday parties and guided hikes for kids. During the winter and summer, Armand Bayou also holds nature camps for kids.

The nature center is located at 8500 Bay Area Blvd., Pasadena (281-474-2551; www.abnc .org). General admission costs $3 for visitors 13 to 59 years old and $1 for children ages 4 to 12 and seniors 60 and older. There's no admission fee for children three and under. Free parking is available on-site.

Colori Street Painting Festival in November. See the "Annual Events" chapter for more information on these events.

Free parking is available off Allen Parkway as you enter downtown. The parking lot is behind a big white brick building—the Kellum-Noble House.

SESQUICENTENNIAL PARK
400 Texas Ave.
www.sesquicentennialpark.org
Located in the downtown Theater District along Buffalo Bayou, Sesquicentennial Park was established in 1986 to celebrate the 150th birthday of both Houston and Texas. This park is less of a recreation destination than most other local parks, but it is worthy of a visit if have some extra time downtown. A peaceful sanctuary in the midst of the city, this 22.5-acre park is filled with grassy slopes for afternoon picnics and frolicking, as well as bridges, cascading waterfalls, meandering sidewalks, native plants, natural water pools, and spectacular views of downtown. Those in need of a quiet space to contemplate can gaze out on Buffalo Bayou and watch canoers and kayakers paddle by or stop at the park. Art lovers will appreciate artist Dean Ruck's photographic display on the railings overlooking Buffalo Bayou, as well as the "seven wonders." Each of the seven wonders is a 70-foot-tall pillar featuring 150 children's drawings that illustrate the city's history of agriculture, energy, medicine, transportation, manufacturing, philanthropy, and technology.

i Bring lots of water along whenever you visit one of Houston's parks. When the mercury starts to soar—especially in sparsely shaded parks—visitors tend to get dehydrated quickly.

Sesquicentennial Park's beauty makes it a popular place for weddings, special events, and photo shoots. Many downtown events are also held here throughout the year. Parking is available in the Theater District parking garages; the most convenient is garage number 8. Parking costs up to $9 during the week and $7 for special events and on weekends. See the downtown parking map on page vii.

TERRY HERSHEY PARK
15200 Memorial Dr., at Memorial Mews St.
(281) 496-2177
www.pct3.hctx.net
Much like George Bush Park and Cullen Park, Terry Hershey Park is built on flood control land in west Houston. The park, previously named Buffalo Bayou Park, was renamed in 1991 to recognize the work of conservationist Terry Hershey, who successfully fought to prevent the paving and channeling of Buffalo Bayou in the 1960s.

Today Terry Hershey Park is a popular place to bike and train for marathons. The park's trails, which stretch from TX 6 to the Sam Houston Tollway, now measure nearly 11 miles. A good chunk of the trails are cooled off by trees as well as the breeze blowing off the bayou, but many sections are not well shaded. There's also quite a bit of litter along the trails. Harris County continues to expand the park in hopes of making it easier for people living in Wilcrest, Kirkwood, and Dairy Ashford to bike to the Metro's Addicks Park and Ride Lot. Although the hiking and biking trails are the biggest draw here, Terry Hershey Park also has a playground, picnic areas, and green space for throwing a Frisbee. While the park runs along Buffalo Bayou, it is not safe to swim or drink the water here.

TRANQUILITY PARK
Downtown between Bagby and Smith
Streets and Rusk and Walker Streets
Located downtown, just across the street from City Hall and the Hobby Center, Tranquility Park pays homage to Houston's role in space history. The park first opened in 1979 to commemorate the tenth anniversary of the first moon landing.

The park's entire design subtly continues this celebration some three decades later. Bronze plaques at the park's entrance include Neil Armstrong's first words from the moon—"Houston, Tranquility Base here. The Eagle has landed."—in 15 languages and a replica of Armstrong's footprints on the moon are displayed at the park. Even the park's grounds—green as they are—bear a slight resemblance to the moon: Mounds and craters dot the park and the giant Wortham Fountain is surrounded by large stainless cylinders-turned waterfalls resembling rocket boosters. Towering trees line the park's perimeter and shade several wooden benches, where downtown office workers often eat lunch or decompress. Many special events and festivals, including the Houston Children's Festival and the Houston International Festival, are held here throughout the year. Learn more about the Houston Children's Festival in the "Kidstuff" chapter, and about the Houston International Festival in the "Annual Events" chapter. Parking is available in the nearby Theater District garages, including two located at Rusk Street at Bagby Street, one at Walker at Bagby Street, and one at Capitol Street and Smith. A map of these garages can be found on page vii. Parking costs up to $9 during the week and $7 on weekends and holidays and during special events.

i Canoeing and kayaking fans, take note: Throughout the year, the Buffalo Bayou Conservancy—the organization that developed Buffalo Bayou Park, Sesquicentennial Park, Memorial Park, and other parks along Buffalo Bayou—hosts special events revolving around boating on the bayou. These include a 15-mile canoe and kayak regatta in March, canoe and kayak trips, and a dragon boat competition. Learn more by visiting the Buffalo Bayou Conservancy Web site (www.buffalobayou.org) or calling (713) 752-0314.

Close-up

Dog Parks

Maybe your dog is getting stir-crazy while staying in a hotel or living in a home with little to no backyard. Or maybe you just want your dog to socialize. Whatever the case, there's plenty of space for your dog to run free, sniff, and socialize at Houston's more than one-dozen off-leash dog parks. Some local dog parks, like the Discovery Green Dog Park and Millie Bush Dog Park at George Bush Park, occupy a small, gated section of a larger made-for-humans park. Others are freestanding parks. Millie Bush Dog Park is considered one of the best dog parks in the city, if not the country. This 15-acre park has plenty of space for dogs to run, as well as three shallow water pools and a gated area for small dogs. As with most of Houston's dog parks, though, there's not a lot of shade here.

No matter which dog park you visit, be sure to bring water and be prepared to clean up after your dog. Poop bags and water are available for the taking at many parks but on hot days, dogs overheat quickly, so it's always a good idea to bring your own water and a bowl. Some parks, such as Congressman Bill Archer Bark Park, prohibit owners from bringing in treats, so be sure to read the signs before entering the park.

Below are the names and addresses of dog parks in the Houston area. Listed first are parks in Houston; parks in the major suburbs follow. New dog parks open fairly often, so for the latest dog park news, visit the Houston Dog Park Association Web site (www.houstondogpark.org).

HOUSTON

Buffalo Bayou Dog Park
2700 block of Allen Parkway at Studewood

Congressman Bill Archer Bark Park
3201 Highway 6, just north of Groeschke Rd.

Danny Jackson Family Dog Park
4828 1/2 Loop Central Dr., inside Loop 610 just south of 59

Discovery Green Dog Runs
Downtown between McKinney and Lamar, 1 block east of Austin at La Branch Street
www.discoverygreen.com

Ervan Chew Dog Park
4502 Dunlavy, east of Shephard and south of Richmond

Levy Park Dog Park
3801 Eastside, just south of Richmond

Maxey Bark and Run Dog Park
601 Maxey Rd., next to the Park and Ride

Millie Bush Dog Park
16756 Westheimer Pkwy.

Officer Lucy Dog Park
4337 Lafayette, near Beechnut, entrance off Edith Street

DEER PARK

Ella and Friends Dog Park
500 block of 13th Street next to Jimmy Burke Activity Center

KATY

Katy Dog Park
5414 Franz Rd.

KINGWOOD

AABY Bark Park
619 Lakeville Dr., off Russell Palmer Road
www.kingwoodkennels.com/dogpark.htm

PEARLAND

Independence Dog Park
3919 Liberty Dr.

Pearland Dog Park
1131 Country Rd. 94, off TX 288

Southdown Dog Park
2150 Country Place Parkway
www.pearlandparks.com/southdown.asp

THE WOODLANDS

Bear Branch Dog Park
5200 Research Forest Dr., west of I-45

Cattail Dog Park
9323 Cochrans Crossing Dr., across from Palmer Golf Club House in Cattail Park
www.thewoodlandsdogparkclub.org

RECREATION

No matter how you like to get in shape and relax, you're sure to find plenty of recreational and fitness opportunities in Houston. Thanks to Houston's Buffalo Bayou location and its proximity to the Gulf of Mexico and area lakes, fans of water-based activities such as fishing, kayaking, canoeing, waterskiing, windsurfing, and boating can get their fix here. There are plenty of opportunities for those who prefer to relax under drier conditions as well: Hunters can pursue deer, fowl, and other animals around these parts, and campers can pitch a tent or sleep in bunk beds at a few area parks. Runners can participate in races—and prepare for them by following the miles of trails in the city's parks. Cyclists can use many of these same trails while also preparing for competitions at the local velodrome. Skaters can take advantage of several skate parks, join a roller or hockey league, or skate for fun at one of the local roller- or ice-skating rinks. And rock climbers? Houston's got two rock-climbing gyms just for you.

If golf or tennis is more your thing, rest assured: There are plenty of opportunities to practice and play here. Several public golf courses and tennis courts are located around Houston. Some of these are operated by the city, making them available at a reduced cost.

In addition to all of these recreation options, Houston is home to many gyms and yoga studios. A few of the gyms are owned by the city, making them available for little to no cost. Others are big chains or independent businesses that charge a bit more. Together, Houston's many yoga studios cover just about every style imaginable (pilates included). They even mix things up occasionally with special classes such as partner yoga, rock 'n' roll yoga, and pre- and postnatal yoga.

This chapter highlights some of the different recreational opportunities in the Houston area. It would take several volumes to list and describe every possible recreational sport, league, and site in town, but the activities and locales listed in this chapter are some of the most popular (in the case of sites and activities) and best (in terms of sites). This chapter also includes a number of Web sites to help you find additional locations or information on participating in your recreational activity of choice in Houston.

Most of the activities listed here require some sort of gear. While there are some good independent sporting goods stores in Houston, you will find far more large sporting good chains here. Among them are REI, Academy, Gander Mountain, Sports Authority, and the Bass Pro Shop in Katy. Many of these stores have several locations in Houston, so check out the phone book to find the store nearest you. A few additional independent shops—including a kayak shop and two great fishing shops—can be found on page 208 of the "Shopping" chapter.

CAMPING

If you savor the chance to sleep in the great outdoors, you're in luck. **Lake Houston Wilderness Park, Brazos Bend State Park,** and **Lake Conroe** cater to campers with campgrounds and cabins. Both Lake Houston Wilderness Park and Brazos Bend offer campsite facilities that sleep small groups as well as large groups, such as scout troops, and that include lantern lighting. For those who don't like roughing it, there are air-conditioned and heated lodges at Lake Houston. You'll need to bring your own camping equipment to both sites. More information about these parks can be found in the "Parks" chapter.

The **Lake Conroe KOA Campgrounds** serve guests with their own RVs, as well as those who want to rent a cottage. Located just a few minutes from the lake, these somewhat fancy camping accommodations include a health club, pool, and water slide. Learn more about the Lake Conroe KOA Campgrounds by calling (936) 582-1200 or visiting the Web site (www.houston northkoa.com).

CYCLING

Because city ordinances prohibit biking on sidewalks where businesses are located, biking around Houston can be challenging. Luckily recreational cyclists have plenty of other options. Not only is biking easy in more suburban residential areas; Houston's parks also give bikers plenty of trails to choose from. Most of the major parks here—including all of those listed in the "Parks" chapter of this book—include extensive trails for biking. Many of these are fairly flat trails but mountain bikers and those looking to build some leg muscle can find more challenging trails on the southwest side of **Memorial Park,** which has a number of ravines. Color-coded maps at the park alert bikers to the difficulty of different trails. Memorial Park closes its Mountain Bike Trails if bad weather has made them dangerous. Before your visit, call the park's Mountain Bike Trail Line (713-437-6588) to find out if the trails are open or closed. Those training for bicycle races—as well as those who just like to bike quickly for fun—should head to Cullen Park on the city's west side. This is the site of **Alkek Velodrome,** one of just 19 velodromes in the country. The banking of this 333-meter outdoor cement spans from 33 degrees around the turns to 9 degrees in the straights. Since opening in 1986, the Alkek Velodrome has been the site of a number of Olympic qualifiers; local races are also held here throughout the year. Learn more about these races on the Greater Houston Cycling Foundation's Web site (www.houstoncycling.org) or by calling (281) 646-7790. See the "Parks" chapter for information about Memorial Park, Cullen Park, as well as the trails at other major parks around Houston.

GOLF COURSES

Thanks in part to its mild temperatures and bustling business climate, Houston is home to dozens of golf courses. Although some are located in country clubs or areas that are off-limits to the general public, visitors and residents who don't belong to a club have plenty of publicly accessible golf courses to choose from. In total there are more than 50 public golf courses in Houston. Seven of these—plus a junior training course—are operated by the Houston Parks and Recreation Department. Many of the nonmunicipal courses are located in the suburbs.

Generally local courses are open throughout the week and on weekends. Greens fees vary depending on the day of the week or time of the day you tee off. Some include golf cart rental; others do not. Most golf courses require guests to reserve a tee time in advance. Since golfers tend to come out in droves when the weather is nice, it is a good idea to reserve your time as far in advance as possible. Keep in mind that temperatures can be particularly hot from noon to sunset during the summer.

While there are far too many public golf courses in Houston to discuss them all here, a small sampling of the city's publicly accessible golf courses is included below. For a complete list of public golf courses in the area, visit the Web site, Golfersweb, at www.golfersweb.com/golfhous.

HERMANN PARK GOLF COURSE
2155 N. MacGregor St.,
at Almeda Road in Hermann Park
www.houstontx.gov/municipalgolf/hermann
One of the country's first desegregated courses, Hermann Park Golf Course is also one of the city's oldest and most popular courses. In 1997 the course was renovated by golf architect Carlton Gipson, who designed a number of attractive courses around Texas. Hermann Park Golf Course has a gold slope rating of 117 and a gold rating

of 67.9. Like the rest of Hermann Park, the well-manicured course is filled with oak trees that offer small pockets of shade during the heat of the summer. The course's Hermann Park location makes the course easily accessible from the Medical Center, the Museum District, and Rice University. Greens fees here vary depending on the day and time, as well as the age of the golfer. Pricing is fairly inexpensive, though, ranging from $6 for ages 18 and under to $30.63 for adults on Friday, Saturday, Sunday, and weekends. Electric carts and range balls are available for rental.

MEADOWBROOK FARMS GOLF CLUB
23230 Meadowbrook Farms Club Dr., Katy
(281) 693-4653
www.meadowbrookfarmsgolfclub.com
Since opening in 1999, Meadowbrook Farms Golf Club has been widely regarded as one of the best courses in the Houston area. The par-72 course, which plays 7,100 yards, was designed by golf legend Greg Norman. Your shot here will be challenged by a range of trees, creeks, lakes, sodwall bunkers, and white sands. The clubhouse is an attractive ranch house, where guests can dine at a full-service grill. Lessons are available. Greens fees range from $49 to $89, depending on the day and time. Half cart rental is included. The club's popularity makes tee times tough to come by so schedule yours several days or even weeks in advance, if possible. Reservations can be made online or by phone.

MEMORIAL PARK GOLF COURSE
1001 E. Memorial Loop Dr., in Memorial Park
(713) 862-4033
www.memorialparkgolf.com
One of the best-rated municipal golf courses in Texas is located right inside Memorial Park. Since opening in 1923, this 18-hole, 600-acre course has hosted the likes of Jack Nicklaus and Arnold Palmer. Renovations in 1995 gave the course a lighted driving course, putting and chipping greens, a golf museum, and a new clubhouse. A practice range and lessons are available for beginners and more experienced golfers looking to improve their game. The course is open in the evenings. Fees vary and don't include golf carts, which can be rented for $4 (for a pull cart) to $22 for a full 18-hole round. Balls can also be rented for $3 to $7, depending on the number of balls. Visit the Web site or call to find out how much your visit will cost. Tee times can be booked online.

WILDCAT GOLF CLUB
12000 Almeda Rd.,
off the South Sam Houston Tollway
(713) 413-3400
www.wildcatgolfclub.com
Located 10 minutes from downtown in southeast Houston, Wildcat Golf Club offers 36 holes of great golf. The club is home to two courses—the Highlands Course and the Lakes Course. Both offer picturesque views of the downtown skyline, significant elevation changes, and fast greens, but the Lakes Course throws in some water to make things more challenging. There are also four putting greens where guests can practice before teeing off. Greens fees range from $42 to $75 on Friday, Saturday, Sunday, and from $32 to $63 Monday through Thursday, depending on the time of day you tee off. Special rates are also available for seniors and children. Call up to two weeks in advance to schedule your tee time.

WORLD HOUSTON GOLF COURSE
4000 Greens Rd.
(281) 449-8381
www.worldhoustongolf.com
This par-72, 6,700-yard course is one of the oldest courses in town. Golf at this 70.8-rated course and you'll be challenged by 37 bunkers and water on 13 holes. The course has a 119-slope rating from the championship tees. On Wednesday through Saturday, the course's Ranch Grill serves up burgers and sandwiches. Greens fees include golf cart rentals and range from $12 to $34, depending on when you play. Teeing off after 5 p.m. will get you the low end of that scale, while tee times on weekends before noon cost more. Special rates are offered for students and seniors 60 and older. Visit the Web site to book your tee time online.

GYMS/WORKOUT FACILITIES

You don't have to abandon your workout routine when you come to Houston. Here you'll find dozens of gyms and fitness centers—some owned by the city, others private facilities that allow short-term visitors to purchase a day- or sometimes even a week- or monthlong pass. Some even offer free day or week trial memberships, although you should be prepared for endless phone calls encouraging you to up your membership if you opt for a free trial.

Community Fitness Centers

The Houston Parks and Recreation Department runs four fitness centers, as well as more than a dozen smaller community center weight rooms and gymnasiums, around the city. The price of using these gyms varies. Some are free and others charge a day or monthly membership fee that is significantly lower than what private gyms charge. Hours vary and most of the fitness centers have limited weekend hours. All four fitness centers, which require guests to be at least 18 years old, are listed below. Call ahead to find out the schedule of your fitness center of choice.

There are far too many community center weight rooms and gymnasiums to list here but a complete list can be found on the Houston Parks and Recreation Department's Web site (www .houstontx.gov/parks/fitnesscenters.html).

FONDE RECREATION CENTER
110 Sabine, just off Memorial Drive
(713) 226-4466
Fonde Recreation Center is home to well-maintained basketball courts, where amateurs and pros alike come to play pickup games. Don't worry if basketball isn't your sport of choice: The center also features a great weight room, aerobics and tai-chi classes, pickle games for seniors, volleyball and badminton games, and plenty of free activities each month. Not only is the Fonde Recreation Center free to the public, but its downtown location also makes this a convenient place to work out during your lunch break or

before or after work. Call the center for information on upcoming events.

JUDSON ROBINSON, JR., FITNESS CENTER AT HERMANN PARK
2020 Hermann Dr., off Main Street
(713) 284-1997
Maybe you work in the Medical Center or are visiting a friend or family member there. Or maybe you want to work a run around Hermann Park into your workout. Either way, the Judson Robinson, Jr., Fitness Center, located in Hermann Park, is a great place to work out. Here you'll find a full gym and weight room, as well as a racquetball court. A monthly membership costs just $20; alternatively, one-time and infrequent guests can pay $1.50 per half hour for early morning workouts. Use of the racquetball court costs $3 per hour. The center is closed evenings, on Sunday, and is only open until 2 p.m. on Saturday.

MacGREGOR FITNESS CENTER
5225 Calhoun, in MacGregor Park
(713) 747-8650
Located just south of the University of Houston's main campus in MacGregor Park, the MacGregor Fitness Center is home to a fully loaded weight room. A little cardio can be added to your workout with a pickup game in the covered, full-court basketball pavilion or a run on the 1.25-mile jogging trail located in the park. There are even tennis courts available next door at the Homer Ford Tennis Center. Use of MacGregor Fitness Center is free; showers and lockers can be used at Homer Ford Tennis Center for 75 cents each. The fitness center is only open on weekdays.

MEMORIAL PARK FITNESS CENTER
6402 Arnot St., off Westcott Street on the eastern border of Memorial Park
(713) 802-1662
If you need even more exercise options than Memorial Park itself offers, pay a visit to the Memorial Park Fitness Center. Here you'll find weights and aerobic machines, such as treadmills, stairmasters, and ellipticals, as well as opportuni-

ties to work with a personal trainer. You can even swim laps at the swim center in the morning during the summer and at select times throughout the year. Call to find out when the pool is available for lap swim. Memorial Park Fitness Center is open daily, although it closes at noon on Sunday. A monthly membership costs $20; daily memberships are available for $1.75.

Private Gyms

In addition to the community centers, Houston is home to many other gym and personal fitness facilities. Chains such as Gold's Gym (www.golds gym.com), Bally's (www.ballyfitness.com), and 24 Hour Fitness (www.24hourfitness.com) all have several locations in and around Houston. Houston also has a number independent health clubs and gyms, many of which cost a little more than the larger chains. These gyms offer a broad range of workout equipment and classes and offer personal training opportunities for an additional cost. A small sampling of some of the most popular independent gyms in town can be found here. See the phone book for more gyms near you.

THE DOWNTOWN CLUB
www.clubcorp.com
340 W. Dallas, at the Met
(713) 652-0700

1100 Caroline St., at the Houston Center
(713) 654-0877
The Downtown Club is the name for three different facilities downtown, two of which have extensive fitness facilities. The Downtown Club at the Met is home to a gym and weight room, group fitness classes, and courts for squash, basketball, tennis, and racquetball. The Downtown Club at the Houston Center offers a gym and weight room, basketball and racquetball courts, and group classes. Both also have a dining room and snack bar. Visit the Web site to get a free trial membership, which can be used to work out at both locations.

FIT ATHLETIC CLUB
1532 W. Gray St. at Waugh Street
(713) 782-9348
www.fithouston.com
Located between River Oaks and downtown, FIT Athletic Club is a popular place to socialize and work out. In addition to a state-of-the-art gym with great personal trainers, FIT offers a variety of classes in yoga, pilates, martial arts, cardio and conditioning, and cycling. Guests can prolong their visit with a trip to FIT's cafe, which offers healthy meals, snacks, coffee, comfortable couches, and Wi-Fi access. FIT offers a free three-day pass for first-time visitors.

MEMORIAL ATHLETIC CLUB
14690 Memorial Dr.
(281) 497-7570
www.fitmac.com
Workout possibilities are endless at the Memorial Athletic Club, where you'll find racquetball and basketball courts, a weight room, and a cardiovascular center with treadmills, ellipticals, bicycles, and stairmasters galore. Yoga, pilates, and spinning classes are offered in two aerobics studios; there's a jogging trail outside and two heated pools—one indoor and one out. Memorial Athletic Club also offers ballet, tumbling, jazz, and a variety of other fitness and conditioning classes for kids. In addition to its main campus, Memorial Athletic Club has a sister club called **MAC for Women,** located just down the street at 14520 Memorial Dr. This second location offers nursery care for babies while mothers take pilates classes and work out in the gym. Call MAC for Women for more information (281-558-6691). Membership here does not require a contract.

TIMBERLINE FITNESS
3939 Montrose Blvd.
(713) 523-7007
www.timberlinefitness.com
One of the pricier gyms in Houston, Timberline Fitness is a popular place to enlist the fitness aid of a personal trainer. Guests at this Montrose-area gym can also work out solo or take pilates, yoga, or martial arts classes. Timberline even offers a

boot camp program for those who need some extra discipline to get in shape. Trial memberships are available.

HUNTING

Hunting is a popular pastime in Texas, with thousands of people tracking deer, hogs, doves, turkeys, and other fowl each year. The Texas Parks and Wildlife Department requires all hunters to have a hunting license. The fees for hunting licenses vary, depending on the license type, of which there are dozens. General hunting licenses for Texas residents run $23, while general hunting licenses for nonresidents cost $300. Licenses can be purchased at sporting goods stores, bait and tackle stores, and even many grocery stores and department stores. Alternatively you can purchase a license by calling the Texas Parks and Wildlife Department at (800) 895-4248 or visiting the Web site (www.tpwd.state.tx.us), where you can also find a comprehensive list of different license fees and hunting regulations. Beware, though: Purchasing your license online or by phone may result in a $5 convenience charge.

There's very little government-owned land open for public hunting in Texas, so if you want to hunt, you'll most likely need to find some privately owned land. One option is to ask ranch- or land-owning friends or family to let you hunt on their property. If you don't know anyone with such land, you can get what's known as a deer lease. That is, you can find a landowner in the area who will let you hunt on their land for a certain period for a fee that they set. Area deer leases can be found by visiting one of the local REI stores, which feature maps, ads, and other information about available deer leases. Houston has two REI locations—one in west Houston at 7538 Westheimer Rd. (713-353-2582) and the other in northwest Houston across from Willowbrook Mall at 17717 Tomball Pkwy. (832-237-8833).

Gear and equipment can be purchased at REI, Academy, Gander Mountain, or the Bass Pro Shop in Katy. Many of these stores have several locations in Houston, so check the yellow pages to find the store nearest you.

> **ℹ** Check out the *Houston Chronicle*'s Texas Hunting and Fishing page online (www.chron.com/sports/texashuntingand fishing) to find the forecast for the upcoming hunting and fishing seasons, tips on good hunting and fishing spots, and what gear to use and where to buy or rent it.

ROCK CLIMBING

If you're into extreme sports or preparing for a challenging hike, consider visiting one of Houston's two publicly accessible indoor rock-climbing gyms—**Stone Moves Indoor Rock Climbing** and **Texas Rock Gym.** The faux boulders at both of these first-class facilities will challenge you mentally as you maneuver your body and figure out where to put your hands and feet. Employees at the rock-climbing gyms can spot you and hold the other end of your rope during your climb, but it's more fun to bring along a buddy to help you out. Each facility also offers lessons to give you the skills necessary to be a better climber both at the gym and on real mountains. First-time climbers, rest assured: Both rock gyms emphasize safety and employees will—literally—show you the ropes beforehand and help you out on the ground throughout the climb. In fact, Texas Rock Gym requires all first-time visitors to take a 15- to 20-minute ClimbSafe beginner's class for $7.50. There's no minimum age to rock climb at either location, but parents are required to sign a liability waiver for children under 18. For information on taking kids rock climbing in Houston, see page 184 of the "Kidstuff" chapter.

Be sure you bring a pair of sturdy, tight-fitting tennis shoes or be prepared to pay a little extra to rent a pair at the gym. Also keep in mind that the required harness can't be worn with skirts or dresses. Rock climbing can be a little pricey but a day pass is good for an entire day, even if you leave for lunch and come back. A day pass at Texas Rock Gym is $12.50. That doesn't include the requisite harness, which can be rented for an additional $3.70. Climbing shoes can be rented for $5.54. A day pass at Stone Moves costs $12.

Harness rental costs $2, and shoe rental costs $3. Below are the addresses, Web sites, and phone numbers for Stone Moves and Texas Rock Gym.

STONE MOVES INDOOR ROCK CLIMBING

6970 FM 1960 Rd. West, in northwest Houston, east of Highway 249/Tomball Parkway
(281) 397-0830
www.stonemoves.com

TEXAS ROCK GYM

1526 Campbell Rd.,
off I-10 between Westview and Longpoint
(713) 973-7625
www.texasrockgym.com

RUNNING

Whether you're a leisurely jogger or training for a marathon, Houston is a great place to run. All of the city's parks include runner-friendly trails. Marathoners and distance runners may find the long-running trails at **Terry Hershey Park** particularly useful, and short-distance race runners will find the 0.25-mile concrete asphalt timing track at **Memorial Park** a good place to practice their speed. See the "Parks" chapter for additional information on these training sites as well as additional running trails around Houston.

Throughout the year, several races, as well as one of the country's best marathons, are held in Houston. Learn more about the Chevron Houston Marathon and associated races, as well as the annual Park to Park Run from Discovery Green to Hermann Park, in the "Annual Events" chapter.

i Like to run races or need some moral support to maintain your running routine? Check out the Houston Area Road Runners Association's Web site (www.harra .org), which includes a great list of upcoming races, as well as daily group runs around the city.

SKATING

If you love to skate, you've come to the right city. Houston is filled with tons of skating opportunities for skaters of all stripes—fast or slow, indoors or out, ice or concrete, flat surfaces or in skate parks.

Several skating rinks and ice-skating rinks are located around the city. In addition to being fun places to take skating lessons or skate with friends, family, or a date, most ice-skating rinks also have ice-hockey teams that are open to the public. See the "Kidstuff" chapter for information about local roller-skating and ice-skating rinks.

Women ages 21 and up who prefer to skate competitively off the ice can try out for one of the city's four roller-derby teams—the HaRD Knocks, the Bayou City Bosse$, the Burlesque Brawlers, and the Psych Ward Sirens. Those who want a little more practice before trying out or who want something a little more laid-back can join the Houston Roller Derby Rec League, which practices every Tuesday evening at the Dairy Ashford Roller Rink and occasionally holds scrimmages against the four roller-derby teams. Visit the Houston Roller Derby Web site (www .houstonrollerderby.com) for more information.

Skating opportunities also abound on the trails at Houston's many parks, which are listed in the "Parks" chapter. If you want more of a challenge or want to avoid the bikers and runners, try one of Houston's seven public skate parks. Each of these parks caters to skateboarders, as well as in-line and old-school roller-skaters, with skate ramps and kicker benches, grind boxes, grindrails, and curbs. The names and addresses of Houston's skate parks are listed below. The new Lee & Joe Jamail Skatepark is the city's first in-ground skate park; the other six are above ground. All of the parks listed here are free to the public. Additional information on the individual parks, including special events and competition information, is available online at the City of Houston's Skate Parks page (www.houstontx .gov/parks/skateparks.html).

Central Houston

LEE & JOE JAMAIL SKATEPARK

103 Sabine St., in Buffalo Bayou Park/Eleanor Tinsley Park (just east of downtown)
(713) 222-5500

East Houston

CLIFF TUTTLE PARK

6200 Lyons, just off I-10

CLINTON SKATE PARK

200 Mississippi St., in Clinton Park, just east of Loop 610

EASTWOOD SKATE PARK

5020 Harrisburg, in Eastwood Park

Northeast Houston

DYLAN DUNCAN SKATE PARK

3950 Rustic Woods

Northwest Houston

WATONGA SKATE PARK

4100 Watonga Blvd. off West 43rd Street

TENNIS

Houston is home to dozens of tennis courts. Many are located inside member-only country clubs, schools, or neighborhood parks that restrict court access to residents. However the Houston Parks and Recreation Department owns three tennis centers—including one at Memorial Park, which you can learn more about in the "Parks" chapter. In total these three tennis centers offer 60 courts for public use at no cost. All of these outdoor courts are lighted, and shower and locker use is available for a small fee. Each of these tennis centers has a pro shop and offers tennis lessons, leagues, and tournaments for a relatively low fee. Call the appropriate center's pro shop to sign up for lessons or find out about upcoming events.

In addition to these three tennis centers, the Houston Parks and Recreation Department manages 145 publicly accessible tennis courts in some 78 neighborhood parks around Houston. It is impossible to list all of these tennis courts in this space, so only the three main tennis centers are given below. For a list of courts in neighborhood parks, call the Houston Parks and Recreation Department's tennis office (713-803-1112) or go online to www.houstontx.gov/parks/tennis .html. Additional courts can be found in neighborhood parks in the suburbs, such as Pasadena and more centrally located independent cities, such as Bellaire. If you live in one of these areas, contact your city to find out where the nearest neighborhood park with a tennis court is. A list of the phone numbers and Web sites of other cities in the area can be found in the "Area Overview" chapter.

HOMER FORD TENNIS CENTER (16 COURTS)

5225 Calhoun, in MacGregor Park in southeast Houston
(713) 842-3460

LEE LECLEAR (26 COURTS)

9506 S. Gessner Dr., inside Braeburn Glen Park in southwest Houston
(713) 272-3697

MEMORIAL PARK TENNIS CENTER (18 COURTS)

1500 Memorial Loop, in Memorial Park, just off the Seymour Lieberman Exercise Trail
(713) 867-0440

ℹ Learn about additional courts and clubs—private and public—and leagues around town by calling the Houston Tennis Association (281-580-8313) or visiting their Web site (www.houston tennis.org), which is an excellent resource for information and news about amateur tennis activities around the city.

WATER ACTIVITIES

There are plenty of opportunities for water sports, such as fishing, boating, waterskiing, surfing, Jet-Skiing, and kayaking around the Houston area. While there aren't a lot of opportunities to boat or enjoy other activities that require waves within the city limits, there are miles of water to do just this within an hour's drive of the city. Additional lakes and beach destinations are located within just a couple of hours of Houston, but in the interest of space, only the closest and most popular ones are included here.

The Texas Parks and Wildlife Department regulates fishing and boating in the area. Here's what that means for you: The department requires everyone 17 or older who wants to fish in public water to get a fishing license. A license is not required, however, if you're fishing at a Texas state park, such as Brazos Bend State Park, which you can learn more about in the "Parks" chapter. Fishing license pricing varies depending on whether you want to fish in freshwater or salt water. Residents pay $28 to fish in freshwater and $33 to fish in salt water, while nonresidents pay $55 to fish in freshwater and $60 to fish in salt water. Combination licenses that permit fishing in freshwater and salt water, as well as fishing and hunting license combo packages, are also available. Licenses can be purchased at dozens of locations around Houston, including sporting goods stores, gun shops, bait and tackle shops, and even grocery stores. They can also be purchased by calling (800) 895-4248 or visiting the Texas Parks and Wildlife Department Web site (www.tpwd.state.tx.us), although this may incur a $5 processing charge. The department also limits the number and size of fish you may take out of Texas waters; these numbers vary based on location and fish type. Visit the Texas Parks and Wildlife Department Web site to review these regulations before your trip if you're thinking about taking home more than a few fish.

Aspiring boaters under the age of 18 must take a boater education course before operating any kind of personal watercraft, any vessel over 10 horsepower, or a sailboat over 14 feet. Basic education courses start at $13. Additional information about boating education and requirements for buying and selling boats is available on the Texas Parks and Wildlife Department Web site (www.tpwd.state.tx.us) or by calling (800) 792-1112.

Be sure to wear a life vest and practice water safety when you participate in water activities in and around Houston. Water can rise quickly, especially in lower-lying areas south of Houston and in Buffalo Bayou, so check the weather before you head out. It's not unusual for Houston days to start out sunny before abruptly turning stormy. Also make sure someone on land knows you are on the water, just in case conditions get rough.

Gear for water activities can be rented at smaller vendors on the roads to the parks and bodies of water listed here, as well as at the sporting goods stores mentioned in the "Shopping" chapter. Additional shops can be found in the yellow pages or by contacting the appropriate visitor bureau (listed below). If you're in Houston in January, also be sure to visit the Houston International Boat, Sport & Travel Show at Reliant Center. More details on this widely attended boating extravaganza are included in the "Annual Events" chapter.

Below are some of the most popular spots for water activities in and around Houston. Most of these spots don't charge for entry, but you must bring your own gear and, in some cases, pay for parking.

BRAZOS BEND STATE PARK
21901 FM 762, Needville
(979) 553-5102
www.tpwd.state.tx.us
Located about 30 miles southwest of Houston in Needville, Brazos Bend State Park offers plenty of fishing opportunities, although boats are prohibited. This 5,000-acre park runs along the Brazos River and has three lakes for fishing—Hale, New Horseshoe, and Forty Acre. There's also a fishing

pier at Hale Lake, and New Horseshoe offers shoreline fishing. Among the fish you'll find here are largemouth bass, catfish, crappie, sunfish, and carp. You don't need a license to fish at this state park, but you will have to pay general admission, which costs $5 for visitors 13 and older. Kids 12 and under get in free. Information about additional activities at the park can be found in the "Parks" chapter.

BUFFALO BAYOU
Various locations around Houston
www.buffalobayou.org

Running through Houston from Katy to the Houston Ship Channel, Buffalo Bayou is a fun place to kayak, canoe, or fish without leaving the city. Some people fish at Buffalo Bayou Park, George Bush Park, or one of the other parks along Buffalo Bayou. In addition to plenty of mosquito fish, you'll find catfish, as well as the occasional eel and bass here.

Two of the easiest spots to launch a canoe or kayak along Buffalo Bayou are located in Buffalo Bayou Park, near downtown. See the Buffalo Bayou Park write-up in the "Parks" chapter for more information on kayaking and canoeing there. If you haven't gone canoeing or kayaking in the Bayou before, you might find it helpful to take a guided morning kayak tour through the Buffalo Bayou Partnership. Trips are offered monthly and cost $60, which includes all of the equipment you'll need, as well as a shuttle ride and guided tour. Reservations are required. Learn more or sign up by calling the Buffalo Bayou Partnership at (713) 752-0314.

CLEAR LAKE/BAY AREA
South of Houston off I-45

Nicknamed the "Boating Capital of Texas," Clear Lake is the shining star of the Bay Area, which sits just south of Houston along Galveston Bay. This breezy inlet spans 2,000 acres and includes more than 9,000 marina slips, making it the country's third-largest basin for recreational boating. Visitors don't just come here to kick back in their

boats and yachts, though. The Bay Area is also a popular spot for rowing, Jet-Skiing, waterskiing, and fishing. Fingerling channel catfish are among the most popular fish here; there are also a fair number of largemouth bass.

i Visit the Bay Area Houston Visitors Bureau online (www.visitbayarea houston.com) or call (800) 844-5253 for a list of companies that provide boat rentals and fishing tours in the Bay Area Houston.

GALVESTON ISLAND
South of Houston off I-45

Galveston Island, located about an hour south of downtown, sits right on the Gulf of Mexico, making it a popular destination for lying on the beach, frolicking in the water, and water activities spanning boating to fishing to surfing. Since the destruction of Hurricane Ike in 2008, many parts of the island are in disrepair and have been closed. Still, the city has worked hard to restore and maintain the beaches, and opportunities for water activities here are still abundant. Although some parts of the beaches are closed off to guests at private resorts and to residents of beachfront neighborhoods, most of the beach here is open to the public. Several beachfront parks charge a modest admission in exchange for the opportunity to use shower and bathroom facilities, as well as picnic areas just off the beach. The city permits surfing at several beaches, including those west of 91st Street, between the 17th Street and 21st Street rock groins, between the west edge of the Flagship Pier (25th Street) and 29th Street rock groins, and between the 29th Street and 53rd Street rock groins. Surfboards are available for rental at many shops on Seawall Boulevard, the main street running along the beach. If you're looking to fish, head out to any of the jetties along the beachfront or visit one of the city's commercial fishing piers—Seawolf Park Fishing Pier, the Galveston Fishing Pier, or the 61st Street Fishing Pier. Parking is available on Seawall Boulevard and other streets in Galveston. Watch the weather before visiting Galveston; tides can rise quickly here, making the rock groins and jetties dangerous places to be. Visit Galveston.com & Company online at www.galveston.com or call the Galveston Island Visitors Center at (888) 425-4753 for additional information on renting gear or finding the best spot for your water activities of choice.

LAKE CONROE
North of Houston off I-45

Lake Conroe, a human-made reservoir completed in 1973, offers 157 miles of shoreline. In addition to being one of Texas's most popular boating destinations, this lake is a great place to go Jet-Skiing, waterskiing, sailing, and windsurfing. The best spots for sailing and windsurfing tend to be near the southern portion of Lake Conroe—the side closest to Houston—since winds tend to be heavier here. Lake Conroe is also a popular place to go fishing. Channel catfish and bluegill are particularly abundant.

i Head online to www.lakeconroe.com to learn about everything you need to know about recreation at Lake Conroe. The site is filled with information about upcoming events, as well as the best places to sail, fish, water-ski, and kayak—and buy or rent the equipment you need to do these things.

LAKE HOUSTON
25 miles northeast of downtown, east of US 59

Lake Houston sits on the San Jacinto River, about 25 miles northeast of downtown. Impounded in 1954, this human-made lake spans nearly 12,000 acres. Many people come here to go boating and fishing. The lake is stocked with fish common to the area—predominately largemouth bass, white bass, white crappie, blue catfish, and bluegill. There are also opportunities to kayak, canoe,

camp, and hike on the north side of the lake in Lake Houston Wilderness Park, a city-owned and operated park that is discussed in more detail in the "Parks" chapter. If you plan to boat here, take note: It is not currently possible to enter the lake with your boat from the park.

YOGA STUDIOS

Yogis can breathe easily: There are plenty of opportunities to practice yoga in Houston. In addition to yoga classes offered at many local gyms, there are many studios around the city. Most studios offer classes early in the morning and in the evening on weekdays, as well as at various times on weekends. Individual classes or week-, month-, or yearlong passes are available for purchase. Below are some of Houston's best yoga studios:

BIKRAM YOGA COLLEGE OF INDIA— HOUSTON
www.bikramyogahouston.com
1854 Fountainview, Galleria area
(713) 781-5333

2438 S. Blvd., Rice Village/West University
(713) 664-5333
The only Bikram-certified studio in the Houston area, this studio offers hot yoga classes at two central locations.

JOY YOGA CENTER
4500 Washington Ave., the Heights
713-868-9642
www.joyyogacenter.com
Vinyasa classes are primarily taught here. Joy Yoga Center also offers pilates, yoga for runners, and a Yoga for Singles class, where students strike some poses before mixing and mingling.

TEJAS YOGA
3930 Kirby Dr.
(713) 807-7018
www.houstonyoga.com
Tejas Yoga teaches ashtanga classes primarily in

the Mysore style. Beginners can also take basic ashtanga classes in the Led Primary Series.

YOGA ANANDA
1822 W. Alabama
(713) 527-8280
www.yogaananda.com
Maximize the benefits of yoga here, where you can choose from Power Hour classes for the busy yogi and Power Vinyasa Flow classes taught in the Baptiste Power Flow style.

YOGA ONE STUDIOS
3030 Travis St., in Midtown
(713) 522-0876
www.yogaonehouston.com

Get your fill of yoga variety at Yoga One Studios, which offers hot, hatha, and vinyasa yoga, as well as a belly dancing class. They even offer rock 'n' roll yoga and partner yoga classes a few times a year.

YOUR BODY CENTER
3605 Katy Fwy., at Heights Boulevard
(713) 874-0800
www.yourbodycenter.com
Variety rules at Your Body Center, which offers classes in pilates, beginner and intermediate yoga, pre- and postnatal yoga, hatha, and a variety of hot yoga classes—including hot belly dancing. It also offers several different kinds of massages for everyone from athletes to couples.

SPECTATOR SPORTS

Sports are a serious business in Houston—so serious, in fact, that the city opened three new sports stadiums between 2000 and 2003. These state-of-the-art facilities immediately won national recognition, with the NFL choosing Houston's new Reliant Stadium as the site of the 2004 Super Bowl, the MLB choosing Minute Maid Park as the site of its 2004 All-Star Game, and the NBA tapping the Toyota Center to host its 2006 All-Star Game.

Although these big events have come and gone, Houstonians still find plenty to cheer about. In addition to professional football, baseball, basketball, soccer, and hockey teams, Houston is home to horse, greyhound, and drag racing tracks and countless NCAA Division I events at Rice University and the University of Houston. The city also hosts annual sporting events, such as the annual Chevron Marathon, Texas Bowl, Shell Houston Open golf tournament, and the US Men's Clay Court Championships. Like sports fans just about anywhere, Houstonians have had their share of heartache, but championships won by the Rockets, Dynamo, Aeros, and Rice Owls (baseball) have given fans a few tastes of glory—and a yearning for more—in recent years.

Tickets for most local sports events are sold through Ticketmaster (www.ticketmaster.com or 800-745-3000) and on-site; exceptions are accordingly noted below. The ticket prices listed here do not include convenience charges, which can add an extra $7 or $8 to the price of a ticket. Keep in mind that prices included here are also based on 2009 rates; many teams and sites increase ticket prices marginally every year or two. Almost all of the stadiums and sites listed in this section are located within Houston city limits; exceptions are noted in address lines and descriptions where applicable.

Parking at local sporting events can be tricky. Some events have little to no on-site parking, and just about every team or event charges an additional fee for parking. In the case of Houston Texans football, this parking fee must be paid when you purchase your tickets. Each event and team listed here includes detailed parking information. Be sure to read it closely to avoid any unnecessary parking headaches.

Price Code

$ . . . . under $15
$$ . . . . $15 to $35
$$$ . . . . over $35

BASEBALL

HOUSTON ASTROS BASEBALL   **$–$$$**
Minute Maid Park
501 Crawford, between Texas Avenue and
Congress Street
(877) 927-8767
www.astros.com

Minute Maid Park is the new home of the Houston Astros, who played on Astroturf under the closed domed roof of the Astrodome for nearly 35 years. The move has served the team and its fans fairly well, though it's hard to say whether credit is due to Minute Maid Park's real grass and retractable roof, the stadium's downtown location, or big-name players like Roger Clemens, Andy Pettitte, Lance Berkman, Roy Oswalt, and Jeff Bagwell. More than three million fans came out to cheer on the 'Stros during the 2000 season—their first at Minute Maid Park—and the team made their first trip to the World Series in

2005, before being swept by the Chicago White Sox. The Astros have lost some of their biggest-name—and controversial—players since then, but Minute Maid Park still tends to be the loudest place downtown when the team plays at home. Among the team's biggest fans is former president George H. W. Bush, who can often be spotted cheering on the team from his seat behind home plate.

The ballpark, which was named Enron Field before the Houston-based energy company filed for bankruptcy in 2001, is almost as much of an attraction as the Astros themselves. Nicknamed the Juice Box, Minute Maid Park was once the site of Houston's Union Station, which comprises the stadium's main entrance. Every time the Astros score a run or win a game, a full-size vintage train runs across 800 feet of track atop a wall on the stadium's left-field side. One of Minute Maid's most modern features is the World's Largest Sliding Glass Door. This 50,000-square-foot wall of hurricane-resistant glass spans across left field to make Minute Maid feel like an outdoor stadium even when the "door" is closed.

Hourlong tours of Minute Maid Park offer a close-up look at the press boxes, luxury suites, Union Station, the Astros' dugout, and other spots around the stadium. Tour tickets cost $9 for adults, $7 for seniors 65 and up, and $5 for children 3 to 14. Visit the team Web site for tour dates and times.

Located 1 block west of US 59, Minute Maid Park sits on the east side of downtown, just a few blocks northeast of the George R. Brown Convention Center and the Toyota Center. Minute Maid Park is bordered by Congress Avenue on the north, Texas Avenue on the South, Crawford Street on the west, and Hamilton Street on the east.

i If you attend a game on a Thursday, buy a ticket in section 434 and pay $35 for an All You Can Eat ticket, which allows you and the rest of your party to scarf up all of the peanuts, hot dogs, popcorn, nachos, and soda you can pack in your belly.

The stadium does not have its own parking garage, but paid parking lots and garages—not to mention the occasional open spot on the street—line the area. You can also take the METRORail, which stops on Main Street, 6 blocks from the ballpark.

The Astros play 81 home games from April through September. If the team makes the playoffs, their season extends into October. Tickets range from about $7 on the outfield deck to $52 in the dugout boxes and club level. Kids 3 to 14 can sit in the outfield deck for just a dollar.

i Don't ask your chauffeur to meet you along Texas Avenue near Crawford after the game. This area is closed to traffic for 20 minutes after every game, so plan to get picked up a few blocks away or along Jackson Street on the south side of Minute Maid Park.

BASKETBALL

HOUSTON ROCKETS BASKETBALL $$–$$$
Toyota Center
1510 Polk St.
(877) 622-7625
www.rockets.com

The Houston Rockets don't have quite the following that the Texans and Astros do, but that has far more to do with Houstonians' affinity for football and baseball than with the team's success. The team is the first of the city's major sports franchises to win a national championship—two, in fact—and one of the few to go to the playoffs nearly every year. In 1994 and 1995 Hall of Famer Hakeem Olajuwon led the Rockets to win back-to-back titles. The road to both championships was bumpy and involved rallying back from deep holes in multiple playoff series, so when the Rockets finally won, Houston—known for its sports teams' tendency to choke under pressure—earned the nickname "Clutch City." The Rockets underwent some growing pains in subsequent years, which included a move from the Compaq Center (now a megachurch) to the

Toyota Center in 2003. But Rockets owner Les Alexander has continued to stock the team with some of the best (and biggest) players around. This high caliber of players makes for thrilling—if at times frustrating—visits to the Toyota Center and have guaranteed many trips to the playoffs. In early 2008 the team's 22-game winning streak won the hearts of even the most fair-weather Houstonians.

Basketball may be the main attraction at Rockets games, but the organization also packs in some of the city's best halftime and time-out entertainment. Clutch the Bear, the team's mascot, energizes the fans with humorous signs, stunts, motorcycle rides, or by running around the arena and hamming it up with the kids. Helping out Clutch are the scantily clad Rockets Power Dancers, as well as the 22 tumblers, break dancers, and jump ropers who comprise the Launch Crew. Another popular time-out diversion is the Kiss Camera, which scans the arena for couples and tries to get them to kiss for the camera and, by extension, the jumbotron.

With all of the food at the Toyota Center provided by Levy Restaurants, dining options beat those of the city's other stadiums. Food options range from Chinese to Mexican to salad to smoked meats to huge sandwiches and burgers and then some. The Toyota Center is located downtown, just a couple blocks east of US 59 at the intersection of LaBranch and Polk Streets. It holds 18,300 fans during basketball games. Tickets range from about $15 on the upper level to $350 for seats at center court on the lower level. Courtside seats are priced in the thousands. Many games sell out, but visitors and fans who want to get in on the action can still get tickets by visiting Flash Seats (http://rockets.flashseats.com). On this Rockets-sanctioned Web site, season ticket holders set a price for their tickets or sell them eBay-auction style. Buyers don't have to worry about fraudulent tickets or getting the tickets in time either. Flash Seats' electronic system transfers tickets digitally so you can just swipe your credit card or license at the game.

Limited parking is available in the seven-level Toyota Tundra Garage next door to the Toyota Center for $15. There are plenty of cheaper parking options, though: Several garages within a few blocks of the stadium offer parking for less than $10 for many games. When the Rockets play big-time opponents, though, parking lots and garages around the stadium tend to bump up prices to as much as $25. Regardless of who is playing, free parking can typically be found on the street within just 5 or 6 blocks of the Toyota Center.

The Rockets' season lasts from October through April, although it can extend into May or June if the team makes it deep into the playoffs.

i Arrive at the Toyota Center at least 30 minutes before tip-off to score free giveaways at designated games. The free Rockets loot is usually only given to the first 5,000 fans, so you've got to beat the crowd.

COLLEGE SPORTS

RICE UNIVERSITY $–$$
(713) 522-6957
(713) 522-OWLS
http://riceowls.cstv.com

Rice University has 13 NCAA Division I teams, but by far the most successful of those is the baseball team. When the Rice Owls won the College World Series in 2003, they became the smallest school in 51 years to win a national championship at baseball's highest collegiate level. Since then, the team has continued to make appearances in the tournament, where the Owls finished third in 2006 and 2007.

The school's women's teams also fare pretty well, with the volleyball, soccer, tennis, and basketball teams advancing to their respective NCAA tournaments in the last few years. After a 45-year dry spell, Rice's football team played in bowl games in 2006 and 2008.

Close-up

Red Rowdies

After the Rockets ended the 2005–2006 season with a 15–26 home record, the team's coach, Jeff Van Gundy, knew something needed to be done to energize the crowd and help restore the home-court advantage. Borrowing a page from the San Antonio Spurs' "Baseline Bums," Van Gundy decided to round up the loudest, most rowdy Rockets fans. The team held auditions to find the greatest fans. Van Gundy bought season tickets for the 30 most impressive—that is, loud and colorful to the point of annoying—fans to sit behind the basket closest to the Rockets bench. The Red Rowdies were so loud during the preseason that player Tracy McGrady bought tickets for 20 more Red Rowdies. The move paid off. During the 2006–2007 season, the Rockets went 28–13 at home.

Van Gundy is no longer the Rockets' coach, but the Red Rowdies live on, with auditions for new Rowdies held each fall. Thirty minutes before each home game, the Rowdies gather at the Toyota Center's LaBranch entrance for their noisy ROMP. The Rowdies attend games clad in Rockets red and scream chants for each player on the team. They rarely sit down, which can be annoying for other fans in their section hoping to see and/or sit. But for those looking to be in the heart of the action, section 114 is the place to be.

The Owls compete in Conference USA, a conference that also counts crosstown rival University of Houston (UH) among its members. Games and meets against UH—as well as against Texas A&M and the University of Texas at Austin—always draw large crowds. Tickets for these events are in high-demand and cost $1 to $3 more than tickets to other games.

Rice's teams play at a variety of facilities around campus, including Reckling Park (baseball), Rice Stadium (football), Tudor Fieldhouse (basketball), Jake Hess Tennis Stadium, and Rice Track/Soccer Stadium.

Baseball tickets range from $7 for adult general admission ($5 for children) on up to $17 for adults who want to sit in rows one and two ($7 for kids who sit in those rows). Tickets for men's basketball range from $12 behind the backcourt to $18 for upper seats along the sidelines. Tickets for other events—including games against Rice's Texas rivals—are also pretty cheap. Tickets to all Rice sporting events can be purchased on the school's Web site, by phone, or at the ticket office, which is in Tudor Fieldhouse at 6100 Main St.

The campus is located across the street from Hermann Park and just a few blocks north of the Texas Medical Center. It is bounded by

Main Street, Sunset Boulevard, Rice Boulevard, Greenbriar Street, and University Boulevard. Free public parking for Rice athletic events is available in West Lot 4, accessible from University Boulevard, located between Greenbriar and Main Streets. Adjacent lots are also opened for football games.

UNIVERSITY OF HOUSTON $
(713) 462-6647 (box office)
http://uhcougars.cstv.com

With 16 intercollegiate teams, the University of Houston (UH) is almost always hosting some sort of sporting event. Although the school's football and basketball teams have the largest following, events in nearly every sport see big turnouts, thanks to a large alumni base and the school's winning tradition. The University of Houston Cougars teams play in the NCAA Division I's Conference USA. UH's teams have won an impressive 33 conference titles since the conference formed in 1995. The Cougars have also won 17 NCAA team titles—16 of them in golf—and 55 NCAA individual championships and played in 17 bowl games and five men's Final Four games. This success can be attributed at least partly to the caliber of athletes the school recruits and produces. Among the UH alumni are NBA Hall of Famers (and former Houston Rockets) Hakeem Olajuwon and Clyde Drexler, track and field star Carl Lewis, former Dallas Cowboys coach Tom Landry, golfer Fred Couples, and Heisman Trophy–winner Andre Ware.

The UH football team plays at Robertson Stadium. The men's and women's basketball teams play at Hofheinz Pavilion and the baseball team plays at Cougar Field. All of these facilities are located on the UH campus, about 3 miles southeast of downtown at the intersection of I-45 and Texas Spur 5.

Ticket prices vary by sport and season, but they generally cost $15 or less. UH students get in to all regular season sporting events for free. Men's basketball and baseball tickets range from $10 for general admission to $15 for reserved seats; tickets to women's basketball games are $10 for reserved seats and $5 for general admission. Children can attend basketball games for $5 and baseball games for $7. Tickets for all Cougars sporting events can be purchased on the university's Web site, by phone, or at the ticket office on the first floor of the Athletics/Alumni Center, which is next door to Hofheinz Pavilion. Parking is available in $5 and $10 lots around campus.

FOOTBALL

HOUSTON TEXANS FOOTBALL $–$$$
Reliant Stadium
1 Reliant Park, inner loop of the southern
portion of Loop 610 between Kirby Street
and Fannin Street
(866) 468-3926
(866) GO-TEXANS
www.houstontexans.com
When owner Bud Adams whisked the Houston Oilers—the city's first NFL franchise—off to Tennessee in 1997, Houston football fans were deprived of a team of their own for five long, agonizing seasons. In 2002 the city finally got a new team and a new stadium, complete with a retractable roof that's open on sunny days when the temperature is between 50 and 80 degrees

Fahrenheit. Located just north of the South Loop near the intersection of Kirby Street and McNee, Reliant Stadium sits in Reliant Park, right next door to the Astrodome, the closed-domed stadium that the Oilers called home.

Since the arrival of the new team, Houston football fans have been making up for lost time and then some. In their first seven seasons, the Texans sold out every single game—Houston's longest sellout streak in any professional sport. Just about everyone comes to Reliant Stadium clad in red or navy (the team's colors) and ready to cheer. Many of the 71,500 fans tailgate outside the stadium beginning as many as four hours before kickoff. Not surprisingly Reliant Stadium can be a tough place for the Texans' opponents to play; in recent years the Texans have won the vast majority of their home games.

The cheapest seats run about $30 and can be found in the Gridiron Terrace at the end zone near the roof. The priciest seats—more than $130—can be found in the Directors Club, located on the end zones at field level, and in the Verizon Wireless Club, an exclusive sideline club featuring live music, bars, and fancy food. With games selling out quickly, it's best to buy tickets early. Otherwise, you may have to cough up some extra dough to buy tickets on the resale site StubHub.com.

Ticket holders with prepaid parking passes can park in the Miller Lite Parking Lots. There's no cash parking on-site, so be sure to purchase a parking pass when you buy your tickets. If you don't have a parking pass, you will have to take a cab, bus, or the METRORail to the game. The METRORail stops at Reliant Park every 12 minutes on game day. Train tickets cost just $1 each way.

i **Visit the Texans' Web site or watch the sports segment of the local news before the game to find out if the roof will be open. If it will, be sure to grab sunglasses and a sweatshirt or sweater for the game. The stadium can get chilly for fans sitting in shaded areas and sunny for fans sitting in more open areas.**

TEXAS BOWL $$–$$$

Reliant Stadium
1 Reliant Park, inner loop of the southern
portion of Loop 610 between Kirby Street
and Fannin Street
www.texasbowl.org

At the end of each December, college football fans flock to Reliant Stadium for the Texas Bowl, an NCAA Division I bowl game that features teams from the Big 12, Big East, and Conference USA, as well as the Mountain West division's Texas Christian University. For bowl games held between 2006 and 2009, the Big East Conference and Conference USA made alternating appearances, based on an agreement with the Texas Bowl. The Texas Bowl was first held in 2006 to replace the now-defunct Houston Bowl, which the city hosted from 2000 to 2005.

Although the Texas Bowl lacks the pomp and prestige of, say, the Rose Bowl, it is quickly becoming a Houston tradition. In 2007 and 2008 the game drew nearly 60,000 fans. This family-friendly event kicks off with TexFest, a pregame carnival featuring horseshoes, tailgate competitions, washers, and food in the Reliant Stadium parking lot. And no matter who wins the game, there's always a big fireworks show—dubbed the "Largest Holiday Fireworks Show in Texas" by the Texas Bowl—after the game. Individual tickets range from $15 to $75, and ticket packages that include food and souvenirs range from about $25 per person for families on up to $2,000 for groups of 100. Cash parking is available at the stadium for $20 to $30. See the Houston Texans listing above for directions and METRORail information.

GOLF

SHELL HOUSTON OPEN $$–$$$

Redstone Golf Club
5860 Wilson Rd., Humble
(281) 454-7000
www.shellhoustonopen.com

Since 1946, Houston has hosted the Shell Houston Open, a regular tournament on the PGA Tour. The event has moved around town over the years, and today it is played at Redstone Golf Club, located just outside of Houston in Humble. The tournament always draws some of the biggest names in golf, although much to locals' chagrin, Tiger Woods has been a perennial no-show for scheduling reasons. That's his loss, though. The Shell Houston Open is highly competitive, with recent winners including Fred Couples, Stuart Appleby, and Vijay Singh.

The six-day tournament is held in April. Tickets can be purchased (or, if necessary, reissued or transferred) and printed through the Shell Houston Open Web site. General admission costs $20 early in the tournament and increases to $25 for the final rounds. Better views are available by purchasing Champions Pavilion tickets for $40. If you want to see the entire tournament, purchase a "6 Pack"—tickets to the entire event—for $100 (general admission) or $150 (Champions Pavilion). Kids under 13 get in free, as long as they show up with a paying adult. Redstone Golf Club is located just south of North Beltway 8 East, which intersects with US 59, just north of the city. Free parking is available on-site on Monday, Tuesday, and Wednesday. On Thursday, Friday, and Saturday, guests can park in the Parking Cents Lot at George Bush Intercontinental Airport for $5 and take a free shuttle to and from the tournament. The Parking Cents lot is located on JFK Boulevard (the main road to the airport) at Greens Road.

GREYHOUND RACING

GULF GREYHOUND PARK $

1000 FM 2004, La Marque
(409) 986-9500
www.gulfgreyhound.com

The world's largest greyhound racing park can be found just 30 miles south of Houston at Gulf Greyhound Park. More than 10 million people have come to this four-level, air-conditioned park to cheer (and bet) on the dogs since Gulf Greyhound opened in 1992. Fans haven't done half bad either; together, they've won more than $1.4 billion. In addition to the traditional win, place, and show wagers, the track offers daily double, pick three, trifecta, exacta, $1 superfecta, and a slew of other wager options. The park features both live racing events and simulcasts of races held around the world.

Many guests enjoy the dining opportunities at Gulf Greyhound Park almost as much as they love the gambling. The Terrace Clubhouse on the park's second level offers visitors the chance to dine on fried Gulf shrimp, steak, salads, and desserts while watching the greyhounds race around the quarter-mile sand composition track below. Those in the mood for something more akin to fast food can take advantage of the concession stands on the park's first and second floors.

The park seats 6,600 but standing-room-only admission is available, enabling the park to hold up to 14,000 people. Races are held year-round. Those held Thursday through Saturday evenings start at 7:00 p.m. On Wednesday, Saturday, and Sunday, the park holds matinee races. Wednesday matinees begin at noon; weekend matinees start at 1:30 p.m. The doors open one hour before all races.

Tickets are only sold on-site. General admission costs $2, and clubhouse admission costs $3. General parking is free.

To get to Gulf Greyhound Park from Houston, take I-45 South, then take exit 15. The park is 1 block west of the highway.

i Call in advance to make reservations for the Terrace Clubhouse at Gulf Greyhound Park. Otherwise, your best dining option at the park may be a concession-stand hotdog.

HOCKEY

HOUSTON AEROS HOCKEY $-$$$
Toyota Center
1510 Polk St.
(713) 974-7825
www.aeros.com
Named after the city's successful 1970s World Hockey Association franchise, the Aeros debuted in 1994 as an International Hockey League (IHL) franchise. Today that IHL—at least the rendition that brought the Aeros to town—is no longer

around, so the Aeros play in the American Hockey League as the primary developmental affiliate for the National Hockey League's Minnesota Wild. Despite the league change, the Aeros have maintained a winning tradition that began during the IHL days. In 1999 the team won the IHL Turner Cup and the Aeros continue to make the playoffs just about every year.

The team plays at the Toyota Center, having followed the Rockets there from the Compaq Center in 2003. From Chinese food to pizza to roast beef sandwiches and salad, the team's new home is full of food options that make Aeros games a popular destination for a night out, with or without the kids. The stadium can hold about 17,000 hockey fans, but games don't typically sell out. Tickets range from about $14 for seats behind the goal on the upper level to $61 for seats along the sideline on the lower level. The Aeros' season runs from October to April. Check out the Rockets listing in this chapter for information on parking around the Toyota Center.

i If you're a hockey nut with time to spare, head out to Sugar Land Ice & Sports Center to watch the team practice throughout the season. The arena is located at 16225 Lexington Blvd. in Sugar Land, about 25 miles from downtown off of US 59. Visit the Web site (www.sugarlandice.com) or call (281-265-7465) to find out when the team will be practicing next.

HORSE RACING

SAM HOUSTON RACE PARK $-$$
7575 N. Sam Houston Pkwy. West
(281) 807-8760
www.shrp.com
Dedicated and first-time betters alike get their fix at Sam Houston Race Park, which hosts live thoroughbred races, as well as simulcasts of races held around the world. Each thoroughbred event features 10 races a night. This, combined with the park's alluring dinner options, makes the park a popular evening destination. Dinner options

include a Texas-size buffet filled with carving stations, pasta and vegetable dishes, and a chocolate-fountain dessert bar that will make any chocoholic swoon. On evenings when there isn't a race, the park often holds outdoor concerts featuring country, rock, and classic-rock musicians.

A special park rewards system woos visitors to keep coming back. Participants in this free program earn points each time they wager a bet. Rewards include free admission to the park for simulcast races, monthly contests, food offers, and, for the biggest gamblers, flat-screen TVs, and iPods.

With general admission starting at just $4 and kids 12 and under getting in for free, Sam Houston Race Park is a popular spot for weekend family entertainment. Packages including dinner start at $35 per person. Tickets for all Sam Houston Race Park events are sold online at www.theshowgrounds.com. You can also order tickets by calling the park or heading to the ticket window when you arrive. Parking ranges from $5 for general parking to $10 for premium parking. Valet parking is also offered for $8.

The park is located in northwest Houston, just off the North Sam Houston Tollway at Fairbanks North Houston Road. Significant damage from Hurricane Ike forced the park to cancel its 2008–2009 live racing season, but it reopened for the 2009–2010 season. Live thoroughbred races take place from November through April on Thursday, Friday, Saturday, and Sunday nights. Races start at 7:00 p.m. on Thursday, Friday, and Saturday and at 5:00 p.m. on Sunday. The gates open at 10:30 a.m. on days when there are simulcasts.

MOTORSPORTS

HOUSTON RACEWAY PARK $–$$$
2525 FM 565, Baytown
(281) 383-7223
www.houstonracewaypark.com
Home to a quarter-mile drag strip and a new 3/8-mile dirt oval track, Houston Raceway Park hosts drag racing events. The park holds 30,000 spectators. Masses of spectators come out for the National Hot Rod Association's prestigious

O'Reilly Spring Nationals, which are held—you guessed it—each spring. Between the hot rods and the thousands of fans who show up to cheer and jeer, the park can get pretty noisy. But for those who love drag racing, the park—whose paved pit area holds about 400 pacing rigs—is a great place to get in on the action.

The park's name is somewhat deceiving: Houston Raceway Park isn't actually located in the city; it lies about 30 miles east of downtown Houston in Baytown. To reach the park, take I-10 East and exit at FM 565, going north.

Events are held year-round. Prices vary depending on the event, but tickets start at about $10 for most events and go up to nearly $60 for O'Reilly Spring Nationals. Parking prices also vary depending on the event, with rates running about $5 for smaller events and closer to $20 for big events like O'Reilly Spring Nationals.

RUNNING

CHEVRON HOUSTON MARATHON $–$$
(FREE TO WATCH)
George R. Brown Convention Center
1001 Avenida de las Americas, just off of US
59 between Polk Avenue and Texas Street
(713) 957-3453
www.houstonmarathon.com
On a designated Sunday each January, more than 200,000 people—both runners and spectators—come out for Houston's largest single-day sporting event: the prestigious Houston Marathon. Although the 26.2-mile marathon is the day's biggest draw, the Chevron-sponsored marathon is just one of three races held that day. There is also a half marathon sponsored by the petroleum company Aramco and a 5K run sponsored by El Paso Corporation. Participants in all three races are encouraged to help raise money for more than 40 charities through the Run for a Reason program, and most take this option seriously. In 2008 the three races' combined 25,000 participants raised $1.25 million for charity.

On the day of the marathon, about 200,000 spectators cheer on the runners along their path, which begins downtown near Minute Maid Park and weaves through the Heights before heading down to Rice Village, west to the Galleria and Memorial area, and swinging back downtown by way of Memorial Park and Buffalo Bayou Park. All three races end with festivities (and plenty of water) at the George R. Brown Convention Center, where family and friends meet up with their favorite runners in the Reunion Area in Hall C. During the races, big groups of spectators can be found around White Oak Drive in the Heights, along University Boulevard in West University Place, along Post Oak and San Felipe, and along Memorial Park. Find out approximately when the marathoners will be heading through your neighborhood by visiting the marathon Web site. Friends and family can sign up to receive text messages to find out their favorite runner's progress throughout the marathon and half marathon.

Although the marathon is best known for its Sunday races, marathon weekend actually kicks off one day earlier, on Saturday. That's when Texas Children's Hospital sponsors a 3K kids' fun run (and walk), which covers part of the marathon course and wraps up at the official Chevron Houston Marathon finish line. About 5,000 local youth ranging from 5 to 15 participate in the event, which also features a 1K adaptive run and walk for children with special needs.

Registration for the marathon and half marathon is capped at a combined total of 18,000 runners. Spaces typically fill up more than six months before the race, so sign up as early as possible if you want to run. There is not currently a cap on 5K participants, although a large number of participants may cause the organizers to prohibit additional sign-ups during marathon weekend. Registration for all three marathon-day races opens on the Web site in July. Prices change each year and by event, so check the Web site for the most up-to-date registration pricing information. Parents can register their children to run in the Saturday kids' fun run online for $10 in the fall or at the George R. Brown Convention Center on race day for $15.

SOCCER

HOUSTON DYNAMO SOCCER $–$$
Robertson Stadium
3875 Holman St., between Cullen Boulevard and Scott Street
(713) 276-7500
www.houstondynamo.com

The Houston Dynamo may be the newest team in town, but they're already one of the most successful. In their first two seasons—2006 and 2007—the Dynamo won the Major League Soccer Cup Championship. Of course, it didn't hurt that the team—which was previously known as the San Jose Earthquakes—had won two championships in their old hometown. When it moved to Texas, the Dynamo was originally going to be renamed Houston 1836 as a tribute to the city's founding year. But the local Mexican community took issue with the name since 1836 is also the year that Texas separated from Mexico. So the franchise settled on Dynamo, a name that pays homage to Houston's energy sector and two previous Houston soccer teams, both named the Dynamos.

The season's biggest draws are games against the other Major League Soccer (MLS) team from Texas, FC Dallas. The series of games the two play each season have been nicknamed the Texas Derby, or El Capitán Clasico. The team that wins the most games in the series is awarded a Civil War–era cannon called El Capitán. Unfortunately city regulations prohibit the Dynamo from firing the cannon in Houston. In addition to competing against other MLS teams, the Dynamo plays a number of international soccer teams each year.

The team plays at Robertson Stadium on the University of Houston campus, about 1.5 miles southeast of I-45 (exit 44B) between Cullen Boulevard and Scott Street. Tickets range from about $20 for seats on the end zone to $74 for seats in the Club VIP section on the sideline or in the lower level seating area, rows A through L. The stadium seats 32,000, and although many matches fill close to capacity, they don't typically sell out.

i Leave your umbrella at home even for games played on rainy days. The Dynamo's hard-core security staff will confiscate it, so you're better off showing some team spirit with a bright orange poncho or a raincoat.

TENNIS

US MEN'S CLAY COURT CHAMPIONSHIPS   **$$–$$$**
River Oaks Country Club
1600 River Oaks Blvd.
(713) 783-1620
www.mensclaycourt.com
In early April the River Oaks Country Club hosts the US Men's Clay Court Championships, the last remaining Association of Tennis Professionals (ATP) tournament to be played on a clay court. The highly competitive championships have fea-tured established tennis pros like Andy Roddick and Andre Agassi, as well as up-and-coming players. The tournament lasts a week, with matches held twice a day.

Tickets are sold on the tournament Web site; marked-up tickets can be purchased on StubHub.com. Prices increase as the tournament progresses; tickets to the earliest matches start at $20, and prices rise to $60 for the Finals. A Champ Pass Ticket, which includes admission to all of the matches from the Quarters through the Finals, is available for $150.

Parking can usually be found on the side streets off of River Oaks Boulevard. At night and on weekends, tournament parking is available at Mirabeau B. Lamar High School, located at 3325 Westheimer Rd., between Westheimer and West Alabama and between Buffalo Speedway and Kirby. A free shuttle takes spectators from the school to and from River Oaks Country Club.

ANNUAL EVENTS

When it comes to special events, Houston's got plenty of them. In fact, hundreds of events are held in Houston year after year. The nature of these events are as diverse as the people of Houston themselves: There are car and boat shows, air shows, a marathon and other races, art events, cultural heritage celebrations, holiday events, food festivals, music festivals, shopping extravaganzas, and the world's largest livestock show and rodeo. New events are cropping up each year.

Unfortunately it would take several volumes to list all of the events that take place inside and just outside the city each year. So this chapter offers a sampling of some of the city's largest annual happenings, as well as a few quirky ones. With a few exceptions, the events listed here are held in Houston. A good number are held at downtown venues such as Discovery Green, the George R. Brown Convention Center, and Sam Houston Park; many others are held in Hermann Park or Reliant Park. A few events require venturing outside the city limits; these have been included because they draw so many people from Houston and the surrounding areas.

Almost all the events listed here are family friendly, and many have special activities for children. Additional events that are specifically geared toward children can be found in the "Kidstuff" chapter.

Some events, such as the Ice at Discovery Green, begin in one month and end in another. These have been listed under the month in which they begin. Likewise, a Hanukkah event is listed in December, even though the holiday (and, by association, the event) occasionally falls at the end of November.

A good number of the events listed here are free, and all of them are open to the public. Most charge an admission fee—typically under $15—and proceeds often benefit area charities. The fees listed here are based on 2008 and 2009 event prices, so keep in mind that prices could be slightly higher if you attend in subsequent years. There are almost always discounts for children; some events offer discounts for students and guests 65 or older as well. In most cases tickets can be purchased on-site. Events that require an advance ticket purchase have been flagged as such in the descriptions that follow. Typically admission fees do not include food or other activities. It's a good idea to bring along some extra cash for admission and incidentals since many events and participating vendors don't accept credit cards. Many events, especially those downtown and at Reliant Park, have little to no free parking. Make sure you have cash on hand to pay for parking, as you'll be required to pay when you enter the parking lot or garage at many venues.

Events listed here are wheelchair accessible unless indicated otherwise. It's a good idea to call ahead and double-check, though, as some events change venues or accessibility offerings.

The contact information provided here is for the event organizers. With a couple of noted exceptions, street addresses are those of the event location.

JANUARY

CHEVRON HOUSTON MARATHON

Pre- and postrace festivities held at
George R. Brown Convention Center
1001 Avenida de las Americas, just off of US
59 between Polk Avenue and Texas Street
(713) 957-3453
www.houstonmarathon.com

Each January more than 200,000 people—both runners and spectators—come out for Houston's largest single-day sporting event: the prestigious Houston Marathon, which is always held on a Sunday. Although the 26.2-mile marathon is the day's biggest draw, the Chevron-sponsored marathon is just one of three races held that day. There is also a half marathon sponsored by the petroleum company Aramco and a 5K run sponsored by El Paso Corporation. About 200,000 spectators cheer on the runners along their path, which begins downtown near Minute Maid Park and weaves through the Heights before heading down to Rice Village, west to the Galleria and Memorial area, and swinging back downtown by way of Memorial Park and Buffalo Bayou Park. All three races end with festivities (and plenty of water) at the George R. Brown Convention Center, where family and friends can meet up with their favorite runners in the Reunion Area in Hall C. Some of the largest spectator groups can be found around White Oak Drive in the Heights, along University Boulevard in West University Place, along Post Oak and San Felipe, and at Memorial Park. Find out approximately what time the marathoners will be heading through your neighborhood by visiting the marathon Web site. Friends and family can sign up to receive text messages to find out their favorite runner's progress throughout the marathon and half marathon.

Although the marathon is best known for its Sunday races, marathon weekend actually kicks off one day earlier, on Saturday. That's when Texas Children's Hospital sponsors the 3K Kids' Fun Run (and walk), which covers part of the marathon course and wraps up at the official Chevron Houston Marathon finish line. About 5,000 local youth ranging from 5 to 15 participate in the event, which also features a 1K adaptive run and walk for children with special needs. If you want to run, sign up as early as possible. Registration for the marathon and half marathon is capped at a combined total of 18,000 runners and spaces typically fill up more than six months before the race. Registration for all three marathon-day races opens on the Web site in July. Prices change each year and vary by race, so check the Web site for the most up-to-date registration pricing information. Entry in the Kids' Fun Run 1K and 3K races costs $10 per child for those who register online in the fall or $15 for those who register on race day at the George R. Brown Convention Center.

HOUSTON INTERNATIONAL BOAT, SPORT & TRAVEL SHOW

Reliant Center
1 Reliant Park
(713) 526-6361
www.houstonboatshows.com

Serious boaters and campers flock to the Reliant Center each January and June for the Houston International Boat, Sport & Travel Show, better known as the Boat Show. With just shy of 500 exhibits and more than 150,000 attendees each year, this 10-day event is among the country's largest boat shows. Not only do attendees get a sneak peak at the latest and greatest yachts, sailboats, powerboats, RVs, and camping gear but they also get special discounts. Industry leaders offer seminars on a variety of topics, and special presentations teach boating novices about boating safety and how to buy a boat. When the kids get tired of checking out the boats, they can try their hand at fishing—for live fish—in the Fish-O-Rama competition. Admission is $8 for adults and $4 for kids under 12, and every ticket gets you a one-year subscription to *Boating Life, Salt Water Sportsman, Cruising World,* or *Outdoor Life.*

Cash parking is available at Reliant Park for $8, but you can save money and avoid the crowded parking lot by taking the METRORail. For directions see the write-up on the Houston Texans on page

148 of the "Spectator Sports" chapter; Reliant Center is located just kitty-corner to Reliant Stadium.

i Visit the Boat Show Web site to print a coupon for $2 off admission on designated days.

HOUSTON AUTO SHOW
Reliant Center, on the north side of Loop 610 South between Kirby Drive and Fannin
1 Reliant Park
www.houstonautoshow.com
If you're in the market for a new car or you just like to admire sleek new vehicles, you can get your fix at the Houston Auto Show. This week-long event showcases some of the hottest cars and offers sneak peaks at some cars and trucks of the very near future. During the two weekends of the Auto Show, children's entertainment is available at the Kids Fun Zone, a supervised play area with arts and crafts projects, a giant obstacle course, a Monster Truck Jump, and a 30-foot slide. This isn't free babysitting, though: An adult must accompany every child. The Auto Show is held at Reliant Center at the end of January or the beginning of February. Admission is $10 for adults; kids 12 and under get in free. Park in the Reliant Park parking lots for $8 or take the METRORail to Reliant Park.

i Visit the Auto Show Web site or local car dealerships to get coupons for $2 off admission.

FEBRUARY

PARK TO PARK RUN
(713) 524-5876
www.hermannpark.org
The Hermann Park Conservancy does its part to encourage Houstonians to get fit and love their parks with the Park to Park Run, held each February. The event includes several races—a 5-mile run and wheelchair race, a 2-mile walk for families, and a 1K kids' fun run. The 5-mile race starts downtown at Discovery Green and ends at Hermann Park, where the family and children's races are held. A postrace celebration is held at Hermann Park's Molly Ann Smith Plaza, where participants celebrate their accomplishments with live music and an array of healthy food. Registration is $12 for children and $30 for adults; prospective racers can register online or at the event. Free parking is available at the Toyota Center Tundra Garage, located downtown at Leeland Street and La Branch Street (next door to the Toyota Center). Alternatively, 5-mile racers can park at Hermann Park, then take a free METRORail ride to the downtown Preston Station. For directions to Discovery Green and Hermann Park, see pages 124 and 126 in the "Parks" chapter.

HOUSTON LIVESTOCK SHOW AND RODEO
Reliant Park, on the north side of the South Loop between Kirby Drive and Fannin Street
www.rodeohouston.com
It's been said that everything is bigger in Texas, and that's definitely the case when it comes to the Houston Livestock Show and Rodeo, which is the place to be in late February and much of March. This three-week event kicks off with a three-day barbecue cook-off that begins on the Thursday afternoon before the Houston Livestock Show and Rodeo and wraps up on Saturday. Hundreds of teams compete in the World Championship Bar-B-Que Contest for three days to see who can make the best barbecue ribs, brisket, and chicken. More than 200,000 Houstonians turn out for the cook-off to get a whiff of the barbecue and enjoy free barbecue plates in the Chuck Wagon. Live music performances take place each evening.

Once the cook-off wraps up, the main event begins. The Livestock Show and Rodeo takes over Reliant Park, with daily events held at the Reliant Stadium, Reliant Arena, and Reliant Center. Each night, a different big-name musician—many of them country stars, many not—plays a concert at Reliant Stadium. Tickets aren't always easy to come by so be sure to purchase tickets in advance if there's someone you want to see.

Close-up

Go Texan Day

Since 1954, the Friday before the Houston Livestock Show and Rodeo kicks off—that is, the Friday of the cook-off—has been known as Go Texan Day in Houston. On this day Houstonians get into the rodeo spirit by donning their best (and sometimes, kitschiest) Western getup, including the requisite denim, vest, bolo, cowboy boots and hat, and even spurs. Schools around the city encourage their students to dress up and come ready for rodeo-themed lessons and activities like square dancing. Those attending school or working along the city's major arteries, including Memorial Drive, get an added taste of the Wild West when they look out their windows and see more than 4,000 trail riders in 13 different trail rides coming into town from across Texas, Louisiana, and even Mexico. The trail riders make their way into town along various routes, but they all end up on Memorial Drive until they reach Memorial Park. The trail riders begin entering the park between 10 a.m. and 5 p.m., when the Trail Ride Awards Ceremony is held. The trail riders' arrival certainly makes for some serious traffic throughout much of the day, but against the backdrop of Houston's skyscrapers and freeway system, it is also a sight that shouldn't be missed.

After camping out at Memorial Park for the night, the trail riders rise early Saturday morning to ride the final 5 miles down Memorial Drive to downtown for the official Rodeo Parade. There, dozens of trail riders, stagecoaches, area marching bands, and local dignitaries march the streets of downtown before the trail riders head to Reliant Park for the main event.

Each concert kicks off with some serious rodeo action—roping, riding, and yee-haws included.

Many concertgoers head to Reliant Park early to check out the rest of the Livestock Show and Rodeo, which is about as authentic as they come. At Reliant Center, you'll find milking, spinning and weaving, and cotton gin demonstrations and get an up-close look at the dairy goats, Brahmousin cattle, and Simbrah cattle in between checking out different livestock shows. There's also a daily beef trivia contest, a burger toss, and plenty of beef to sample. A series of educational expos geared toward ranchers takes place each day in Reliant Arena. There's also plenty of rodeo getup and souvenirs to be purchased and food to be eaten at Reliant Center and Reliant Arena each day. Those looking for something a little more sophisticated can also sip wine in the Champion Wine Garden in Carruth Plaza and watch entertainers in the Hideout. Since the Livestock Show and Rodeo celebrates cultural diversity, some of this entertainment celebrates Tejano and black heritage.

Some of the most popular attractions can be found outside, where a Texas-size carnival showcases roller coasters, Ferris wheels, cotton candy, and funnel cake galore. There is also the Kids Country Carnival, which gives kids a taste of life on a farm with pig races, a petting zoo, pony rides, live kid-friendly music, a mechanical bull, and other activities.

Tickets to the barbecue cook-off are $7 for guests 13 and up and $4 for kids ages 3 to 12. Tickets to the carnival, livestock and horse shows, shopping, and food areas cost the same price. If you plan to attend the cook-off and other attractions (concerts excluded) multiple times, consider getting a Houston Livestock Show Season Pass, which costs $25 per person and gets you into the cook-off, carnival, and livestock and horse shows as many times as you want over the rodeo's duration. Tickets to the rodeo concerts are sold through Ticketmaster and can be purchased on the rodeo Web site or by phone. Prices range from $16 for seats high up in the Upper Bowl to $300 for seats in the front row, right behind the bucking chutes. All rodeo concert tickets include admission to Reliant Stadium, Reliant Arena, Reliant Center, and the carnival. Cash parking is available at Reliant Park for $7 during the day on weekdays and for $12 on weekday evenings and weekends.

MARCH

RIVER OAKS GARDEN CLUB AZALEA TRAIL
River Oaks Garden Club Forum of Civics and other locations in the River Oaks area
2503 Westheimer Rd.
(713) 523-2483
www.riveroaksgardenclub.org
Each spring azalea blossoms brighten up Houston neighborhoods with their pink, white, purple, red, and yellow flowers. The River Oaks Garden Club, located in one of the city's most prestigious neighborhoods, celebrates these blooms over three days at the beginning of March with tours of some of the city's most beautiful mansions and azalea-filled gardens. The azalea tours include seven sites, most of which are close to one another, but few of which are within walking distance of one another. Only two of these sites—the River Oaks Garden Club Forum of Civics Building & Gardens and the Bayou Bend Gardens—are wheelchair accessible. Tickets to a single site can be purchased for $5; a ticket for all seven sites can be purchased for $20 during the event or for $15 in advance. Proceeds benefit conservation, horticulture, and beautification efforts around the city. Tickets can be purchased at the River Oaks Garden Club, Randall's, Rice Epicurean grocery stores, the Museum of Fine Arts, Houston, and a number of nurseries around the city. These ticket outlets, as well as the addresses of the seven sites, can be found on the River Oaks Garden Club Web site.

FOTOFEST BIENNIAL
1113 Vine St., Ste. 101 (headquarters)
(713) 223-5522
www.fotofest.org
Held in even-numbered years, the FotoFest Biennial is an internationally acclaimed festival and conference celebrating photography and other image-heavy art. Each year's conference has a different social or aesthetic theme of global relevance. The biennial runs for several weeks from early March to mid-April and features exhibits, a film and video series, a fine print auction, educational workshops, and reviews of participating photographers' and artists' portfolios by curators and critics. The events are held at several venues, including a designated downtown hotel, the Museum of Fine Arts Houston, and Vine Street Studios, which is located downtown at 1113 Vine St. Event prices vary. Visit the Web site or call the FotoFest office for schedule and event pricing information.

BAYOU CITY ART FESTIVAL
March: Memorial Park
October: Downtown around City Hall
www.bayoucityartfestival.com
The semiannual Bayou City Art Festival is regarded as one of the country's best art festivals. More than 300 artists and crafters from around the country participate, and all of them must apply and win the approval of the festival jury. The semiannual festival is held along a 1.1-mile loop in Memorial Park for three days during late March; in mid-October a two-day show is held downtown in front of City Hall around Hermann Square and at Sam Houston Park. In addition to gallery-quality art of all media, both shows feature cooking demonstrations from some of the city's top chefs, food and wine samplings, artist demonstrations, live musical and dance performances, and the Creative Zone, where kids make crafts such as mini art cars and wax hand sculptures. Admission is $10 for guests 12 and up; kids under 12 get in free. All festival profits benefit local charities. Although both festivals are held outdoors, pets aren't allowed.

There is no public parking in Memorial Park for the Bayou City Art Festival. There is, however, a free shuttle that takes guests to and from Northwest Mall (located on Loop 610 North at 18th Street) throughout the three-day event. On Saturday and Sunday, there is free shuttle service between the park and three locations downtown—Memorial Drive at Rusk Street, Smith Street at Capitol Street, and Rusk Street at

Smith Street. Parking information for the October festival can be found in the "October" section of this chapter on page 165.

APRIL

JAPAN FESTIVAL
Japanese Garden at Hermann Park, just west of the Jesse H. Jones Reflection Pool
(713) 963-0121
www.japanfestivalhouston.org
Each April more than 20,000 people head to Hermann Park's serene Japanese Garden for the Japan Festival. This two-day event celebrates Japanese culture—past and present—with traditional Japanese dance performances, food from local Japanese restaurants, martial arts demonstrations, and opportunities to learn about ikebana, origami, calligraphy, and anime. Admission is free, as is parking, which is available in several lots around Hermann Park. Nice weather can make a free parking space tough to come by, though, so take the METRORail to the Rice U/Hermann Park stop if the thought of driving around in search of a parking space stresses you out. For more information on parking in or visiting Hermann Park, see the Hermann Park write-up on page 126 of the "Parks" chapter.

US MEN'S CLAY COURT CHAMPIONSHIPS
River Oaks Country Club
1600 River Oaks Blvd.
(713) 783-1620
www.mensclaycourt.com
In early April the River Oaks Country Club hosts the US Men's Clay Court Championships, the last remaining Association of Tennis Professionals (ATP) tournament to be played on a clay court. The highly competitive championships have featured established tennis pros like Andy Roddick and Andre Agassi, as well as up-and-coming players. The tournament lasts a week, with matches held twice a day.

Tickets are sold on the tournament Web site; marked-up tickets can be purchased on StubHub.com. Prices increase as the tournament progresses; tickets to the earliest matches start at $20, and prices rise to $60 for the Finals. A $150 Champ Pass Ticket will get you into all of the matches from the Quarters through the Finals.

Parking can usually be found on the side streets off of River Oaks Boulevard. At night and on weekends, tournament parking is available at Mirabeau B. Lamar High School, located at 3325 Westheimer, between Westheimer and West Alabama and between Buffalo Speedway and Kirby. A free shuttle takes spectators from the school to and from River Oaks Country Club.

BAYOU CITY CAJUN FEST
7979 North Eldridge Rd.,
accessible from I-10 or 290
(281) 890-5500
www.tradersvillage.com/en/houston
Red beans and rice. Gumbo. Boiled crawfish and fried alligator. Cajun sausage. Boudin. This is the stuff of the Bayou City Cajun Fest, hosted by Traders Village one weekend each April. If the spicy food doesn't give the event a down-home feeling, the live music—fiddles included—and dancing in the rustic Traders Village establishment are sure to do the trick. The event is free to the public. Parking costs $3.

MENU OF MENUS EXTRAVAGANZA
Discovery Green
1500 McKinney St.
(713) 280-2478
www.houstonpress.com/microsites/
menu-of-menus
Each April winos, foodies, and beer lovers flock to the Menu of Menus Extravaganza. The city's alternative newsweekly, the *Houston Press,* hosts this popular one-night event to celebrate Houston's vibrant restaurant industry with food samples from dozens of the city's best restaurants, as well as wine, beer, and spirits tastings. There's also live entertainment, a cash bar, and the opportunity to meet some of the city's most esteemed chefs. Participating restaurants and bars vary from year to year; each year's participants are featured in the *Houston Press*'s free Menu of Menus supple-

ment, which hits newsstands just a couple of days after the event. Attendees can pick up a free copy at the event, though. Previously held at other venues around the city, the Menu of Menus Extravaganza was held downtown at Discovery Green in 2009.

General admission costs $35. For $75 you can get in an hour early to sample signature dishes and gain access to the VIP room, which offers top shelf liquor and pricey bottles of wine. Purchase tickets in advance online, as Menu of Menus tends to sell out. All proceeds benefit local charities. Be sure to bring your ID and leave the kids at home. Because the liquor flows freely here, you must be 21 or older to attend. For information on parking at Discovery Green, see page 124 of the "Parks" chapter.

SHELL HOUSTON OPEN

Redstone Golf Club
5860 Wilson Rd., Humble
(281) 454-7000
www.shellhoustonopen.com

Since 1946, Houston has hosted the Shell Houston Open, a regular tournament on the PGA Tour. The event has moved around town over the years, and today it is played at Redstone Golf Club, located just outside of Houston in Humble. The tournament always draws some of the biggest names in golf, although much to locals' chagrin, Tiger Woods has been a perennial no-show for scheduling reasons. That's his loss, though. The Shell Houston Open is highly competitive, with recent winners including Fred Couples, Stuart Appleby, and Vijay Singh.

The six-day tournament is held in April. Tickets can be purchased (or, if necessary, reissued or transferred) and printed through the Shell Houston Open Web site. General admission costs $20 for early rounds and increases to $25 for the final rounds. Better views are available in the Champions Pavilion, for which admission costs $40. If you want to see the entire tournament, purchase a "6 Pack"—tickets to the entire event—for $100 (general admission) or $150 (Champions Pavilion). Kids under 13 get in free, as long as they show

up with a paying adult. Redstone Golf Club is located just south of North Beltway 8 East, which intersects with US 59, just north of the city. Free parking is available on-site on Monday, Tuesday, and Wednesday. On Thursday, Friday, and Saturday, guests can park in the Parking Cents Lot at George Bush Intercontinental Airport for $5 and take a free shuttle to and from the tournament. The Parking Cents lot is located on JFK Boulevard (the main road to the airport) at Greens Road.

> **i** Pick up a *Spectator's Guide* at the tournament for $3 to get a list of tee times and golfer groupings, as well as restroom and concession stand locations.

HOUSTON INTERNATIONAL FESTIVAL

Downtown Houston in City Hall, Tranquility Park, and Sam Houston Park
(713) 654-8808
www.ifest.org

The Houston International Festival, also known as iFest, celebrates the city's diversity and encourages goodwill with the United States' international trade partners. Each year's festival pays tribute to a different country with interactive exhibits, music, dance performances, fashion shows, cooking demonstrations, and food from the honored country. Many local teachers integrate the honored country into their teaching throughout the year by using a festival-developed curriculum guide and, in April, taking their students on a field trip to iFest.

While the selected country may be the guest of honor, the festival's offerings highlight plenty of other cultures and interests as well. iFest is broken into six entertainment zones, each featuring the music, art, and food of a different region. One zone is always reserved for the honored country. Other zones include Africa and the Caribbean, Texas/Latin America, International, Louisiana, and Jamaica. There's also a Kids Zone, which features a petting zoo, pony rides, inflatable games, a NASA exhibit, and sugary festival treats, such as funnel cakes and candied apples.

Close-up

Cinco de Mayo

Houston's large Latino population makes for lots of Cinco de Mayo celebrations on and around May 5. On that day in 1852, the Mexican army overcame steep odds to defeat the French at the Battle of Puebla. Today that victory is celebrated in different ways at venues and events around the city. On May 5, just about every Tex-Mex restaurant in town has a wait as Houstonians—many of whom aren't quite sure what they're celebrating—line up to enjoy margarita specials and Mexican food galore.

Elsewhere around Houston, several family-friendly events celebrate Latino and Hispanic culture. Exact dates vary, as many venues celebrate Cinco de Mayo on the weekend closest to May 5. Miller Outdoor Theatre in Hermann Park celebrates with an afternoon full of mariachis and musical and dance performances by artists from Mexico. The event is always free. Visit the Miller Outdoor Theatre Web site (www.milleroutdoortheatre.com) for more information.

Traders Village serves up fresh fajitas, margaritas, live music, games, and community service exhibits for adults, and tasty treats and games for little ones. The event is free; on-site parking costs $3. Learn more at the Traders Village Web site (www.tradersvillage.com/en/houston).

Univision, the Spanish radio broadcasting network, sponsors one of the state's largest Cinco de Mayo celebrations downtown at the George R. Brown Convention Center (1001 Avenue of the Americas). The color-filled event features arts and crafts activities, tons of Mexican food, live Latino music, and games for the kids. Learn more by calling (713) 407-1455.

In addition more than 500 jewelry designers, photographers, painters, ceramicists, and other artisans sell their work throughout the iFest area. Some of the best art at the festival can be found along the so-called Fine Arts Avenue, a juried show featuring the work of some of the country's most talented artists.

iFest is held for two consecutive weekends in late April; the first Friday prior to the festival is iFest Preview Day. Held at City Hall, this free event takes place during lunchtime and features an opening ceremony, concerts, and a chance to savor some of the international fare that will be served at the main event.

Admission costs $15 for ages 13 and up. Tickets can be purchased on the festival Web site and at local H-E-B grocery stores. Kids 12 and under get in free. Be sure to purchase coupons for food and drinks at the festival. iFest's food and beverage vendors don't accept cash or credit cards. Coupons are $1.50 each and $10 for sheets of nine.

Parking is available for $7 in the Theater District Parking Garages downtown. The most convenient parking is available in Garage 2 at Rusk Street between Bagby Street and Smith Street and in Garage 3, located behind the City Hall Annex at Bagby Street and Walker Street. See the downtown map on page vii to navigate your way to these garages.

i Visit the iFest Web site a few weeks before the festival to get discounted admission tickets, which are good for any single day of the event.

MAY

ART CAR PARADE
Allen Parkway near downtown, between Taft and Bagby Streets
www.orangeshow.org/artcar.html
On a Saturday in early May, some 250 souped-up cars—airbrushed and decorated in the loudest, most unexpected ways—make Houstonians *ooh*, *ah*, and laugh hysterically. A Toyota Rav4 turned

into a hippopotamus? Check. A car transformed into a loader? Ditto. The parade runs along Allen Parkway from Taft Street to Bagby Street, where the cars turn around to head back to Taft. There's no fee to stand along Allen Parkway and watch.

Even better views are available at the VIPit Party, which is held at the Heritage Society at 1100 Bagby St. The party starts a couple of hours before the parade and runs until the parade is over. Tickets cost $125 in exchange for one of the city's best views of the parade, drinks, and food from some of the Houston's best restaurants. VIPit Party tickets help offset the costs of the parade and can be printed from the Web site.

For a sneak peak of the cars, head downtown to Discovery Green (discussed on page 124 of the "Parks" chapter) on the Friday evening before the parade. This free event also features live music and Art Car movies.

i **Make your own wacky art—er, trophies—for the Art Car Parade winners by volunteering for the free Art Car Trophy Workshop, held in mid-April. Find out the date and sign up on the parade Web site. You can also make your own mini art car at the Bayou City Art Festival in March (page 158).**

JUNE

HOUSTON PRIDE FESTIVAL AND PARADE
Montrose
(713) 529-6979
www.pridehouston.org

The Houston Pride Festival and Parade features Houston's gay, lesbian, bisexual, and transgender communities and supporters. Held on the fourth Saturday in June, the event takes place in Montrose, a district with a strong gay and lesbian

i **Check out more art cars year-round at the ArtCar Museum (www.artcar museum.com), which features some of its own art cars, as well as other unusual contemporary art. The museum is located in the Heights at 140 Heights Blvd. Admission is free.**

community. The celebration begins with the festival, which is broken down into several sections. The Festival Latino section features traditional Latin cuisine and music—rock, salsa, pop, and traditional Latin tunes—from Houston's southern neighbors. The Gender Block shares information and exhibits geared toward transgender individuals, while Community Street offers lots of food options, crafts, and the main stage. Art exhibits—including crafts, sculptures, and other work available for sale—fill the artSpace section. There are also two kid-friendly areas: Kids Zone is home to inflatable bouncers, face painting, balloons, and snacks, and the Family Retreat is an alcohol-free section featuring live, family-friendly music.

In the evening the festival ends and the Southwest's biggest pride parade begins. Each year's parade has a different theme and participants vie for awards in categories such as Ruby Slipper (best walking), Stonewall (best social commentary), and Pink Diamond (best float for a for-profit). The community selects the parade's grand marshal through online voting. The parade runs through Montrose on Westheimer Road between Dunlavy and Crocker Streets. Limited parking is available on side streets near the parade route.

Admission to both the parade and festival is free.

i **In the weeks and months leading up to the festival and parade, Pride Houston hosts several events, including a wine tasting, Houston Pride Idol (a takeoff on _American Idol_), and a song-and-dance production. Learn more about these events by visiting the festival Web site.**

JULY

FREEDOM OVER TEXAS
Eleanor Tinsley Park at Buffalo Bayou on Allen Parkway, just west of downtown
www.houstontx.gov/july4

There are plenty of ways to celebrate the Fourth of July in Houston but the "official" celebration—that is, the one sponsored by the mayor's

(Q) Close-up

Juneteenth

President Abraham Lincoln issued the Emancipation Proclamation in September 1862, but it wasn't until June 19, 1865—more than two years later—that Texans first learned that the slaves were free. Since 1980, Juneteenth, as that historic day is now called, has been an official state holiday in Texas. Although offices do not close, some employees use a floating holiday to take the day off. Twenty-eight other states have subsequently made June 19 a holiday, but no state celebrates Juneteenth quite like Texas does.

Celebrations of black culture and freedom take place throughout the Houston metropolitan area and Galveston—the first Texas city to learn of the Emancipation Proclamation. Many churches hold special events, as do civic centers in some of the outlying areas. Some events are held on June 19; others take place on the days before or after.

Among the largest Juneteenth celebrations is the Freedom Parade in downtown Houston. The colorful parade is accented by boisterous music. Some parade participants also seek to remind onlookers that racism isn't dead by passing out flyers and carrying banners about the impact of war and the death penalty on the African-American community. The parade begins at Texas and Hamilton Streets. Learn more at www.june19thtexas.com or by calling (713) 901-4863.

Another big Juneteenth event is held downtown at Discovery Green: The Houston Juneteenth Multicultural Health Festival (www.houstonhealthfestival.org) seeks to raise public awareness about health problems faced by blacks, Latinos, and Asian Americans. To promote good health, the one-day festival offers free health screenings and immunizations, exhibits, and a conference. There's also a "Real Men Cook" competition, a Guinness World Record Couples Salsa Dance, fitness demonstrations, and live music. Admission is free. More information is available online at www.houstonhealthfestival.org.

One of the best celebrations in town is A Gulf Coast Juneteenth, sponsored by the Houston Institute for Culture. Held at Hermann Park's Miller Outdoor Theatre, this evening event showcases soul, blues, jazz, rock, and gospel music by some of today's most-talented black musicians. A Gulf Coast Juneteenth is free, and parking is available around Hermann Park, although you may have to drive around to find a space. Learn more by visiting www.houston culture.org/juneteenth or www.milleroutdoortheatre.com, or by calling (713) 521-3686.

office—is the Freedom Over Texas. On Fourth of July afternoon, thousands of Houstonians begin staking out their spots in Eleanor Tinsley Park at Buffalo Bayou and laying out their blankets and lawn chairs to watch about four hours of musical performances by pop, Latin, country, oldies, and classic-rock artists. The festival also includes rides, games, and food booths. After the sun goes down, the sky lights up with a magnificent 20-minute fireworks show that can be seen around much of the city.

Admission to Freedom Over Texas costs $8 at the gate. Kids under 10 get in free.

Food, drink, and game vendors only accept special event coupons as payment. Packs of nine coupons can be purchased for $10. The city closes off many streets around the park on the day of Freedom Over Texas, so close parking can be tough to come by. A better bet is to park in one of the Theater District parking garages downtown. The most convenient one is Garage 2, located along Rusk Street between Bagby and Smith Streets. See the downtown map on page vii. To avoid significant congestion on your drive to the event, listen to the local traffic on 740 AM, or watch one of the local TV stations beforehand to find out which streets have been closed off.

i Since the fireworks are the main event and the heat can be intense in July, crowds don't usually start to show up for Freedom Over Texas until about 5:30 or 6 p.m.—two hours after the gates open. Find a better parking spot—and seating area—by lathering on the sunscreen, bringing a bottle of water and a deck of cards, and showing up early.

FOURTH OF JULY AT MILLER OUTDOOR THEATRE

Miller Outdoor Theatre in Hermann Park
(713) 284-8350
www.milleroutdoortheatre.com

If you like a great symphony, great fireworks, and money in your wallet, Miller Outdoor Theatre might be more your Fourth of July scene than Eleanor Tinsley Park. Each year the Hermann Park–based theater and the Houston Symphony—along with thousands of Houstonians sitting outside on blankets and lawn chairs—celebrate Independence Day with a night of all-American tunes. Among the highlights are the symphony's rousing performance of Tchaikovsky's *1812 Overture* and a 16-cannon salute. The patriotic evening wraps up with a vibrant fireworks display. Admission is free. Refreshments and drinks are available for purchase, but it's even more fun to pack a picnic and eat under the stars while listening to the music. Sit near the top of the hill and you might even get a glimpse of the Freedom Over Texas display at Eleanor Tinsley Park. See the Hermann Park write-up on page 126 of the "Parks" chapter for parking information.

i If you want to avoid the traffic but refuse to take the METRORail to the Fourth of July at Miller Outdoor Theatre celebration, start walking to your car as soon as the cannons go off. You'll still be able to see the fireworks display, but won't have to stare at the taillights of the car in front of you for a half hour.

ARTHOUSTON
Various locations
(713) 522-9116
www.arthouston.com

Each July nearly 40 Houston galleries participate in ArtHouston. During this one-day event, participating galleries launch new exhibits showcasing the work of up-and-coming regional artists and established artists from around the world. The selected works span a variety of media, including painting, sculpture, drawing, photography, and mixed media. Many of the galleries celebrate with evening receptions the night of—or the night prior to—ArtHouston. Unfortunately not all of the participating galleries are within walking distance of one another, but many are clustered in the Museum District, the Heights, or along Gallery Row in Upper Kirby. All of the exhibits are free to the public. Visit the ArtHouston Web site for a map of participating galleries.

AUGUST

HOUSTON INTERNATIONAL JAZZ FESTIVAL
Discovery Green
1500 McKinney St.
(713) 839-7000
www.jazzeducation.org

The rest of the country celebrates Jazz Month in April, but Houston holds off until August, when the Houston International Jazz Festival is held downtown at Discovery Green. Jazz may have originated in the United States but as the festival demonstrates, people around the world make and play jazz music. This three-day event showcases international jazz musicians, who hail from several continents. Be sure to bring a blanket to sit on, sunscreen, and sunglasses.

Tickets can be purchased in advance for $20 through Ticketmaster or at the gate for $25. Proceeds benefit Jazz Education, a local organization that promotes music education in schools. Information on parking around Discovery Green can be found on page 124 of the "Parks" chapter.

HOUSTON SHAKESPEARE FESTIVAL

Miller Outdoor Theatre at Hermann Park
100 Concert Dr., just south of the Houston
Museum of Natural Science
(281) 373-3386
www.houstonfestivalscompany.com

A perennial summer favorite, the Houston Shakespeare Festival takes place at Miller Outdoor Theatre in Hermann Park during the first part of August. Two different Shakespeare plays are performed every summer; each play is performed multiple nights to accommodate the thousands of Houstonians who flock to the festival, each year. A good number of these folks get their first exposure to Shakespeare through the festival, and many are repeat guests, some of whom bring along a picnic dinner to eat before or during the performance. Bring blankets to sit on, as the grass can be moist. The festival is free. See page 126 of the "Parks" chapter for information about parking around Hermann Park.

SEPTEMBER

QFEST

Museum of Fine Arts Houston
1001 Bissonnet St.
www.q-fest.org

One of the city's most popular gay, lesbian, bisexual, and transgendered cultural events takes place in late September. Previously known as the Houston Gay and Lesbian International Film Festival, the annual event was renamed QFest in 2007 to reflect the festival's commitment not just to film, but also to art and music. Still the festival is best known for showcasing full-length movies and shorts promoting sexual diversity and the work of LGBT and female filmmakers. Films are typically screened at the Museum of Fine Arts Houston. Tickets cost $10 per movie for adults. Museum members and guests 65 and older get in for $8. Tickets can be purchased through the QFest Web site or at the museum. For parking information, see the Museum of Fine Arts Houston write-up on page 101 of the "Museums" chapter.

OCTOBER

BAYOU CITY ART FESTIVAL

March: Memorial Park
October: Downtown in front of City Hall and along Walker, Bagby, and McKinney Streets
www.bayoucityartfestival.com

The semiannual Bayou City Art Festival is regarded as one of the country's best art festivals. More than 300 artists and crafters from around the country participate, and all of them must apply and win the approval of the festival jury. The semiannual festival is held along a 1.1-mile loop in Memorial Park for three days during late March; in mid-October, a two-day show is held downtown in front of City Hall around Hermann Square and at Sam Houston Park. In addition to gallery-quality art of all media, both shows feature cooking demonstrations from some of the city's top chefs, food and wine samplings, artist demonstrations, live musical and dance performances, and the Creative Zone, where kids make crafts such as mini art cars and wax hand sculptures. Admission is $10 for guests 12 and up; kids under 12 get in free. All festival profits benefit local charities. Although both festivals are held outdoors, pets aren't allowed.

Parking for the Bayou City Art Festival downtown in October is available in the Theater District Parking Garages 2 (Rusk Street at Bagby Street), 3 (Walker Street at Bagby Street), and 5 (Capitol Street at Smith Street). Look at the downtown map on page vii to see exactly where these garages are located. All-day parking costs $7.

THE ORIGINAL GREEK FESTIVAL

Annunciation Greek Orthodox Cathedral
3511 Yoakum Blvd., 1 block east of Montrose
between Harold and Kipling Streets
(713) 526-5377
www.greekfestival.org

It's all Greek to Houston for four days at the beginning of October. That is when the Annunciation Greek Orthodox Cathedral complex holds the Original Greek Festival—not to be confused with the smaller Greek festival held in Clear Lake in May. Highlights include cathedral tours, Greek folk dancing, and the Athenian Playground, where children play and enjoy crafts and other activities. Perhaps the biggest draws of all are the souvlaki, Greek salad, gyros, and other Greek food and pastries made by the cathedral's parishioners using generations-old recipes.

Admission costs $5; kids 12 and under get in free. Food isn't included in the price of admission. However, some advance planning and $18 will get you a presale ticket, which includes admission and a dinner plate. Visit the cathedral in advance or call to order presale tickets.

There is no parking at the complex, although limited parking can be found along the street. Just be sure to watch for the No Parking signs that are put up around the area for the event. Your safest bet is to park at Mirabeau B. Lamar High School, located at 3325 Westheimer, between Westheimer and West Alabama and between Buffalo Speedway and Kirby, and take the free shuttle to the cathedral.

HOUSTON WOMEN'S MUSIC FESTIVAL
Jones Plaza
601 Louisiana St., at Texas Avenue
www.hwfestival.org
Since 1995, the Houston Women's Music Festival has celebrated the artistic contributions of independent female musicians from the Gulf Coast region. Hosted by the Athena Art Project, this daylong event features performances by about 10 solo artists and groups, as well as wine tastings, art displays, and food. Although the festival is usually held in October, it sometimes takes place in September. About 1,000 people—mostly women—attend each year. The event is held outside at Jones Plaza, so it tends to be hot and humid. Tickets cost $15 in advance and $20 at the door and parking is available for $7 in the Theater District Parking Garage in front of Jones Hall. Use entrance 4 on Texas Avenue or entrance 7 on Capitol Street.

TEXAS RENAISSANCE FESTIVAL
21778 FM 1774, Plantersville
(800) 458-3435
www.texrenfest.com
Take a trip back to 16th-century England with a visit to the Texas Renaissance Festival. Held for seven weekends in October and November, the festival features all things Renaissance: music, cuisine, games, rides, and dancing. There are even gardens designed to look like those of King Henry VIII and the English queen of fairies. Everyone working at the festival dresses as if it were the 1500s, which makes glassblowing, blacksmithing, metal forging, and broom making demonstrations, among others, seem all the more authentic.

The festival is held in Plantersville, about 55 miles northwest of downtown. That is a bit of a drive, but it's worth every mile if you've got children. Visit the Web site for detailed directions from numerous points in the Houston area.

Tickets can be purchased at the gate for $23 for adults and $11 for children 5 to 12. Children four and under get in free. Weekend passes cost $32 for guests of all ages. Save several dollars by purchasing tickets in advance by phone, on the festival Web site, or at local H-E-B and Randall's stores.

i Extend your stay and celebration at the Texas Renaissance Festival by camping on-site beneath the trees. There's no air-conditioning, water, or restrooms but there is a Quickie Mart for all of your 21st-century snack food needs. Camping on-site costs $10 per vehicle with the purchase of a festival ticket.

WINGS OVER HOUSTON AIR SHOW
Ellington Airport, located just southeast of the Sam Houston Tollway/Beltway 8 at FM 1959 and TX 3/Old Galveston Road
(713) 266-4492
www.wingsoverhouston.com
At the end of October, the U.S. Air Force Thunderbirds and Blue Angels put on a one-of-a-kind

show. During this weekend-long event, planes swoop up and down like acrobats, fly in formations, and pull off some cheer-worthy landings. The show is put on at Ellington Airport (formerly Ellington Field), an air base used primarily by the military and NASA. It is located about 15 miles south of downtown, near Pasadena and toward Clear Lake and Galveston Island. General admission costs $20 for adults and $5 for children ages 5 to 11. Kids under five get in free. Be sure to bring your own lawn chairs; the show is standing room only, unless you shell out $40 for an assigned seat at the "50-yard line" and reserved parking. For $125 you can get a seat in a covered area, reserved parking, and free food and drinks. Purchase and print tickets online or order them over the phone or at the gate. Convenience charges are added to the price of tickets purchased online or over the phone.

i Get into the Halloween spirit by taking one of Discover Houston Tours' Ghost Walks on the third Friday of October. As you walk around downtown, you'll learn about some of the city's urban legends, unsolved mysteries, and spooky stories about dead Houstonians. The tour costs $30 and starts and ends at the Spaghetti Warehouse at 901 Commerce St., which has a few ghost stories of its own. Purchase tickets at the Spaghetti Warehouse at 6:30 p.m.; parking is free. Call (713) 222-9255 or visit www.discoverhouston tours.com for more information.

INTERNATIONAL QUILT FESTIVAL
George R. Brown Convention Center
1001 Avenida de las Americas, just off of US 59 between Polk Avenue and Texas Street
(713) 781-6864
www.quilts.com
Quilters and quilt collectors can find their little piece of heaven downtown at the George R. Brown Convention Center each year in mid-to-late October or early November. The International Quilt Festival showcases thousands of beautiful quilts, cloth dolls, and other art made from fabric.

Most are available for purchase. There are also more than 400 demonstrations and classes for quilters and quilt collectors alike. General admission costs $10 for adults and $8 for students and seniors 65 and over.

RE/MAX BALLUNAR LIFTOFF FESTIVAL
Johnson Space Center
1601 NASA Pkwy.
(281) 488-7676 (Clear Lake Chamber of Commerce)
www.ballunarfestival.com
Every October dozens of hot air balloons lift off at NASA's Johnson Space Center and inspire awe in the thousands of Houston- and Galveston-area residents who come out to watch them. During the weekend-long event, these balloons celebrate our shared fascination with flight. The balloons participate in several competitions in hopes of being named Event Champion of the RE/MAX Ballunar Festival. This family-friendly event has a carnival aura, complete with concession stands, arts and crafts exhibits, live entertainment, skydiving exhibits, and the enchanting evening balloon glows, which light up the sky. Admission is $10 per vehicle, which includes parking at the Lyndon B. Johnson Space Center and a special space center tour. To reach the festival, take I-45 South and exit at NASA Parkway (formerly NASA Road 1). Take NASA Parkway east and follow the signs to the Johnson Space Center.

NOVEMBER

NUTCRACKER MARKET
Reliant Center
1 Reliant Park
(713) 535-3231
www.houstonballet.org/nutcracker_market
More than 300 artists and merchants from across the country—and a few from around the globe—kick off Houston's holiday shopping season by peddling everything from Christmas ornaments to jewelry to knickknacks and food at the Nutcracker Market, held at Reliant Center over a four-day period in early November. With products ranging from kitschy to artsy to luxurious, the Nutcracker

Market offers something for just about everyone on your gift list. Proceeds benefit the Houston Ballet Foundation. There are several food and alcohol vendors, as well as a few fashion shows and special events, which cost anywhere from $35 to $150 per person. Beware, though: With more than 65,000 shoppers attending each year, the crowds can be intimidating. General admission tickets cost $11 at the door and $10 if purchased in advance at any local Randall's store. Kids under six get in free, but strollers aren't allowed inside. Cash parking is available at Reliant Park for $8; those who want to save money and avoid the crowded parking lot can take the METRORail. For directions, see the write-up on the Houston Texans on page 148 of the "Spectator Sports" chapter.

i Visit the Nutcracker Market three hours before closing on any of the event's four days and get in for half price.

VIA COLORI STREET PAINTING FESTIVAL
Sam Houston Park at Bagby Street and
Allen Parkway (downtown)
(713) 523-3633
www.houstonviacolori.com

The streets around Sam Houston Park look like they belong in an art museum for a few days each November, thanks to the Via Colori Street Painting Festival. Around the middle of the month, more than 175 artists—hobbyists and professionals alike—spend a weekend downtown "painting" the streets around Sam Houston Park. The festival provides them with pastels, and they create elaborate illustrations and designs on the concrete. Each "square" that they color corresponds to a donation made to the Center for Hearing and Speech, which teaches children with hearing issues to speak and listen without using sign language. Houstonians show up in droves to watch the artists work their magic during this free event. Although the art is the main draw, there is also live entertainment, a section where children can play and color, and food and drinks. Anyone who is college age or older can color in the festival for free; sign-up begins in May on the Via Colori Web site.

H-E-B HOLIDAY PARADE
Downtown
(713) 654-8808
www.hebparade.com

Many Houstonians begin their Thanksgiving morning with a trip downtown for the H-E-B Holiday Parade. As the parade travels some 20 blocks through downtown, Houstonians of all ages cheer on colorful floats and high-flying balloons, marching bands, and the Houston Texans Cheerleaders and the Rockets Power Dancers. Little ones also get a thrill from seeing costumed characters, including the hottest cartoon characters of the moment and Santa, as well as local celebrities and athletes. The parade begins at Minute Maid Park at Hamilton and Texas and ends up at Rusk and Crawford Streets, a block north of Discovery Green. See the parade Web site for a route map. The parade is free to the public, although reserved seats can be purchased for $14 on the parade Web site. Parking is available on the street and in many garages and paid lots throughout downtown.

UPTOWN HOLIDAY LIGHTING
Uptown District/Galleria
Post Oak Boulevard between San Felipe
Street and Westheimer Road
(713) 621-2504
www.uptown-houston.com/about/events

After their Thanksgiving feasts, many Houstonians and their out-of-town visitors head to Uptown to watch the lighting of the 80 trees along Post Oak Boulevard right by the Galleria. Adding to the festive air is a fireworks display, Christmas music, and visits by reindeer, elves, 12-foot-tall snowmen, and even Santa. For those who still have room in their stomachs, concession stands sell carnival foods such as kettle corn, cotton candy, and funnel cakes. The free event is always held on Thanksgiving evening and the trees remain lit throughout the holiday season, making Post Oak Boulevard a lovely—if sometimes congested—route to and from the Galleria for holiday shopping. Free parking is available at the Galleria mall and several adjacent buildings and shopping centers.

THE ICE AT DISCOVERY GREEN
Discovery Green
1500 McKinney St., between La Branch Street and Avenida de Las Americas
www.theiceatdiscoverygreen.com
Snow is rare in Houston, but the Ice at Discovery Green might almost make you forget that. From Thanksgiving to Martin Luther King Jr. Day, a 7,200-square-foot ice-skating rink is set up at Discovery Green, with a smaller area for younger children to play in the snow. Live music; open-air movies; a gift shop; and seasonal treats, like hot cocoa and apple caramel cider, add to the festive air. Admission is $10, which includes skate rental, and neophytes can take 20-minute skating lessons for $20. Parking is available around Discovery Green at meters and in paid lots and parking garages.

MAYOR'S HOLIDAY CELEBRATION
City Hall
901 Bagby St., between Walker and McKinney Streets
(713) 437-6367
www.houstontx.gov/specialevents
In late November or early December, Houston's mayor kicks off the holiday season with an outdoor celebration at City Hall. Held around the reflection pool, the event features musical, theatrical, and dance performances before the lighting of the City Hall Christmas tree. The evening wraps up with a fireworks display, creating a spectacular backdrop for the newly lit tree. The event is free and open to the public. See the City Hall write-up on page 114 of the "Attractions" chapter for information on parking in the area.

DECEMBER

CITY HALL MENORAH LIGHTING
City Hall
901 Bagby St., between Walker and McKinney Streets
(713) 774-0300
www.chabadhouston.org
During the eight-night holiday of Hanukkah, the Chabad-Lubavitch Outreach Center of Houston sponsors a series of menorah lightings around the city. The biggest of these takes place outside City Hall, where a giant menorah stands to commemorate the Jewish festival of lights. In addition to a symbolic lighting, the evening boasts Hanukkah treats like jelly rolls and latkes, craft demonstrations, and live entertainment. The lighting may be held anywhere from late November to the end of December, depending on when Hanukkah falls. The event is free and open to the public. See the City Hall write-up on page 114 of the "Attractions" chapter for information on parking in the area.

TEXAS BOWL
Reliant Stadium
1 Reliant Park, inner loop of the southern portion of Loop 610 between Kirby Street and Fannin Street
www.texasbowl.org
At the end of each December, college football fans head to Reliant Stadium for the Texas Bowl, an NCAA Division I bowl game that features teams from the Big 12, Big East, and Conference USA, as well as the Mountain West division's Texas Christian University. The Texas Bowl was first held in 2006 to replace the now-defunct Houston Bowl, which the city hosted from 2000 to 2005.

Although the Texas Bowl lacks the pomp and prestige of, say, the Rose Bowl, it is quickly becoming a Houston tradition. In 2007 and 2008 the game drew nearly 60,000 fans. This family-friendly event kicks off with TexFest, a pregame carnival featuring horseshoes, tailgate competitions, washers, and food in the Reliant Stadium parking lot. After the game, there's always a big fireworks show—dubbed the "Largest Holiday Fireworks Show in Texas" by the Texas Bowl. Individual tickets range from $15 to $75, and ticket packages that include food and souvenirs range from about $25 per person for families on up to $2,000 for groups of 100. Cash parking is available at the stadium for $20 to $30.

i City ordinances don't allow dogs in city parks and plazas, so leave Fido at home for any events held downtown or at city parks.

KIDSTUFF

Houston is a great place to be a kid. The mild weather here spells endless opportunities to run around outside and play in the water. Plus, there are plenty of parks and playgrounds, festivals and carnivals, water parks, skating rinks and bowling alleys, and plenty of spots to see—and pet—some unusual animals. There are even theaters especially for kids. This chapter highlights some of the most fun ways for your kids to blow off some steam in Houston. With categories highlighting carnivals and festivals, parks and playgrounds, mental stimulation, physical activities, circuses and other shows, and animal hot spots, you're sure to find something in this chapter that satisfies even the pickiest child.

Entertaining your kids in Houston can be an expensive endeavor if you go to a carnival or a family fun center where you have to pay for each game and activity, not to mention food. But there are plenty of ways and places you can entertain your children here for less than $10 or $15. Often you can cut costs by not spending money on yourself, although many children's entertainment spots do charge for admission for both children and parents. Look at all of the activities included in this chapter and you're sure to find something in your budget—even if that budget is $0. Free parking is available on-site unless noted otherwise.

The activities listed here are by no means all-inclusive. There are plenty of other neighborhood destinations and spots in the exurbs where kids can have fun. The ones listed here draw some of the biggest crowds and tend to put big smiles on little faces. You might notice some overlap between this chapter and the "Annual Events" and "Attractions" chapters. That's because many attractions and events are perfect for kids but also shouldn't be missed if you don't have children in tow. Likewise, you should give the "Annual Events" and "Attractions" chapters a second look even if you have children with you all the time. Plenty of the activities listed in those chapters—especially the San Jacinto Battleground State Historic Site ("Attractions" chapter), the Houston International Festival, the Art Car Parade, the Wings Over Houston Air Show, the RE/MAX Ballunar Liftoff Festival, and the H-E-B Holiday Parade (all listed in the "Annual Events" chapter)—make for great family outings. Also be sure to read up on Hermann Park and Discovery Green in the "Parks" chapter; both offer endless fun for families and children.

If your child's idea of fun is a visit to the toy store, there are plenty of great ones in Houston. You can find a complete rundown in the "Shopping" chapter, which also includes a section on children's clothing stores.

Price Code

$	$5 to $8
$$	$9 to $12
$$$	over $12

WHERE THE WILD THINGS ARE

Horses. Butterflies. Sharks. Pigs. Panda bears. Name your child's favorite animal and there's almost certainly at least one opportunity to see it in action in Houston. The city is home to a world-class aquarium and zoo, as well as a fantastic nature center. And in late February and March, the Houston Livestock Show and Rodeo comes to town, with plenty of cattle, bulls, horses, and other livestock ready to be watched and petted by kids. These aren't the only places to see exotic creatures, though. You can also watch butterflies flutter by and insects crawl around at the Houston Museum of Natural Science, which is described in the "Mental Buzz" section of this chapter. Below are the best places in town to take your kids to see their favorite creatures.

DOWNTOWN AQUARIUM $–$$$
410 Bagby St., at Memorial Drive (Downtown)
(713) 223-3474
www.aquariumrestaurants.com/down townaquariumhouston

Houston's Downtown Aquarium is a popular spot for school field trips, birthday parties, and family fun. Here you'll find eight one-of-a-kind "adventure exhibits," a couple of which pay homage to the Gulf of Mexico region. The Louisiana Swamp exhibit, for instance, celebrates Texas's eastern neighbor with recreated Gulf Coast marshes and bayous that introduce you to some of the state's slimier residents—alligator snapping turtles, crayfish, spotted gar, and some good old dwarf alligators. The Gulf of Mexico exhibit gives visitors a look at the nurse sharks, snapper, and other aquatic creatures that live around the gulf's offshore rigs. Also not to be missed are the aquarium's more international exhibits, which include a sunken temple that showcases a 20-foot tiger reticulated python and other species from a lost Mayan civilization, as well as the white tigers— yes, tigers—that strut around the replicated ruins of an ancient Indian temple. Fans of sharks and those looking to transform fear into admiration will enjoy the aquarium's shark offerings: A ride on the CP Huntington train will take you through the Shark Voyage exhibit, where you can gaze at zebra sharks, blacktips, and sandtigers as they swim in a 200,000-gallon habitat, and Discovery Rig's shark nursery lets you check out baby bamboo sharks and shark eggs.

When all of the marine biology lessons start wearing you or the kids out, head outdoors to play the aquarium's carnival-style games, ride the carousel on a plastic alligator's back, or take in some of the best views of the Houston skyline on the Diving Bell Ferris. If you're hungry, head to the Aquarium restaurant, where you'll dine surrounded by a 150,000-gallon aquarium filled with thousands of smaller fish. Not surprisingly, seafood comprises a large portion of the menu here, but don't worry if you're uneasy about eating fish while you watch their brethren swim. There are also plenty of salad, pasta, burger, and steak options. The food is much better than you might expect since the Aquarium is owned by Landry's Restaurants, a solid national seafood chain that began right outside of Houston in Katy. Entrees range from about $9 for a burger to $32 for seafood and steak platters. Kids' meals are $5.99 and include typical kiddie fare with underwater names, like Coral Reef Chicken, Barracuda Burgers, and Surfer's Mac & Cheese.

In addition to these usual admission offerings, the Downtown Aquarium features a number of special offerings, including schools and scout trips. Inquisitive children can participate in the Marine Biologist for a Day and Zoologist for a Day programs, overnight adventures, and a weeklong Sea Safari Camp during the summer. Camps range from $49.95 for a day to $200 for a week. The aquarium also hosts children's birthday parties, which range from $28 per child for admission, dinner, cake, a few rides, and a group photo on up to $79.95 per child for a slumber party, complete with nighttime snacks, T-shirts, and breakfast.

The aquarium's ballroom is a popular spot for bar mitzvahs and other special events.

Admission to the aquarium is $6.25 for kids ages 2 to 12, $9.25 for adults, and $8.25 for seniors 65 and up. Kids under 2 get in free. Don't

i   **Take the kids to the free Art Car Trophy Workshop in mid-March or early April. They'll get to make their own wacky art—er, trophies—for winners of the Art Car Parade (held in May, see the "Annual Events" chapter). Find out the date and sign up on the parade Web site (www.orangeshow.org/artcar.html).**

be fooled by the prices, though. A trip to the aquarium can add up quickly. Rides—including the Shark Voyage—aren't included in general admission, so you'll wind up paying $2.99 to $4.99 per ride. If you're planning to make a day of it, your best bet is to shell out $15.99 for an All-Day Adventure Pass, which allows you to see all of the exhibits and ride as many rides as you want. There are no discounts on the All-Day Adventure Pass for children.

The aquarium is located downtown, just east of I-45 North and just north of Memorial Drive at Bagby Street, making it easily accessible from both I-45 and I-10. Parking is available for $6 in a lot on-site; valet parking is available in front of the aquarium for $8.

HOUSTON ARBORETUM & NATURE CENTER
4501 Woodway Dr., on the western edge of Memorial Park
(713) 681-8433
www.houstonarboretum.org

If your kids love to catch bugs, watch birds, and discover new things, be sure to take them to the Houston Arboretum & Nature Center. Located on the western edge of Memorial Park, this 155-acre nature preserve is a fun place to explore the creatures living in forest, pond, wetland, and meadow habitats as you walk along the shady trails. The arboretum also offers educational programs that teach children and adults about nature and conservation through guided tours and hands-on activities. During spring break and in the summer, the arboretum offers camps for kids as young as three years old to learn about everything from tadpoles to ecology through hands-on activities. The arboretum, which hosts scout troops and school groups as well, is a fun place to have an amphibian, bird, or snake-themed birthday party. Learn more by visiting the Web site. Admission is free but donations are encouraged. Free parking is available on-site.

HOUSTON LIVESTOCK SHOW AND RODEO (FEB–MAR)
Reliant Park, on the north side of the South Loop between Kirby Drive and Fannin Street
www.rodeohouston.com

For many big kids—er, adults—the chili cook-off and concerts tend to be the most fun part of the Houston Livestock Show and Rodeo, held at the end of February and early March each year. (See the "Annual Events" chapter for more information.) Not so for the little kids, who tend to go for the animals, the rides, and the cotton candy. Many families head to Reliant Park to check out the rest of the Livestock Show and Rodeo, which is about as authentic as they come. At Reliant Center the kids can watch milking, spinning and weaving, and cotton gin demonstrations and get an up-close look at the dairy goats, Brahmousin cattle, and Simbrah cattle in between checking out different livestock shows. And yes, your kids can pet them. Don't worry if your little ones show up looking like city slickers: They'll leave looking like they belong—that is, if they can talk you into buying some of the rodeo gear and souvenirs for sale at Reliant Center and Reliant Arena.

When the kids get tired of the livestock show, take them outdoors to the rodeo carnival, which is filled with roller coasters, Ferris wheels, merry-go-rounds, cotton candy, and funnel cake galore. Also be sure to stop by the Kids Country Carnival so your kids can get a taste of life on a farm. They'll have the chance to ride a mechanical bull, cheer on some cute oinkers in the pig races, pet even more animals at the petting zoo, and ride ponies—all while listening to live kiddie music.

Tickets are $7 for guests 13 and up and $4 for kids ages 3 to 12. Kids under three get in free. If you plan to attend the livestock show and carnival multiple times, consider getting a Houston Livestock Show Season Pass, which costs $25 per person and gets you into the cook-off, carnival, and livestock and horse shows as many times as you want over the rodeo's duration. Cash parking is available at Reliant Park for $7 during the day on weekdays and for $12 on weekday evenings and weekends.

HOUSTON ZOO

**6200 Golf Course Dr., at North MacGregor
Drive in Hermann Park
(713) 533-6500
www.houstonzoo.org**

Located in the Museum District amid the lush grass of Hermann Park, the Houston Zoo is home to more than 4,500 animals from more than 900 species. Here you can introduce your little ones to all the usual suspects, as well a number of rare breeds, including an adorable red panda named Toby and a young sifaka family. The 55-acre zoo is also the only zoo in the state to have a giant eland exhibit and one of just 14 worldwide to have a leucistic American alligator exhibit. The Texas Wetlands exhibit features some local amphibians, and the Pheasant Run offers a fun place for children to watch pheasants interact. But perhaps the most popular spot is the John P. McGovern Children's Zoo, where children can touch and pet sheep and goats, play on the playground, ride a wildlife carousel, and check out different animal habitats.

As part of its commitment to educate and entertain the public, the zoo hosts more than two dozen "Meet the Keeper" talks each day. During these kid-friendly "talks," zookeepers from different sections of the zoo tell guests about the animals they work with and, in some cases, offer hands-on demonstrations. A list of scheduled talks can be found online at www.houstonzoo .org/chats.

The zoo offers many other hands-on programs to learn more about the animals. On Tuesday and Thursday mornings at 9:15, you can get some exercise and learn about the animals as you push your newborn- to 30-month-old children through a section of the zoo. Dubbed Wild Wheels, the hourlong stroll concludes in the Children's Zoo, where the kids can pet and play with the animals. Wild Wheels costs $7 per child. Parents get in for the regular cost of admission.

Also popular among little ones are the New Beginnings programs, held on Wednesday and Saturday mornings. During these hour-long sessions, kids learn about animals through songs, games, stories, and the occasional hands-on demonstration. Classes cost $20 per child and require advance registration, available online.

When you visit the zoo, be sure to budget some time to feed the ducks at the duck pond, rent a paddleboat and go for a ride around the duck pond, and take the kids for a ride (or three) on the Hermann Park Railroad—an open-air, kid-size train that travels around Hermann Park, just outside Houston Zoo. The sleek red train runs from 10 a.m. to 6:30 p.m. every day and costs $2.50 per ride.

General admission to the zoo is free for infants, $6 for kids 2 to 11, $10 for guests 12 to 64, and $6 for seniors 65 and up. Save $1 on kids' tickets and $2 on adult admission by purchasing tickets up to a year ahead at any local Fiesta Mart. The zoo is open every day except Christmas and stops admitting visitors one hour before closing each evening.

The zoo can be reached by car by taking I-59 or I-45 to TX 288 South, exiting at North MacGregor, and taking a right, or by taking the South Loop to TX 288 North, exiting at North MacGregor, and taking a left. Free parking is available in a lot on Golf Course Drive, but spots fill up quickly in the summer and on busy days. Paid parking can be found near the Houston Museum of Natural Science or at Memorial Hermann Medical Plaza at 6400 Fannin St. Those who don't want to mess with parking can also take the METRORail to the Memorial Hermann Hospital/Houston Zoo stop.

i **Avoid the zoo on Martin Luther King Jr. Day, Presidents' Day, Columbus Day, the day after Thanksgiving, and New Year's Day. The zoo is a mob on these days because admission is free and just about every kid in town is out of school.**

MENTAL BUZZ

Houston's got plenty of brain food for little Einsteins, aspiring meteorologists, mad scientists, future astronauts, and dinosaur lovers. Several of the city's museums, as well as Space Center

Houston, offer some great exhibits and hands-on activities that are sure to keep inquisitive little minds asking questions. There's even a fantastic museum just for kids. Below are some of the best spots to take your little ones to learn while having tons of fun.

CHILDREN'S MUSEUM OF HOUSTON $
1500 Binz St., at La Branch Street in the Museum District
(713) 522-1138
www.cmhouston.org

If you take your kids to just one place in Houston, make sure it's the Children's Museum of Houston. Every moment in this quirky, brightly hued building is a learning experience—and an incredibly fun one, at that. Kids are encouraged to use their imaginations and touch the exhibits, which teach them about everything from math to the environment by engaging all five of their senses.

In March 2009 the museum doubled in size—and fun—with a new building that adds more than 37,000 square feet of exhibit space. The new space is filled with innovative exhibits—seven of which are permanent—that mesmerize kids of every background and interest. At the Kidtropolis, USA exhibit, kids learn about money management and personal responsibility as they run a city for kids by kids. Little builders will enjoy visiting the Invention Convention exhibit, where they can invent and build all sorts of contraptions, ranging from Styrofoam cups and water bottles to colored gels and gears. For kids who can't get enough, the museum offers an Inventor's Workshop, where children learn to make soda, build robots, and design glowing jewelry. Check the museum calendar for information about upcoming workshops. Those kids with lots of energy should head straight to the Power Play exhibit, a three-story installation that teaches kids about their bodies and the importance of physical fitness through a series of activities. They can climb the 40-foot Power Tower, for instance, or find out how strong they really are at the Grip It station.

In addition to being home to some amazing permanent and special exhibits, the Children's Museum hosts special events and workshops. From story time to face painting and puppet shows to special holiday events, there are dozens of things to do here just about every day of the year. Each year on Halloween evening, the museum stays open late to host Monster Mash Bash. Not only do kids get to make scary 3-D monster sculptures, spider hats, ghost bubbles, and slime, but there is also the *Ronald McDonald Magic Show* and a chance to dance as DJ Beetlejuice plays his favorite Halloween tunes—"Monster Mash" included. Kids can even trick-or-treat—in or out of costume—right inside the museum, where they can collect treats and toys from each exhibit.

Special events like Monster Mash Bash are typically included in the cost of admission, which runs $7 for everyone who is one-year-old or older. Kids under one and museum members get in free. Seniors ages 65 and up pay $6. On Thursday evenings from 5 to 8 p.m., everyone gets in free. The Children's Museum of Houston is also included on the Houston CityPass, which allows you to visit six local attractions for a reduced price. See page 111 of the "Attractions" chapter for more information about the Houston CityPass.

The museum is located in the Museum District. Plenty of parking is available in the museum garage, which charges $5 for one hour of parking, $6 for two hours, and $7 for three hours or more.

i   **Find out about upcoming kid-centered events throughout the Houston metropolitan area online at Kid's Directory (www.kids-houston.com) and GoCityKids (www.gocitykids.parentsconnect.com). Or check out the "Preview" section in Thursday's *Houston Chronicle* to find out about activities taking place the upcoming weekend.**

THE HEALTH MUSEUM $
1515 Hermann Dr., between LaBranch and Crawford Streets, just east of the Hermann Park Golf Course in the Museum District
(713) 521-1515
www.thehealthmuseum.org

With a long history of providing some of the world's best health care and health-care education at the Texas Medical Center, it's only fitting that Houston has one of the country's only museums devoted to health. For 21 years Houston celebrated its commitment to health and medicine at the Houston Museum of Natural Science in what was known as the Museum of Medical Science. But since medicine is such a big part of the city's economy and identity, members of the medical and science community—including Dr. John P. McGovern—lobbied hard for a museum devoted to health and medicine. In 1996 Houston finally got its Health Museum, which was dedicated to McGovern five years later. With a variety of interactive exhibits and activities designed to help visitors better understand their bodies, the Health Museum is one of the city's can't-miss spots—and a place sure to entertain even the littlest guests.

You: The Exhibit offers a one-of-a-kind chance to see one's own internal organs in real time using a body scanner. Elsewhere in the exhibit, kids can learn how living in Houston affects their bodies. The Amazing Body Pavilion gives curious little visitors the chance to walk through an enormous human body and discover the importance of keeping arteries unclogged, the brain challenged, and bones exercised. Inside the McGovern 4D Theater, you and the kids can watch films about the body—and don't worry, these are nothing like those old movies you watched in biology class. These movies come complete with real scents, rain, lightning, and, of course, surround sound. Little braniacs love the Challenge Gallery, where they can test their reflexes, play some Dance Dance Revolution, and work some puzzles. The museum hosts additional fun exhibits and events throughout the year.

Admission costs $8 for adults and $6 for kids ages 3 to 12 and seniors 65 and up. Museum members get in free. The museum is also included on the Houston CityPass. Parking is available in the museum parking lot for $3 with the purchase of an admission ticket. Metered parking is also available along the streets surrounding the museum.

HOUSTON MUSEUM OF NATURAL SCIENCE $$–$$$
1 Hermann Circle Dr., between Caroline and San Jacinto Streets in Hermann Park just east of Main and Fannin Streets
(713) 639-4629
www.hmns.org

From dinosaurs to insects to butterflies, the Houston Museum of Natural Science is a favorite among kids. One of the museum's biggest draws is the Cockrell Butterfly Center and Brown Hall of Entomology, where kids are mesmerized as they watch butterflies flutter around, sip nectar, and rest inside a simulated tropical rainforest, complete with a 50-foot waterfall and exotic plants. If your kids are true insect lovers, don't miss the Brown Hall of Entomology, which is located in the Cockrell Butterfly Center. Brown Hall is filled with live insects and spiders of all varieties, including walking sticks, cockroaches, and tarantulas. Kids can also play with insect-themed toys and read insect-themed books. Parents, beware: Strollers aren't allowed in the Cockrell Butterfly Center. Butterflies sometimes pay visits to the humans down below, so you can probably imagine why strollers are a no-go. A McDonald's is located inside the museum, just in case you need to refuel.

Inquisitive kids with the patience for exhibits will also get giddy about some of the museum's permanent exhibits, which cover all things science—astronomy and space, oil and energy, chemistry, paleontology, shells, Texas wildlife, rare gems and minerals, and, most importantly, the requisite dinosaurs. The museum hosts two or three special exhibits at any given time, although these are typically geared toward adults and older kids rather than little ones. Recent special exhibits featured the famous Lucy fossil, have given visitors the chance to try their hand at forensic science, and showcased gifts designed for, given to, and used by Tibet's Dalai Lamas over the past nine centuries.

If your kids like to pretend they're on a big adventure, they're likely to be thrilled with a visit to the Burke Baker Planetarium, where they can identify constellations, watch science-themed movies, and listen to music. Or they might prefer to watch a fast-moving, adventure-filled IMAX film about nature in the Wortham Theater. Most IMAX films are screened just once or twice a day, so be sure to check the schedule online or by calling (713) 639-IMAX before your visit. IMAX movies do sell out, so be sure to purchase tickets and line up early to get a good seat.

The Houston Museum of Natural Science also has two satellite educational campuses. The Woodlands Xploration Station, located just north of Houston, features some 13 dinosaur skeletons, live frogs, as well as exhibits on minerals and gems. About an hour south of the city in Fort Bend County's Brazos Bend State Park is the George Observatory, which boasts three domed telescopes. Among them is the 36-inch Gueymard Research Telescope, one of the country's largest telescopes available for public viewing. The George Observatory is also home to the Challenger Learning Center, which teaches visitors about space exploration and science through simulated missions. Both the Woodlands Xploration Station and the George Observatory are a bit of a drive for many Houstonians, so the two campuses cater largely to school and scout groups. Learn more about both of these satellites on the museum's Web site.

Admission to the main campus's exhibits is $15 for adults and $9 for college students, adults 62 and up, and children ages 3 to 11. Members get in free. The museum is also included on the Houston CityPass, which is discussed in the introductions to the "Museums" and "Attractions" chapters. Admission to the Cockrell Butterfly Center, Burke Baker Planetarium, and Wortham Theater IMAX movies requires the purchase of additional tickets, which cost $8 for the butterfly center, $7 for the planetarium, and $10 for an IMAX movie. Seniors, students, and children under 11 pay $6 to see the butterflies, $6 to visit the planetarium, and $8 to see an IMAX movie.

Parking is available in the museum garage on Caroline Street; museum members pay $5 and nonmembers who show their museum ticket stub pay $10. Those without a ticket pay $20

for parking. Limited parking is available on the streets around the museum. You can also take the METRORail to the Museum District rail stop, located just 3 blocks from the museum.

JOHN C. FREEMAN WEATHER MUSEUM $
5104 Caroline St., between Southmore Boulevard and Palm Street 3 blocks east of Main Street in the Museum District
(713) 529-3076
www.weathermuseum.org

If you're the parent or grandparent of an aspiring meteorologist or a child who wants to understand how those hurricanes form in the Gulf of Mexico, take note: Houston's got the country's only museum dedicated to weather. The John C. Freeman Weather Museum, which opened in 2006, was founded and is now run by meteorologists from the Weather Research Center, a Houston-based nonprofit organization devoted to educating the public about weather and weather safety. The museum is particularly popular among children, who enjoy the museum's many hands-on activities. And who can blame them? Here kids can record their own weather broadcast in a simulated studio, touch a simulated tornado vortex in the Tornado Chamber, and watch meteorologists perform experiments in the Weather Wizard Corner. Other exhibits shed light on the history of meteorology and teach inquiring minds how tornadoes form and how to track hurricanes. Throughout the year, the museum also offers kids the chance to learn more about the weather at weather camps.

Self-guided tours of the museum are $5 for adults, $3 for students and seniors 65 and older, and free for kids under 3. Guided tours cost $8 for adults and $5 for students, teachers, and seniors. Guided tours last an hour to an hour and a half and must be booked in advance by phone. Parking is available on the streets around the museum.

SPACE CENTER HOUSTON $$$
1601 NASA Pkwy.
(281) 244-2100
www.spacecenter.org

For an adventure that's out of this world, take the kids to Space Center Houston, the visitors center of NASA's Lyndon B. Johnson Space Center. This 100-building complex is where all U.S. astronauts train. It is also the home of NASA's Mission Control, which coordinates and tracks all of the United States' human spaceflight and directs all space shuttle missions and International Space Station activities.

Space Center Houston offers dozens of hands-on and information exhibits and activities tracing the history of spaceflight. A film in the Space Center Theater offers a crash course on aerospace technology and equipment, as well as the challenges that astronauts face. In the Blast Off Theater, your family will feel like they're traveling in space as large monitors air live updates about current shuttle missions and simulated shuttle exhaust blows into the room. The Feel of Space exhibit lets visitors discover for themselves how astronauts shower, eat, and live in outer space, and the Kids Space Place lets kids practice flying a space shuttle. Also not to be missed are exhibits featuring old spacesuits, artifacts, and space shuttle hardware. As you walk through the exhibits, get the scoop on what you're seeing by taking an Astronaut Audio Tour. These digital tours are narrated by astronaut legends like John Glenn, Gene Cernan, Alan Bean, Gene Kranz, Shannon Lucid, Eileen Collins, and Barry Corbin; different versions are available for kids and adults.

During the summer, spring break, and other school holidays, the center hosts daylong, half-day, and weeklong day camps and scout camps where kids can participate in hands-on activities and check out some special space exhibits.

General admission costs $19.95 for adults, $18.95 for seniors 65 and older, and $15.95 for kids 4 to 11. Print your tickets online before your visit, and get $3 off admission. Space Center Houston is located about 25 miles south of downtown near Clear Lake. To get there, take I-45 South toward Galveston, then take exit 25 for NASA Parkway/TX-1. Drive east and follow the signs for the Johnson Space Center.

CELEBRATION BUZZ

What kid doesn't like a good festival, carnival, or other celebration? Just about every festival listed in the "Annual Events" chapter of this book includes activities geared toward kids but there are a few events that are especially popular among—or in some cases designed just for—kids. Among them are the Easter Orange Hunt, two outdoor kids' festivals, and a Renaissance Festival. Also fun is the Houston Livestock Show and Rodeo, listed in the "Where the Wild Things Are" section of this chapter. The fun doesn't have to stop when these seasonal events wrap, though. The Kemah Boardwalk in the Houston Bay Area is home to a huge amusement park and, of course, cotton candy. Below are some of Houston's best festivals and carnival atmospheres for kids.

i NASA Parkway was previously named NASA Road 1 so some maps and GPS systems don't account for the fairly recent name change.

EASTER ORANGE HUNT (MAR/APR)   FREE
Orange Center for Visionary Art
2402 Munger St.
(713) 926-6368
www.orangeshow.org/events.html
Want your kids to go easy on the Easter candy? Skip the traditional Easter egg hunt and opt for the Orange Show Center's Easter Orange Hunt. Held on the Saturday afternoon before Easter, the zany event features a maze of hidden oranges and the occasional piece of candy. There's also a bunny petting zoo, an Art Car Trophy Making Workshop, and some sweet puppies begging to be adopted. The Easter Orange Hunt is free and free parking is available on-site. To reach the Orange Center, take I-45 South toward Galveston, then take exit 43A toward Telephone Road. Merge onto the Gulf Freeway and take a right at Munger Street.

HOUSTON CHILDREN'S FESTIVAL (APR) $
Downtown Houston
www.houstonchildrensfest.com

Imagine a weekend packed with games, rides, kiddie karaoke and live music, arts and crafts, science experiments, a petting zoo, and autographs and hugs from Nickelodeon stars, Houston Rockets and Dynamo players, and the likes of Dora the Explorer and Mickey Mouse. That's the Houston Children's Festival, a weekend-long extravaganza that overtakes the streets and sidewalks of downtown Houston in early April. With some 350 activities and thousands of Houston kiddos and their families in attendance, it's the largest outdoor children's festival in the country. The weekend can get a little pricey, so be sure to make a trip to the ATM beforehand. Admission is $8 per person; kids under three get in free. There are plenty of free activities, but food, drinks, and many games and rides cost between $1 and $5 each. Your best bet is to buy a pack (or several) of nine food, drink, and ride coupons, which will cost you $10. If the event seems expensive, keep in mind that all proceeds go to Child Advocates, an organization that supports abused children. The most convenient parking is available in Theater District Parking Garage 2 at Rusk Street between Bagby Street and Smith Street and Theater District Parking Garage 3, located behind the City Hall Annex at Bagby Street and Walker Street. Parking in these, or any of the other Theater District parking garages, is $6 during the festival. See the downtown map on page vii.

i   Save $3 off the price of admission to the Houston Children's Festival by picking up a discount coupon at any Houston area McDonald's.

KEMAH BOARDWALK $$–$$$
217 Kipp Ave., Kemah
(877) 285-3624
www.kemahboardwalk.com

Located about 30 miles south of downtown in Galveston County, the Kemah Boardwalk is where many Houston families head to escape the city (or the suburbs) for an afternoon or evening. With dining options aplenty, amusement park games and rides, souvenir shops, occasional live music, and soothing views of Galveston Bay, this entertainment district offers something for just about everyone. Kemah suffered significant damage from Hurricane Ike, but by March 2009, just about everything was up and running again.

Kids love the Stingray Reef, where they can watch—and touch—live stingrays. Perhaps the biggest draws are the amusement park games and rides. Little ones enjoy riding the two-story carousel, the Kemah Train, and the Balloon Wheel, and older kids—and kids at heart—get a thrill from scream-inducing rides, such as the Broadway Bullet roller coaster and quick-falling Drop Zone. Individual rides cost between $3 and $4.75, which can add up quickly. A better bet is to purchase an all-day ride pass, which costs $16.99 for guests under 48 inches tall and $18.99 for guests 48 inches and taller.

If your kids are a little older and love a good thrill, hop onboard the *Boardwalk Beast,* an open deck speedboat that's painted to look like a shark, albeit a rainbow-hued one. This 25-minute ride takes guests out into Galveston Bay at a speedy 40 miles an hour and almost no one gets off the boat dry. But between the music, views, and other entertainment, few find reason to complain. Those who ride the *Boardwalk Beast* in the evening enjoy a slower ride. Tickets can be purchased on-site; they cost $12 for adults and $9 for kids 12 and under.

All of the restaurants here are owned by Landry's, the popular seafood chain that launched in nearby Katy in the 1980s before going national. Currently there are about 10 restaurants—plus two coffee shops—at the Kemah Boardwalk and they include a number of kid-friendly options such as Pizza Oven, Joe's Crab Shack, and Saltgrass Steak House.

To reach Kemah, take the South Loop to TX 225 East, then take TX 146 South to Bayport Boulevard. Take a left at 6th Street and another left at Bradford Street. Free parking is available on-site most days. On weekends and holidays, parking in the lots closest to the boardwalk will cost you $7.

KIDS DAY ON BUFFALO BAYOU (JUNE) FREE
Sabine-to-Bagby Promenade downtown
(713) 752-0314
www.buffalobayou.org/kidsday.html
Help your kids find a new outdoor hobby or enjoy an old one with a visit to Kids Day on Buffalo Bayou. Held downtown each June, this event is a fun chance to celebrate the outdoors and the many recreational possibilities Houston has to offer. In addition to the requisite face painting, jugglers, and arts and crafts activities, Kids Day features boat rides and scavenger hunts along Buffalo Bayou, kayaking demonstrations, fishing lessons, skateboarding and hiking opportunities, as well as the chance to meet stars from the Houston Dynamo soccer team and the Houston Rockets basketball team. Gardeners of all ages can also help plant wildflowers to make the bayou even more scenic. With so many activities to choose from, Kids Day makes for a fun family outing. Your kids might even go home begging to do some of the festival activities more often. Admission is free, and the event runs from 10 a.m. to 2 p.m. The Sabine-to-Bagby Promenade is located downtown along Buffalo Bayou between Sabine Street and Bagby Street just south of I-45 and north of Tranquility Park. Parking is available in City Lots H and C, both of which are located off Memorial Drive at Houston Avenue as you enter downtown.

TEXAS RENAISSANCE FESTIVAL $$–$$$
21778 FM 1774, Plantersville
(800) 458-3435
www.texrenfest.com
Take the kids to 16th-century England with a visit to the Texas Renaissance Festival. Held for seven weekends in October and November, the festival features all things Renaissance: music, cuisine, games, rides, and dances. There are even gardens designed to look like those of King Henry VIII and the English queen of fairies. Everyone working at the festival dresses as if it were the 1500s, which

makes glassblowing, blacksmithing, metal forging, and broom making demonstrations, among others, seem all the more authentic. The festival is held in Plantersville, about 55 miles northwest of downtown. That is a bit of a drive, but it's worth every mile for most children. Visit the Web site for detailed directions from numerous points in the Houston area. Tickets can be purchased at the gate for $23 for adults and $11 for children 5 to 12. Children four and under get in free. Weekend passes cost $32; there are no children's prices for weekend passes. Save several dollars by purchasing tickets in advance by phone, on the festival Web site, or at local H-E-B and Randall's stores.

CURTAIN CALLS

Kids who live to see clowns, ice skaters, ballerinas, and stage actors are sure to get their fix in Houston. There's almost always some sort of kids production going on. Some of these are put on by big tours; others are the work of small local theaters that stage productions especially for kids.

For those who love clowns and animals, **Ringling Bros. and Barnum & Bailey** circus comes to Houston's Reliant Stadium about once a year. The circus typically stays in town for about 10 days and tickets are often in demand, so it's a good idea to get yours early. Tickets are sold through Ticketmaster (www.ticketmaster.com). Find out about the circus's next stop in Houston on the Ringling Bros. Web site at www.ringling.com.

If you've got aspiring figure skaters or your kids just love all things Disney, you'll also want to grab tickets for **Disney on Ice,** which comes to town once or twice a year. Each tour has a different theme, like princesses, *High School Musical*, or *Finding Nemo*. Shows are held at Reliant Stadium. There are typically eight or nine performances over about five days, but it's a good idea to get tickets early so you can see the performance you want in the seats you want. Tickets are sold through Ticketmaster.com. Find out when the next Disney on Ice show is coming to town by visiting www.disney.go.com/disneyonice.

Another big-ticket show is the Houston Ballet's annual performance of ***The Nutcracker,*** which parents, grandparents, and even schools whisk children to see each December. Even if your kids aren't wowed by the ballerinas' leaps and twirls, they are likely to feel a little starry-eyed as they watch Clara, Franz, and the Sugar Plumb Fairy impart a classic story of holiday cheer. Visit the Houston Ballet Web site (www.houstonballet .org) and see the Houston Ballet description on page 89 of the "Performing Arts" chapter for more information.

Some of the best children's performances in town are put on by smaller local theaters. Each Saturday, for instance, **Company OnStage's Children's Theater** holds professional-caliber performances of old classics like *Snoopy!* as well as more contemporary scripts like *The Little Mermaid*. This volunteer-run theater has been around since 1978, when former Alley Theatre associate director Joyce Randall McNally began offering acting classes and putting on plays for children. More than 30 years later, it still has some great performances for children, thanks to the support of the Houston Arts Alliance, the Texas Commission on the Arts, and local actors who live to entertain kids. Company OnStage hosts two children's theater performances each Saturday—one at 11:00 a.m., the other at 1:30 p.m. Each show runs for about five weeks. Tickets cost $8 for adults and children and can be reserved online at www.companyonstage.org or by phone (713-726-1219). Don't sweat it if you miss the chance to order tickets in advance. As long as you show up at the theater a few minutes early, you should be able to snag a few. The theater is located in southwest Houston at 536 Westbury Sq. near the corner of West Bellfort and Burdine.

Another popular children's theater venue is **InterActive Theater Company,** which pays homage to the city's diversity with multicultural performances. Shows here range from classics like *Alice's Adventures in Wonderland* to more historical tales like *Harriet Tubman's Freedom Train* and *The Story of the Lone Star State.* The theater is supported by the National Endowment for the Arts, the Houston Arts Alliance, the Houston Foundation, and a number of local foundations

and corporations. Performances take place on weekday and Saturday mornings inside Talento Bilingüe de Houston just east of downtown at 333 South Jensen Dr. Tickets cost $7 for adults and children during the week. On Saturday tickets are also $7, but they're buy one, get one free. Visit the Web site (www.interactivetheater.org) or call (713) 862-7112 to find out about upcoming performances and times. Advance reservations are required.

If your kids enjoy books, such as *If You Give a Pig a Party* and *Sideways Stories from Wayside School,* take them to **Main Street Theater.** The Youth Theater here is guaranteed to make you and your kids laugh at its adaptations of popular children's books. If your kids become inspired by what they see, you just might consider sending them to Kids on Stage, the theater's popular summer camp, which is held at four different locations around the city. Tickets to Youth Theater performances cost $12 for adults and $10 for seniors 65 and up and kids. Unfortunately the theater doesn't admit guests under three. Tickets can be purchased by phone (713-524-6706) or online (www.mainstreettheater.com). The theater has two locations—one in Montrose, the other in Rice Village—but all Youth Theater performances are held at the Montrose location at 4617 Montrose Blvd. in the Chelsea Market complex behind Danton's Gulf Coast Seafood Kitchen.

Also popular among families and school groups are **Stages Repertory Theatre**'s Early-Stages shows for children. This top-notch River Oaks theater company produces folktales, multi-cultural tales, plays, and musicals. Recent shows include the regional premiere of *Panto Cinderella,* a wacky musical based on Kate Hawley's book of the same name, and *Peter and the Wolf.* Ticket prices vary. While tickets to non-premiere shows like *Peter and the Wolf* cost just $8, prices for bigger shows run around $30—the same price that Stages charges for admission to its adult-oriented productions. Tickets can be purchased on Stages' Web site (www.stagestheatre.com), by phone (713-527-0123), or at the theater, which is located at 3201 Allen Pkwy., just off Waugh.

Think your child has a future in the theater biz? Send him or her to acting classes at Theater Under the Stars (listed in the "Performing Arts" chapter) or HITS Theatre in the Heights (713-861-7408; www.hitstheatre.org).

BOWLING

Houston has been known to have more than a couple of rainy Saturdays and parents here plan birthday parties with a chance of rain in mind. Whether you're in town with the kids on one such day or you just want to plan a rainproof birthday party, consider taking the little ones to one of Houston's many bowling alleys. Most local bowling alleys stand alone and are pretty standard fare, with bumpers and ramps to help the kids bowl. There's also plenty of fun to be had bowling in Pasadena and Sugar Land at Incredible Pizza Company and in southwest Houston at the Grand Event, both of which offer many other activities and are described in the "Family Fun Centers" section below.

Since the Houston area has so many bowling alleys, there isn't room to discuss each one here. Below you'll find the locations, phone numbers, and Web sites of several local bowling alleys located in the city limits. The bowling alleys listed under broad ordinal categories are located pretty far from downtown. Call ahead for pricing and hours. Consult the yellow pages to find a bowling alley if you live or are staying in the outlying suburbs.

Bellaire
PALACE BOWLING LANES
4191 Bellaire Blvd.
(713) 667-6554
www.palacebowlinglanes.com

TROPICANA BOWLING CENTER
4189 Bellaire Blvd.
(713) 667-3072

Memorial
300 HOUSTON
925 Bunker Hill Rd., just off I-10
(713) 461-1207
www.3hundred.com

Avoid 300 Houston in the evening if you've got little ones in tow. The wait to get a lane can be long since young adults flock here after work and on weekend nights for the loud music and mixed drinks.

North Houston
DIAMOND LANES
267 N. Forest Blvd., off I-45
(281) 440-9166

Northwest Houston
DEL MAR LANES
3020 Mangum Rd.
(713) 682-2506

WILLOW LANES
19102 West Montgomery Rd.
(281) 955-5900

WINDFERN LANES
14441 Northwest Fwy.
(713) 466-8012

Southeast Houston
ARMADILLA LANES
10055 Fuqua
(713) 944-7100

CLEAR LAKE LANES
16743 Diana Lane
(281) 488-1331

FAMILY FUN CENTERS

Sometimes the easiest way to entertain kids is to take them to a place that offers a variety of games and activities, such as go-karts, minigolf, and inflatables for bouncing around. This way they can choose what they want to do (within reason, of course) and you can kick back and watch them burn off all that excess energy. There are three great family fun centers in the Houston area. Two—the Grand Event and Incredible Pizza Company—are fun for the whole family and kids of all ages. The third, Monkey Bizness, is perfect for younger children who love to jump around in inflatable castles.

THE GRAND EVENT $$–$$$
13700 Beechnut St.
(281) 530-7777
www.thegrandevent.net

Formerly known as Fun Plex, this newly renovated fun complex is now called the Grand Event. The perfect place to go on rainy days, The Grand Event is Texas's biggest indoor family fun center. It's easy to find something to satisfy everyone in your family here. In addition to the usual rides, go-karts, arcade, and concession food, The Grand Event offers paintless paintball, a movie theater that shows new movies, pool tables, a skating rink, and a bowling alley. With the exception of the arcade games and rides, The Grand Event charges by the number of activities you do. One activity costs $6.99, two cost $10.99, four cost $17.99, six cost $24.99, and eight cost $31.99. Individual rides cost $2.50; unlimited rides (excluding go-karts) cost $7.99.

INCREDIBLE PIZZA COMPANY $$–$$$
3412 TX 6 South, Sugar Land
(281) 313-0631
www.ipcsugarland.com

5950 Fairmont Pkwy., Pasadena
(281) 998-2424

Imagine a place where your kids can go bowling, play minigolf, ride bumper cars and go-karts, play air hockey and Skee-Ball, win big stuffed animals, jump around in the gym, and ride a little train. Then throw in a huge pizza buffet with more than 30 kinds of pizza. That little slice of kid heaven is called Incredible Pizza Company. It might sound a lot like Chuck E. Cheese, but the Incredible Pizza Company offers more choices that keep kids busy for hours. Not surprisingly this is a very popular place for birthday parties. A buffet and drink purchase is required for admission. This costs $7.99 for ages 13 to 54, $5.99 for kids 12 and under, and $4.99 for adults 55 and up. Bring extra money, though—the activities will require a constant flow of cash. Prices vary for the different attractions but range from $2.50 to $5.50 per person. There are two Incredible Pizza Company locations in the Houston metropolitan area—one in Pasadena and one in Sugar Land.

MONKEY BIZNESS $
9750 W. Sam Houston Pkwy. North
(832) 237-0100
www.monkeybizness.com

Located inside an office building next door to Coldwell Banker, Monkey Bizness has 15,000 square feet where younger kids can do what they do best—run, jump around, play, and have fun. The several custom-made inflatable play zones include a huge obstacle course and a 24-foot slide. There's also an air hockey table and rock climbing, although the latter is usually only open during birthday parties and on special holidays. Speaking of birthday parties, this is a great place to have one—all you have to do is bring the cake. So many parents like this idea, though, so it's a good idea to reserve the party room well in advance of your child's special day. Admission for open play is $7.50 for children ages 1 to 18; parents get in free. Kids under 1, as well as kids under 2 with a paying sibling, get in free. Show up before 11 a.m. on Monday, Thursday, or Friday and pay just $5 per child.

FUN RUNS

PARK TO PARK RUN (FEB)
Hermann Park
(713) 524-5876
www.hermannpark.org

The Hermann Park Conservancy does its part to encourage Houstonians of all ages to get fit and love their parks with the Park to Park Run, held each February. The event includes several races—a 5-mile run and wheelchair race, a 2-mile walk for families, and a 1K kids' fun run. The family and children's races are held at Hermann Park; afterward, everyone who participates gets to celebrate with live music and tons of healthy snacks. Registration is $12 for children and $30 for adults; prospective racers can register online or at the event. Free parking is available at Hermann Park. For directions to Discovery Green and Hermann Park, see pages 124 and 126 in the "Parks" chapter.

TEXAS CHILDREN'S HOSPITAL KIDS' FUN RUN (JAN)
Pre- and postrace festivities held at George R. Brown Convention Center
1001 Avenida de las Americas, just off of US 59 between Polk Avenue and Texas Street
(713) 957-3453
www.chevronhoustonmarathon.com/kidsRun
Each January more than 200,000 people—both runners and spectators—come out for Houston's largest single-day sporting event: the prestigious Houston Marathon, which is always held on a Sunday. But marathon weekend actually kicks off one day earlier, on Saturday. That's when Texas Children's Hospital sponsors the 3K Kids' Fun Run (and walk), which covers part of the marathon course and wraps up at the official Chevron Houston Marathon finish line. About 5,000 local youth ranging from 5 to 15 participate in the event, which also features a 1K adaptive run and walk for children with special needs. Parents can register their children for the Kids' Fun Run 1K and 3K races online for $10 per child in the fall or at the George R. Brown Convention Center on race day for $15 per child. There are no fees for accompanying parents.

PARKS AND PLAYGROUNDS

Have kids with jungle gym fever? You've got options. Many neighborhoods around the city are also home to smaller parks with the requisite monkey bars, swings, and slides, and in some cases, pools, tennis courts, and basketball courts, although the latter are often only available to members of the neighborhood association that supports the park.

The most noteworthy neighborhood park is **Firetruck Park at Southside Place.** Here you'll find the usual playground equipment, as well as a 1935 fire truck. This isn't the kind of antique you should discourage your kids from touching, though. This fire truck is meant for climbing, sliding, and letting little imaginations run wild. You'll also see a pool and tennis courts at the park, but access to these is limited to residents of the surrounding neighborhood who belong to the Southside Park Association. The park is located in the Southside Place neighborhood at 3743 Garnet St. between Edloe and Auden Streets.

You don't have to scope out neighborhood parks to find a good jungle gym or slide in Houston. Most of the city's parks also have a good playground or two. Check out the "Parks" chapter to find out about some of Houston's great parks, many of which have playgrounds designed to accommodate kids of all physical abilities, including those in wheelchairs.

No matter which parks you visit, be sure to pack some extra juice boxes and water during the summer. Temperatures can get very hot and running around outside may make your kids overheat faster than you might expect.

SKATING

Ice-Skating

Whether you've got a little one who wants to be a figure skater or a hockey player or you just want your kids to have a little cold fun on the ice, Houston—hot and humid as it may be—is a great place to take the kids ice-skating. The city is home to several ice-skating rinks. Some of the local rinks, like the Aerodome Ice Skating Complex, are destinations by themselves. Others, like the rinks at the Galleria and Memorial City malls, can be a fun treat when the kids are tired of shopping and running errands. And the Ice at Discovery Green is set up outside during the winter holidays, adding to the season's festive spirit.

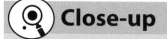 Close-up

Rock Climbing

If your kids are always showing you how strong they are or are climbing all over the place like monkeys, Houston may have a challenge just for them. The city is home to two publicly accessible indoor rock-climbing gyms—Stone Moves Indoor Rock Climbing and Texas Rock Gym, both of which cater to kids (and parents) with walls and classes geared toward beginners. Monkey Bizness, a 15,000-square foot family fun center just for kids, also has a 24-foot rock climbing wall, although it is open to the public for climbing only sporadically—typically during spring break and other holidays. See the Monkey Bizness write-up on page 182 of this chapter and call ahead (832-237-0100) to find out when rock climbing will be available next.

Pay any of these rock-climbing walls a visit and odds are your child will beg for a sequel. He or she might even demand a trip to rock-climbing camp or a rock-climbing birthday party—both of which are among the offerings at Stone Moves and Texas Rock Gym. Not only is rock climbing fun, but it also challenges kids mentally as they figure out how they'll make their next move. Rock climbing isn't one of those activities where you can kick back and watch while your kids brum off steam. As your child uses a rope, a belt, and his or her arms and legs to climb up and down a faux rock wall, you'll hold the other end of the rope to keep your child from falling onto one of the cushion-like mats. Don't worry, though. Both rock gyms emphasize safety and will—literally—show you and your child the ropes beforehand and help you out on the ground throughout the climb. In fact, Texas Rock Gym actually requires all first-time visitors—kids and parents alike—to take a 15- to 20-minute ClimbSafe beginner's class for $7.50.

There's no minimum age to rock climb at either location, although it's worth noting that the Texas Rock Gym requires kids to be at least 10 years old to attend one of its rock-climbing day camps. And anytime your child visits either rock gym, you'll be required to sign a liability waiver if your child is under 18. Anyone who is climbing must bring a pair of sturdy, tight-fitting tennis shoes or plan to rent a pair at the gym. It's also a good idea to wear comfortable shoes if you're just holding the rope. Keep in mind that the harness that climbers must wear can't be worn with skirts or dresses.

Rock climbing can be a little pricey, but a day pass is good for an entire day, even if you leave for lunch and come back. A day pass at Texas Rock Gym is $12.50 per person; you'll also need to rent a harness for $3.70 for the climber(s) in your crew. Climbing shoes can be rented for $5.54. Stone Moves charges $12 per person for a day pass, $2 for harness rental, and $3 for climbing shoe rental. Parents who are not climbing do not need to pay for a day pass or equipment rental for themselves.

Stone Moves Indoor Rock Climbing
6970 FM 1960 Rd. West, in northwest Houston, east of TX 249/Tomball Parkway
(281) 397-0830
www.stonemoves.com

Texas Rock Gym
1526 Campbell Rd., off I-10 between Westview and Longpoint
(713) 973-7625
www.texasrockgym.com

Houston's ice-skating rinks cater to families with kids of all ages and skill levels. Beginner ice-skating lessons are a staple at every rink, although you typically have to call in advance to sign up for classes or find out when a coach can give your child private lessons. Most of the rinks offer figure-skating and ice-hockey classes; a couple also offer hockey leagues. With the exception of the two temporary outdoor ice rinks, all of the rinks listed here will help throw your child a birthday he or she is sure to remember.

Even if your kids aren't taking (or don't need) classes, going ice-skating requires some advanced planning. Most rinks have very limited hours for public skating. So it is a good idea to call ahead or visit the Web site to find out about the latest hours, as these tend to change monthly and seasonally. Parking at all of these rinks is free, although parking at the Ice at Discovery Green may require parking on the street or in a paid garage. See the "Parks" chapter to learn more about parking around Discovery Green.

The rinks listed here are not the only ones in town, but they are the best and, for the most part, centrally located.

AERODOME ICE SKATING COMPLEX
8220 Willow Place Dr. North, at Willowchase (Northwest Houston, off TX 249, just northeast of FM 1960)
(281) 847-5283
www.aerodromes.com
Even the littlest hockey and figure skater wannabes can get a head start on their careers on the Aerodrome's rink, which features open skating hours, beginner figure-skating and ice-skating lessons, and ice-hockey classes that teach kids basic ice-skating skills and body control.

Throughout the year the Aerodrome features themed evenings and special events. Bring the whole family on Friday evenings for Friday Night Live. For these fun-filled evenings, the Aerodrome dims the lights, plays some lively tunes, and breaks up the ice-skating with games and dancing on the ice. No matter what day you visit, admission is $7 and skate rental is $3.

THE ICE AT DISCOVERY GREEN
Discovery Green
1500 McKinney St., between La Branch Street and Avenida de Las Americas
www.theiceatdiscoverygreen.com
Spread some holiday cheer by taking your kids to Discovery Green between Thanksgiving

i Save $25 on a beginner ice-skating class at the Aerodrome by signing your kids up online.

and Martin Luther King Jr. Day. That's when a 7,200-square-foot ice-skating rink known as the Ice at Discovery Green is set up in Houston's beloved downtown park. Little ones who prefer to play in the snow can do just that in a special snow play area set up just for them. Be sure to check out the seasonal treats like hot cocoa and apple caramel cider. Admission is $10, which includes skate rental, and beginners—young and old—can take 20-minute skating lessons for $20. Parking is available around Discovery Green at meters and in paid lots and parking garages.

i If you're living or staying out near the Woodlands, about 32 miles north of downtown Houston, visit the Ice Rink at the Woodlands Town Center. It's run by the same people who operate the Ice at Discovery Green and is open from mid-November to mid-January. Admission is $9.50, which includes skate rental. Visit www.thewoodlandsicerink.com or call (281) 419-5630 for more information.

ICE SKATE USA
Memorial City Mall
303 Memorial City, off I-10 at the Gessner Road exit
(713) 463-9296
www.iceskatememorialcity.com
Ice Skate USA is one of the city's newest ice-skating rinks; it was added in 2003 as part of Memorial City Mall's remodeling. To ensure your kids actually get to skate here, though, you have to plan your trip just right. The public skating schedule varies by month and season; during the year, the rink doesn't stay open for public skating past 4 or 5 p.m., except on Friday evenings. When the rink isn't open for public skating, it is typically being used for classes for beginners, as well as aspiring figure skaters and ice-hockey players. In the winter

the rink is home to the Hitmen (www.houston hitmen.com), a winter hockey league for kids 12 and under. Visit the Web site to get the latest class schedules, as well as the current month's open skating schedule. Ages 11 and up skate for $7 here, and kids under 10 skate for $6. Skate rental costs $3. Free parking is available at the mall.

POLAR ICE GALLERIA
The Galleria—Level 1
5015 Westheimer Rd.
(713) 621-1500
www.polaricegalleriahouston.com
Polar Ice Galleria gets kids: This rink, located on the first floor of the Galleria mall, doesn't make kids wait several days to go ice-skating. The only rink in town that is open to the public seven days a week, Polar Ice Galleria offers public skating every morning, afternoon, and evening, no matter the season. Public skating is a no-go for two or three hours each day, though, so be sure to check the schedule on the Web site or call ahead to make sure the rink will be open when you plan to visit.

Polar Ice Galleria offers beginner ice-skating classes for kids as young as three, as well as ice-hockey and figure-skating classes. For kids who need a little more personal attention, as well as those who are more advanced, Polar Ice Galleria offers private lessons. If your kids really love skating, consider sending them to Camp Blizzard for a day, week, or longer during the summer. Geared toward kids ages 6 to 14, Camp Blizzard includes free skating time, ice-skating lessons, arts and crafts, movies, and games.

Socks are required to skate here. Luckily, if your kids show up sockless, you can purchase a pair at the rink for $3. Skates can also be rented for $3. Skating costs $8 for ages 13 and up and $7 for kids 12 and under. Free parking is available in the Galleria parking garages.

SUGAR LAND ICE & SPORTS CENTER
16225 Lexington Blvd., Sugar Land, about 25
miles from downtown off of US 59
(281) 265-7465
www.sugarlandice.com

Sugar Land Ice & Sports Center isn't the most conveniently located ice-skating rink in town, but it is one of the best, especially for kids who love hockey or figure skating. The Houston Aeros minor-league hockey team practices on one of the two rinks here, and many kids come to watch the team in action and yearn for their own pro hockey careers. In addition to in-house hockey developmental leagues for kids ages 7 to 12 and a developmental league for girls 12 to 19, the center offers drop-in sessions, where young hockey players of all levels can come play with their equipment and work on their skills. The center also offers a long list of classes for kids ranging from toddlers on up, as well as on- and off-ice training classes in ballet, spin, power building, and ice jumping.

One of the rinks is open for public skating about four hours each day. With all of the classes and other activities going on, the center's schedule is pretty packed and constantly changing so call ahead for current public skating times. It costs $7 to skate here, plus $3 for skate rentals.

Roller-Skating
Houston is home to several roller-skating rinks. The days and hours that the rinks are open typically vary by month or season. Most are open primarily on the weekends and a couple of weekdays during the school year. They are usually open most days during the summer, spring break, winter break, and other school holidays. Occasionally the rinks host themed events, such as retro music nights or dress-up days. Some, like the Dairy Ashford rink, host Mommy and Me or family skating times. Call ahead or visit the rink's Web site, where applicable, to find out the monthly schedule.

Just about all of the skating rinks have variable admission prices: They typically charge between $3 and $7 to skate, depending on the day and time. Admission is generally most expensive on Friday and Saturday evenings when there are big crowds; weekday mornings and afternoons tend to be the least expensive. The rinks typically have skates—both in-line and old-school roller skates—available for rental for $2 or $3. Since some people bring their own skates, this fee isn't typically included in the cost of admission. Group and private skating lessons are offered for beginners at many rinks.

Most rinks here host birthday parties and other special events. Some, like the Dairy Ashford Roller Rink and the Bear Creek Roller Rink, also host hockey leagues. The Bear Creek rink is home to the Cy Fair Roller Hockey League (www .cyfairhockey.com), which is open to kids ages 6 to 18. The Dairy Ashford rink is home to the Houston Roller Derby Rec League. Although the league's members are adults, younger guests are welcome to watch the team practice. Call the rink to find out practice times.

There are close to two-dozen roller-skating rinks in the greater Houston area. In the interest of space, this list is confined to those inside the city limits, although even these are located in more suburban areas. A complete list of rinks in the Houston exurbs can be found online at www .skatingfitness.com or in the yellow pages. With the exception of The Grand Event, which features a variety of activities for children, all of locations listed here are stand-alone skating rinks.

North Houston
AIRLINE SKATE CENTER
10715 Airline Dr., in Greenspoint, just southwest of George Bush Intercontinental Airport
(281) 448-7845
www.airlineskatecenter.com

i Have a child who likes to glam it up? Consider throwing a birthday party at Olive Anne & the Pink Pokka Dot. This Heights shop throws really fun birthday parties; they can even bring the party to you. Each party is unique and depending on your child, could revolve around pedicures and facials (seriously), karaoke, disco, tea parties, and more. Call the shop (713-802-2021) or visit the Web site (www.pinkpokka dot.com) for more information.

Northeast Houston
LOCKWOOD SKATING PALACE
3323 E. Lockwood Dr.
(713) 673-2232

Northwest Houston
TRADE WINDS ROLLER PARK
5006 W. 34th St., just off the Northwest Freeway/TX 290
(713) 682-5312

Southeast Houston
ALMEDA SUPER RINK
10750 Almeda Genoa Rd., off I-45, just southeast of William P. Hobby Airport
(713) 941-7000

West Houston
BEAR CREEK ROLLER RINK
5210 TX 6 North
(281) 463-6020
www.bearcreekskate.com

DAIRY ASHFORD ROLLER RINK
1820 S. Dairy Ashford, between Westheimer and Briar Forest
(281) 493-5651
www.skatedarr.com

THE GRAND EVENT
13700 Beechnut St., just west of Eldridge Parkway
(281) 530-7777
www.thegrandevent.net

WATER PARKS

When the mercury starts to rise, there's nothing more fun than a day at a water park. Houstonians used to have a few water parks to choose from, but some have closed in recent years. If you're willing to make a little bit of a drive, though, you can give your family a memorable day of sliding, floating, tubing, and swimming at one of two nearby water parks. Both of the area waterparks are open primarily in the summer, although they are typically also open on designated holidays and weekends in the spring and early fall. Check the Web sites or call ahead for the latest schedules.

SCHLITTERBAHN GALVESTON WATER PARK
2109 Lockheed Rd., Galveston
(409) 770-9283
www.schlitterbahn.com/gal
If you've got a day to spare and want to get out of town, make the 45-minute to one-hour drive to Galveston and visit Schlitterbahn. This popular water park is divided into three zones with German-sounding names: Blastenhoff and Surfenburg are the outdoor areas and Wasserfest is a heated indoor area. Each zone is filled with a range of slides and activities to keep everyone happy—from the biggest adventurers to the littlest tikes to those looking for a lazy day. Toddlers love to slide down the short Beached Boat Slide, splash around in the shallow activity pool in the Wasserfest Kids' Area, and get sprayed with water as they slide down some more tot-sized slides in Tiki Tikes. For older adventurers, Schlitterbahn is filled with huge slides with twists and turns galore, whitewater adventure, and even bodysurfing in the Boogie Bahn. When you need a break from all the action, head over to Kristal Beach and sit in a lounge chair on the sand beside Kristal River. Or pay a visit to Arcadia, where video games, Dance Dance Revolution, and air-conditioning await kids (and parents) who need to get out of the sun but still have energy to burn. There are concessions at the park but if you've got picky eaters or want to avoid buying a bottle of water every half hour, bring a cooler with food and drinks of your own. The entire park is open from late April to late September. From March to April and late September to December, the Wasserfest section

of the park is open for indoor, heated adventures. Ticket prices vary. During the indoor season, day passes for adults and kids 12 and up cost $25.99, and passes for kids 3 to 11 are $21.99. Summer day passes are $37.99 for kids and adults ages 12 and up and $29.99 for kids ages 3 to 11. Tickets can be purchased on-site, but you can avoid the lines by ordering them online.

i Schlitterbahn can get really crowded, especially in the summer and on weekends, so get to the park early and, if at all possible, visit on a weekday to avoid long waits.

SPLASHTOWN
21300 I-45, Spring
(281) 355-3300
www.splashtownpark.com
SplashTown doesn't have quite as many rides, slides, and activities as the other area water park—Schlitterbahn—but it can be fun nonetheless. Here little ones can climb net ladders on Treehouse Island, swing and play in the Blue Lagoon Activity Pool, and swim past the relatively authentic-looking crocs at Crocodile Island. Bigger kids—that is, anyone 48 inches or taller—can float on a raft along the river, ride in the eye of a tornado as they travel down a 132-foot tunnel, or go for a wild ride on the Ripqurl tube slide. The park is located about 30 minutes north of downtown on I-45 North. Admission at the gate is $32.99 for adults, $24.99 for kids under 48 inches, and free for kids under two. Tickets purchased online cost $2 less. Parking costs $10 or, if you don't want to walk far after a long day at the park, $20. Bring cash because the parking lot attendants don't take credit cards or checks.

SHOPPING

The vast amount of stores in Houston—including a number of luxury ones—makes the city a great place to shop. In fact, many people visit from other parts of the state or the region just to restock their closets. The reason? Just about anything you want or need can be purchased in Houston.

If you drive around town, you're likely to notice lots of familiar stores. Houston is, in fact, home to many chain stores, ranging from cheap retailers like Payless and Target to higher-end shops like Tiffany and Neiman Marcus. Most of these are located in strip malls, shopping centers, and malls. The best and most prestigious mall in the city is the Galleria (5085 Westheimer Rd.; 713-622-0663; www.simon.com), located on Westheimer Road just off West Loop 610 South. The Galleria is home to elite tenants like David Yurman, Prada, Neiman Marcus, and Nordstrom, as well as less-expensive vendors, such as Ann Taylor, Gap, Urban Outfitters, J. Crew, Macy's, Dillard's, and Gymboree. Many other stores—most chains, some not—are located on streets around the mall. Smaller, more specialized chain stores, such as Williams-Sonoma, Anthropologie, Lucy, Pottery Barn, and James Avery, are about a mile east of the Galleria in a shopping center known as Highland Village (www.shophighlandvillage.com).

Other popular malls in the area include Memorial City Mall in Memorial (www.memorial citymall.com), which is anchored by Target, Macy's, and Dillard's and has many typical mall chain stores, such as Abercrombie & Fitch and American Eagle. A couple of miles west along Memorial Drive is Town & Country Village (www.townandcountryvillage.com), an outdoor shopping area that includes big chains like Barnes & Noble, Restoration Hardware, and Chico's, as well as the cute children's store, Chocolate Soup, which is described in this chapter. There are a good number of other malls throughout the city. Since the stores in these malls are not unique to Houston and can easily be found by flipping through the phone book or calling information, they are not the focus of this chapter. This chapter focuses on the stores you might not discover without this book. These are primarily independent stores and smaller local and regional chains that give the city its unique flavor. Many of them are places where you can find special, one-of-a-kind things.

OVERVIEW

In the pages that follow, you will find stores in just about every category. These include antiques stores and commercial art galleries, thrift and resale shops, comic book shops, flea markets, toy stores, jewelry stores, shoe stores, gift shops and garden shops, specialty food stores, sporting goods stores, music shops, bookstores, and clothing stores for men, women, and children. You'll even find out where to buy cowboy boots and hats—used, new, and custom-made. The stores listed here are by no means the only ones in town, but they are some of the best in their respective categories. Together the stores included here span from inexpensive to luxurious, giving you options no matter what your budget is. The stores are organized by type and then divided by neighborhood, or, in the case of less-central locales, the general geographic direction. A good number of the stores included here are located in the Heights, Rice Village/West University, Memorial, Upper Kirby, Montrose, or around the Galleria area. All of these areas are discussed in the "Area Overview" chapter and can be found using the maps in this book.

Because many of the stores listed here are small, family-owned and operated shops, some of them are closed one or two days a week. These closure days have been noted when appropriate in the descriptions that follow. Keep in mind, however, that stores often change their hours, especially during the holidays. It's a good idea to call ahead and make sure the store will be open when you plan to stop in. Most stores in Houston have parking lots or free street parking available.

ANTIQUES

Memorial

CAROLINE THOMPSON'S ANTIQUE CENTER OF HOUSTON
1001 W. Loop North at I-10 West
(713) 688-4211
http://antiquecenteroftexas.tripod.com
See thousands of antiques under one roof at Caroline Thompson's Antique Center of Houston. This 120,000-square-foot warehouse space features more than 200 dealers offering a diverse selection of antiques, including furniture, decor, china, silver, jewelry, and old toys. Take a break by getting a sandwich or a drink at the center's full-service restaurant, the Radio City Café.

Midtown

ADKINS ARCHITECTURAL ANTIQUES AND TREASURES
3515 Fannin St. at Berry Street
(713) 522-6547
www.adkinsantiques.com
Located in a three-story house dating back to 1912, Adkins Architectural Antiques and Treasures has been helping Houstonians, movie studios, restaurant owners, and photographers find period design pieces and architectural treasures since 1972. Among the embellishments offered here are old street lamps, patio furniture,

doors, Anduze French pottery, and ornamental fixtures—many of which come from notable homes and buildings that have been renovated. Adkins also has a full wood shop that restores customers' architectural antiques. The worldly salespeople here speak French and Spanish, as well as English.

Montrose

ANTIQUE WAREHAUS
1714 Westheimer, at Park Street
(713) 522-6858
www.turningleaffurniture.com
As Antique Warehaus's tagline "Trash and Treasure since 1947" suggests, you'll find plenty of things you don't want here and a few that you do. If you're willing to rummage through the floor-to-ceiling stacks of antiques here—and can tolerate the store's dirt and dust—you'll find a great selection of furniture, flatware, dishes, old-timey decor, and old cameras. Best of all, you won't have to shell out your life savings.

TEXAS JUNK COMPANY
215 Welch St.
(713) 524-6257
For more than two decades, Houstonians have come to Texas Junk Company to find everything from yard art, old picture frames, and telephones to an eclectic collection of cowboy boots, animal hides, and reptile skin. Browse this well-organized warehouse's ever-changing selection to find unique gifts—and things you never knew you needed. The store can get hot in the summer so it's best to shop earlier in the day. Texas Junk Company is only open on Friday and Saturday, though this changes seasonally.

i In addition to the antiques stores listed here, there are several small antiques stores in Montrose along Westheimer between Woodhead and Dunlavy Streets.

Northwest Houston

MORTON KUEHNERT AUCTIONEERS & APPRAISERS

2801 W. Sam Houston Pkwy. North
(North of I-10)
(713) 827-7835
www.mortonkuehnert.com

If you're looking for one-of-a-kind antique furnishings, art, fine jewelry, silver, porcelain, or architectural finds from around the world, pay a visit to Morton Kuehnert Auctioneers & Appraisers. The company holds estate auctions every Thursday at 7 p.m., and each one features antique, estate, contemporary, and/or traditional pieces. Attendance and bidding are free, and there's no minimum bid. The company's staff is happy to help first-time bidders. Visit Morton Kuehnert's public gallery on the Wednesday or Thursday before the auction to familiarize yourself with the items up for auction. The company is closed Sunday.

Upper Kirby

MADE IN FRANCE

2912 Ferndale St., at West Alabama Street
(713) 529-7949
www.madeinfranceantiques.com

If you want to give your home a French country feel, visit Made in France. This shop's yellow walls and checkered floors are lined with fine French antiques, including furniture, paintings, and tapestries. Made in France doesn't change its inventory much; new shipments arrive from France each April and November. The shop is closed on Sunday.

i Attend the Houston Antiques Dealers Association's shows, held at the George R. Brown Convention Center each spring and fall, to see great antiques from more than 150 dealers. Learn about upcoming shows and other special events by visiting the association's Web site (www.hadaantiques) or by calling (713) 764-4232.

ART GALLERIES

Montrose

BARBARA DAVIS GALLERY

4411 Montrose Blvd.
(713) 520-9200
www.barbaradavisgallery.com

Barbara Davis Gallery specializes in contemporary visual art. Here you'll find an extensive lineup of emerging artists, as well as established artists doing bold new things with new techniques. Among the many artists represented by the gallery are Jonathan Borofsky, Andrea Bianconi, Paul Fleming, Joseph Cornell, and Kiki Smith. The gallery is closed Sunday and Monday.

DE SANTOS GALLERY

1724-A Richmond Ave.
(713) 520-1200
www.desantosgallery.com

Fine art photography is De Santos Gallery's raison d'être. Located inside a contemporary stucco building, the gallery touts work from the United States and abroad, but it shows a particular affinity for Spanish photographers as well as a selection of Iranian photographers. The gallery is particularly interested in helping newbie photography aficionados build their collections. The De Santos Gallery is closed Sunday, Monday, and Tuesday.

Rice/West University

GREMILLION & CO. FINE ART

2501 Sunset Blvd.
(713) 522-2701
www.gremillion.com

Gremillion & Co. Fine Art's contemporary American art is considered some of the country's best. For nearly 30 years, Gremillion has brought Houstonians an extensive selection of sophisticated sculpture, art furniture, paintings, and printmaking. Work is displayed in two galleries—the main gallery and the annex. Both are available for rental for special events. Gremillion is closed Monday.

River Oaks

TEXAS GALLERY
2012 Peden St.
(713) 524-1593
www.texgal.com
Texas Gallery is considered one of the city's best galleries. Here you'll find avant-garde and more contemporary works by artists from around the country, as well as a few like Rachel Hecker from Texas. The gallery has featured notable New York artists, such as abstract painter Elizabeth Murray, contemporary painter Jeff Elrod, and contemporary landscapist Ellen Phelan.

Upper Kirby

GERHARD WURZER GALLERY
1217 S. Shepherd
(713) 523-4300
www.wurzergallery.com
The Gerhard Wurzer Gallery specializes in original prints by significant 19th- and 20th-century artists, including some of art's biggest names such as Pablo Picasso, Joan Miró, and Marc Chagall. The gallery also showcases the work of rising stars and notable artists who are not household names. Among them are *Divine Comedy* illustrator Alfredo Muller and 19th-century Parisian painter Jean-François Raffaëlli, who is best known for his cityscapes. The gallery is open by appointment only.

GOLDESBERRY GALLERY
2625 Colquitt St., at Lake Street
(713) 528-0405
www.goldesberrygallery.com
Goldesberry Gallery is the city's premiere source for craft-based fine art. The gallery represents local, regional, and national artists who create three-dimensional pieces in media such as ceramics, glass, fiber, wood, metal, painting, mixed media, and collage. Goldesberry also showcases handcrafted jewelry. The gallery is closed Sunday and Monday.

HOOKS-EPSTEIN GALLERIES
2631 Colquitt, at Lake Street
(713) 522-0718
www.hooksepsteingalleries.com
Hooks-Epstein Galleries has been around since 1969, making it one of the city's longest-operating galleries. Many of the best art collections in the city include pieces acquired here. Hooks-Epstein specializes in representational American, European, and Latin works from the 19th and 20th centuries. The gallery is closed Sunday and Monday.

JOHN CLEARY GALLERY
2636 Colquitt, at Lake Street
(713) 524-5070
www.johnclearygallery.com
John Cleary Gallery is Houston's leading gallery for fine art photography. Photographs here range from vintage prints by famed photographers, like Henri Cartier-Bresson, Elliott Erwitt, and Dorothea Lange, to new work by contemporary photographers, like Brent Phelps and Rodney Smith. John Cleary Gallery is closed Sunday and Monday.

MEREDITH LONG & COMPANY
2323 San Felipe
(713) 523-6671
www.meredithlonggallery.com
Described by the *Houston Chronicle* as "a pillar in the landscape of Houston art," Meredith Long & Company is the gallery that many significant private art collectors turn to when they want to add to their collections. Meredith Long & Company specializes in 19th- and 20th-century American art, including paintings and sculptures. Among the many artists whose work the influential gallery has exhibited and sold are Thomas Cole, Georgia O'Keeffe, Alexander Pope, and Mark Rothko. The gallery is closed Sunday and Monday.

MOODY GALLERY
2815 Colquitt, at Lake Street
(713) 526-9911
www.moodygallery.com
Since Betty Moody opened this gallery in 1975, it has showcased work by American artists in a range

of media. With a large amount of work produced by Texas artists like Lisa Ludwig, Lucas Johnson, and Luis Jiménez, Moody Gallery is considered one of the best places in Houston to find work by Texas artists. It is closed Sunday and Monday.

BOOKSTORES

Downtown

BROWN BOOKSHOP
1517 San Jacinto St.
(713) 652-1917
www.brownbookshop.com

Dating back to 1946, Brown Bookshop is one of Houston's oldest bookstores, though it doesn't cater to the general interest. Books sold here are geared toward technical professionals, such as engineers, electricians, construction workers, and computer scientists. If you can't find the technical publication, codes, or standards that you need, just ask. Brown Bookshop might be able to order it for you. The bookshop is closed Saturday and Sunday.

The Heights

KABOOM BOOKS
www.kaboombooks.com
3116 Houston Ave., at Bayland
(713) 869-7600

733 Studewood St.
(713) 869-1700

Kaboom Books was a New Orleans establishment, until Hurricane Katrina came and the owner fled west. Now Houstonians enjoy two Kaboom stores, located just a few blocks away from each other in the Heights. Each store has a well-organized collection of hard-to-find, scholarly, children's, and used books by authors ranging from Danielle Steele to Henry Miller. The prices here are reasonable. If you have books to sell, bring them here: Kaboom will give you more for your books than competitors like Half Price Books.

i If you're looking for a specific book at Kaboom, call ahead to find out which of the two stores—if either—has it in stock.

Montrose

DOMY BOOKS
1709 Westheimer Rd.
(713) 523-3669
www.domystore.com

Don't go to Domy Books looking for the latest bestseller. The obscure titles sold at this popular hipster hangout focus largely on off-the-beaten-path art and comics from around the world. Domy also offers a good selection of first-edition books, zines and other hard-to-find periodicals, and other media. Check out the gallery to see new contemporary—and quirky—art on display.

HALF PRICE BOOKS
1011 Westheimer Rd.
(713) 520-1084
www.halfpricebooks.com

If you've ever visited a Half Price Books elsewhere in the country, you probably know that these stores are great places to find both rare and popular books at a steep discount. The family-owned chain has eight stores in and around Houston and two in particular are worthy of a visit: the Montrose location and the store in Rice Village. Both have especially good selections ranging from cookbooks to novels and everything in between, thanks in part to the large number of students and bookish types living nearby. The Montrose store can also be a fun place to people watch, although seating is limited. The Rice Village location is listed below; see the Half Price Books Web site or the yellow pages for the addresses of other locations in the area.

ISSUES MAGAZINE STORE
3425 S. Shepherd
(713) 521-9900
www.issuesmagazinestore.com

It's not exactly a bookstore, but Issues caters to Houston's reading population. Here you'll find mainstream magazines like *Vogue, GQ,* and *Martha Stewart Weddings* sandwiched between indie and obscure magazines, scholarly journals, and literary journals, like *Bitch, Farm Ranch Living,* and *JPG.* Issues also offers a selection of gay and straight pornography. Beware, though: There's not really room to sit and read here and there's no coffee shop to speak of, so plan to stand or buy and take your finds home.

Rice Village and West University
BRAZOS BOOKSTORE
2421 Bissonnet
(713) 523-0701
http://brazos.booksense.com
One of Houston's few independent bookstores, Brazos Bookstore is dedicated to maintaining what it calls a "careful, intelligent book selection." This includes a unique collection of literary fiction and nonfiction, biographies, poetry, history, literary criticism, philosophy, travel, art, and architecture books. The knowledgeable staff is happy to make suggestions or help you find exactly what you are looking for. The store also holds a number of author events and has a monthly book club. Recent authors showcased at Brazos include Andre Dubus III *(House of Sand and Fog),* Douglas Brinkley *(The Great Deluge: Hurricane Katrina, New Orleans, and the Mississippi Gulf Coast),* and Emily Fox Gordon *(Are You Happy? A Childhood Remembered).* On the first Wednesday of each month, Brazos hosts book club meetings that are free and open to the public. See the Web site to learn about upcoming meetings and events.

HALF PRICE BOOKS
2537 University Blvd.
(713) 524-6635
www.halfpricebooks.com
See the Half Price Books description in the "Montrose" section.

MURDER BY THE BOOK
2342 Bissonnet St.
(713) 524-8597
www.murderbooks.com
Since 1980, Murder by the Book has offered one of the largest collections of mystery books around, many of these being signed first editions. Titles here include everything from Agatha Christie classics to graphic thrillers. Nominated for *Publishers Weekly*'s Bookseller of the Year honor three years running, Murder by the Book sells a lot of books and, as a result, is able to recruit a lot of mystery authors to stop here on their book tours. Murder by the Book also hosts a free book club once a month. See the Web site to learn about upcoming meetings.

Upper Kirby
THE ALABAMA THEATRE BOOKSTOP
2922 S. Shepherd Dr.
(713) 529-2345
The Alabama Theatre Bookstop is owned by Barnes & Noble, yet its location in an old theater has enabled it to retain an independent flair. As you walk around this spacious bookstore looking at titles found at other Barnes & Noble stores, you'll see remnants of the old art deco–style theater, including bookshelves organized along seat rows, easy-to-trip-on stairs, and old carpet between aisles. There's often talk of demolishing the building, but for now it remains a staple of Houston book culture. The store frequently hosts author events, which are listed on the old marquee outside. Head upstairs to have a cup of coffee or use the free Wi-Fi.

BOOTS AND WESTERN WEAR
Various locations
CAVENDER'S BOOT CITY
www.cavenders.com
2505 S. Loop West 610
(Southeast Houston near Reliant Park)
(713) 664-8999

13580 E. Fwy. (East Houston)
(713) 450-3434

2345 W. FM 1960
(North Houston near Spring)
(281) 444-4588

12141 Katy Fwy. (West Houston, between Memorial and Katy)
(281) 597-1110

14045 Northwest Fwy.
(Northwest Houston near Jersey Village)
(713) 462-1122

This Texas chain is owned and run by a family of ranchers who dress in Western wear themselves, and make sure the clothes sold at Cavender's stores are authentic and durable. With their large selection of boots, blouses, shirts, and denim, Cavender's caters to everyone from farmhands to those looking to dress up for a Western-themed gala.

Galleria

THE HAT STORE

5587 Richmond, at Chimney Rock
(713) 780-2480
www.thehatstore.com

Find the perfect cowboy hat at the Hat Store, which specializes in custom-made, hand-shaped hats. This family-run business has designed hats for celebrities, such as former president George H. W. Bush and basketball star Shaquille O'Neill. Hats come in more than 25 colors. Although the store specializes in cowboy hats, the Hat Store offers hats in a variety of shapes and styles, including felt hats, fedoras, and dress hats. It is closed Sunday.

PINTO RANCH

1717 Post Oak Blvd.
(713) 333-7900
www.pintoranch.com

This spacious Western wear store sells what it bills as "Fine Western Wear." Pinto Ranch's inventory includes Stetsons, boots, jewelry, buckles, jeans,

Western shirts, and rhinestone- and turquoise-covered dresses and blouses—everything you might ever need for a hoedown or rodeo. Decorative logs inside and out give the store a rustic, ranchlike feel to get you in the mood to buy.

Montrose

TEJAS CUSTOM BOOTS

208 Westheimer Rd.
(713) 524-9860
www.tejascustomboots.com

Tejas Custom Boots is the place that celebrities and athletes call when they want a one-of-a-kind pair of cowboy boots made of ostrich, alligator, or other exotic leather. Former Houston Rockets basketball star Hakeem Olajuwon purchased more than 30 pairs made to fit his size 22 feet. Tejas also makes leather belts and buckles. Although the boots here are some of the finest around, they're not cheap. Prices start at $750 per pair.

Southwest Houston

WHEELER BOOT COMPANY

4115 Willowbend
(713) 665-0224
www.wheelerboots.com

Since it opened in 1960, this family-run custom-boot business has created one-of-a-kind boots for everyone from celebrities to ranchers and Texans with a strong sense of personal style. Master boot maker Dave Wheeler treats each boot as a piece of art and makes them according to customers' specifications. The world-renowned company has been written up in magazines ranging from *Playboy* to *Forbes*. Wheeler Boot Company is closed Sunday and Monday, although you can try to schedule an appointment on these days.

> **i** Find a pair of unique cowboy boots at a steep discount at Texas Junk Company, listed in the "Antiques" section of this chapter.

COMICS/COLLECTIBLES

Northwest Houston

BEDROCK CITY
4683 FM 1960 West
(281) 444-9763
www.bedrockcity.com
Bedrock City's two Houston stores—and a third in nearby Webster—aren't in the most convenient locations, but they are well worth the trip for true comic fans. Here you'll find an extensive collection of comic books, old and new, as well as a great selection of figures and collectibles from your favorite series. You will also find friendly staff who knows its comics. See "West Houston" for the address of the second Houston store.

Upper Kirby/Greenway

NAN'S GAMES & COMICS TOO
2011 Southwest Fwy.
(713) 520-8700
Get in touch with your inner geek at Nan's Games & Comics Too. In addition to comic books and figures aplenty, Nan's offers an extensive collection of board games, many of which you've probably never heard of. They also have a great selection of novelty toys. The shop's shelves can be tough to navigate at times, but the staff is happy to help. Beware, though: Nan's can be pricey.

THIRD PLANET
2718 Southwest Fwy., near Lakewood Church
(713) 528-1067
www.third-planet.com
From *Star Wars* to *Superman* to everything obscure and in between, Third Planet is the best place in town to find out-of-print comic books. The store also offers a great collection of comic figurines and novelty toys—that is, if you're willing to spend some time browsing. Third Planet has so much merchandise that toys here are stacked from floor to ceiling. Luckily, the staff is very helpful at this sometimes-overpriced store. Third Planet occasionally hosts author events. Call ahead or visit the Web site to find out about upcoming events.

West Houston

BEDROCK CITY
6517 Westheimer Rd., near Hillcroft
(713) 780-0675
www.bedrockcity.com
See the Bedrock City description in the "Northwest Houston" section on this page.

FARMERS' MARKETS

Downtown

GREEN MARKET
Discovery Green, Andrea and Bill White Promenade
1500 McKinney St.
www.centralcityco-op.org/discoverygreen.html
On Sunday from 12 p.m. to 4 p.m., the Andrea and Bill White Promenade at Discovery Green transforms into a marketplace where local farmers sell organic produce. In addition to produce, vendors here sell eggs, organic dog treats, locally roasted coffee, cookies, pimento cheese, and orchids and other plants. Some even sell craft products, jewelry, clothes, and bath products. See the Discovery Green description in the "Parks" chapter for information on parking in the area.

The Heights

HOUSTON FARMERS MARKET
Behind Onion Creek Coffee House at 3106 White Oak, between Studewood and Heights Boulevard
www.farmersmarket.rice.edu
Houston Farmers Market is the city's first Texas State Certified Farmers Market. Open on Saturday from 8 a.m. to 12 p.m., the market sells an array of organic produce, humanely raised chicken and beef, fair trade coffee, homemade dog biscuits, fresh herbs and gelato, and homemade bread and desserts. You can even get your knives sharpened while you shop. Parking is available in the Onion Creek Coffee House parking lot.

Midtown

MIDTOWN FARMERS MARKET

T'afia

3701 Travis St., just north of West Alabama

www.tafia.com/mfm.html

On Saturday from 8 a.m. to noon, head to the Midtown Farmers Market. Held inside and just outside T'afia restaurant, the market offers a little of everything—fresh-picked produce from more than 20 local farms, fresh roasted coffee, baked bread from Krafts'men Baking (highlighted in the "Restaurants" chapter of this book), free-range eggs, drug-free meats, and plenty of Texas cheeses. Several vendors here sell crafts and bath products. Plenty of parking is available on-site. You can also take the METRORail to the HCC/Ensemble stop. The market is open rain or shine.

Upper Kirby

BAYOU CITY FARMERS MARKET

Behind the office building at 3000 Richmond, between Kirby and Buffalo Speedway

(713) 880-5540

www.urbanharvest.org

Considered the best farmers' market in town, Bayou City Farmers Market is open every Saturday from 8 a.m. to noon, rain or shine. In addition to mouth-watering seasonal produce from local farms, Bayou City sells grass-fed meats, honey, coffee, and baked goods. The market is constantly adding new vendors, especially ones who practice organic and sustainable growing. On one Saturday each March, Bayou City hosts a free Kid's Market Day, where kids can learn about the environment and where their food comes from,

i Join the Central City Co-op and get great organic produce every Wednesday between 9 a.m. and 6:30 p.m. The makeshift co-op is located inside Ecclesia at 2115 Taft St. in Midtown. You can even place your order online. Visit the co-op Web site (www.centralcityco-op.org) to learn more.

participate in hands-on cooking demonstrations, get their faces painted, and pet some baby animals. See the Web site to find out the date of the next Kid's Market Day.

FLEA MARKETS

North Houston

SUNNY FLEA MARKET

8705 Airline Rd.

(281) 447-8729

www.sunnyfleamarket.com

More than 50,000 people visit the Sunny Flea Market each weekend, making it one of the country's largest open-air markets. The vendors here sell everything from vinyl records, old Nintendo sets, and garage sale–type goods to cowboy hats and beauty supplies. Most vendors will gladly bargain with you. There are also produce stands, tax prep services, pony rides, and an old-fashioned carousel. Don't worry about getting hungry: You'll find plenty of food here, including fresh cooked churros, fajitas, Chinese food, and chicken on a stick. Sunny Flea Market is open every weekend.

Northwest Houston

TRADERS VILLAGE

7979 N. Eldridge Rd.

(281) 890-5500

www.tradersvillage.com/en/houston/fleamarket

One of the most popular flea markets in town is Traders Village, which has been around since 1989. Each weekend more than 2,500 dealers show up to sell their goods, which include everything from old tires, silk plants, and collectibles to army surplus items, crafts, and comic books. There are also more than 15 food stands that sell spicy fajitas, huge turkey legs, homemade corndogs, cake, ice cream, beer, and more. Traders Village is open every Saturday and Sunday from 7 a.m. to dusk.

GARDEN SHOPS

The Heights

ANOTHER PLACE IN TIME
1102 Tulane
(713) 864-9717
www.anotherplaceintime.com
Named the best small nursery in town by the *Houston Chronicle,* Another Place in Time sells a beautiful array of orchids, tropical plants, herbs, annuals, and perennials. The staff is knowledgeable and can help you find plants for your garden's unique growing conditions. Be sure to stop in the gift shop, which sells Texas-made candles in all shapes and scents, vintage and decorative pottery, and garden decor. Another Place in Time also carries quite a bit of seasonal decor.

BUCHANAN'S NATIVE PLANTS
611 E. 11th
(713) 861-5702
www.buchanansplants.com
Buchanan's Native Plants specializes in organic gardens and, as the business's name suggests, native plants—those that can survive serious heat and humidity. In addition to native trees and shrubs, Buchanan's offers some lovely wildflowers, antique roses, and heirloom vegetables. The garden shop sells unique garden art, bird feeders, windchimes, candles, jewelry, scents, and handmade crafts.

JOSHUA'S NATIVE PLANTS AND GARDEN ANTIQUES
502 W. 18th St.
(713) 862-7444
www.joshuasnativeplants.com
Joshua's Native Plants and Garden Antiques offers plants that can sustain Houston's heat and humidity. The owner, Joshua, visits local farms each week to scope out and purchase new plants, which he then makes available to customers. Garden accessories that are available for purchase include concrete landscape pieces, recycled tumbled glass, and fountains. Joshua's Native Plants is also home to an 8,500-square-foot warehouse full of antiques, American and European pottery, handblown glass, and unique gifts.

River Oaks

THOMPSON & HANSON
3600 W. Alabama
(713) 622-6973
www.thompsonhanson.com
This upscale nursery sells both native and unusual annuals and perennials, as well as some sophisticated pots in which to plant them. In Thompson & Hanson's garden shop, you'll find unusual gifts, antiques, and fine housewares. If you have time, have lunch at the nursery's Tiny Boxwoods Café, which offers a delicious range of sandwiches and salads. More information about Tiny Boxwoods can be found on page 59 of the "Restaurants" chapter.

GIFT SHOPS

Galleria and Uptown Park

BERING'S
6102 Westheimer Rd.
(800) 237-4647
www.berings.com
Walking into the front of Bering's, you might mistake this for just another hardware store, but you'd be wrong. In addition to pet supplies and outdoor, patio, and hardware products, Bering's sells beautiful china, crystal, and silver. Just a few feet away from the elegant showroom where these products lie, there's a great selection of kitchenware and epicurean delights, such as coffee and unusual candy. Bering's also offers an extensive selection of stationery and invitations for special events, as well as gifts and toys for children and babies, home decor, and a large selection of Jon Hart luggage and accessories.

HANSON GALLERIES
1101–10 Uptown Park Blvd.
(713) 552-1242
www.hansongalleries.com
Handblown perfume bottles. Meticulously crafted earrings and necklaces. Glass cheeseboards.

Wooden kaleidoscopes and hand-carved boxes. These are just a few of the artisan gifts you'll find at Hanson Galleries. You'll also find some one-of-a-kind wall art, dazzling glass vases and bowls, and unusual scarves and ties. Since everything here is handcrafted, it can be tough (but not impossible) to find anything under $50. Free gift wrap is available.

JEFFREY STONE
5000 Westheimer Rd.
(713) 621-2812
www.jeffreystoneltd.com
Located across the street from the Galleria, Jeffrey Stone sells luxury gifts for men. Here you'll find some fine leather sporting bags and apparel, cigars from around the world, and pens by Cartier, Dunhill, and Montblanc. Jeffrey Stone also sells some high-end belts, clocks, and desktop decor. It is closed Sunday.

LÉRÁNT
5000 Westheimer Rd.
(713) 626-1377
Silver, china, picture frames, and a hodgepodge of other upscale home gifts can be found at this shop across from the Galleria. Léránt also offers a good selection of Judaica, including handcrafted menorahs and mezuzahs. Walk carefully and leave strollers at home: The store is narrow and lined with breakables. Léránt is closed Sunday and Monday.

THE MONOGRAM SHOP
5860 San Felipe St.
(832) 251-8771
www.monogramshophouston.com
Houston has many monogram stores, but this is one of the very best. From towel wraps to duffle bags to coolers, the Monogram Shop sells plenty of gifts ready to be monogrammed. The store also sells a wide selection of personalized sorority and college gear, as well as seasonal gifts, baby and children's gifts, jewelry, hand lotions, and Vera Bradley bags. The helpful saleswomen will even gift wrap your purchases for free. The shop is closed Sunday.

OLIVINE
1151 Uptown Park Blvd.
(713) 622-7776
www.olivineliving.com
This French-inspired store offers a variety of beautiful lifestyle items—beaded jewelry, bedding, furniture, glasses for the bathroom or bedside, candles and body scents, baby clothes, and even unique dog leashes. You may have to sift through the linens in this cozy store to find exactly what you want, but the salespeople are very helpful.

The Heights
TANSU
321-B W. 19th St.
(713) 880-5100
www.tansustyle.com
For the gift recipient who likes unique gifts, visit Tansu. This fun-to-visit store sells Japanese-themed gifts, such as origami, fountains, and lanterns, as well as stylish handmade jewelry, stationery, picture frames, furniture, and unusual items for the home and office.

Memorial
HANSON GALLERIES
Memorial City Mall
746 Memorial City Mall, near Starbucks
(713) 984-1242
www.hansongalleries.com
See the Hanson Galleries description in the "Galleria and Uptown Park" section.

HEART'S DELIGHT GIFTS
9600 Westheimer Rd.
(713) 974-0591
www.heartsdelightgifts.com
If you're shopping for someone who likes hearts, this is the place to go. Heart's Delight sells jewelry, vases, frames, and other gifts for the home—and most (though not all) of them include hearts in some form. The store carries quite a bit of merchandise by Brighton, Jeep Collins, and Jon Hart. Heart's Delight is closed Sunday.

OUT OF THE BOX
5709 Woodway Dr.
(832) 252-6222

Out of the Box isn't a big store, but it's got a huge array of gifts. The selection here includes bath and body products, stationary, flip-flops, kitchen decor, decorated aprons, jewelry, toys, and baby blankets. Many of these gifts can be monogrammed. Out of the Box is closed Sunday.

THE VILLAGER
9311 Katy Fwy.
(713) 461-2022

With a selection that includes stationery, jewelry, bath scents, serving dishes, and mosaic picture frames, the Villager is packed with great gift options. This popular Memorial gift shop also sells cards, women's clothing, Vera Bradley bags, unique seasonal decor and gifts, children's toys, and baby gifts. The saleswomen here are friendly and happy to wrap your gifts for free. The Villager is closed Sunday.

Montrose
CANDYLICIOUS
1837 W. Alabama St.
(713) 529-6500

Candylicious is a good place to find neat but inexpensive gifts for your favorite sugar addict. Here you'll find M&Ms, jelly bellies, rock candy—both on the stick and off—in a variety of colors, novelty toys, retro candy, and some unusual types of candy you have probably never tried before. Candylicious also sells carefully crafted baskets and gift packages combining different candies for every kind (and age) of sweet tooth.

PH DESIGN SHOP
3306 S. Shepherd
(713) 522-8861
www.phdesignshop.com

Just about any stationery, greeting card, and journal addiction can be fed at ph Design Shop. This small shop sells greeting cards, notebooks, stationery, desk products and gifts, and other paper products with funky designs. ph Design also has a full-service graphic-design studio that will custom design invitations and announcements for weddings, bar and bat mitzvahs, holidays, births, and special events. It is closed Sunday.

Rice Village and West University
BERING'S
3900 Bissonnet
(713) 665-0500
www.berings.com

See the Bering's description in the "Galleria and Uptown Park" section.

CANDYLICIOUS
2515 University Blvd.
(713) 784-1988

See the Candylicious description in the "Montrose" section on this page.

EMBELLISHED
2514 Rice Blvd.
(713) 523-2200
www.embellishedgifts.net

Embellished specializes in monogramming and personalizing everything from pillows to bloomers to dog tags to stationery. The shop also sells items like wallets, jewelry, and picture frames that don't need to be personalized. You'll find Jon Hart and Vera Bradley bags and accessories here as well. Embellished is closed Sunday.

LA TASTE
2417 Rice Blvd.
(713) 520-0027

Prepare to be soothed by lavender and other scents when you visit La Taste, where you'll find bath soaps, gels, lotions, and even a little bath confetti. The French-inspired shop sells well-known brands like L'Occitane, as well as some more offbeat scents. La Taste also sells colorful pottery for the kitchen and bathroom, unique candies, and dried flowers and potpourri. Free gift wrap is available.

PAULA FRIDKIN DESIGNS
2534 Amherst
(713) 520-6150
www.paulafridkindesigns.com

Costume jewelry and relatively inexpensive yet chic handbags are among the biggest sellers at Paula Fridkin Designs. The shop also sells a hodgepodge of gifts, ranging from candles and notepads to the latest in flip-flop fashion. New products arrive every day. Paula Fridkin has a second location in River Oaks.

SURROUNDINGS
1710 Sunset Blvd.
(713) 527-9838
www.surroundings.cc

Located a couple blocks from Rice Village, Surroundings is a great spot to find eclectic contemporary and ethnic gifts that are reasonably priced. Wooden tables, painted and designed by artist David Marsh, are scattered throughout the spacious shop. These are often used to showcase some of the store's other goods: one-of-a-kind painted lamps and mirrors, Talavera pottery, painted crosses, salt and pepper shaker sets in the form of animals, textiles, handpainted mugs, and bowls made from tree stumps. Surroundings also has a great collection of inexpensive earrings, including some from Latin and South America. The owners are frequently at the store, and like the rest of their staff, are knowledgeable and great at dishing out gift suggestions. They'll even gift wrap your purchases for free. Surroundings is closed Sunday.

THE VILLAGE FIREFLY
2422 Rice Blvd.
(713) 522-2808
www.thevillagefirefly.com

One of the newest shops in Rice Village, the Village Firefly is a great place to shop for artsy and unique gifts, including wall art, jewelry, Texana, seasonal decor, and home gifts ranging from glass cutting boards to painted gourds to papier-mâché dogs. Everything sold here is made by

artists from the United States and many of the featured artists hail from the Gulf Coast region. The selection changes regularly. The shop owner knows about each piece and artist, and she'll gladly tell you all about them.

River Oaks

EVENTS
1966 W. Gray
(713) 520-5700
www.eventsgifts.com

Some of the most elegant gifts in town can be found at Events. The large River Oaks shop has a beautiful collection of stationery, china, silver, crystal, linens, and handblown glass and pottery. Events also sells unique handmade jewelry, specialty photo albums, and ornamental gifts for men and women. Many couples register for their wedding gifts here. Nothing here is cheap but there are some fairly inexpensive tchotchkes. Events is closed Sunday except during the winter holiday season.

INDULGE
2903 Saint St.
(713) 888-0181
www.indulgedecor.com

Find the perfect gift for those who like to feel pampered at Indulge. This shop, which makes its home in a French garden, sells unique jewelry, linens, soaps and scents, children's toys, furniture, glassware, home decor, and garden gifts that owner Cynthia Davis has carefully selected during her trips to New York and France. Even if you don't buy anything, the beautifully decorated shop is worthy of a look. Indulge is closed Sunday.

PAULA FRIDKIN DESIGNS
2022 W. Gray
(713) 490-1070
www.paulafridkindesigns.com

See the Paula Fridkin Designs description in the "Rice Village and West University" section.

Upper Kirby

KUHL-LINSCOMB
2424 W. Alabama
(713) 526-6000
www.kuhl-linscomb.com

Kuhl-Linscomb is one of the more unusual shops in Houston. The 70,000-square-foot shop occupies five different buildings—three of them old houses—each showcasing different products. The main showroom is best. Here you'll find some unique gifts, beautiful—if pricey—handmade jewelry, quirky books, and a large selection of delicious smelling lotions and bath scents. The other showrooms feature unusual—and often retro—contemporary furniture, linens, and other home decor.

GROCERY STORES AND SPECIALTY FOOD STORES

Dairy Ashford

LEIBMAN'S WINE & FINE FOODS
14529 Memorial Dr.
(281) 493-3663
www.leibmans.com

Leibman's offers some of the best in gourmet food and wine. At this West Houston store, you can order a delicious sandwich or soup for lunch, pick up a nice bottle of wine and some gourmet cheese, or order gourmet gift baskets and party platters. Leibman's also caters and offers special menus and foods for major holidays.

> **i** You can't purchase beer or wine before noon on Sunday in Texas so plan ahead if you need to pick up a bottle or a six-pack for a Sunday gathering.

The Heights

ASIAN MARKET
1010 W. Cavalcade St.
(713) 863-7074
www.asiamarket-hou.com

Hard-to-find Asian spices are easy to find at the Asian Market, which supplies groceries to local

> **i** Need a nice bottle of wine? Stop into one of the dozens of Spec's Liquors locations around Houston. In addition to an extensive selection of wines from around the globe, Spec's boasts a knowledgeable sales staff that can help you find the perfect wine for your meal. It also sells cigars, spirits, gourmet treats, and, at some locations, deli sandwiches. Visit the Spec's Web site (www.specsonline.com) or consult the yellow pages for a list of the company's many Houston stores.

Thai, Laos, and Cambodian communities. It's not the best-looking store in town, but the Asian Market sells plenty of fresh galangal, chilis, Kaffir lime leaves, and Thai basil for reasonable prices. The market also sells some of the best-prepared (and most-authentic) Thai food in town.

Highland Village

CENTRAL MARKET
3815 Westheimer Rd.
(713) 386-1700
www.centralmarket.com

Central Market is a big slice of foodie heaven. Here you'll find some of the best fresh-baked breads and tortillas in town, an overwhelming array of tasty prepared foods and sandwiches, hard-to-find spices and gourmet foods, an extensive beer and wine selection, and staff who can help you find the perfect bottle for your meal. Central Market also sells gift baskets and flower arrangements consisting of some of the most beautiful blooms in town. It even offers cooking

> **i** Central Market's sister store, H-E-B, recently opened a location in Memorial that offers many of the same specialty foods, spices, and vast beer, wine, and cheese selections. It also sells the standard name brands. If you're in Memorial, stop in at 9710 Katy Fwy. (713-647-5900).

classes taught by some of the best chefs in the region. The store can be a little pricey though, and it doesn't carry a lot of standard name brands that you'd find at other grocery stores.

Memorial

SUPER H-MART
1302 Blalock Rd.
www.hmart.com
One of the best Pan-Asian groceries in town, Super H-Mart has a huge selection of Asian foods and spices. The large assortment of Korean, Chinese, and Japanese food products include everything from Korean pickles to garlic-infused Chinese cabbage to sushi-grade fish, as well as deliciously prepared Asian dishes. Super H-Mart is very clean and well arranged and the prices are very reasonable.

i Many additional Asian groceries and shops can be found in West Houston along Bellaire Boulevard between Boone and Fondren.

JEWELRY STORES

Bellaire

I W MARKS
3841 Bellaire
(713) 668-5000
www.iwmarks.com
I W Marks bills itself as Houston's "Hometown Jeweler," and rightfully so. For more than 30 years, this family-owned business has been South Texas's largest independent jeweler—and a popular place to buy wedding and engagement rings. The more than 100 showcases at the Bellaire store house diamonds, platinum, semiprecious stones, gold, and watches manufactured by the likes of Tag Heuer, Bertolucci, Omega, and Raymond Weil. I W Marks's success recently led the company to open a second location in Sugar Land. Both locations are closed Sunday.

Galleria

A.A. BENJAMIN
1775 St. James Place, Ste. 105
(713) 965-0555
www.aabenjaminjewelry.com
If you're looking for a one-of-a-kind engagement ring or another special piece of jewelry, visit A.A. Benjamin. Twice named the "Best Place to Buy an Engagement Ring" by the *Houston Press* and named the "Best Place to Buy Estate Jewelry in Houston" by *HTexas* magazine, this small Galleria-area shop sells exquisite estate, period, and antique jewelry, much of it designed in the art-deco, Georgian, and Edwardian styles. The shop also does jewelry appraisals. It is closed Sunday.

ZADOK JEWELERS
1749 Post Oak Blvd., at San Felipe
(713) 960-8950
www.zadokjewelers.com
Seven generations of the Zadok family have been fine jewelers, which means you get some serious expertise—not to mention great service—when you shop at this family-owned jewelry shop. Zadok's has an extensive collection of everything from platinum and gold wedding and engagement rings to Swiss watches by more obscure and creative designers like Gregg Ruth, Roberto Coin, and Yvel, as well as familiar names like Bulgari, Montblanc, Baccarat, and Lalique. Zadok is closed Sunday.

Memorial

MARNIE ROCKS
1415 S. Voss Rd., at San Felipe
(713) 533-0550
www.marnierocks.com
This airy boutique features trendsetting gemstone, gold, and silver jewelry designed by owner Marnie Greenwood, whose work has been purchased by celebrities such as Justin Timberlake, Jessica Alba, Rachel Ray, and Brooke Shields. The store also has a limited selection of home decor and baby toys. Don't worry if you don't know what to buy: The saleswomen here are knowl-

edgeable and happy to offer suggestions. Marnie Rocks is closed Sunday.

Sugar Land

I W MARKS
2623 Town Center Blvd.
(281) 275-5000
www.iwmarks.com
See the I W Marks description in the "Bellaire" section. This location is closed Sunday.

Upper Kirby

PAST ERA ANTIQUE JEWELRY
2311 Westheimer Rd.
(713) 524-7110
www.pastera.com
Brides, antiques collectors, and those looking for a special piece of jewelry head to Past Era Antique Jewelry, which sells one-of-a-kind rings, earrings, necklaces, brooches, bracelets, and objects dating as far back as the 17th century. The store's extensive offerings include many pieces designed in the Georgian, Victorian, arts-and-crafts, art-deco, Edwardian, and belle-epoque styles. The daughter of London jewelers, owner Marion Glober handpicks each piece she sells and goes as far as Europe to find many of her collection's exquisite pieces. Past Era is closed Sunday and Monday.

KIDS' CLOTHING

Galleria and Uptown Park

LITTLE LORDS N' LADIES
6100 Westheimer Rd.
(713) 782-6554
www.littlelordsladies.com
Little Lords N' Ladies sells runway-worthy children's clothing for boys ages 0 to 7 and girls 0 to 14. The store also sells an extensive array of accessories, including whimsical jewelry, trinkets, and gifts. This is also one of the best places in town to get your children's hair cut, although it charges more than other kids' chains. Little Lords N' Ladies is closed Sunday.

MINT BABY
1121-09 Uptown Park Blvd.
(713) 622-3580
From taffeta dresses to tutu skirts and cute shorts and shirts, Mint Baby offers children's couture that's perfect for a portrait session or special event. The store also sells everything first-time parents could need from hip diaper bags to beautiful beds. Service here is great, but that's to be expected, given how pricey most of the merchandise is. After shopping for baby, head next door to Mint (listed in the "Women's Clothing" section) to find some clothes for Mom. Mint Baby is closed Sunday.

SECOND CHILDHOOD
1922 Fountainview
(713) 789-6456
www.secondchildhoodtexas.com
This aptly named children's store sells new and used clothes and shoes for young kids—and buys your kids' old clothes on consignment. Most of the merchandise is used, but the clothes and shoes are good quality and tend to run anywhere from about $4 to $20. There is a limited selection of maternity clothes as well. A big play area in the middle of this small store is filled with toys that will occupy the kids while you shop. Second Childhood is closed Sunday.

The Heights

TULIPS AND TUTUS
833 Studewood
(713) 861-0301
Instead of focusing on trends and labels, this ecofriendly shop seeks to give kids (and their parents) lots of options for embracing their individuality. Style and fun are never sacrificed, though: The clothes, tutus, and toys sold at Tulips and Tutus are among the cutest in town and the service and prices here are terrific. Free gift wrapping is available.

Memorial

CHOCOLATE SOUP

12850 Memorial Dr.

(713) 467-5957

After you've been to some of Houston's smaller children's boutiques, Chocolate Soup can seem overwhelming. The spacious store is packed with oft-disorganized racks of clothes, but they're worth a look. The cute clothes here are made by brands such as Baby Lulu and Le Top, and the prices are hard to beat. Chocolate Soup also has adorable accessories, including a big hair-bow collection.

COTTON TOTS

6510 Woodway Dr.

(713) 785-8686

www.bestdressedkids.com

Located in Memorial at the intersection of Woodway and Voss, Cotton Tots is a great place to buy children's clothes, shoes, and even a few gift items—if you're willing to look. Most of the cute cotton clothes in this high-ceilinged store are stacked high in bins and baskets labeled by size. Luckily the staff here is eager to help find exactly what you need.

Montrose

BEBÉ VERDE

1741 W. Alabama

(713) 522-7373

www.bebeverde.com

One of Houston's newest children's boutiques, Bebé Verde sells ecofriendly products for babies. In addition to toys, clothes, and accessories, the shop sells nursery furniture, as well as hygiene and skin-care products. It also sells cloth, bamboo, and biodegradable disposable and hybrid diapers—and hosts chats to teach new and soon-to-be parents about diaper options. Bebé Verde is closed Sunday and Monday.

LITTLE PATOOTIES

2608 Westheimer, near Kirby

(713) 520-8686

www.littlepatooties.com

If you like children's outfits that look like they're meant for adults, Little Patooties is the place to go. Here you'll find boys' and girls' couture ranging from formal evening wear to casual styles. Sizes are available for infants through preteens. Little Patooties is closed Sunday.

Rice Village and West University

HIP HOP LOLLIPOP

6207 Edloe

(713) 218-7800

www.thehiphoplollipop.com

Hip Hop Lollipop sells some of the most hip, casual clothes in town for young girls, tweens, and women. The store is constantly increasing its cute quotient with new merchandise. At the back of the store, Hip Hop Lollipop hosts birthday parties that make little girls go gaga. Themes include Groovy Girl Rock Star, Hannah Montana, Glamour Girl, PJs and Pancakes, and Spa Party. Hip Hop Lollipop is closed Sunday.

PURPLE MANGO

2410 Rice Blvd.

(713) 529-9188

Find cute, brightly colored clothes for toddlers and young children at this well-organized Rice Village shop. In addition to an array of clothes, Purple Mango sells backpacks, bags, bows, and tutus, and offers an extensive selection of children's shoes, including boots. Be sure to check out the dressing rooms, which resemble a fairy tale castle. Purple Mango is closed Sunday.

MEN'S CLOTHING

Galleria and Uptown Park

A. TAGHI

5116 Westheimer Rd.

(713) 963-0884

www.ataghi.com

A. Taghi, as its tagline suggests, sells "fine clothing for men and ladies." Men can find slacks, suits, sport coats, and shirts, as well as shoes, by brands such as Zanella, Mobro, Santoni, and Bruno Magli here. If you don't want to look through the neatly manicured racks to find exactly what you need, A. Taghi's salespeople will do it for you. They'll also see to it that the clothes you select fit perfectly. A. Taghi has a second store in the Four Seasons Hotel downtown, although it is open by appointment only. If you want to schedule an appointment to visit that location, call (713) 650-1300.

M PENNER
1180-06 Uptown Park Blvd.
(713) 527-8200
www.mpenner.com
Recognized by *Esquire* magazine as one of the best stores in its class, M Penner sells men's suits, slacks, sport coats, and sportswear by designers such as John Varvatos, Luigi Borrelli, Tailorbyrd, and Versace. M Penner also custom designs clothing and sells shoes by Alden, Michael Toschi, Romano Martegani, and others. It is closed Sunday.

The Heights
HAROLDS IN THE HEIGHTS
350 W. 19th St.
(713) 864-2647
www.haroldsintheheights.com
Since 1950, Houston men have been going to Harolds in the Heights to find suits. Even former president George H. W. Bush buys his suits here. Harolds prides itself on selling only the best brands, including Canali, Trussini, and Ravazzolo. Service here is second to none: The sales staff is knowledgeable and will make sure your suit really fits before making the sale. Tailoring and free gift wrapping are available on-site. Harolds is closed Sunday.

Upper Kirby/Greenway
NORTON DITTO
2425 W. Alabama, at Kirby Drive
(713) 688-9800
www.nortonditto.com
Since 1908, Norton Ditto has been one of Houston's premiere fine clothing stores for men. It carries everything you could possibly need, including shoes, dress shirts, coats, pajamas, suits,

sport coats, slacks, and casual wear. Here you'll find brands like Trussini of Italy, Orvis, Tommy Bahama, Cole Haan, and Kenneth Gordon. If none of the brands available suit your needs, Norton Ditto's Custom Shop can design clothes especially for you. Don't have time to stop by to get fitted for your custom clothing? Someone from Norton Ditto will come to you—at your office, hotel, or home. The shop is closed Sunday.

MUSIC SHOPS

Midtown
SIG'S LAGOON
3710 Main St.
(713) 533-9525
www.sigslagoon.com
Named after the late *Houston Press* and *Houston Chronicle* columnist Sig Byrd, this campy Midtown music shop boasts a large collection of local and more obscure music on CD and vinyl. Sig's also sells some novelty toys. The store hosts a number of in-store performances by touring and local musicians.

Montrose
ALL RECORDS
1955 W. Gray, at Driscoll Street
(713) 524-4900
For more than 20 years, All Records has been one of Houston's leading independent music stores. It sells everything from classical and international music to big band, rock, pop, and folk. In addition to CDs, All Records offers an expanding vinyl collection as well as cassettes. Owner Fred Allred is always happy to talk music and will order anything you can't find. All Records is closed Sunday.

SOUND EXCHANGE
1846 Richmond, at Hazard Street
(713) 666-5555
www.soundexchangehouston.com
You won't find the latest top-40 tunes at Sound Exchange, but you will find an enormous selection of hard-to-find blues, punk rock, jazz, obscure

folk, psychedelic and rock, experimental, and local music. Some of this comes in CD format, but a sizeable chunk of the store's inventory is vinyl. Ask the staff for recommendations; they're likely to introduce you to some great new tunes. Sound Exchange also repairs turntables and offers appraisals for CD and record collections. It will even buy your old CDs and records—if your albums are the kind of music the staff likes.

SOUNDWAVES
3509 Montrose Blvd.
(713) 520-9283
www.soundwaves.com
Part surf shop, part music shop, Soundwaves sells a large selection of rock, country, classical, and jazz tunes, just about all on CD. The store has a very small selection of records and a selection of used CDs that's nearly as small. Soundwaves also has a decent DVD selection, including a shelf of used DVDs. There's a small coffee stand inside the store, but there is nowhere to sit while you sip. Soundwaves has two additional locations—one in the Clear Lake area and one in north Houston on East Crosstimbers. See the "Sporting Gear" section of this chapter for these locations' addresses.

Northwest Houston
VINAL EDGE RECORDS
13171 Veterans Memorial Dr., near FM 1960
(281) 537-2575
www.vinaledge.com
Located in far northwest Houston, Vinal Edge Records isn't in a particularly central location, but it's well worth the drive if you collect vinyl records. It doesn't even matter what kinds of music you like—the collection here is so expansive that you are sure to find whatever you want, as well as a few things you never knew you wanted until now. Finding such music will require you to thumb through what seems like miles of cardboard boxes lining the floor, though. Vinal Edge is constantly getting in new records, so the collection here is constantly growing and changing.

Upper Kirby/Greenway
CACTUS MUSIC AND VIDEO
2110 Portsmouth St., at Richmond
(713) 526-9272
www.cactusmusictx.com
For many years, Cactus Records stood next door to the Bookstop at Alabama Theatre as a staple of the Houston music scene. It shut down in 2006, but a few former Cactus staffers have since reincarnated the store, naming it Cactus Music and Video and setting up shop not far from the old location. The new Cactus is every bit as good as the old one: Here you'll find tons of independent and obscure music, as well as an extensive collection of Texas and Houston music. Although much of this music is available on CD, Cactus has an entire room of vinyl, dubbed the Record Ranch. The store also has a large stage, which it uses for in-store performances by local musicians and bigger acts peddling their latest album.

SHOE STORES

Bellaire
SHOE CENTS
3851 Bellaire Blvd. at Stella Link
(713) 666-5856
www.shoecents.com
Shoe Cents is a popular local chain among those who want casual, work, or athletic shoes at an affordable price. Service is do-it-yourself at this discount store so be prepared to look at the walls of shoes and find your size. Shoe Cents also sells handbags. Brands sold here include everything from Converse and Adidas to Nine West and Franco Sarto. There are 12 locations around Houston; the River Oaks location is listed in this chapter. For additional locations, see the Shoe Cents Web site.

Galleria
BRUCETTES SHOES
4920 San Felipe
(713) 993-0022
www.brucettes.com

Brucettes Shoes serves Houstonians with narrow and wide feet. This small Galleria-area shop has a big selection of dress, casual, and even tennis shoes in sizes 2 to 15 in widths ranging from AAAAA to WW. Many are made by well-known brands such as Stuart Weitzman, Nina, and Keds. The store also has a decent selection of dyeable and bridal shoes, as well as handbags. Brucettes has a second location out in Friendswood. Call (713) 941-1170 for more information on that location.

Rice Village

ARIEL'S VILLAGE SHOE SHOP

2507 Rice Blvd.

(866) 528-8424

www.arielsvillageshoeshop.com

Ariel's Village Shoe Shop doesn't carry a large variety of shoes. That's because the store specializes in comfortable shoes, especially those designed for people with diabetes or orthopedic problems. Among the brands sold here are Rockport and Birkenstock. The store's resident pedorthist can also design custom orthotics. Ariel's Village Shoe Shop does shoe and luggage repairs, as well as fabric dying. It is closed Sunday.

PREMIUM GOODS

2416 Times Blvd.

(713) 523-8825

www.premiumgoods.net

Premium Goods offers a good selection of Nikes, Adidas, and Pumas in all the latest colors. Just don't come here in search of your next pair of running shoes. Aside from a few pairs of Air Jordans, most of the shoes sold here are meant purely to make a fashion statement. The store sells a limited selection of men's and women's clothes.

River Oaks

SHOE CENTS

1560 W. Gray St., at Waugh Street

(713) 522-0250

www.shoecents.com

See the Shoe Cents description in the "Bellaire" section.

SPORTING GEAR

Bay Area

FISHING TACKLE UNLIMITED

12800 Gulf Fwy.

(281) 481-6838

www.fishingtackleunlimited.com

See the Fishing Tackle Unlimited description in the "Memorial" section.

SOUNDWAVES

1331 Bay Area Blvd., Webster

(281) 332-4200

www.soundwaves.com

Soundwaves is a music store but it is also Texas's largest surf and skate shop. Here you'll find more than 600 surfboards, some of them used. Soundwaves also has a great collection of Reef sandals and board shorts, women's clothes by Quicksilver, and all the latest skaters' shoes. The store has additional locations in Montrose and Northwest Houston.

Bellaire

AUSTIN CANOE & KAYAK (CANOESPORT)

5822 Bissonnet

(713) 660-7000

www.austinkayak.com

Whether you're looking for a whitewater kayak, a fishing kayak, a sit on-top kayak, or a canoe, you'll find it at Austin Canoe & Kayak, also known as ACK Canoesport. This small Texas chain rents and sells just about every kind of kayak and canoe imaginable, as well as all of the accessories you need, whether you're going for a ride down the Buffalo Bayou or heading to Clear Lake. Depending on what kind of canoe or kayak you want, rentals range from $30 and $40 a day for one to two days and $25 to $35 a day for three or more days. Paddles, cell phone cases, and dry bags are also available for rental. Each month, ACK offers a two-day introduction to sea/touring kayaking class that will teach you about navigation, safety, and equipment as you paddle around Independence Lake near Sugar Land. The class costs $93 per person, which includes equipment use; sign up on the Web site.

Downtown
IFLY, THE ANGLER'S EDGE
728 Travis St., at Rusk Street
(713) 224-4359
www.ifly.org
This small store is packed with all things related to fly-fishing. Here you'll find friendly but not overly aggressive salespeople, a large selection of poles, fishing line, and men and women's clothing by brands such as Patagonia, as well as a few unique gift items such as carved wooden boxes. IFLY, the Angler's Edge also has a travel services arm that helps fly-fishing fanatics plan personalized and guided trips.

Galleria
IFLY, THE ANGLER'S EDGE
5000 Westheimer Rd.
(713) 993-9981
www.ifly.org
See the IFLY, the Angler's Edge description in the "Downtown" section above.

WHOLE EARTH PROVISION CO.
2501 Post Oak Blvd.
(713) 526-5440
www.wholeearthprovision.com
Whole Earth Provision Co. sells a hodgepodge of products—travel and spirituality books, windchimes, sunglasses, children's puppets and toys, hammocks, and camping gear, like stoves, cook sets, and luggage. The store carries many products by the likes of Birkenstock and North Face, as well as some more obscure lines. Not only are the durable and functional items sold here useful for an active lifestyle, but they also often make great gifts.

Memorial
FISHING TACKLE UNLIMITED
8933 Katy Fwy.
(713) 827-7762
www.fishingtackleunlimited.com

Fishing Tackle Unlimited has aisles and aisles of gear for fly, in-shore, freshwater, and offshore fishing, including some tough-to-find tackle and accessories. The store also sells kayaking gear and rents kayaks for $50 a day. Inside Fishing Tackle Unlimited's Flywater Outfitters shop, you'll find clothing by brands like G. Loomis and Abel. The store has a second location in southeast Houston near the Bay Area.

Montrose
SOUNDWAVES
3509 Montrose Blvd.
(713) 521-9890
www.soundwaves.com
See the Soundwaves description in the "Bay Area" section.

Northwest Houston
SOUNDWAVES
20 E. Crosstimbers
(713) 694-6800
www.soundwaves.com
See the Soundwaves description in the "Bay Area" section.

Upper Kirby
WHOLE EARTH PROVISION CO.
2934 S. Shepherd Dr.
(713) 526-5226
www.wholeearthprovision.com
See the Whole Earth Provision description in the "Galleria" section.

Several major sporting goods chains are located in Houston, including Sports Authority, Academy, Bass Pro Shop, REI, and Gander Mountain. Consult the yellow pages to find a location near you if none of the independent sporting gear stores listed here sells what you need.

TOY STORES

Bellaire/Meyerland

IMAGINATION TOYS AND SHOES
3849 Bellaire Blvd.
(713) 662-9898
Imagination Toys and Shoes sells tons of toys and cute shoes for everyone from infants to preadolescents. While you shop, the kids can run loose and use their imaginations at the Thomas the Train table or in the kids' play kitchen. Some of the toys and shoes here can be a little pricey. If you're looking for something in a particular price range, just tell the salespeople, who will gladly help you find something within your budget. Free gift wrap is available.

Galleria

TOYS TO LOVE
1715 Post Oak Blvd.
(713) 599-0099
www.toystolove.net
Toys to Love lives up to its name. With merchandise ranging from remote-control dinosaurs, art project kits, and toy cars to cute T-shirts, pj's, stuffed animals and pillows, you could literally spend hours here and not see everything. The store also helps put together special gifts, including Easter baskets. Free gift wrap is available.

Highland Village

LEARNING EXPRESS TOYS
3838 Westheimer Rd.
(713) 572-9800
www.learningexpress.com
No matter your price range, you can do all of your gift shopping for kids at Learning Express Toys. This popular store sells stationery, toys and games, stickers, and personalized gifts galore. The salespeople here are happy to help you find the perfect gift or toy—and gift wrap it for free. You can even register for gifts for an upcoming baby shower or birthday party. This Texas franchise has 10 stores in the Houston area; the Memorial and Rice Village/West University locations are listed below. Visit the Learning Express Web site or consult the yellow pages for the locations of the stores in the outlying suburbs, including Katy, the Woodlands, Pearland, Cypress, and Copperfield.

Memorial

LEARNING EXPRESS TOYS
6531 Woodway, at Voss
(713) 463-7300
www.learningexpress.com
See the Learning Express Toys description in the "Highland Village" section.

Rice Village/West University

LEARNING EXPRESS TOYS
2402 Rice Blvd.
(713) 521-7200
www.learningexpress.com
See the Learning Express description above in the "Highland Village" section.

River Oaks

FUNDAMENTALLY TOYS
1963 W. Gray
(713) 524-4400
www.fundamentallytoys.com
Since opening in 1995, Fundamentally Toys has sold toys and games geared toward children's mental and physical development. This well-organized store sells lots of books, as well as a range of children's gifts. Fundamentally Toys will even host a themed birthday party for your child. The staff takes care of the registry, decorations, cupcakes, and fun; you just show up. Gift wrapping here is always free.

VINTAGE, THRIFT, AND RESALE SHOPS

The Heights

RETROPOLIS
321 W. 19th St.
(713) 861-1950
www.myspace.com/retropolishouston
If you live and breathe vintage, Retropolis is the place to shop. This two-story Heights store sells

a hodgepodge of clothes, accessories, records, and novelty items. All of the clothes are thrown together, so you have to search to find something special. If you invest the time and energy, though, you're likely to find a few keepers. Prices aren't the lowest in town, but they're not bad given the quality and uniqueness of the clothes.

WEAR IT AGAIN SAM
373 W. 19th St.
(713) 862-9327

Some of the best vintage clothes for men and women in town can be found at Wear It Again Sam. This Heights store has a huge collection of clothes from the 1950s through the 1980s, as well as lots of great accessories, including hats, purses, and shoes. They even sell retro home decor. Prices aren't quite Salvation Army cheap, but they're still pretty reasonable.

Memorial

ENCORE
6415 San Felipe, at Winrock
(713) 334-9327
www.encorehouston.com

For high-end clothing at reasonable prices, visit Encore. Here you'll find well-maintained clothing and accessories by Prada, Louis Vuitton, Gucci, David Yurman, Manolo Blahnik, and Tracy Reese—all secondhand. Owner Terry Rambin, a former Tootsies employee, will help you put together the perfect outfit.

Montrose

BLUE BIRD CIRCLE
615 W. Alabama
(713) 528-0470
http://thebluebirdcircle.com/resale_
shop.html

It's not uncommon to find brands like Banana Republic and Talbots on the rack at Blue Bird Circle. Clothes here are clean and well organized. The prices aren't the best in town, but Blue Bird Circle does mark down clothes the longer they're on the floor. The store also offers some nice used

furniture, wall art, and other home items. It is closed Sunday.

CHARITY GUILD RESALE SHOP
1203 Lovett Blvd.
(713) 529-0995

Not to be confused with the nearby Guild Shop, the Charity Guild Resale Shop is a good place to put together a costume. In addition to great accessories, Charity Guild offers a solid selection of vintage and newer clothes, including wedding dresses. Prices are marked down pretty regularly but the best items tend to get snapped up before they are marked down. The Charity Guild Resale Shop is closed Sunday.

THE GUILD SHOP
2009 Dunlavy St.
(713) 528-5095
www.theguildshop.org

Visit the Guild Shop for a good deal or an unusual piece of decor. This Montrose shop has a sizeable selection of previously owned clothes; rugs; jewelry; household items, like dishes and lamps; and even lithographs and original art. They also have some nice furniture, some of which is antique. The prices here are cheap, but if you wait a week or two, you'll likely find what you want marked down for even less—that is, if someone else doesn't beat you to it. The shop is run entirely by volunteers, and it frequently makes donations to charities. Call ahead to find out about selling your wares on consignment.

ℹ️ There are tons of thrift shops in Montrose, including several on Westheimer Road between Dunlavy and Mandell. Park your car and walk around the area to find the treasure you've been looking for.

Rice Village/West University

MEN'S RESALE BY THE VILLAGE
2437 Bissonnet St.
(713) 522-5645

Men who shop at Men's Resale by the Village can look like a million dollars without shelling out more than $20 or $30. This well-organized shop sells previously worn men's clothing, especially suits, slacks, dress shirts, and sport coats. Much of the merchandise here is by designers such as Zanella and Zegna, so prices tend to be closer to $20 or $30 than the $2 to $3 you might spend at other thrift shops. Men's Resale is closed Sunday.

Upper Kirby

MORE THAN YOU CAN IMAGINE
2817 Westheimer Rd.
(713) 668-8811
www.mtyci.com
Want to dress like Carrie Bradshaw without breaking the bank? More Than You Can Imagine is the place to do just that. This consignment shop sells secondhand clothes, shoes, accessories, and even home decor by designers such as Louboutin, Prada, Juicy Couture, and Louis Vuitton. Sizes range from 0 to 20. Although everything here was previously owned, many items have never been worn. Yet, even for these items, the price is just a small fraction of what you'd pay retail. More Than You Can Imagine is closed Sunday.

WOMEN'S CLOTHING

Galleria

A. TAGHI
5116 Westheimer Rd.
(713) 963-0884
www.ataghi.com
A. Taghi, as its tagline suggests, sells "fine clothing for men and ladies." Here you'll find shoes and casual and formal wear by designers such as Zanella, Brioni, Belvest, and even some clothes designed by A. Taghi. The salespeople are great about finding your size and pairing separates. They'll also make sure that whatever you select fits just right. A. Taghi has a second store in the Four Seasons Hotel downtown, though it

is open by appointment only. If you want to schedule an appointment to visit that store, call (713) 650-1300.

GREEN BY ADELINE
5136 Richmond Ave., at Sage
(713) 871-1888
www.greenbyadeline.com
Dedicated to environmental responsibility, everything at Green By Adeline is made with environmentally friendly materials, such as Austrian beech tree, certified organic cotton, bamboo, and wood pulp. The boutique doesn't sacrifice fashion, though. The dresses, blouses, and pants sold here are stylish, if at times preppy.

JEANS COUTURE
5000 Westheimer Rd.
(713) 626-5326
www.m2mfashion.com
Located across the street from the Galleria mall, Jeans Couture sells clothes for the younger, hip gal looking for jeans or something to wear for a night out. The store has a large selection of jeans by a variety of designers, as well as lots of brightly colored tops and dresses by brands ranging from Miss Sixty to Lacoste. It also sells big chunky jewelry and designer sunglasses. Jeans Couture has three additional stores—one in Rice Village (listed below), another in Katy, and a third in northwest Houston off FM 1960. Consult the phone book or visit the Web site for the addresses for the Katy and FM 1960 locations.

MINT
1121-7 Uptown Park Blvd.
(713) 977-4460
www.minthouston.com
From the moment you ring the bell to enter Mint, you'll see that this women's boutique is exclusive—and serious about fashion. The clothes here range from casual slacks and blouses to colorful suits and sundresses by designers like Hugo Boss, Moschino Jeans, and Cynthia Rose and just

(Q) Close-up

Variety Fair 5 & 10

Nestled in the hustle and bustle of the Rice Village of the 21st century is an old relic: Variety Fair 5 & 10 (2145 Rice Blvd.; 713-522-0561; www.varietyfair.com). Ben Klinger opened this five-and-dime store in 1948, when such stores could be found on many a corner. More than 50 years later, the store—now run by Klinger's daughter, Cathy Irby—still retains its mid-20th-century charm. The store's inventory is a floor-to-ceiling assortment of odds and ends. This includes everything from makeup, politician masks, coloring books, stickers, paper dolls, garden gnomes, and retro Pez dispensers to housewares, games, sewing kits, tea infusers, egg poachers, hammers, screwdrivers, hairpins, yo-yos, and kites. If you need something, there's a good chance you can find it at Variety Fair 5 & 10. What you want might not be easy to find given the store's haphazard organization, but the salespeople know where everything is and will point you to it. Little if anything here still sells for a nickel or a dime, but few things sell for more than a few quarters or dollars. Variety Fair 5 & 10 is closed Sunday.

about everything is pricey. Mint also has a small selection of jewelry and accessories. Mint Baby is located next door. Mint is closed Sunday.

M PENNER
1180-06 Uptown Park Blvd.
(713) 527-8200
www.mpenner.com
M Penner offers a good collection of dresses, suits, and casual clothing by some of today's leading designers. From Badgley Mischka to Hugo Boss to Paul Smith, the brands sold here offer women a variety of styles. M Penner is closed Sunday.

The Heights
HAROLDS IN THE HEIGHTS
350 W. 19th St., (the Heights)
(713) 864-2647
www.haroldsintheheights.com
Although Harolds is best known for its men's clothing, the store also offers a noteworthy collection of women's clothes, which includes fine suits, evening wear, dresses, and business casual clothes. Here you'll find brands such as St. John, Isabella Fiore, Audrey Talbott, and Zanella. Service is excellent. Tailoring and free gift wrap are available. Harolds is closed Sunday.

Highland Village
TOOTSIES
4045 Westheimer Rd.
(713) 629-9990
www.tootsies.com
Tootsies is Houston's premier women's boutique. While some women come here for casual wear and jeans, others head to Tootsies to find fine suits and ball gowns. No matter what you come here in search of, you'll have your pick of esteemed American and European designers and styles ranging from classic to contemporary. Complete your look with some of Tootsies beautiful jewelry, accessories, and shoes. The sales staff will make sure that you find exactly what you want. Tootsies also has an excellent Alterations Department.

Rice Village/West University
ALEXANDRA KNIGHT
2449 S. Blvd., #103
(713) 527-8848
www.alexandraknightonline.com
Actresses like Hilary Swank and Michelle Williams have purchased modish leather handbags from former *Vogue* and *Vanity Fair* stylist Alexandra Knight, who designs her unique handbags right here in Houston. If you call ahead, you can visit her West University studio to purchase a hand-

bag or talk to her about custom designing one just for you.

JEANS COUTURE
2511 University Blvd.
(713) 526-5355
www.m2mfashion.com
See the Jeans Couture description in the "Galleria" section.

LANGFORD MARKET
2715 University Blvd.
(713) 520-5575
Cotton and silk dresses, jeans, and trendy blouses comprise just part of this spacious Rice Village boutique. Much of the casual clothing here is vintage inspired. Langford Market also sells panties, swimsuits, jewelry, and other accessories. The store is decorated with comfortable chairs and contemporary paintings, and all of them are for sale. The hip salespeople wear outfits worthy of emulation, and they'll gladly help you put together one of your own.

VILLAGE GIRLS BOUTIQUE
2509 Rice Blvd.
(713) 533-1163
www.villagegirlsboutique.com
If you are looking for something fun to wear to a dressy casual party or for a night on the town, visit Village Girls Boutique. The dresses, blouses, sweaters, skirts, and jewelry here are every bit as bright and fun as the fuchsia-hued walls. You won't find much by familiar designers, but everything is reasonably priced and stylish. Village Girls is closed Sunday.

River Oaks
MUSE
2411 W. Alabama St.
(713) 520-6873
www.musehouston.com
Muse is a fun place to shop for funky clothes and accessories you won't find anywhere else in Houston. In addition to brands such as YA-YA, Nanette Lepore, and Tracy Reese, Muse sells dresses, tops, skirts, and pants by New York– and Los Angeles– based designers like B with G and Swati Argade. Muse also sells great jewelry, handbags, and accessories, as well as some home decor. You'll get lots of personal attention here, both on the sales floor and while you're trying on your finds in the boudoir-inspired dressing rooms.

Upper Kirby/Greenway
NORTON DITTO
2425 W. Alabama, at Kirby Drive
(713) 688-9800
www.nortonditto.com
Best known for its men's clothing, Norton Ditto recently added a Women's Department. Much like the Men's Department, the Women's Department offers high-end business and casual clothes by brands such as Audrey Talbott. Norton Ditto is closed Sunday.

i If you crave a good knockoff handbag and costume jewelry that won't cost you more than a few dollars, head down to Harwin Drive from Hillcroft to Gessner Road. Cheap perfume, knockoffs, and other quirky fashion finds are abundant here.

RELOCATION

People move to Houston for many different reasons: Some, like my stepfather, come for the promise of warm weather year-round. Others come for job opportunities in aerospace, architecture, medicine, law, business, education, or the arts. Many choose Houston for the low cost of living and the good quality of life. Some are sold on the cultural, social, and culinary offerings—the parks, the museums, the Theater District, the shopping, the restaurants, the festivals, the sports teams, the friendly people. Others come because Houston is a good place to raise a family. And more than a few come here to get an education and then stay. No matter why you have decided to move—or are thinking about moving—to Houston, you're likely to be able to find your niche in this city of millions of opportunities and people.

You are also likely to see why Houston topped *Kiplinger*'s 2008 list of the "Best Cities to Live, Work and Play." From an economic standpoint, Houston is about as good as it gets. The city's cost of living index is 88.1—well below the national average of 100. In 2007 the city's booming energy, aerospace, health-care, and technology sectors helped create 100,000 new jobs. Those new hires had their choice of affordable housing—some new, some old, almost all significantly less than comparable homes in other cities of Houston's size. While Houston hasn't escaped the recession of 2008 and 2009 entirely, it has weathered the storm far better than most of the country. And recession or not, Texans don't pay a state income tax.

The city is also committed to providing residents a great quality of life. In the last few years, the city has given downtown the most magnificent of makeovers, building a serene urban park, new sports stadiums, and a light-rail system. New restaurants, clubs, hotels, and residential developments have been quick to move in and make downtown a place where Houstonians want to spend their time. The city isn't stopping here, though: In the next few years, Houston will be adding more light-rail lines, making it even easier to get around downtown. Elsewhere in the city, you'll find all of those other things that make for a good life: good primary and secondary schools, world-class colleges and universities, some of the best health-care facilities in the world, great grocery stores and farmers' markets, festivals, shops, live music, restaurants, parks, and playgrounds.

OVERVIEW

One's quality of life depends on more than just finding the right city. You also have to find the right place to live in that city, a place that caters to your needs, wants, and pocketbook. So where should you live? Greater Houston is filled with dozens of neighborhoods, subdivisions, and suburbs that continue to expand along with Houston's population, which has grown nearly 15 percent since 2000. In the pages that follow, you'll learn about some of the most desirable neighborhoods in the city. You'll also learn about real estate agencies and other resources that can help you find your new home, whether you are renting or looking to buy. Keep in mind that most neighborhoods aren't for everyone. If you're young or you and your family like to be in the middle of the action, you would probably be far happier in a central, happening area like Midtown, the Heights, or downtown than you would be in a suburb like Sugar Land or Katy.

This chapter also covers some of the things you will need to do once you have moved to Houston—things like registering your car, registering to vote, licensing your pet, getting a driver's license, and finding a place of worship. In subsequent chapters you will learn about the city's education, child-care, higher education, and health-care offerings—all factors that could affect your decision about where to live.

NEIGHBORHOODS

Houston and the surrounding area are filled with dozens of neighborhoods, ranging from eclectic urban communities with lofts and luxury hotels to distant suburbs with houses with swimming pools. To give you some direction in deciding where to live, a few of the most desirable and popular residential neighborhoods are listed in this section. Most housing in these neighborhoods is single-family homes. However, most neighborhoods have some apartments and condos. Apartments in Houston tend to be located in large complexes with on-site management. Many have facilities such as gyms, laundry rooms, and pools; the vast majority includes parking—often gated.

With so many neighborhoods and rapidly growing suburbs, it is impossible to list every desirable neighborhood here. So as you read the following pages and begin to search for a place to live, keep in mind that there are plenty of neighborhoods and suburbs in the Houston area that would be great places to call home. Be sure to study the "Area Overview" chapter for additional insight on these neighborhoods. If you have school-age children, take a close look at the "Education and Child Care" chapter, too.

Bellaire

Located just off the Loop, Bellaire is an independently run city. While there is a strong sense of community here, Bellaire is hardly disconnected from the rest of Houston. Residents enjoy easy access to the Medical Center, downtown, and the Galleria, as well as many other neighborhoods inside the Loop. This makes Bellaire an attractive option for many doctors, as well as

professionals who work downtown. The area, which is home to a couple of synagogues and the Jewish Community Center, is also home to a sizeable Jewish community. The City of Bellaire is primarily residential, although there are a number of retail businesses and restaurants in the area. Single-family homes comprise more than 94 percent of the housing here, but there are some apartments in the area. While there are a number of older, smaller houses in Bellaire, there has been a trend toward tearing these down and building bigger houses in recent years. The median home value here is $545,000; the median condo value is $245,000. Bellaire is served by the Houston Independent School District, and most students are zoned to attend Bellaire High School. You can learn more about Bellaire at www.ci.bellaire.tx.us.

Clear Lake

The heart of Houston's Bay Area is Clear Lake, located about 20 miles southeast of Houston on I-45. Many residents work at nearby NASA, and a good number enjoy sailing, waterskiing, and other water-based recreational activities in Clear Lake and Galveston Bay. Housing in this family-oriented area ranges from smaller, older homes to large new homes in planned communities. There are even some houses right on the water, although you'll typically pay a premium for such a location. The broad array of single-family homes in Clear Lake makes for quite a variation in pricing: You can find homes here for anywhere from $150,000 on up to $3.5 million for newer mansions. Most homes, though, fall below the $1 million mark. The area is served by Clear Creek Independent School District and Dickinson Independent School District.

Cypress

Located about 20 miles northwest of downtown off US 290, Cypress is an unincorporated area of Harris County. Extraterritorial jurisdiction gives the City of Houston control over this major suburban area. Cypress is divided into many neighborhoods and subdivisions, such as Jersey Village, Klein, and Copperfield. Up until the 1950s, Cypress was farmland, so the houses here are pretty new and range from smaller two- and three-bedroom homes to larger brick houses. Many of the neighborhoods here are master-planned communities with their own recreational facilities and offerings, such as parks and neighborhood swimming pools. There's quite a bit of commercial development in the area, including a new outlet mall with 120 stores. The median single-home value here is $208,500; the median condo value is $193,500. Two school districts serve the area—Cypress Independent School District and Klein Independent School District.

Downtown

Downtown's revitalization in the early 2000s resulted in many new lofts and luxury condos, and with them people who actually wanted to live downtown. Many Houstonians opt to live downtown because it means easy access to the office. Residents also enjoy easy access—not to mention light-rail, sidewalk, and underground tunnel access—to some of the city's best offerings, including the Theater District, the Houston Rockets and Astros, great restaurants and clubs, and Discovery Green and other parks. More than 87 percent of the housing here is condos; the median downtown condo value is $258,000. Rent downtown ranges from just under $1,000 per month on up to more than $11,000 per month for luxury penthouses. More than two-thirds of downtown residents are married, although there's also a sizeable population of young single professionals. Children living downtown are zoned to attend school in the Houston Independent School District.

Galleria/Uptown

The Galleria area is anchored by the Galleria mall and the many restaurants, shops, hotels, and other businesses that surround this prestigious shopping district. Since the 1990s, the Galleria/Uptown area has become home to a number of new residential developments. Most of these are luxury high-rise condos, condos, apartments, lofts, and town houses. In fact, nearly half of

Houston floods often, so be sure to get flood insurance if you rent or buy a home in the area. Not all insurance companies provide this, especially if you live in a flood zone, so you might have to shop around. All it will take is one storm to realize that it was worth every hour and dollar it took to get that coverage.

the residences here are condos; only about 37 percent are single-family homes. More than a third of the neighborhood's residents are single, making this an attractive area for young professionals to live. The median condo value in the Galleria area is $177,500, while the median value for single-family homes is $537,000. Rent for the area's apartments ranges from about $650 per month for smaller, less-luxurious apartments farther away from the Galleria to as much as $5,000 a month for luxury rentals with a doorman and other amenities. While close proximity to great shopping and dining is part of the neighborhood's allure, many people move here for easy access to other parts of the city. Located just off of the West Loop, the Galleria area is just minutes from downtown, the Medical Center, Memorial, River Oaks, and many other central locations around the city. Children in the area are zoned to attend school in the Houston Independent School District.

The Heights

The Heights is one of the city's most unique and historic neighborhoods, making it an attractive option for many people in search of a fairly central eclectic location. While many older homes around the city have been bulldozed and replaced with newer cookie-cutter homes, that hasn't been the case with the Heights. In the 1970s Heights residents began a campaign to restore the beautiful Victorian homes—some mansions—in their neighborhood. Residents here tend to be very community minded and know one another's faces, if not names. The neighborhood even has its own civic association and opera, as well as a neighborhood fun run and art events throughout the year. Single-family houses comprise more than 90 percent of the housing in the Heights, where the median home value is $284,000. These homes include a mix of old bungalows, Victorian homes, and enchanting cottages. The Houston Independent School District serves the Heights. Visit the Heights' civic organization at www.houstonheights.org to learn more.

Katy

Over the last two decades, Katy has attracted large numbers of families with its relatively new master-planned communities, such as Cinco Ranch, Memorial Parkway, and Grand Lakes. Located about 25 miles west of downtown off of I-10, these affluent communities boast amenities such as swimming pools, golf courses, parks, rec centers, and playgrounds. More than 90 percent of housing in Katy is single-family homes, which are fairly large in many of the developments. Less than 1 percent of housing is comprised of condos; the rest are apartments. A median home value of $133,500 makes Katy an affordable option for many people who want relatively easy access to downtown. There has been tremendous commercial development in the area over the last few years, with a number of retail vendors and restaurants setting up shop in Katy. Part of what's now considered the Katy area is located in the City of Katy, which is an independent municipality; the rest of the area is an unincorporated area controlled by the City of Houston. Children in the area are zoned to attend school in the Katy Independent School District.

Kingwood

Located in northeast Houston about 23 miles from downtown, Kingwood is home to several master-planned communities. The neighborhood—which was annexed by the City of Houston in 1996—is divided into several villages, each of which is heavily wooded. Housing here is comprised largely of single-family homes, although about a quarter of Kingwood residents rent apartments, condos, or houses. The median home value is $143,010. Each year, the community holds several events in Town Center Park. Among them are Mardi Gras, Fourth of July, and picnics. Most of Kingwood is located in Harris County, but a small part lies in Montgomery County. Students are zoned to attend school in the Humble Independent School District.

Medical Center and South Loop

Some of the most affordable, centrally located apartments in Houston can be found near the Texas Medical Center. Many medical center staff and students live in new developments along Hermann Park or in the nearby South Loop area, which, as its name suggests, is located along the south side of Loop 610. The South Loop neighborhood runs along South Main and Fannin Streets near the Reliant Center, where the Houston Texans play football and the Houston Livestock Show and Rodeo is held each year. Developers have moved in and begun renovating older apartments and building new, yet affordable ones. The neighborhood is easily accessible on the METRORail and has a number of METRO bus stops. There are many retail businesses and restaurants here, too. Children in the South Loop are zoned for the Houston Independent School District. Apartments and condos for rent in the area run between about $750 and $1,200 per month, although you'll find a few here and there that are outside of this range.

Memorial

This wealthy neighborhood on Houston's west side is home to large as well as beautiful landscaping and old trees. Many of the houses in Memorial were built 50 years ago, but contractors have begun to move in and tear down the original houses to replace them with enormous homes. While housing here consists largely of single-family homes, a number of upscale apartment complexes have cropped up recently, with rents ranging from about $1,000 to upwards of $2,000. Memorial is divided into many smaller neighborhoods, and in a few cases, independently run villages with their own municipal governments. In 2008 Forbes.com named two of these villages—Bunker Hill and Hunters Creek—"Top Suburbs to Live Well." A number of prominent people live in Memorial, including former baseball All-Star Roger Clemens. Single-family homes in Memorial have a median home value of $877,000, but there are many homes in the multimillions, as well as some that cost well below the median. The median condo value here is $181,500. The majority of Memorial is zoned for the Spring Branch Independent School District, although some parts of the area are zoned for the Houston Independent School District. Many Memorial parents send their children to private schools, such as The Kinkaid School and Second Baptist Church. Often people who can't quite afford a Memorial mortgage or rent live on the north side of I-10 in Spring Valley. This enables families to send their children to Spring Branch schools and pay less for housing. The median home value in Spring Valley is $464,000; the median condo value is $302,500.

Midtown

Victorian-style homes dating back to the early 20th century once lined the streets of this urban neighborhood, but with Midtown's revamp in the 1990s came their demolition. Today these old homes have been replaced with upscale apartments, town houses, and lofts. This mixed-use area is considered one of Houston's most hip neighborhoods, with popular bars and restaurants lining the area. Midtown residents are largely 20- and 30-somethings who work downtown or in the nearby Medical Center, but you'll find families here, as well as a large Vietnamese population. Close to half of Midtown's residents are single, and about 60 percent of residents live in single-family homes. Another 30 percent live in condos. The median home value is $231,000; the median condo value is $118,500. Apartments in Midtown range from about $650 per month to more than $2,000 per month. Midtown youth attend school in the Houston Independent

School District. Visit www.houstonmidtown.com to learn more about Midtown.

Montrose

Montrose's proximity to downtown, Rice University, Midtown, River Oaks, the Medical Center, and the Museum District makes it an attractive place to call home. The neighborhood, which has a large gay and lesbian population, is one of the city's most diverse. Many new apartments and condos have recently been built in the eastern part of Montrose near Midtown, pricing out many of the artsy types and students who have historically called this eclectic neighborhood home. In their stead are a growing number of young professionals. About half of Montrose's residents are single and about two-thirds live in single-family homes, which range from restored mansions dating back to the early 1900s to cute cottages. Even as Montrose has become a pricier place to live, it has remained eclectic and community oriented. Many families also live in the area, particularly in Neartown, a neighborhood with tree-lined streets and homes that range from mansions to cottages. Among the people who have lived here are reclusive aviator Howard Hughes and former U.S. president Lyndon B. Johnson. The median Montrose home value is $336,000; the median condo value is $217,500. Apartments here range from about $800 per month to $2,000 per month although there are certainly some apartments that cost quite a bit more. The neighborhood is served by the Houston Independent School District.

Check out www.swamplot.com for the latest news on Houston real estate, architecture, home design, and renovation.

Pearland

One of the fastest growing cities in the country, Pearland is located about 20 miles south of downtown. The independent city is filled with master-planned communities with parks and recreational facilities, as well as retail locations. Larger homes here are more affordable than they are in more central locations, making Pearland an enticing option for many families. The median home value is $178,500; the limited number of condos here has a median value of $114,500. Residents also enjoy relative quietude, a family-friendly community, and easy access to jobs in the Medical Center and downtown via TX 288. Pearland is served primarily by the Pearland Independent School District; parts of the area are served by the Alvin Independent School District. You can learn more about Pearland by visiting the city's Web site at www.cityofpearland.com.

River Oaks

Located inside the Loop, River Oaks is in one of the country's wealthiest zip codes. Close to a quarter of the residents make $800,000 or more a year. Residents are typically big business professionals, lawyers, and doctors; many belong to the exclusive River Oaks Country Club. Throughout River Oaks are older stately mansions embellished with lavish landscaping. The Houston Independent School District serves River Oaks. Many children in the neighborhood attend Mirabeau B. Lamar High School, which is one of the best public high schools in the area. A number of others attend St. John's School, which is located in River Oaks. Although houses make up the majority of River Oaks housing, there are some condos and apartments in the area. The median single-family home value is $698,000; the median condo value is $235,000. Learn more about living in River Oaks at www.ropo.org.

Sugar Land

Situated about 20 miles southwest of downtown, Sugar Land is an independent municipality in Fort Bend County. The city is home to master-planned communities with houses that have largely been built within the last 20 years. Each community has retail and recreation facilities, such as tennis courses, golf courses, pools, and clubhouses. Many people move here because they can get a bigger home for less than they might pay in the city. About 15 percent of people in Sugar Land rent houses or apartments. The median home value here is $236,000 and

i Visit www.movehouston.com to compare rates on utilities and order service for your home phone, cable TV, satellite TV, electricity, and high-speed Internet.

the median condo value is $127,500. There are plenty of homes in Sugar Land that cost in the millions, making this a popular place for professional athletes to live. In 2008 Forbes.com named Sugar Land one of the "Top Suburbs to Live Well" (along with two Memorial neighborhoods) and in 2006 *Money* magazine ranked Sugar Land third on its list of "100 Best Cities to Live in the United States." Sugar Land is served by the Fort Bend Independent School District. You can learn more about Sugar Land by visiting the city's Web site at www.sugarlandtx.gov.

West University

This neighborhood just west of Rice University is one the most lovely—and priciest—areas of the city. Many streets in West University—aka West U—are lined with large oak trees and homes here are eclectic in design and steep in price. Houses vary in size, but many have small yards. More than 85 percent of the housing here is single-family homes; another 9 percent is condos. The median home value in West U is $646,000; the median condo value is $143,000. Most West U residents are professionals (and in some cases, Rice professors) with families who appreciate the neighborhood's proximity to the Medical Center, Museum District, Hermann Park, and downtown. Close to 40 percent of residents here make $600,000 or more a year. Children in West U are zoned to attend school in the Houston Independent School District and its well-regarded Mirabeau B. Lamar High School. You can learn more about West U by visiting www.westu.org.

The Woodlands

Located nearly an hour northeast of downtown off I-45, this master-planned community offers a serene retreat from the city. The Houston exurb, as its name suggests, is highly wooded and beautiful, with plenty of community-oriented offerings and amenities. The vast majority of Woodlands residents are families living in single-family homes, although there are some condos and apartments in the area. Residents often choose The Woodlands, in part, because it is a less-expensive alternative to living in the city. The area has its own mall, several golf courses, a country club, and plenty of other recreational facilities. The median home value is $235,000; the median condo value is $124,000. The Woodlands is served by three school districts: Tomball, Conroe, and Magnolia. Learn more about The Woodlands by visiting www.thewoodlands.com.

REAL ESTATE AGENCIES AND RESOURCES

Finding a new home can be a big endeavor, especially in a city as big as Houston. Luckily, there are thousands of knowledgeable Realtors in the Houston area who can help you buy or sell a home or rent an apartment or loft. Below is a list of a few of the biggest and best-known real estate brokerage firms in the area. At these firms and many others, you'll find Realtors who speak many languages, so if you need someone who speaks a language other than English, just ask. Note that the list here is by no means all-inclusive. There are dozens of other reputable companies and agents who can also help you find a new home.

To find additional agents and agencies, contact the **Houston Association of Realtors** (HAR), which helps Houstonians and soon-to-be Houstonians find real estate agents and new homes. The service is free and is available for people looking to buy, as well as those looking to rent apartments, lofts, and houses. Visit the Web site www.har.com to search for houses, apartments, real estate companies, or agents or call (713) 629-1900 for free assistance.

Many Realtors distribute publications from a series called **Houston Newcomer Guides,** which highlights everything you need to know about moving to areas such as Clear Lake, Fort Bend County (where Sugar Land is located), Northeast Houston, Northwest Houston, West

Houston, and the area along TX 288 South, which includes the Texas Medical Center and Pearland. You can also request a free paper copy or view the electronic version online at www.houstonnewcomerguides.com.

Apartment hunters can find apartments through **Apartment Whiz,** which offers free apartment locating services. Call (713) 688-5585 or visit www.apartmentwiz.com to get started. Other apartment-hunting resources include the Web site **Houston Apartments** (www.houstonapartments.com) and the local **Apartment Guide** magazine, which you can pick up for free in most grocery stores. While you're picking up Apartment Guide, you might want to grab a copy of the Houston Press and the Greensheet and look for apartments in their respective classified sections. Also be sure to pick up the Sunday Houston Chronicle, which includes real estate ads, or visit the Chronicle's Web site (www.chron.com/realestate), where you can browse for homes in the neighborhood of your choice and learn about the latest local real estate trends.

CENTURY 21 BALLARD & ASSOCIATES
5930 Hwy. 6 North, Ste. A1
(281) 855-6100
www.century21ballard.com
Century 21 Ballard & Associates was opened by veteran property manager and licensed Realtor Darrell Ballard in 1991. Today the firm has more than 30 agents who speak many different languages, including Arabic, French, Spanish, German, and Italian. Located on the west side of town, Century 21 Ballard & Associates sells homes and helps buyers find homes in Cypress, Houston, and Katy.

CENTURY 21 THE MORTON GROUP
www.c21morton.com
14525 FM 529, Ste. 200 (Northwest)
(281) 582-9999

2425 W. Loop South (Galleria)
(713) 297-8866
Century 21 the Morton Group has two offices—one in Northwest Houston, the other in the

Galleria area. The firm has more than 25 agents who speak many different languages, including German and Spanish. The Morton Group serves clients seeking to buy and sell in the Houston and Katy areas.

CENTURY 21 PREMIER GOLD PROPERTIES
8118 Park Place, Ste. 300
(713) 644-0084
www.century21.com
With almost 100 agents who speak 27 languages, Century 21 Premier Gold Properties is Houston's largest Century 21 firm. Agents here specialize in everything you might need: relocation, construction, resales, vacant land, and rentals. The firm serves the Houston, Pasadena, South Houston, and Livingston areas.

CENTURY 21 ROSS GROUP
12623 Jones Rd.
(281) 469-7677
www.century21ross.com
The Century 21 Ross Group has been recognized for its sales volume and excellent service. The company has agents who speak Arabic as well as Spanish. It serves the Clear Lake, Cypress, Houston, Kemah, Klein, Nassau Bay, River Oaks, Spring, Tomball, and Seabrook areas.

COLDWELL BANKER UNITED
http://houston.cbunited.com
Coldwell Banker United has nearly 20 offices in the Houston area. Each office serves a different area of the city or one of the Houston suburbs. Greenway Plaza, the Heights, Clear Lake, Bellaire, Pearland, Katy, the Woodlands, and Memorial are among the neighborhoods covered by Coldwell Banker United. Visit the Web site or consult the phone book to find the office for the neighborhood you're interested in.

GREENWOOD KING PROPERTIES
www.greenwoodking.com
3201 Kirby Dr. (Upper Kirby)
(713) 524-0888

1616 S. Voss, Ste. 900 (Memorial)
(713) 784-0888
1801 Heights Blvd. (Heights)
(713) 864-0888
Greenwood King is one of the foremost names in Houston's high-end real estate market. The private firm, which was founded in 1984, has three offices and nearly 200 agents. Greenwood King provides financial support for a number of community organizations and schools and founded the Lobby, the city's only full-service real estate resource center for homeowners. Although Greenwood King specializes in expensive homes, these properties aren't limited to just a few neighborhoods. Agents here help clients buy and sell houses and condos all over the Greater Houston area and surrounding counties.

JOHN DAUGHERTY REALTORS
www.johndaugherty.com
520 Post Oak Blvd., 6th Floor (Uptown)
(713) 626-3930

13130 Memorial Dr. (West Houston)
(713) 935-4100

Since its founding in 1967, John Daugherty Realtors has led the way in home sales in areas such as Bellaire, West University, Memorial, and River Oaks. More than 170 agents currently work for the firm, which has offices in Uptown and in West Houston. While the firm specializes in high-end real estate, John Daugherty has been branching out to serve emerging neighborhoods and cater to clients with a broad range of budgets and lifestyles.

KELLER WILLIAMS METROPOLITAN
550 Post Oak Blvd., Ste. 350
(713) 621-8001
www.kwmet.com
Keller Williams Metropolitan has more than 300 agents, many of whom are multilingual. They sell and help clients buy homes all over the Greater Houston area.

MARTHA TURNER PROPERTIES
www.marthaturner.com
12506 Memorial Dr. (Memorial)
(713) 520-1981

1440 Lake Front Circle, Ste. 190 (the
Woodlands)
(281) 367-7637

1801 Kingwood Dr., Ste. 120, Kingwood
(Northeast)
(281) 359-6800

1345 Space Park Dr., Ste. B, Nassau Bay
(Bay Area)
(281) 333-3034

Relocation services
50 Briar Hollow Lane, Ste. 700W (Galleria/
River Oaks)
(800) 927-2774

This privately owned real estate company is a big player in Houston's high-end market. In 2007 Martha Turner Properties booked more than $1.15 billion in closed sales transactions. The company has several offices around the Greater Houston area; the Galleria/River Oaks location specializes in relocation. The company works with home buyers, sellers, developers, and builders. Although Martha Turner Properties is known for its success in the high-end market, the company helps clients in all price ranges buy and sell homes. Martha Turner publishes *PROPERTIES*, a full-color magazine featuring articles and listings of interest to local home buyers and sellers. The magazine is sent to more than 50,000 households in the area; copies can also be picked up at the Martha Turner offices.

INFORMATION FOR NEWCOMERS

If you're new to the Houston area, here are a few things you need to know:

Pet licenses: The City of Houston requires that all dogs and cats have and wear a license. You can purchase your pet's license by filling out an application online at www.petdata.com/cs/hst and submitting it by mail. Or you can get

i Houston does not permit households to have more than three dogs older than six months.

a license in person at the animal shelter at 3200 Carr St., located north of downtown, just off of US 59 North. The office is open from 11:30 a.m. to 5:30 p.m. Monday through Friday and from 12:00 p.m. to 4:00 p.m. on Saturday and Sunday. Whether you acquire a license in person or by mail, you'll need to provide your pet's rabies vaccination certificate, as well as your spay/neuter certificate, if you have one. Licenses cost $50 a year for pets that have not been spayed or neutered and $10 a year for pets that have been. With a valid ID seniors can purchase a license for $5 the first year and $2 for subsequent years; licenses are free for seeing/hearing assistance pets. You must purchase your license within 30 days of moving to the city and renew your license within 30 days of your previous license's expiration or your pet's most recent rabies vaccination. In addition, Houston requires all pets to be on a leash or in a fenced yard. If your pet is found roaming the streets—or hanging out in an angry neighbor's yard—he or she may be impounded, and you may be fined up to $100.

Auto Insurance: The State of Texas requires all vehicles to be covered by liability insurance. The minimum liability requirement is $25,000 for bodily injury or death of one person, $50,000 for bodily injury to or death of two or more persons, and $15,000 for property damage or destruction. On January 1, 2011, these minimums will increase to $30,000 for bodily injury for each injured person, $60,000 per accident, and $25,000 for property damage. You will need proof of your liability coverage to obtain or renew your Texas driver's license, register your car, and get your vehicle inspected. A new database called SafeTexas makes it easier for police to verify insurance coverage. If your policy has expired, expect to get a ticket when you get pulled over.

Vehicle Registration: The State of Texas requires new residents to register their vehicles and get Texas license plates within 30 days of ℹ️ **You must have liability insurance before you can register your vehicle or get your driver's license.**

moving to the state. Prior to registering, you'll need to visit a state-approved Safety Inspection Station for a vehicle safety inspection and a visual verification of the vehicle identification number. To find the Safety Inspection Station nearest you, look in the yellow pages under "Automobile Inspection Stations." At the inspection station, you will receive a Vehicle Identification Certificate, which you must then submit to the Harris County Tax Office along with an Application for Texas Certificate of Title and your out-of-state title or registration. Your Texas vehicle registration can be acquired in person at any Harris County Tax Office or by mail; you'll also need to supply proof of liability insurance. Registering your vehicle will cost a new resident fee of $90, or a sales tax fee of 6.25 percent of the price you paid for the vehicle. The Harris County Tax Office is located downtown at 1001 Preston. Call the office at (713) 368-2000 or visit the Web site (www.tax.co.harris.tx.us) for more information. You are required to renew your registration each year and keep a registration sticker on your vehicle window. You can renew your registration at the tax office or on the Web site.

Vehicle Inspection: Texas requires all vehicles to be inspected each year. Your first inspection will occur during the vehicle registration process; subsequent inspections can be conducted at the same Safety Inspection Station you visited initially, or at one of many gas stations and oil change businesses around the area. The inspections include both safety and emissions testing. Safety testing costs $14.50; emissions testing costs up to $39.75. You'll need to provide proof of insurance to get an inspection.

Driver's Licenses: The State of Texas requires all permanent residents to get a Texas driver's license within 30 days of moving to the state. If you've already got a driver's license and are 18

or older, you'll need to take proof of identity and social security number, proof of Texas vehicle registration, and proof of liability insurance. You can find a complete list of acceptable forms of ID on the Texas Department of Public Safety's Web site (www.txdps.state.tx.us). To obtain a license, you will also be required to pass a vision exam, surrender your out-of-state license, and be thumb-printed. Applicants under 18 with a valid license from another state must also supply proof that they've completed a driver's education course and verification of current enrollment and attendance in school. The fee for a driver's license is $24 for adults 18 and up; licenses expire after six years. New Texans under 18 pay just $5 for a license but must renew each year until they turn 18.

ℹ️ **Avoid a hassle and an even longer wait by taking cash when you visit the Department of Public Safety to get your license.**

The Texas Department of Public Safety has several locations at which you can obtain or renew a driver's license; they are listed below. Take note: None of the locations are open on the weekend, though most are open until 7 p.m. at least one day a week. Call ahead to find out the hours for your location since these vary by day and by location.

12220 South Gessner (Southwest)
(713) 219-4100

10503 Grant Rd. (Northwest)
(281) 890-5440

1601 Townhurst (West)
(713) 465-8462

9206 Winkler (Southeast)
(713) 943-0631

8825 Tidwell (Northeast)
(713) 633-9872

15403 Vantage Pkwy. East Ste. 300 (North)
(281) 449-2685

i If you have a good driving record, you may be able to renew your driver's license online. You'll receive a notice in the mail when your renewal date approaches if you're eligible to do so.

Religious Institutions: With thousands of places of worship and religious organizations, the Greater Houston area serves just about every religion and denomination. The city's churches, synagogues, temples, and mosques have congregations ranging from the low hundreds to several thousand, so you can find a place to worship that suits your preferences. Jewish newcomers may find the Jewish Federation (www.houstonjewish .org; 713-729-7000) and the Jewish Community Center (www.jcchouston.org; 713-729-3200) to be useful resources for finding a synagogue and getting involved in the community. Muslim newcomers will find the Islamic Society of Greater Houston (www.isgh.org; 713-524-6615) helpful. You can find a complete directory of Houston's many houses of worship and religious organizations at www.houston.com/religion/business-directory or by consulting the yellow pages.

Registering to Vote: You may register to vote in Texas by calling (713) 368-8683 and requesting an application or by downloading an application from www.tax.co.harris.tx.us and mailing it to the Tax Assessor-Collector and Voter Registrar. You can also register to vote in person at 15 Tax Office branch locations around the city. Call (713) 368-2000 to find the office closest to you. If you live outside of Harris County, you can download an application from the Texas secretary of state's Web site (www.sos.state.tx.us) and mail it to the address listed on the application.

EDUCATION AND CHILD CARE

Whether you're moving to Houston with children or you plan to raise a family here in the future, you are probably concerned about the city's education and child-care offerings. Rest assured: You are in good company. Houstonians place a high value on education and child care. No matter how unique your child's learning needs are, you will almost certainly find an appropriate school or child-care facility in Houston. Between the 26 school districts, 300 private schools, and 1,500 licensed day-care facilities that serve the area, Houston is home to many excellent learning environments. Around these parts, you will find schools that cater to just about every demographic and neighborhood. Read on to learn about the city's public-school, private-school, preschool, and day-care offerings.

PUBLIC SCHOOLS

If you haven't quite grasped how big Houston is yet, the public education system should give you some idea: Some 26 school districts serve Harris County. (Six of these districts lie only partly in the county.) By far the biggest district is the Houston Independent School District, which also happens to be the largest district in Texas and the seventh largest in the country. Many Houston suburbs, such as Katy, have their own school districts. These districts vary in size and the number of schools within them. Some include charter schools and magnet schools. Students are required to attend school in the district in which they live, although some magnet schools and charter schools make exceptions to this rule.

Public schools here are typically organized in three levels: pre-K through 5th grade (elementary school), 6th through 8th grade (middle school), and 9th through 12th grade (high school). Texas children are not required to attend kindergarten, unless they are at least six years old on September 1. The curriculum and activities for all grade levels are regulated by the State Board of Education and Texas Education Agency. Among these regulations: Classes for grades four and lower never have more than 22 students per teacher. While wealthier districts try to maintain comparable class sizes for the older-grade levels, some poorer districts may have closer to 30 students in a classroom. Just like students elsewhere in the state and country, public school students are required to take a number of aptitude and achievement tests throughout the course of their K-12 education. Students in grades 3 through 10 take the Texas Assessment of Knowledge and Skills (TAKS) in math and reading each year and in writing, social studies, and science once each in elementary, middle, and high school. The freshman class of 2011–12 and all future high school classes are also required to take end-of-course assessments in algebra I, algebra II, geometry, biology, chemistry, physics, English I, English II, English III, world geography, world history, and United States history.

Texas high school students are also required to earn at least 26 credits to graduate. Students with special challenges or who attend lower-performing schools may only be required to complete 22 credits. The requisite 26 credits include four years of English, math, and science; three-and-a-half years of social studies, including three history classes and a U.S. government course; economics; at least two years of a foreign language; a year-and-a-half of physical education; a semester of speech or another communications course; a technology course; a fine arts class; and several electives.

Because there are so many school districts in the Houston area, it is impossible to discuss them all in the space of a chapter. A few notable districts are listed below to give you an idea of the educational terrain in the area. To enroll your child in a public school in Houston, contact your local school district. You'll need a copy of your child's birth certificate, immunization records, social security number, and proof of residence to enroll him or her in school. You can find out what district you're zoned in, the contact information for that district, and other essentials by contacting the Harris County Department of Education (713-694-6300; www.hcde-texas.org).

ℹ Before deciding where to live, check out the ratings of local school districts on the Texas Education Agency's Web site at www.tea.state.tx.us.

School Districts

HOUSTON INDEPENDENT SCHOOL DISTRICT
4400 W. 18th St.
(713) 556-6005
www.houstonisd.org
Houston Independent School District—better known as H.I.S.D.—serves more than 300 square miles of the city and parts of the suburbs. That means if you live inside Houston or Bellaire, odds are high that your child is zoned to attend an H.I.S.D. school. The district served nearly 200,000 students in 2008. About 60 percent of the district's students are Latino, 28.4 percent are black, 8 percent are Caucasian, and 3.2 percent are of Asian origin. The district has a strong bilingual education program for its many Spanish-speaking students. H.I.S.D. is divided into five regional districts—Central, East, North, South, and West—each with its own regional superintendent. Each of the district's 300-plus schools belongs to one of these regional districts. Like other urban districts of its size, Houston Independent School District has its share of problems, ranging from underperforming schools to dropouts to schools in need of

repair. The district's high dropout rate appeared to decline considerably in the late 1990s and early 2000s, but an audit of these numbers revealed that the district misreported and misrepresented their dropout rates.

Some of the best schools in the district are magnet schools, such as the High School for Performing and Visual Arts, the Michael E. DeBakey High School for Health Professions, and Carnegie Vanguard, which serves gifted and talented students. To attend an H.I.S.D. magnet school, students must apply and be selected from a competitive applicant pool. All told, there are more than 100 magnet schools in H.I.S.D., nearly half of which are for elementary school students. These schools, which began as a way to encourage integration three decades ago, give otherwise indifferent or at-risk students the chance to attend a school that focuses on something they're passionate about. They also give talented students the chance to hone their gifts at a young age. (Just ask Beyoncé Knowles: She's a graduate of the High School for Performing and Visual Arts.) Budget concerns have forced the district to curtail bus transportation for magnet-school students living two miles or farther away from their school, causing some Houstonians to worry about additional cuts.

H.I.S.D. also operates more than 30 charter schools. Achievement standards at these schools tend to be higher than at other schools in the district or state. That's at least partly because H.I.S.D. charter schools are exempt from many of the regulations that other schools in the district are required to follow. Families must apply to send their children to an H.I.S.D. charter school, which shouldn't be confused with the many independently run charter schools throughout the state. If there are more applicants than available spots, students are selected by lottery.

KATY INDEPENDENT SCHOOL DISTRICT
6301 S. Stadium Lane
(281) 396-6000
www.katyisd.org
The Katy Independent School District serves an 181-square-mile area west of Houston's city limits,

predominately in the city of Katy. This is one of the state's fastest-growing school districts, with enrollment increasing by about 6 percent each year. Currently the district's 47 schools enroll close to 55,000 students, about half of whom are Caucasian and a third of whom are Latino. Although close to 40 percent of Katy students are considered at-risk, students in the district—on the whole—perform consistently well on the statewide TAKS test. Many schools in the district receive "exemplary" or "recognized" ratings in the Texas accountability system each year. The suburban district is particularly notable for its emphasis on drawing in volunteers from the community to mentor students and give them fresh perspectives and opportunities. Thanks to the district's unique approach to junior achievement, more than half of the district's students participated in junior achievement classes taught by community volunteers during the 2007–2008 school year.

SPRING BRANCH INDEPDENDENT SCHOOL DISTRICT
955 Campbell Rd.
(713) 464-1511
www.springbranchisd.com

The Spring Branch Independent School District enrolls more than 32,000 students on the city's west side. The district's 44-square-mile area covers the Memorial area, as well as an area north of the Katy Freeway and west of 290. About half of Spring Branch students are Latino and a third are Caucasian. The district serves everyone from wealthy students to poorer students living in apartments, although it's rare that both ends of this spectrum are represented in large numbers at the same school. Spring Branch's 46 campuses include four high schools, an alternative high school, a career and technology education center for high school–age students, a charter middle/high school, seven regular middle schools and a middle school–only charter, 26 elementary schools for grades K through five, and five schools for children in pre-K. While high schools like Northbrook and Spring Woods have histori-

cally had some problems with underperforming students, many of the district's schools are quite good. Memorial High School, for instance, is consistently rated one of the best high schools in the country in national rankings. The district touts 17 National Exemplary "Blue Ribbon" Schools and produced 32 National Merit Scholarship semifinalists during the 2006–2007 school year.

PRIVATE SCHOOLS

The Houston area is home to more than 300 private schools, giving you options galore for educating your child outside the public–school system. Some independent schools serve students from preschool through high school; others offer only high school classes. Many schools are affiliated with a particular religion or religious organization; others are secular. The city is home to several schools for students with learning and physical challenges, as well as schools that serve gifted types. The price tags at these schools vary almost as much as their focuses and their student bodies do. Many private schools require students to wear uniforms.

Unfortunately, it's impossible to list all 300-plus private schools here, but the top-notch schools listed below should give you a flavor for the types of learning environments offered. Use this list merely as a starting point, then find additional suggestions by consulting the yellow pages, friendly neighbors and colleagues, and www.houstonprivateschools.org, the Web site of Houston Area Independent Schools (HAIS). The HAIS is composed of 68 private schools in the area, and its Web site includes information about each member school. Every fall the HAIS hosts a "preview" day, where parents and students can meet representatives from more than 100 private schools and boarding schools in and beyond Houston.

THE BRIARWOOD SCHOOL
12207 Whittington Dr.
(281) 493-1070
www.briarwoodschool.org

The Briarwood School serves students who have learning and developmental disabilities. The school houses three different programs, each referred to as a "school": The Lower School educates kindergarteners through sixth graders. Students in grades 7 through 12 attend the Middle/Upper School, while students ages 5 to 12 who have developmental delays attend the Tuttle School. Each school offers small classes, typically comprised of less than 10 students. Teaching approaches are adapted to meet each child's individual needs. In addition to standard curriculum requirements in reading, math, science, and social studies, students take electives and participate in extracurricular activities. Each of Briarwood's three schools also focuses on helping students build social and motor skills. The Briarwood School is located on the Westside in the Dairy Ashford area.

THE EMERY/WEINER SCHOOL
9825 Stella Link
(832) 204-5900
www.emeryweiner.org
The Emery/Weiner School is a Jewish community school for middle- and high-school age students. The curriculum at this southwest Houston school focuses on both general and Jewish studies. The school also emphasizes *Tikkun Olam*—the Jewish value of repairing the world—through community service requirements and opportunities. Students often participate in experiential learning opportunities, including trips to Poland, Israel, and elsewhere. The classes here are small, which makes for a close-knit community. Emery/Weiner recently built a new $14-million campus, featuring art and music studios, a high-tech audio/video room, and top-notch computer and science labs.

EPISCOPAL HIGH SCHOOL
4650 Bissonnet
(713) 512-3400
www.ehshouston.org
Episcopal High School enrolls approximately 640 students and offers a 7-to-1 student-to-faculty ratio. The school, which is affiliated with the Episcopal Diocese of Texas, requires students to participate in daily chapel and sacred studies. While religion is a big part of the curriculum, the school also emphasizes academics, the arts, and athletics. The 35-acre campus is located in Bellaire.

THE FAY SCHOOL
105 N. Post Oak Lane
(713) 681-8300
www.thefayschool.org
This secular preparatory school serves students from age three to fifth grade. Small nurturing classes and individualized attention help students discover and hone their intellectual, physical, social, ethical, and artistic abilities. Students at this challenging school study math, social studies, Spanish, music, language arts, library, multimedia, and art. The Fay School's first-class facilities include an outdoor classroom, which is a screened-in area where students learn while interacting with the environment.

THE KINKAID SCHOOL
201 Kinkaid School Dr.
(713) 782-1640
www.kinkaid.org
The Kinkaid School educates bright—and typically wealthy—students from preschool through high school before sending many of them off to the Ivy League. About 1,280 students are enrolled here each year and admission is highly competitive. As a nonsectarian college preparatory day-school, Kinkaid offers a curriculum filled with English, math, science, social studies, foreign language, computer, and fine arts requirements. In addition to the usual courses, students have opportunities to take classes in subjects such as Chinese, philosophy and ethics, art history and philosophy, astronomy, JAVA and robotics, and filmmaking. The school also offers top-notch extracurriculars and competitive teams in everything from debate to lacrosse to football. The campus is located in Memorial and is divided into three separate schools—Lower School, Middle School, and Upper School. Each school has its own classrooms, faculty, and close-knit community.

i Thinking about sending your child to a charter school? Check out the list of Houston charter schools—some public, some private—at www.charterstexas.org.

ST. JOHN'S SCHOOL
2401 Claremont Lane
(713) 850-0222
www.sjs.org

Considered one of the best—if not *the* best—private school in Houston, St. John's School is a college preparatory school serving students from kindergarten through high school. Students here often end up going to some of the country's best universities. The admissions process at this River Oaks school is highly competitive and academics are rigorous. Regardless of what grade they're in, students take classes in math, science, language arts, social studies, and the arts. The school also has a number of athletic teams and extracurricular events. Particularly ambitious students in grades 10 through 12 can undertake an Independent Studies Project, where they spend a semester or year studying a subject of interest in-depth and at their own pace.

CHILD CARE AND PRESCHOOLS

There are hundreds of licensed child-care centers in the Greater Houston area—1,500 in Harris County alone. Some of these are national chains such as Crème de la Crème, Kindercare Learning Center, LaPetite Academy, and Montessori. Many community organizations such as the YMCA, churches, synagogues, and other religious institutions also offer excellent child-care and preschool programs. While it is impossible to list all of the child-care centers and preschools here, a sampling of some of the most popular programs can be found in the next few pages.

Before enrolling your child in a child-care program or preschool, be sure to visit the school and do some research to make sure the school is licensed and has not had any health or safety violations. If you do not know any other local parents yet, contact the referral agency listed at the end of this section. A representative can help identify the best early childhood programs for your child.

i The Texas Department of Family and Child Protective Services maintains a searchable database of licensed child-care providers. Search the database at www.dfps.state.tx.us/child_care, then look into licensing history and compliance with health and safety standards by calling (866) 892-4453.

Child-Care Providers
BECKER EARLY CHILDHOOD CENTER
1500 Sunset Blvd.
(713) 535-6400
www.beckerschool.org

The Becker Early Childhood Center is the preschool of Congregation Emanu El, a Reform synagogue across the street from Rice University. There is often a waiting list to attend the school, which serves more than 200 children ages 15 months to 5 years. While many of the children are Jewish and come partly for the Jewish education and programming, many non-Jewish families send their children here as well. Becker Early Childhood Center is accredited by the National Association for the Education of Young Children.

i Many public schools offer prekindergarten programs; consult your school district to find out if your local elementary school offers this option.

ESPERANZA SCHOOL
639 Heights Blvd.
(713) 868-3276
www.esperanzaschool.com

This popular school in the Heights offers child care for kids ages six weeks through pre-K, as well as after-school and summer camp programs for children in elementary school. Esperanza School also offers child care on Saturday evenings for kids ages 18 months to 10 years.

ℹ For nanny or babysitting services, child development or music classes, baby nurses, or new parent support, contact the Motherhood Center at (713) 963-8880 or www.motherhoodcenter.com. This local organization provides programming that helps parents from pregnancy through their child's early years.

KOMPANY KIDS
2030 Post Oak Blvd.
(713) 621-4006
www.kompany-kids.com
Kompany Kids, which has a second location in Atlanta, serves children ages six weeks to prekindergarten. The classes have low teacher-to-child ratios. Children eat hot, healthy meals that are prepared at the school. The center is located in the Galleria area.

MONTESSORI SCHOOL OF DOWNTOWN
Various locations
(713) 520-6801 (downtown/Medical Center campuses)
www.montessoridowntown.com
Since opening its first campus downtown in 1984, the Montessori School of Downtown has opened a second downtown campus and three campuses in the Silverlake, Clear Lake, and Pearland suburbs. The school ascribes to the Montessori philosophy. Programs are offered for infants, toddlers, preschoolers, and elementary school students through the fifth grade. Summer programs are also available.

Referral Agencies
COLLABORATIVE FOR CHILDREN
3800 Buffalo Speedway, Ste. 300
(888) 833-6805
www.collabforchildren.org
As a member of the Texas Association of Child Care Resource and Referral Agencies, Collaborative for Children helps parents find quality child care and provides resources related to child development and learning. This nonprofit organization offers parenting classes and supports and trains early childhood teachers and care providers. The Collaborative for Children works to improve early childhood care and education through policy initiatives, too. Visit the Web site or call to speak with a consultant who can guide you in your search for a child-care program or other early childhood resources.

HIGHER EDUCATION

No matter what you want to study or where you are in your life, Houston is a great place to continue your education. Close to a dozen colleges and universities, three major community college systems, and several nationwide technical institutes and distance-learning universities have campuses here. With some of the world's leading hospitals located in Houston's Texas Medical Center, many of these colleges and universities offer students an unrivaled opportunity to study medicine. Two medical schools—Baylor College of Medicine and the University of Texas Health Science Center at Houston—are located in the Texas Medical Center, as is Prairie View A&M College of Nursing. Plenty of other professional, graduate, and associate's degree programs in the health sciences are available through the University of Texas Health Science Center at Houston, the Texas A&M Institute of Biosciences and Technology, and local community colleges.

There are also plenty of opportunities to work on a law degree or an M.B.A. in Houston. In addition to the business programs at the large universities here, Houston is home to satellite M.B.A. programs affiliated with Tulane University, Texas A&M University, and the University of Texas at Austin. Two of the city's universities have their own law school, and a third university—South Texas College of Law—is a law school unto itself.

Houston educates far more than doctors, nurses, lawyers, pharmacy technicians, and physician's assistants, though. Here you'll find higher-education institutions that educate college students, older adults, and recent high school graduates or GED recipients pursuing associate's degrees and future doctors and medical practitioners, aspiring lawyers and M.B.A.s, established professionals seeking continuing education credits, as well as curious adults who just want to learn something new. Those seeking a Christian education also have two options in Houston.

Many institutions of higher education here offer night classes and special programs geared toward students who work full-time and have families. The city's colleges and universities also cater to students of all financial backgrounds and offer a good deal of financial aid. A few of the universities here are pricey private schools, but many are public schools, with low tuition rates for students who hail from Texas and still-reasonable prices for those who come here from elsewhere in the country or the world. Unless indicated otherwise, tuition prices listed in this chapter are based on 2009 rates and do not include room and board, books, or other fees.

Below you will find a rundown of the different colleges and universities in Houston—including medical, law, and business schools—followed by community colleges. Several national technical colleges and distance-learning programs have campuses in Houston; a list of these can be found here as well.

COLLEGES AND UNIVERSITIES

BAYLOR COLLEGE OF MEDICINE
1 Baylor Plaza in the Texas Medical Center
(713) 798-4951
www.bcm.edu

Baylor College of Medicine—also referred to as BCM or Baylor—consistently ranks among the top 15 medical schools in the country. This is due in part to the school's location in the heart of the internationally acclaimed Texas Medical Center, allowing for affiliations with several outstanding teaching hospitals. While groundbreaking research projects and teaching (and learning) opportunities are abundant at these affiliated hospitals, significant research is also undertaken at Baylor, which receives more than $300 million in research support. This funding helps support Baylor's more than 90 patient-care and research centers.

Baylor's outstanding reputation makes it a dream school for many aspiring doctors in the region, even before they begin college. Several Texas colleges—including Baylor University in Waco and Rice University in Houston—offer joint bachelor's degree/M.D. programs in affiliation with the medical school. When aspiring doctors apply to these schools' undergraduate programs, a few are also provisionally accepted to Baylor, allowing them to bypass the stress and hassle of taking the MCAT and applying to medical school when they graduate from college.

Despite these affiliations, Baylor College of Medicine shouldn't be confused with Baylor University, a Baptist university located in Waco, about 90 minutes north of Austin in central Texas. The medical school—then located in Dallas and called the University of Dallas Medical Department—became affiliated with Baylor University in 1903, before becoming an independent institution in 1969, some 26 years after moving to Houston. In the spring of 2009, Baylor and Rice University began discussing the possibility of a merger.

Baylor enrolls approximately 3,000 students, the majority of which are medical students, postdoctoral fellows, and bright-eyed physicians completing their residency training. The school also trains about 600 students pursuing Ph.D.s,

as well as a smaller number of nurse anesthesia and physician assistant students. Students seeking an M.D. have the option of also pursuing a second degree—a Ph.D., a Master of Business Administration, a Master of Public Health, or a law degree—in conjunction with another school in the area. Tuition and other enrollment fees vary depending on the program and the student's year in the program. Out-of-state medical school students pay between $25,000 and $30,000 a year, while Texas residents pay between $12,000 and $17,000 a year. Ph.D. students pay about $16,000 per year no matter where they're from, while physician assistant and nurse anesthetist students pay more than $26,000 during their first year of school, with tuition and other fees dropping to just over $10,000 in their third year.

HOUSTON BAPTIST UNIVERSITY
7502 Fondren Rd., just off US 59
(281) 649-3000
www.hbu.edu

Since its founding in 1960, Houston Baptist University—also known as Houston Baptist or HBU—has prided itself on providing students a solid liberal arts education infused with Christian ideals. The university isn't a liberal arts school in the true sense, though: There are plenty of major and degree offerings beyond liberal arts staples like literature, history, and philosophy, including an array of preprofessional and professional programs. Undergraduates can choose from more than 40 majors in music, business administration, liberal arts, and the sciences. The university also offers both bachelor's and associate's degree programs for aspiring nurses. Graduates enroll in master's degree programs in Christian counseling, accountancy, psychology, theology, business and management, liberal arts, and education, as well as a teacher certification program. With just 2,000 undergrads and graduate students enrolled at Houston Baptist, students tend to enjoy small classes with lots of personal attention. Not surprisingly, students here are almost entirely Christian, and the vast majority attend school full-time. Many undergrads live on campus, especially during their first couple of years of college.

Annual fees for tuition and room and board total about $28,000.

The verdant campus, which is located in southwest Houston just off of US 59, has been expanding with the addition of new residence halls, the Morris Cultural Arts Center, and a university academic building. There are also plans to build new athletic facilities, a new student center and library, and new buildings and facilities. Luckily for students, the expansion hasn't really cut into green space; the university is simply buying up more land and expanding its perimeter toward US 59.

PRAIRIE VIEW A&M COLLEGE OF NURSING
6436 Fannin St., in the Texas Medical Center
(713) 797-7000
www.pvamu.edu/pages/290.asp
The main campus of Prairie View A&M—a member of the Texas A&M University system—is located in a small town northwest of Houston, but the university's nursing students enjoy big learning and research opportunities in the Texas Medical Center, where the College of Nursing makes its home. The college offers both undergraduate and graduate degree programs in nursing; students pursuing bachelor's degrees include those fresh out of high school, as well as registered nurses from two-year programs who seek a B.S.N. Undergrads must first complete their basic science/prenursing requirements on the main campus or another university, then transfer to the College of Nursing. Graduate students may pursue degrees that will allow them to work as family nurse practitioners, nursing administrators, or nursing educators. Currently, the College of Nursing is expanding its programs and facilities to give students and professors even better research and learning opportunities.

A historically black university, Prairie View A&M was the first university west of the Mississippi River to admit black students to nursing school when the College of Nursing opened in 1918. Today the student body is still predominately black, but the College of Nursing's 8,000 students also represent a number of other racial and ethnic backgrounds.

College of Nursing students pay Prairie View A&M tuition rates, which are relatively low and are determined by the number of credit hours a student takes. Texas residents pay less than students from out-of-state. Undergrads from Texas pay about $17,420 per year for tuition, room and board, and other fees, while out-of-state undergrads pay nearly $27,000 per year. Graduate students from Texas pay about $16,200 per year, while out-of-state grad students pay closer to $23,000.

RICE UNIVERSITY
6100 Main St., at Sunset Boulevard
(713) 348-0000
www.rice.edu
Rice University is one of Houston's educational gems. Thanks to its large endowment, small classes, and top-notch professors, the university consistently ranks among the top 15 universities in the country. Add to that the promise of mild temperatures, limitless artistic and intellectual opportunities, a beautiful sprawling campus, and a great baseball team, and it's easy to understand why so many students choose to be Rice Owls instead of heading to the Ivy League.

The university enrolls just over 3,000 undergrads in six schools—architecture, engineering, humanities, music, natural sciences, and social sciences. Rice also enrolls about 1,500 graduate students in research-centered Ph.D. and master's degree programs, as well as for professional degrees in the sciences and business management. Rice undergraduate tuition used to be exceptionally affordable for a private school of its caliber, but the cost of attending the university has gone up quite a bit in recent years. Tuition, room and board, and other fees for undergraduates totaled $45,685 for the 2009–2010 academic year. Tuition varies for the different graduate programs. The vast majority of graduate students receive some sort of fellowship or tuition waver, though.

The Susanne M. Glasscock School of Continuing Studies offers top-notch educational opportunities for older adults and professionals, who can take professional development courses and work toward certificates in a wide range of fields. The school also offers foreign language and English as a Second Language courses for businesspeople and non-businesspeople alike, as well as a limited number of classes for high school students. Adults who want to learn something new can also take courses on everything from wine to music to personal finance; most courses are offered at night, though some daytime courses are available as well. Working adults with inquisitive minds can also work toward a Master of Liberal Studies, an evening degree program designed for busy adults who want to learn and talk about important issues in the humanities, sciences, and social sciences. Glasscock courses are open to people throughout the Houston community, not just Rice alumni. Tuition and fees vary, depending on the program.

SOUTH TEXAS COLLEGE OF LAW
1303 San Jacinto St., at Clay Street in downtown
(713) 659-8040
www.stcl.edu
When South Texas College of Law opened in 1923, it became Houston's first law school and Texas's third. Originally, the school was geared toward people who worked full-time and needed to be able to take classes in the evening. Today about two-thirds of South Texas students enroll full-time, many coming straight out of college. A small number of these participate in the "3 and 3" program with Texas A&M University, which allows undergraduates to receive both a bachelor's and a law degree in six years, with three years spent at each institution. One-third of South Texas students are enrolled part-time, most taking evening classes so they can work other jobs or care for their families. The school's downtown location is particularly convenient for these students. A small number of part-timers enroll in daytime classes, as space permits. South Texas admits new students in both the fall and the spring. Each year South Texas enrolls about 400 new students, close to a quarter of which are minorities. Most students here hail from Texas or somewhere else in the Southwest.

South Texas is one of the easier law schools in the state to get into, but students here get a good education and have the opportunity to participate in a number of solid clinical programs. The school has a particularly strong trial law program: The Trial Advocacy Program regularly ranks in the *U.S. News & World Report*'s top 10, and the mock trial team has won the American Association for Justice's Student Trial Advocacy Competition and the National White Collar Crime Mock Trial Invitational in recent years.

Annual tuition was $24,390 for full-time students for the 2008–2009 academic year; part-time students paid $16,260 for tuition during the same period.

SPRINGFIELD COLLEGE SCHOOL OF HUMAN SERVICES
2122 E. Governors Circle
(713) 681-1120
www.spfldcol.edu
Massachusetts-based Springfield College opened up a campus of its School of Human Services in Houston in September 2008. The school offers both a bachelor's and a master's degree in human services; students seeking the graduate degree may opt for a concentration in organizational management and leadership. Students in the undergraduate program are expected to complete their degree within 16 to 24 months of enrollment, so it's practically a requirement to have at least 30 hours of prior college coursework credits that can be transferred. The school offers courses only on weekends, so most students are older or work full-time. Like any school just starting out in a new city, the School of Human Services' student body is tiny but is expected to grow over time. A semester's tuition for the bachelor's degree program was $4,200 in the fall of 2008; tuition for the master's degree program was $4,275 for the same period. The campus is located just northwest of the North Loop in the Philips Leadership Center, a space shared with the YMCA of Greater Houston.

TEXAS A&M UNIVERSITY INSTITUTE OF BIOSCIENCES AND TECHNOLOGY

2121 West Holcombe Blvd., in the Texas Medical Center
(713) 677-7700
www.ibt.tamhsc.edu

Since opening the Institute of Biosciences and Technology in the Texas Medical Center in 1992, Texas A&M University has given aspiring bio-medical science scholars the chance to work with leading scientists and other practitioners specializing in biomedicine and biotechnology. The institute offers a Ph.D. program in biomedical sciences, which requires students to develop theoretical and practical research skills. Students here specialize in one of four areas: cell and developmental biology, microbiology and immunology, environmental and molecular genetics, or biochemistry and molecular biology. The institute's research revolves around the work of its five centers—the Center for Cancer and Stem Cell Biology, the Center for Environmental and Genetic Medicine, the Center for Genome Research, the Center for Infectious and Inflammatory Diseases, and the Center for Molecular Development and Disease. Scientists and families collaborate to study the causes of spina bifida and anencephaly through the university's Spina Bifida Research Resource. Each senior faculty member has a relationship with at least one biotechnology company, giving students access to the most cutting-edge research and trailblazers in their field.

The institute's students are enrolled in the Texas A&M University System Health Science Center's Graduate School of Biomedical Sciences. The Health Science Center also facilitates other graduate programs in dentistry, public health, medicine, and biomedical sciences on the main A&M campus in College Station and other campuses around the state.

Tuition here is low, especially for in-state students. In the spring of 2009, a semester's tuition for Texas residents cost about $1,750, while out-of-state students paid about $4,560.

TEXAS A&M UNIVERSITY MAYS BUSINESS SCHOOL MBA PROGRAM

Lone Star College—University Center
3232 College Park Dr., The Woodlands
(888) 551-9998
http://emba.tamu.edu

Like its rival University of Texas, Texas A&M's Mays Business School offers an M.B.A. program in the Houston area—The Woodlands, to be exact. A&M's program is an executive M.B.A. program geared toward molding students into strong managers who are savvy when it comes to communication, problem solving, self-management, financial acumen, and teamwork. Classes are held on alternating weekends in the fall and spring at Lone Star College's University Center in The Woodlands. There are no summer classes. In addition to class time in The Woodlands, students are required to spend a week at Texas A&M's College Station campus at the beginning of the program and another week in Washington, D.C., where they can see federal policies in action.

Texas residents enrolling in August 2009 paid $67,500 for the two-year program. This relatively low tuition gives the Mays M.B.A. students one of the highest returns on investment, according to the *Wall Street Journal*. Non-Texas residents pay a bit more to attend the program. Applicants are not required to take the GMAT. The admissions committee prefers applicants who have at least 10 years of professional work experience, with at least 7 of those involving managerial responsibilities.

TEXAS MBA AT HOUSTON

The Houstonian
111 North Post Oak Lane
(866) 881-6224
www.mccombs.utexas.edu/houstonmba

A new program offered by the University of Texas at Austin allows Houston professionals to earn an M.B.A. from the top-ranked McCombs School of Business without moving to Austin. Students in the Texas MBA at Houston program take team-based classes taught by the well-regarded faculty of McCombs School of Business on alternating weekends for two years. In addition to an array of business, management, and accounting classes, the curriculum includes a one-week trip and seminar abroad; the destination is chosen based on student input. Classes meet year-round at the luxurious Houstonian hotel, where students spend the night on Friday evenings and receive gym access on Friday and Saturday.

Admission is limited to students with some full-time business experience. The total, two-year cost for students entering in August 2009 was $88,500, including Friday night room and board at the Houstonian. Enrollment costs the same for Texas and non-Texas residents.

TEXAS SOUTHERN UNIVERSITY
3100 Cleburne St., in the Third Ward
(713) 313-7011
www.tsu.edu
With more than 9,500 students, Texas Southern University is one of the country's largest historically black colleges. Today the university gets credit for producing 27 percent of all black pharmacists and the majority of Houston's black lawyers and teachers in the Houston Independent School District. While most Texas Southern students are native Texans, the school is becoming increasingly diverse, with a growing number of students coming from other states and abroad.

Texas Southern is home to nine schools and colleges, including programs in the liberal arts, education, and sciences, as well as the Barbara Jordan–Mickey Leland School of Public Affairs, the College of Pharmacy and Health Sciences, the Jesse H. Jones School of Business, the Tavis Smiley School of Communications, and the Thurgood Marshall School of Law, which *U.S. News & World Report* has recognized as one of the country's most diverse law schools. The school also touts cutting-edge programs and centers devoted to urban planning, entertainment management, and research related to astronaut health.

Sprawling across some 150 acres, Texas Southern is situated in the Third Ward, a historically black neighborhood near downtown. Tuition varies, depending on the number of credit hours a student is taking, field of study, whether the student

is a graduate student or undergraduate, where the student lives, and whether the student is a Texas resident. In 2009 tuition for undergrads from Texas was roughly $7,000 a semester. Graduate students from Texas paid about $8,000 per semester during the same period. Out-of-state undergrads paid about $11,200 per semester, while out-of-state grad students paid close to $11,500.

TULANE UNIVERSITY FREEMAN SCHOOL OF BUSINESS—HOUSTON
1700 W. Loop South, on the 610 Loop at San Felipe Street in the Galleria area
(713) 586-6405
www.houston.tulane.edu
Businesspeople, take note: You can now earn a graduate degree in business from Tulane University without spending more than a weekend or two in Louisiana. That's because the New Orleans–based university recently opened a branch of its Freeman School of Business in Houston's Galleria area. Tulane in Houston, as the school is often called, offers small classes taught by leading business experts. Students work toward a degree in one of three programs—a 23-month professional M.B.A., an 18-month executive M.B.A. for managers and executives, or a 14-month Master of Finance program. An accelerated seven-month Master of Finance program is available for students who have completed an M.B.A. at Tulane no more than three years prior to applying for the program. Each program has alternate weekend classes, so students don't have to spend every weekend in the classroom. Students in the M.B.A. programs are also required to participate in special weeklong international seminars, as well as a couple of seminars in New Orleans.

The programs are geared toward young professionals with at least two years of full-time work experience. Tuition and fees vary depending on the program. Tuition for the professional M.B.A. program was roughly $37,000 per year for students enrolling in 2009. The executive M.B.A. program costs a total of $74,000, while the finance program costs $43,000 for students entering the program in 2010.

UNIVERSITY OF HOUSTON
4800 Calhoun Rd., in southeast central
Houston (main campus)
(713) 743-2255
www.uh.edu
With more than 36,000 students enrolled in a combined total of nearly 300 undergraduate and graduate programs, the University of Houston (U of H) is by far the largest university in town. The university's main campus is located in southeast central Houston; there are also three other campuses—one downtown, another just south of downtown in Clear Lake, and a third in Victoria, located about two hours southwest of Houston. All four campuses in the University of Houston system are served by teaching centers in Cinco Ranch (near Katy) and Sugar Land, located about 25 miles southwest of Houston.

Thanks to a strong alumni base and a huge endowment, U of H students—also known as Cougars—enjoy a wealth of resources, opportunities, and sports teams. The university is constantly undertaking renovations to ensure its students and faculty enjoy the most state-of-the-art facilities. Each U of H campus serves many nontraditional students—both undergrads and graduate students—so courses are typically offered both during the day and in the evening.

Undergraduates at U of H's main campus have their pick of more than 100 majors and plenty of extracurricular activities, student organizations, and internship opportunities. People seeking to pursue graduate work have plenty of options here as well. In addition to highly ranked programs in creative writing, clinical psychology, kinesiology, and business, U of H offers strong programs in optometry, law, and pharmacy. In total the university offers 128 master's degree programs, 50 doctoral programs, and 3 professional degree programs. There has also been talk of opening a University of Houston medical school in the Texas Medical Center.

Undergraduate students at the other U of H campuses in the greater Houston area don't enjoy quite as many academic options, but they still have plenty of choices. Graduate offerings are more limited at the University of Houston–Downtown, however. The downtown campus offers four master's degree programs in criminal justice, professional writing and communication, security management, and teaching. Offerings at University of Houston–Clear Lake are more extensive, with graduate coursework being offered in more than a dozen fields, including environmental sciences, business, engineering, and art and design.

Tuition at the University of Houston is relatively low, especially for Texas residents. Tuition and room and board was a little over $15,000 a year for in-state students and just shy of $21,000 for out-of-state students in 2009.

UNIVERSITY OF ST. THOMAS
3800 Montrose, in the Museum District
(713) 522-7911
www.stthom.edu
The University of St. Thomas is a small Catholic school that sits on the edge of Houston's Museum District, which makes for an attractive campus with easy access to the local arts and culture scene. The university enrolls only about 3,250 students, the majority of which are undergraduates. Despite the school's size, students have an abundance of academic options. St. Thomas's 31 undergraduate majors and minors include the standard fare, as well as more unusual offerings, such as environmental science and studies, pastoral studies, social justice, medieval studies, and, fittingly, Catholic studies. The university offers nine graduate programs, including divinity, business, pastoral studies, and theological studies. With a 12-to-1 student-to-faculty ratio, St. Thomas offers students the benefits of small classes and a fairly close-knit campus. Although the university is a Catholic institution, nearly a third of students here are not Catholic. Tuition is fairly reasonable for a private university. Undergrads pay $673 per credit hour—around $10,000 per semester—and graduate students pay $753 per credit hour, which comes out to around $11,300 per semester. These costs don't include room and board or other fees.

UNIVERSITY OF TEXAS HEALTH SCIENCE CENTER AT HOUSTON
7000 Fannin St., in the Texas Medical Center
(713) 500-4472
www.uthouston.edu
Founded in 1972, the Health Science Center is the main health science arm of the University of Texas, one of the state's two largest university systems (the other being Texas A&M University). Thanks to its location in the Texas Medical Center, the Health Science Center offers some unrivaled learning and research opportunities for students pursuing just about any career in the health sciences. Among the center's research facilities are the Brown Foundation Institute of Molecular Medicine for the Prevention of Human Diseases and the UT Harris County Psychiatric Center.

No other university in Texas has as many health science schools on one campus as the Health Science Center does. Students here can pursue a variety of degrees in the UT Dental Branch, the Graduate School of Biomedical Sciences, the School of Public Health, the School of Nursing, the School of Health Information Sciences, and the Medical School. With the exception of a few certificate programs, the Bachelor of Science in dental hygiene, and the Bachelor of Science in nursing, all of the Health Science Center's programs are geared toward graduate-level students.

Students seeking certificates or bachelor's degrees in additional health professions are served by the closely affiliated University of Texas M.D. Anderson School for Health Professions. The School of Health Professions offers certificate and Bachelor of Science degrees in eight health professions: clinical laboratory science, cytogenic technology, cytotechnology, diagnostic imaging, histotechnology, medical dosimetry, molecular genetic technology, and radiation therapy. About 100 students graduate from the School of Health Professions each year. More information on the School of Health Professions is available online at www.mdanderson.org/prof_education/healthscience.

As part of its effort to encourage interdisciplinary studies, the Health Science Center offers a number of joint degree programs, including a Master of Social Work with a Master of Public Health and a Doctor of Law with a Master of Public Health in conjunction with the University of Houston. Health science professionals also have opportunities to work on continuing education credits and participate in educational community service opportunities here.

Tuition for the University of Texas Health Science Center varies by program and by the student's year in the program. Out-of-state students pay roughly four times as much as Texas residents, but their tuition is still relatively low. A complete tuition breakdown can be found on the Health Science Center's Web site (http://sfs.uth.tmc.edu).

COMMUNITY COLLEGES

HOUSTON COMMUNITY COLLEGE
Various locations
(713) 718-2000
www.hccs.edu
Houston Community College, also known as HCC, is the primary community college system serving the Houston area. The system's 57,000 students attend HCC for a variety of reasons: Some are fresh out of high school and need to earn a couple of year's credits before they can transfer to a university. Others are working on an associate's degree, certificate, or license program so they can begin careers in the technical sector. Some are high school age or older students working toward their GED; others come for the Adult Basic Education or English as a Second Language programs. And a fair number are ambitious high school students trying to rack up a few college credits in summer school or through HCC's dual-credit program, which allows courses taken at the student's high school to count toward college credits.

The HCC system includes six colleges: Central College, Coleman College for Health Sciences, Northeast College, Northwest College, Southeast

College, and Southwest College. With the exception of Coleman, which is located in the Texas Medical Center, each college's name corresponds to the region of the Houston metropolitan area that it serves. The system caters to Houstonians living in seven area school districts—Houston Independent School District, Stafford Municipal School District, Spring Branch Independent School District, Alief Independent School District, North Forest Independent School District, Katy Independent School District, and the part of Fort Bend Independent School District that covers Missouri City.

Each college, aside from Southeast, has at least two campuses. In total HCC offers courses in about 70 fields. All of the colleges in the Houston Community College system also offer distance-learning classes. Course offerings vary by campus to some extent, but just about all of them offer liberal arts and science courses that fill basic requirements at most universities. The exception is Coleman, where classes prepare students to work in about 20 different health-science fields. Coleman students go on to become clinical lab technicians, dental assistants, emergency medical service providers, health-information technicians, mammographers, massage therapists, pharmacy technicians, occupational-therapy assistants, registered nurses, and more.

None of HCC's campuses offer housing, but students have the opportunity to participate in university-wide sporting events and attend special activities, such as film screenings and guest talks. Tuition varies depending on where the student makes his or her permanent residence and the number of credit hours. Students who live in one of the seven school districts served by HCC pay the lowest price, students who live in Texas but outside of the seven districts pay nearly twice as much, and out-of-state students pay even more. In 2009 the cost for 15 credit hours was $843 for in-district students, $1,653 for out-of-district students, and $1,953 for out-of-state students.

LONE STAR COLLEGE SYSTEM
Various locations
(832) 813-6500
www.lonestar.edu
The Lone Star College System is one of the fastest-growing community college systems in Texas. The system's five colleges serve north Houston and areas just north of the city limits in Harris and Montgomery Counties. With almost 50,000 students enrolled in credit courses and 14,000 taking continuing education classes, Lone Star is also one of the state's largest community college systems. The five Lone Star colleges are Lone Star College–CyFair, Lone Star College–Kingwood, Lone Star College–Montgomery, Lone Star College–North Harris, and Lone Star College–Tomball. There are also six satellite campuses.

Students here are a pretty diverse bunch; a good chunk are college age but there are also a many older adults and younger parents taking continuing education classes or working toward associate's degrees, enhanced skills certificates, or other professional certificates. Students seeking an associate's degree here don't work toward a specific major. Instead, they take basic required courses that easily transfer to most four-year colleges. Exceptional students can participate in the Honors Program, which offers the opportunity to work closely with professors, take a special honors course, and receive a special designation on their transcript. Students who want to learn more about a particular topic and get to know their peers at this nonresidential college can enroll in one of Lone Star's Learning Communities. Participating students take at least two related classes in different disciplines, giving them the opportunity to learn about different angles of a common theme. Through Lone Star College–University Center, a partnership with six of the area's biggest universities, students can complete their associate's degrees at one of Lone Star's campuses, then work toward their bachelor's and even master's degrees at one of the partner universities. Lone Star also offers GED prep classes,

Technical Schools

A few nationwide technical institutes and distance-learning universities have campuses in Houston. Contact information for these schools is listed below. Some schools have multiple campuses in Houston; each campus is included beneath the name of the institute or university.

COURT REPORTING INSTITUTE– HOUSTON CAMPUS
13101 Northwest Fwy.
(713) 996-8300
www.crid.com

EVEREST INSTITUTE
www.everest.edu

Houston Bissonnet
9700 Bissonnet St.
(713) 772-4200

Houston Greenspoint
255 Northpoint Dr.
(281) 447-7037

ITT TECHNICAL INSTITUTE
www.itt-tech.edu

Houston North
15651 North Fwy.
(281) 873-0512

Houston West
2950 South Gessner
(713) 952-2294

REMINGTON COLLEGE
www.remingtoncollege.net

Houston
3110 Hayes Rd.
(281) 899-1240

North Houston
11310 Greens Crossing Blvd.
(281) 885-4450

UNIVERSITY OF PHOENIX
www.phoenix.edu

Clear Lake Learning Center
16055 Space Center Blvd.
(713) 465-9966

Houston Campus
11451 Katy Fwy.
(713) 465-9966

Houston Northwest Learning Center
7900 N. Sam Houston Pkwy. West
(713) 465-9966

West Loop Learning Center
4888 Loop Central Dr., Ste. 300
(713) 465-9966

WESTWOOD COLLEGE
www.westwood.edu

Houston South Campus
1 Arena Place
7322 Southwest Fwy.
(713) 777-4433

as well as dual-credit and tech-prep programs for high school students looking to earn some college credits.

Tuition varies depending on where the student makes his or her permanent residence and the number of credit hours taken. Students who live in one of the following school districts pay the lowest prices: Aldine, Conroe, Cypress-Fairbanks, Humble, Klein, Magnolia, New Caney, Splendora, Spring, Tomball, or Willis. Students who live in Texas but outside of these districts pay nearly twice as much, and out-of-state students pay even more. During the spring 2009 semester, 15 credit hours cost $702 for in-district students, $1,602 for out-of-district students, and $1,827 for students who don't hail from the Lone Star State.

SAN JACINTO COLLEGE
Various locations
(281) 998-6150
www.sjcd.edu

San Jacinto College is a local community college system, serving residents of the Channelview, Deer Park, Galena Park, La Porte, Pasadena, Sheldon, and Clear Creek School Districts. The college has three campuses—one in south Houston, one in north Houston, and a third in Pasadena, which is just southeast of the city. There are also five extension centers—two in Clear Lake, one southeast of Houston in Webster, and two east of Houston in Galena Park.

Each of the three campuses offers courses that can be transferred to four-year colleges, as well as continuing education courses and job-training programs that prepare students for careers in industries such as agriculture, food, natural resources, hospitality, and construction. SanJac, as the college is nicknamed, also offers dual-credit programs for high school students, as well as GED courses. For students who work full-time or have family obligations that prevent them from attending classes on weekdays, all three colleges offer what's known as the Weekend College—a broad array of classes offered Friday, Saturday, and Sunday during the morning, afternoon, and evening. SanJac offers students more extracurricular activities and campus activities—including special speakers, festivals, sporting events, and fine arts events—than other community colleges in the area.

As with the other community colleges in the area, tuition here varies depending on where the student makes his or her permanent residence and the number of credit hours taken. Students living in the Channelview, Deer Park, Galena Park, La Porte, Pasadena, Sheldon, or Clear Creek School Districts pay low in-district tuition rates. Students living in Texas but outside of these districts, as well as students from out of state, pay more. In the fall of 2008, 15 hours of course credits cost $625 for in-district students, $1,000 for out-of-district students, and $1,750 for out-of-state students. This does not include the additional fees required for some courses.

HEALTH CARE

If you need to see a doctor, you've come to the right place. Houston is home to dozens of hospitals and urgent-care facilities—many of which are so good that people travel from across the globe to receive treatment. Hospitals here conduct groundbreaking medical research and surgeries time and again, consistently earning them recognition among the top hospitals in the country—and the world.

Most of the best hospitals here are located in the Texas Medical Center, the world's largest medical complex. Located inside the Loop near Hermann Park, this 1,000-acre medical complex is home to 46 independent institutions, including 13 hospitals, 2 specialty institutions, and medical, nursing, public health, dentistry, and pharmacy schools. Together, hospitals in the Medical Center perform more heart surgeries than any other place in the world. The Texas Medical Center isn't just a leader when it comes to cardiology, though. Other top-ranked specialties here include pediatric care, woman's health, urology, gastroenterology, oncology, endocrinology, psychiatry, and neurology. The Medical Center is also home to two level-one trauma centers.

While the Medical Center is the center of Houston's medical universe, it is hardly the only place to receive great medical care in Houston. Around the city you'll find many other excellent hospitals, many of which are satellites of Medical Center institutions. A sampling of some of the city's best hospitals can be found in this chapter.

Fortunately not all symptoms and medical circumstances demand a trip to the hospital. A number of urgent-care/walk-in clinics around the city serve patients with relatively minor medical problems like broken bones, the flu, and asthma attacks. You will find a list of some of these clinics in this chapter. The city and county health departments also operate several community health clinics that cater to lower-income Houstonians. If you're interested in visiting one of these facilities, be sure to consult the "Health Departments" section in this chapter.

Elsewhere in this chapter you'll find a list of physician referral services, which newcomers as well as longtime residents will find useful. Call any of these services and you're likely to be paired up with a great doctor, whether you need a general practitioner or a specialist. Keep in mind that Houston is home to thousands of doctors and dozens of hospitals, so this list—like the clinic list and hospital list—is hardly exhaustive. Use this chapter to start your search for a doctor or a medical facility, but don't discount the value of seeking doctor recommendations from friends and colleagues who have been in the city for many years.

At the end of this chapter is a list of important emergency numbers such as poison control, animal control, and the local rape crisis hotline.

HEALTH DEPARTMENTS

HARRIS COUNTY PUBLIC HEALTH AND ENVIRONMENTAL SERVICES DEPARTMENT
2223 W. Loop South
(713) 439-6000
www.hcphes.org

The Harris County Public Health and Environmental Services Department promotes health and seeks to prevent injury and illness throughout Harris County. The department provides resources for the community to learn about communicable diseases, prenatal care, HIV screening, and immunizations, as well as how to avoid unhealthy conditions created by storms and other environmental conditions. Also handled by the department: the all-important mosquito control. Six health clinics run by the department on behalf of the county provide preventative health-care services for low-income residents. A list of these clinics can be found by calling the department or visiting its Web site.

HOUSTON DEPARTMENT OF HEALTH AND HUMAN SERVICES
8000 N. Stadium Dr.
(713) 794-9320
www.houstontx.gov/health

The Houston Department of Health and Human Services works with the community and health-care providers to promote good health and health services among Houstonians. The department implements programs geared toward reducing the prevalence and impact of communicable diseases ranging from the standard flu to HIV to H1N1 (swine flu). The city health department also leads public health programs; monitors environmental conditions, such as air quality and allergens; and oversees animal control. Inspections of local restaurants and food establishments are conducted by the health department to ensure food isn't a threat to diners' health. As part of its efforts to ensure that all Houstonians have access to quality health care, the Houston Department of Health and Human Services operates several preventative-care clinics and primary-care clinics for low-income residents. A list of these can be found by calling the department or by visiting www.houstontx.gov/health/HealthCenters.

HOSPITALS

BEN TAUB GENERAL HOSPITAL
1504 Taub Loop (Medical Center)
(713) 793-2000
www.hchdonline.com/about/facilities/
bentaubgh.htm

Located in the Medical Center, Ben Taub General Hospital is owned and operated by the Harris County Hospital District. It is one of just two level-one trauma centers in the county and the only hospital in the Medical Center with a 24-hour psychiatric emergency room. With 650 beds Ben Taub treats more than 108,000 emergency room patients each year, making it one of the country's busiest trauma centers. Faculty and residents from Baylor College of Medicine comprise the hospital's staff. Specialties here include endocrinology, oncology, pulmonary, cardiology, renal, and gastroenterology. Ben Taub also has a children's center.

CHILDREN'S MEMORIAL HERMANN HOSPITAL
6411 Fannin (Medical Center)
(713) 704-5437
www.memorialhermann.org/locations/
childrens

Each year more than 37,000 children receive treatment at Children's Memorial Hermann Hospital, located in the Memorial Hermann–Texas Medical Center complex. The hospital, which has 178 beds, handles everything from neonatal care to common childhood ailments and injuries to transplants and potentially fatal diseases and injuries. The hospital is home to the Children's Heart Institute and the Children's Neuroscience Center, as well as a woman's center, which provides prenatal and maternal care and ob/gyn and breast-health services. Families also have access to support services here.

DUBUIS HOSPITAL OF HOUSTON
1919 LaBranch (Downtown)
(713) 339-7000
www.dubuis.org

Dubuis Hospital of Houston is part of a Catholic-affiliated hospital system that has hospitals and health centers in several states. This location specializes in long-term acute care and palliative care, as well as wound care and rehabilitation. The hospital has 30 beds and is located on the seventh floor of St. Joseph Medical Center.

MEMORIAL HERMANN HOSPITAL

www.memorialhermann.org
6400 Fannin (Medical Center)
(713) 790-7700

7789 Southwest Fwy. (Southwest Houston)
(713) 343-3100

1631 N. Loop West (Northwest Houston)
(713) 343-1086

920 Frostwood (Memorial)
(713) 932-3000

23920 Katy Fwy. (Katy)
(281) 644-3200

17510 W. Grand Pkwy. (Sugar Land)
(281) 238-1600

9200 Pinecroft (the Woodlands)
(281) 297-9500

With 11 hospitals around the Houston area, Memorial Hermann Hospital is Texas's largest hospital system. Anchored by the Medical Center campus, the system operates one of Houston's two level-one trauma centers, as well as 7 cancer centers, 3 heart institutes, 27 sports medicine and rehabilitation centers, a substance abuse treatment center, 25 patient imaging centers, a children's hospital, and a neuroscience institute. The Urology Department at Memorial Hermann–Texas Medical Center ranked among the country's best in *U.S. News & World Report*'s 2008 hospital rankings. In 2007 Memorial Hermann treated more than 1 million patients and delivered more than 25,000 babies. Several of the Memorial Hermann hospital locations are listed here; visit the Web site to find additional hospitals and specialty facilities.

i Download a map of the Texas Medical Center (www.tmc.edu) and figure out where to park before you visit.

THE METHODIST HOSPITAL

www.methodisthealth.com
6565 Fannin St. (Medical Center)
(713) 790-3311

18220 Tomball Pkwy. (Northwest Houston)
(281) 477-1000

16655 Southwest Fwy. (Sugar Land)
(281) 274-7000

4401 Garth Rd. (Baytown)
(281) 420-8600

Anchored by the Methodist Hospital campus in the Texas Medical Center, this renowned hospital system is responsible for groundbreaking research in areas ranging from heart disease to cancer treatment and is home to a level-three trauma center. This teaching hospital's main campus is nationally ranked in 12 specialties, including urology; neurology and neurosurgery; opthamology; psychiatry; gastrointestinal disorders; rheumatology; cardiovascular care and surgery; kidney disease; cancer; orthopedics; geriatrics; and ear, nose, and throat. The Medical Center branch has nearly 900 beds.

ST. JOSEPH MEDICAL CENTER

1401 St. Joseph Pkwy. (downtown)
(713) 757-1000
www.sjmctx.com

When it opened in 1887, St. Joseph Medical Center was Houston's first hospital. Today the hospital provides comprehensive medical and surgical care, including neonatal and pediatric care, women's care, behavioral care, intensive care, neurosurgery, and orthopedics. The Obstetrics Department here delivers close to a third of babies born in Houston. St. Joseph has 420 beds and can hold up to 792 patients. This teaching hospital is staffed by more than 600 board-certified physicians.

ST. LUKE'S EPISCOPAL HOSPITAL

6720 Bertner Ave. (Medical Center)
(832) 355-1000
www.sleh.com

Since the Episcopal Diocese of Texas founded it in 1954, St. Luke's Episcopal Hospital has become one of the country's best hospitals and one of the world's leaders in heart surgery and the treatment of heart disease. Today the hospital has 640 beds, including 143 in the intensive care unit. In addition to providing outstanding cardiac care, St. Luke's is known for specialties such as neurology and neurosurgery, gastrointestinal disorders, geriatrics, endocrinology, respiratory disorders, urology, and kidney disease. The hospital, which is located in iconic O'Quinn Medical Tower, trains residents at Baylor Medical School. St. Luke's is the principal hospital in the St. Luke's Episcopal Health System, which includes the Texas Heart Institute, hospitals in the Woodlands and Sugar Land, St. Luke's Diagnostic & Treatment Center, several urgent-care clinics, and Kelsey-Seybold Clinic, which provides primary care and specialty care in an outpatient setting. Visit the Web site or call to find for additional St. Luke's facilities.

TEXAS CHILDREN'S HOSPITAL
6621 Fannin St. (Medical Center)
(832) 824-1000
www.texaschildrens.org
With 465 beds, Texas Children's Hospital is the country's largest children's hospital and a global leader in pediatric care. The hospital's specialty care centers focus on cancer, fetal care, cardiology, maternity care, neurology, and newborns. *U.S. News & World Report* has ranked Texas Children's Hospital in the top-10 hospitals when it comes to performing surgery and treating pediatric respiratory disorders, cancer, heart problems, neurology, and neonatal care. The hospital lays claim to trailblazing accomplishments, such as inserting the world's smallest pacemaker in a child and operating on conjoined twins. Texas Children's is affiliated with Baylor College of Medicine.

THE UNIVERSITY OF TEXAS M.D. ANDERSON CANCER CENTER
1515 Holcombe Blvd. (Medical Center)
(713) 792-6161
www.mdanderson.org

People from around the world visit the University of Texas M.D. Anderson Cancer Center for cancer treatment. Ranked the number-one hospital for cancer care in the country by *U.S. News & World Report,* this leader in cancer research evaluates more cancer-fighting drugs than any other institution in the country. The hospital specializes in everything from the most common to the most obscure cancers, as well as pediatric cancer care. M.D. Anderson has more than 500 beds at its Medical Center location; it served more than 89,000 patients in 2008. The cancer center has several satellites, specialty clinics, and treatment centers in Houston and elsewhere in the state. Visit the Web site to learn about these additional care centers or to find a clinic near you.

THE WOMAN'S HOSPITAL OF TEXAS
7600 Fannin (Medical Center)
(713) 790-1234
www.womanshospital.com
As Texas's leading hospital focused solely on the care of women and newborn infants, the Woman's Hospital of Texas specializes in gynecology, regular obstetrical care, high-risk pregnancies, and minimally invasive surgery. In 2007 Woman's Hospital delivered more babies than any other hospital in Harris County. The hospital has a 91 percent success rate with babies weighing 1,500 grams or less at birth. Woman's Hospital has 275 beds and is adding 92 more in 2009, as part of a $75-million, 145,000-square-foot expansion.

URGENT-CARE/WALK-IN CLINICS

Houston has several urgent-care facilities, which serve Houstonians and visitors suffering from minor illnesses and injuries, saving them the time and hassle of sitting in a hospital emergency room. The clinics treat medical problems, such as burns, broken bones, migraines, swallowed objects, splinters, urinary tract infections, fever, and the flu. They also provide immunization and diagnostic services. Although it's a good idea to call ahead, you don't need an appointment to visit one of these clinics, where you will be treated by board-certified physicians and licensed nurses. Most accept health insurance plans with major insurance companies, as well as Medicare and Medicaid. The clinics listed below are typically open seven days a week. 24 Hour Emergency Room and St. Luke's Community Emergency Center are open 24 hours. Houston Urgent Care, Texas Urgent Care, and Wells Walk-In Clinic close relatively early in the evening, so call ahead to make sure the clinic will be open for your visit.

HOUSTON URGENT CARE
www.urgentcarehouston.com
1826 Wirt Rd. (West Houston)
(832) 428-4546

16125 Cairnway, Ste. 100
(Northwest Houston)
(832) 428-4546

ST. LUKE'S COMMUNITY EMERGENCY CENTER
www.stlukesemergency.com
6363 San Felipe St., at Winrock (Memorial)
(713) 972-8300

2727 W. Holcombe (West University)
(832) 355-7525

11713 Shadow Creek Pkwy. (Pearland)
(713) 793-4600

10701 Vintage Preserve Pkwy. (Northwest Houston)
(281) 379-7200

10710 Kuykendahl Rd. (The Woodlands)
(281) 681-770

TEXAS URGENT CARE
10906 FM 1960 West, at Jones Rd.
(Northwest Houston)
(281) 477-7490
www.texasurgentcare.com

24 HOUR EMERGENCY ROOM
www.24houremergencyroom.com
1635 South Voss Rd., at San Felipe
(Memorial)
(713) 972-0911

16000 Southwest Fwy. (Sugar Land)
(281) 277-0911

24727 Tomball Pkwy., Tomball (Northwest of Houston)
(281) 516-0911

WELLS WALK-IN CLINIC
10311 North Eldridge Pkwy. (Northwest Houston)
(281) 890-3822
www.wellswalk-inclinic.com

Kelsey-Seybold Clinic, an affiliate of St. Luke's Episcopal Hospital, and Baylor Clinic, Baylor College of Medicine's adult outpatient care facility, both offer excellent primary and specialty care. To find a doctor or schedule an appointment, contact Kelsey-Seybold (713-442-5440; www.kelsey-seybold.com) or Baylor Clinic (713-798-1000; www.baylorclinic.com).

REFERRAL SERVICES

Whether you're new to town or a longtime Houstonian, finding a good doctor can be tough. Below is a list of hospitals and organizations that provide referral services those looking for local physicians and specialists. Most participating doctors are affiliated with specific hospitals in the city and many teach at local medical schools, such as Baylor College of Medicine and the University of Texas Health Sciences Center.

BAYLOR CLINIC PHYSICIAN REFERRALS
(713) 428-6411

HARRIS COUNTY MEDICAL SOCIETY REFERRAL SERVICE
(713) 524-4267

HCA HOUSTON NETWORK REFERRAL SERVICE
(800) 265-8624

Emergency Phone Numbers at a Glance

Abuse and Neglect Hotline
(800) 252-5400

Adult Protective Services–Aged and Disabled
(713) 767-2700

Animal Control
(713) 229-7300

Children's Protective Services
(713) 664-5701

Domestic Violence Hotline
(713) 528-2121

Harris County Hospital District's 24-Hour Nurse Help Line
(713) 633-2255

Household Hazardous Waste Hotline
(713) 551-7355

Houston Health Department
(713) 794-9320

Houston Rape Crisis Hotline
(713) 528-7273

Mental Health/Mental Retardation Crisis Center
(713) 970-4600

Missing Persons Information
(713) 526-8300

Poison Control
(800) 222-1222

Police/Ambulance
911 (emergency)
(713) 461-9992 (nonemergency)

Runaway Hotline
(800) 392-3352

Suicide Prevention Hotline
(713) 228-1505

Teen Crisis Hotline
(713) 529-8336

MEMORIAL HERMANN HOSPITAL REFERRAL SERVICE
(713) 222-2273

PLANNED PARENTHOOD
(713) 522-6363

TEXAS CHILDREN'S HOSPITAL REFERRAL SERVICE
(832) 824-7700

ST. LUKE'S EPISCOPAL HOSPITAL PHYSICIAN REFERRAL SERVICE
(832) 355-4343

THE WOMAN'S HOSPITAL OF TEXAS REFERRAL SERVICE
(281) 238-4357

Veterans can receive treatment for everything from post-traumatic stress disorder to cancer at the Michael E. DeBakey VA Medical Center in the Texas Medical Center. Visit the Web site (www.houston.va.gov) or call (713) 791-1414 for more information. The VA center also offers 24-hour telecare at (713) 794-8985.

INDEX

ABOUT THE AUTHOR

Born and raised in Houston, Laura Nathan is a freelance writer and editor whose articles have appeared in national publications, such as *Redbook* and *Cooking Light*. Although Nathan currently resides in upstate New York, she spends several weeks at home in Houston each year. During these visits, she cheers on her Houston Rockets and seeks out new local haunts and spots where she can bask in the sandal-friendly weather.